NEPAL
WITH REFERENCE TO KASHMIR AND SIKKIM

ADARSH BOOKS

Rhododendrons at 12,000' framing Kangtega (22,340') in the Everest National Park, E. Nepal.

BIRDS OF NEPAL

WITH REFERENCE TO KASHMIR AND SIKKIM

BY

ROBERT L. FLEMING, SR.,
ROBERT L. FLEMING, JR.,
LAIN SINGH BANGDEL

FOREWORD BY

ELVIS J. STAHR
FORMER PRESIDENT
NATIONAL AUDUBON SOCIETY, NEW YORK

ILLUSTRATED BY

HEM POUDYAL and HIRA LAL DANGOL with
ROBERT L. FLEMING, JR.

AND

MARGARET FLEMING WALDRON
LINDA FIRTH FLEMING

ADARSH BOOKS

© Robert L. Fleming, Jr.

All rights reserved. No part of this publication, including its texts and plates, may be reproduced in and form or by any means, electronically or mechanically, including photocopying, recording or any information storage or retrieval system, without prior permission in writing from the publisher Adarsh Enterprises, Delhi.

**Birds of Nepal
With Reference to
Kashmir and Sikkim**

First Adarsh Impression - 2000

ISBN - 81-87138-12-2

Published By :
Nirmal Kumar Karn
Adarsh Enterprises
E-22-C, Jawahar Park, Laxmi Nagar,
Vikas Marg, Delhi -110 092.
Phones : 2469733, 2464961.
E-mail : nirmal@ndb.vsnl.net.in
adarshbooks@vsnl.com

Printed By :
Gaurav Offset
Laxmi Nagar,
Delhi - 92.

Royal Palace
Nepal

An extract from His Majesty King Birendra Bir Bikram Shah Dev's message on the occasion of the publication of the first edition of this book:

In our view, birds show the perennial beauty of Creation and together with other fauna, flora and their landscape, they make up the natural heritage of a nation. Universally, birds also embody the esthetic principle in colour. I have, therefore, no doubt that the publication of a book on the subject will greatly add to the body of knowledge on Nepal.

The Flemings deserve our appreciation and I wish their venture all success.

DEDICATED TO
BETHEL HARRIS FLEMING, M.D.
WIFE, MOTHER AND FRIEND

who enthusiastically encouraged and supported
our study of Nepal birds

I will lift up my eyes to the hills.
From whence cometh my help?
My help cometh from the Lord
Who made heaven and earth.
—Psalms 121

Inasmuch as ye have done it unto
one of the least of these my brethren,
ye have done it unto Me.
—Matthew 25:40b

PREFACE TO THE THIRD EDITION

Birds new to Nepal, along with additional data, continue to emerge from the lowlands and mountains of Nepal, thanks to dedicated observers spending many hours searching through various parts of the country. The Kosi Barrage in southeastern Nepal still rates as the finest birding area in Nepal and within recent years has produced seven species new to the Nepal list. Unfortunately the area around the Barrage remains unprotected and this habitat, unique in Nepal, is rapidly being overrun and destroyed. Properly organized and controlled, the Kosi Barrage area has the potential of being one of the great bird sanctuaries in Asia; we wish it could be so.

Many people have contributed to our understanding and knowledge of the birds of Nepal and we wish to thank the following: Tim and Carol Inskipp (Kathmandu, Nepal lowlands), Francis Lambert, Richard Grimmett, Dick Filby, Les Norton (Kathmandu, Pokhara, Chitwan, Kosi), Nigel Redman, Chris Murphy (Kathmandu, Chitwan, Kosi, Ilam District), Mogens Henriksen, Oluf Lou, Niels Krabbe (Kathmandu, Pokhara, Kosi, Arun Valley), K. Curry-Lindahl (Chitwan), Jim Hall (Kosi), Dick Byrne (Kosi), J. Thiollay (Annapurna area), Fairbank (Manang), Paul Hagan (Surkhet, Butwal), Delos McCauley (Butwal, Jumla, Kosi, East Nepal), Tony Lelliott (Machapuchare area), Johnathan Ross, Robert Wicks (Chitwan, Kosi, East Nepal), Werner and Dorothy Suter (Kathmandu, Kosi), David Pritchard, D. M. Brearey (Jumla, Rara, Chankheli Lekh), Peter Pyle (Pokhara, Jomsom), H. S. Nepali (Kathmandu, Mustang), John Halliday (Chitwan, Kathmandu), Andy White (Khumbu), Brian Finch (Kathmandu, Chitwan), Matt Ridley (Chitwan), Andrew and Claudea Cassels (Kosi, Biratnagar), Nigel Hopkins, Geraldine Tuma (Kosi), Steve LeClerq (East Nepal), Richard Isherwood (Arun-Makalu Trek), Goran Holmstrom (Kathmandu), David Percival (Pokhara), Hashim Tyabji (Chitwan), Devendra Basnet (Chitwan), Tim Finnegan (Api-Nampa), Gunter Groh (Manang Trek), Valentine Russels (Jumla-Rara), Adrian del-Nevo, Peter Ewins (Chitwan, Pokhara), Tony Baker, David Mills, Nick Preston (Kathmandu, Jomsom, Pokhara), James Wolstencroft (Pokhara, Kagbeni, Mahendranagar), Kathleen Munthe (Dang Valley, Butwal).

The above list comprises largely foreign observers but an outstanding exception is Hari Sharan Nepali from Kathmandu who continues to collect birds new to Nepal and other valuable data. A heartening note, too, is a growing band of young Nepalese who are taking a strong interest in birds and conservation and who will be soon in a position to contribute to our knowledge of the birds of their country.

FOREWORD

NEPAL is a land of great altitudinal and scenic contrasts. Jagged peaks, the highest in the world, delineate the northern border while placid streams meander through hot, tropical forests and lowland cultivations in the south. Within this unique setting live nearly 800 species of birds.

Nepal can boast of exceptional beauty as well as unusual diversity in its flora and fauna. This variety is due to altitude fluctuations and also to Nepal's geographical position in Asia. In a biogeographical sense, Nepal is at the center of Asia. This can be seen from a study of its birds. Included in this book for example, are Accentors from north Asia, Barbets of tropical, southeast Asia, numerous Timaliids from east Asia as well as Nuthatches from Europe and west Asia and Storks from south Asia.

Nepal shares its fauna and flora with other areas. In fact, as a meeting point of Asian animals and plants, it is so unusual that of all the birds here only the Spiny Babbler is thought to be endemic to the country. This means that studies of particular species as well as conservation principles evolved for Nepalese fauna and flora will be of interest far beyond the borders of the country.

The work of conservation in Nepal has been strongly underlined by the recent formation of a National Parks system under the enlightened leadership of His Majesty King Birendra and his Government. National Parks along with Wildlife Preserves and Sanctuaries protect the vital habitat upon which birds as well as other species depend for their living.

Birds form an important part of Nepal's natural beauty. It is my hope that this book, by stimulating an increased interest in the birds of Nepal, will thereby assist in their preservation through the continuing development of appropriate conservation measures so necessary for their survival.

                                    ELVIS J. STAHR
Former President
National Audubon Society
950, Third Ave.
New York, N.Y.

INTRODUCTION

Nepal is a land of great interest, beauty and visual variety. At an elevation of 76 meters (250') above sea level, the sands of the lower Kosi shimmer through summer heat waves, while around the top of Everest, only 145 kilometers (90 mi.) away, gales whip spindrift snow through a permanent deep freeze. There are few places in the world where snowy-white egrets perch in front of giant peaks, both turning pink in the setting sun. And very few places where one can observe birds at 8235 meters (27,000') and still be on the ground.

To describe Nepal requires, in effect, a summary of Asia: the heat of south Asia, the moist tropical forests of southeast Asia, the dry valleys complete with olive trees reminiscent of west Asia and the cold from the central Asian tablelands and north Asia. For convenience of discussion, Nepal may be divided broadly into three regions: the Lowlands, Midlands and Highlands. The Lowlands include the Tarai, Bhabar, Churia, Duns and the Mahabharat Range up to 915 meters (3,000'). The Midlands cover the Mahabharat Range above 915 meters as well as the "Middle Hills" or Pahar zone that extends up to 2745 meters (9,000'). The Highlands include all of Nepal over 2745 meters.

The Lowlands

The *Tarai* is defined as a belt of well-watered alluvial soil stretching from the Indian border northward to the first slopes of the Bhabar. Because of the proximity of precipitation-producing mountains, the Tarai is wetter than much of the adjoining Gangetic plain.

The Tarai, one of the richest bird areas in Nepal, is also intensely interesting from an anthropological point of view. On a trip to the Tarai one sees an extensive farming region producing a major rice crop in summer and a wheat harvest in winter. Small Tarai hamlets are surrounded by mango groves and other fruit trees while major towns near the border such as Biratnagar, Birganj and Nepalganj attract bustling commerce. One need visit only a few of the unique ethnic groups—the Tharus, Maithilis, Rajbunchis and Mechis—to see that over hundreds of years the Tarai people have developed complex and sophisticated cultural and social structures.

The Tarai was once widely forested or grass-covered and sheltered many large mammals. A small portion of the original Tarai vegetation still remains and recently His Majesty's Government established two wildlife sanctuaries, Shuklaphanta in the west and Kosi Tappu in the east, to preserve unusual Nepalese animals and plants. If one follows the principle that a portion of every unique area in a country should be preserved as a part of that

Artists Hem and Hira Lal at 3,000' elevation near Machapuchare (22,980').

country's natural heritage, then these two sanctuaries are of utmost importance.

Shuklaphanta is a roughly circular preserve of about 60 square miles encompassing both hardwood forest on upland levels and low, flooded tracts complete with tall marsh grass. This preserve not only protects a sample of Tarai vegetation but also the last of the Swamp Deer *(Cervus duvauceli)* in Nepal as well as a number of tigers, leopards, wild boar and numerous birds. The rare Swamp Partridge, for instance, is found now in Nepal only in the southwest.

The Kosi Tappu Reserve, a 12 sq. mi. strip of land along the Kosi River, protects a remnant population of Wild Water Buffalo *(Bubalus bubalis)*. It is an area of seasonally inundated grassland with acacia and shisham trees. Just downstream from Kosi Tappu we come to one of the finest bird areas in Nepal. Indeed, when spring migration is on, this is one of the spectacular bird sights in south Asia. During a week's count in 1971 we listed 32,000 ducks of 19 species, not to mention shore birds, herons, gulls, terns, gallinules, hawks and eagles. It is hoped that protection might be extended some day to these thousands of birds in what would be Nepal's first bird sanctuary.

While little extensive forest remains in the Tarai, considerable Sal *(Shorea robusta)* growth exists in the *Bhabar*. The Bhabar is a gently sloping, very stony band of land between the Tarai and the first uplift of the Churia Hills. In most areas it is about 13 kilometers (8 mi.) in width. The Bhabar has very little surface water; its stream beds, their round boulders and pebbles baking in the hot sun, stand dry for nine months of the year. These conditions are not conducive to agriculture and few people live here.

The *Churia Range* (Siwalik Hills), the outermost range of the Himalayas, reaches a maximum elevation of about 1220 meters (4,000'); it lies immediately north of the Bhabar. This range, while young by geological time, is still thought to be one of the oldest of Himalayan uplifts. The Churia is perhaps most famous for its fossil deposits of Pleistocene mammals.

At close range the Churia is seen to be completely unstable with small pebbles and boulders giving a conglomerate-like appearance to the soil. This physical condition does not encourage farming or settling; almost no people live here. As a result, the Churia is covered with vegetation—fire resistant Sal as well as Long-leafed Pine and Phoenix Palm. Damp ravines reveal tangles of bamboos, vines and wild bananas. As one would expect, Bhabar birds as well as other animal life, extend into the Churia with additional species found in moist, shaded ravines.

Duns (pronounced "doons") are valleys with fertile, alluvial soils that lie between the Churia Hills to the south and the Mahabharat Range to the north; their elevations rarely exceed 300 meters (915'). The cultivated Dang Dun in the west and the partly forested Chitwan (Rapti) Dun in central Nepal are the best known.

Years ago the Tharus, an ethnic group apparently partly resistant to malaria, settled in the Duns where they cleared patches of forest and raised crops. Today additional people from the hills are moving into the Duns following a malaria eradication program. In most places now, villages, fields and hedgerows have replaced forests.

The Royal Chitwan National Park, located in the Chitwan Dun and encompassing part of the Churia Hills, was officially established in 1973 for the preservation of a remnant population of One-horned Rhinoceroses. Chitwan, once one of the most famous big-game hunting areas in all Asia, now offers habitat protection to a large array of mammals such as the Tiger, Spotted Leopard, Sloth Bear and Gaur as well as numerous unusual birds including the Yellow-bellied Prinia, Crow-billed Drongo and the Rufous-necked Laughing Thrush.

Visitors to the Park may stay at Tiger Tops Jungle Lodge. During a twenty-four hour tour there, one would expect to see large mammals as well as about 100 species of birds. Crocodiles (the Gavial and the Muggar), butterflies and flowering trees near the Lodge add interest to one's visit. Today Chitwan is one of the outstanding wildlife areas of Asia. We trust it will maintain this position.

The Midlands

The oak-crowned crests of the *Mahabharat Range* rise to about 2745 meters (9,000') immediately north of the Duns and Churia Hills. The lower slopes of the Mahabharat are inhabited by many people including Caste Hindus, Tamangs and Chepangs. Their villages perch incredibly, and sometimes rather precariously, on mountain sides while terraced fields spread endlessly beneath the houses. The thousands upon thousands of terraces of Midland Nepal are often referred to as one of the world's agricultural wonders.

As one ascends the range, there is a dramatic change from cultivations to scrub growth to dense oak forests. The branches of oaks growing along the ridges are encased with moss, lichens and ferns which obtain moisture from the mist of low-lying clouds. Winter at these elevations signals clear nights accompanied by frost while three or four storms during the cold season touch the oaks and hanging moss with white accents.

One of the best places to observe Mahabharat bird life and changing vegetation patterns is on the southern rim of Kathmandu Valley. Here, at Godaveri, where the original Schima-Castanopsis subtropical forest has been preserved, one may see White-crested Laughing-Thrushes, Blue-throated Barbets and Rufous-bellied Bulbuls. Then, starting at an elevation of 1525 meters (5,000'), one climbs to the summit of Phulchowki at 2745 meters (9,000'). In the fine oak forest near the top one enjoys the songs of the Black-capped Sibia, the Gray-winged Blackbird and the Red-headed Laughing-Thrush.

As one stands atop the Mahabharat, one is impressed by the waves of blue-hazed ridges which stretch northward to support the giant snow peaks of the Great Himalayan Range. These hills of moderate elevation, rising above deep-shadowed valleys, comprise an area variously called the Pahar or Middle Hills.

The *Pahar zone,* one of the most fascinating in Nepal, is where the majority of the hill people live. In past years a deadly form of malaria made it difficult to survive below 915 meters (3,000') altitude. It was also virtually impossible to exist, except in dry, inner valleys, above about 2745 meters (9,000') as heavy cloud cover precluded crops ripening during the short growing season. Thus over the years a great variety of ethnic types settled in the Pahar zone. Among these, the "Tibeto-Burman" linguistic groups are perhaps the most numerous.

The "Tibeto-Burman" people are thought to be of eastern and northern origin; they become more numerous as one moves eastward through Nepal. The western-most of these people, the Maggars, are found on the slopes of Dhaulagiri and from here eastward one passes through Gurung, Tamang, Sherpa, Rai and Limbu communities. Most interestingly, the eastern trend of these people is strongly paralleled by the flora and fauna. Eastern forms begin to appear in the Dhaulagiri area and then become more prolific through the eastern hills.

It should be mentioned that the Pahar zone is not a uniform entity from east to west. Besides microclimatic variation, there is a substantial difference in the general climate so that even at identical elevations one notes a considerable change in vegetation. In western Nepal, extensive forests of oak and pine remain, possibly due to the comparatively dry conditions that inhibit intensive agriculture. In central and eastern Nepal, where it rains a good deal, we find fields virtually flowing from one terrace to the next and these are flanked by scrub growth in steep gullies.

Kathmandu Valley is a unique part of the Pahar zone. This former lake bed, now a plain of about 204 square miles, supports a human population of more than half a million. While the natural history of the Valley is exciting, the two thousand or so temples and shrines plus the colorful customs of the festival-loving, but hard-working people, have attracted most attention.

Kathmandu Valley is rich in natural history despite the fact that over 500,000 people live here. Botanists of the Department of Medicinal Plants of HMG record in their FLORA OF PHULCHOKI AND GODAWARI, 527 flowering plants in these two small areas. We have listed 412 bird species from the Valley; additions are constantly turning up. During our annual Christmas Bird Count (patterned after those organized by the National Audubon Society in the U.S.A.), we have located up to 180 species in a single day's search. There are surely well over 200 species in Kathmandu Valley during this time of the year. With additional observers we hope to be able to increase our count numbers.

The Highlands

Looking north from Kathmandu, or from a vantage point in the Pahar, one can pick out white ice pinnacles complete with overhangs, avalanche channels and steep, dark rock faces. These peaks, the highest of the Great Himalayan Range, crown Highland Nepal.

It is convenient to start Highland Nepal, or the Himalayan zone, at about 2745 meters (9,000') elevation. Most of the cultivations in Nepal occur below this level so that above this altitude, one finds fine forests of hemlocks, firs, rhododendrons and birches. The timber line in the Himalayas varies to some degree with exposure and other conditions; an average is about 3965 meters (13,000').

Once above 4270 meters (14,000'), Himalayan vegetation often grows dwarfed in form and bird varieties diminish. With rare exceptions, people do not live permanently above the tree line in Nepal but some hardy mammals and birds do—the Himalayan Tahr, Snow Leopard, and Blue Sheep along with the Snow Partridge and snow cocks, to name a few.

Summer is *the* time to visit the Himalayan zone. Rose finches, accentors, Grandalas, and pipits sing here amid broad carpets of wildflowers—poppies, primulas, edelweiss, everlastings, geraniums and dwarf rhododendrons. Little pikas (mouse-hares) scurry about nibbling rumex, corydalis and other plants that grow between lichen-decorated boulders. Few visitors outside of local people venture into these highland meadows during the summer, for travel is somewhat difficult. On a summer trek one is hampered in route by heavy rain, swollen streams and leeches. At high altitudes a constant, drizzling mist reduces visibility. One may be treated, however, on an occasional monsoon morning, to a spectacular view across multiple jagged ridges that are buttressed below by puffy white clouds temporarily stuffed into the valleys. At such times, carpets of Himalayan wildflowers glisten with water, each drop shimmering in the orangy-red rays of the early sun.

Above Himalayan meadows rises a harsh but dramatic land of rocks, snow and ice. Little life is sustained here. The sounds of the region are neither the songs of birds nor the strumming of insects so familiar in south Nepal, but rather the wind whistling over ice cornices, the sudden rush of a rock fall, or the thunder of an avalanche.

This is not to say there are no birds at extreme altitudes. There are. One of the fascinating features of the Himalayas is that birds fly to exceptional heights. Mountain climbers regularly report soaring birds such as choughs, lammergeiers, ravens and eagles up to elevations of 7625 meters (25,000'); some birds go even higher. Apparently birds adapt readily to low oxygen tensions and can adjust without acclimatization to heights that would quickly render a person unconscious. Bar-headed Geese appear to illustrate this phenomenon. We have noted thousands of this migratory species resting within sight of the Churia foothills. From here they take off, heading straight towards the high mountains until lost from view. Circumstantial evidence now suggests that these birds reach heights of at least 7625 meters (25,000') within a short time, then pass over into Tibet without stopping again in Nepal. Terrance Bech of the 1973 American Dhaulagiri expedition, while on the mountain, actually watched "V"s of geese flying over the eastern spur of Dhaulagiri at about 7625 meters. It should be noted that birds are at these altitudes for only short periods.

North of the Great Himalayan Range, in the districts of Dolpo, Mustang and Manang, one looks out on a near-desert landscape. Reduced rainfall combined with high altitude allow Tibetan species to flourish here. Hence one notes the Tibetan Hare *(Lepus capensis)* at 4880 meters (16,000') along with the Himalayan Marmot *(Marmota bobak)* and Siberian Weasel *(Mustela sibirica)*. While the vegetation is somewhat sparse, there is a combination of *Caragana* and *Lonicera* dotting the hillsides up to about 5032 meters (16,500'). Bird life is rather drab-colored in keeping with the surroundings. One looks for Hume's Ground Peckers, Short-toed Larks, Tibetan Twites, Tibetan Snow Finches and Tibetan Partridges. Additional species not yet known from Nepal should occur in these northern areas. One should be on the lookout for, among others, the Tibetan Sandgrouse, the Tibetan Owl and the Pied Magpie.

Zoogeographical Considerations of Nepal Bird Life

Nepal stands alone both from its altitudinal variety as well as its geographical position in Asia. Zoogeographically, Nepal falls close to the center of Asia. The two biogeographical realms of Asia—the Palearctic to the north and the Oriental to the south—interdigitate here.

The flora and fauna of the Himalayan zone is allied with Europe and north Asia. "European" ferns, *Dryopteris acuto-dentata* and *Polystichum prescottianum*, commonly shelter under rocks in high altitude Nepal. European flower genera—edelweiss (*Leontopodium*), forget-me-not (*Cyanoglossum*), *Geranium* and *Corydalis* frequently lend their colors to Himalayan meadows. Likewise, we find accentors, finches, pipits and grosbeaks that range into the Himalayas from northern Asia.

Oriental Realm species are predominant in southern Nepal. Here, minivets and cuckoo-shrikes feed in *sal, terminalia* and *adina* trees. On the forest floor, pittas search through leaf litter as Orange Oakleaf butterflies sun nearby. Occasionally a Green Whip Snake moves gracefully past. These are tropical, warm-climate species.

Biogeographically, the Himalayan Mountain System can be separated conveniently into eastern and western sections. At one time the dividing line between east and west was thought to be near the Arun River in eastern Nepal, as eastern forms apparently rarely occurred west of this boundary. Recent avian data show, however, that the Arun is neither an effective barrier nor a dividing line. Instead, the Kali Gandaki River in central Nepal emerges as a very distinct breaking point in bird distributions. Eastern birds including the Brown Parrotbill, Golden-breasted Tit Babbler, Rufous-bellied Shrike Babbler and the Blood Pheasant extend only as far west as the Annapurnas. Conversely, western birds that reach Dhaulagiri and apparently no further east are the Simla Black Tit, Spot-winged Black Tit, White-throated Tit, Missel Thrush, White-cheeked Nuthatch and the Eurasian Nuthatch. Thus, virtually in the center of Nepal, and also in the center of the 2577 kilometer (1,600 mi.) Himalayan arc, we find a fairly narrow region of considerable species change.

Bird Watching in Nepal

Bird watching in Nepal can be a very rewarding experience for colorful birds live here amid one of the most scenic regions on earth. Bird watching is an activity which requires some energy but little equipment. Binoculars, though, are essential; we tend to choose lightweight varieties due to the Nepalese terrain. Successful bird watching centers on the principle: "don't frighten the quarry." This means that one should proceed as quietly and inconspicuously as possible. Numbers of endemic Himalayan laughing-thrushes, babblers, yuhinas and pheasants are quite shy; your chances of seeing them increase if you move slowly.

Identifications of most adult birds in good light and at close range should not be difficult. Once you have studied the book, you will be looking for important points including size, shape, behavior and plumage details. You will note eye-rings, wingbars and special color combinations. A positive identification may be impossible, though, if the bird does not cooperate. Birds often slip away too soon; one learns to be patient. Identifications will come more easily and accurately with increased experience, especially if you are able to recognize bird calls. Many visually secretive Himalayan species, interestingly enough, are often quite vocal; their presence can be detected instantly by a trained ear.

Getting to the birds is often a challenge in Nepal. From Kathmandu one can drive comfortably to suitable forest areas in the Valley. In addition, a flight to Tiger Tops Jungle Lodge in the lowlands can be worked into a tight schedule. Nepal, though, is the land of the trekker. The term "trek" as used in Nepal denotes an extended hike lasting several days. Supplies usually are carried along with the party. We find this an excellent way to see the country, its people and its flora and fauna.

Several treks offer fine introductions to Nepal and its bird life. Among these, the Everest area presents spectacular mountains along with high altitude birds. Dhaulagiri and Annapurna peaks are striking on the Kali Gandaki trail and one may see Tibetan species of birds around Jomosom which is north of the great Himalayan chain. Main trails of Nepal, especially the Everest, Kali Gandaki, Helumbu and Langtang routes, now sustain heavy tourist pressure. Fortunately there are innumerable other spectacular areas which receive little publicity and so are visited only rarely.

For one interested in seeing as many different birds as possible, we recommend going from low to high elevations. A concentrated three-week visit in Nepal should produce a bird list of between 300 to 400 species.

If one is interested in discovering new data regarding Nepalese birds, there are several places where one could concentrate his efforts. The "Rara-Ringmo finger" is a western belt of coniferous forest that points into the country as far east as Dhaulagiri. Here the vegetation—pine, cedar, juniper, spruce, cypress, yew and fir—reminds one of Kashmir, or even parts of Europe or North America. This entire area needs thorough investigation.

Other places of special interest include the Mai Valley in Ilam District and the southeastern Lowlands in Jhapa and Sunsari Districts. The Tailed Wren Babbler and the Black-spotted Yellow Titmouse are known in Nepal only from the Mai Valley. Likewise the rare Purple Cochoa occurs here. The southeast Lowlands has abundant animal life. Fairy Bluebirds, Blue-eared Barbets and Little Spiderhunters are specialities of the area.

While the bird life, mountains, wildflowers, butterflies and other colorful living things, make Nepal beautiful, it is the people that give the country its distinctive character. The open courteousness and the friendliness of the Nepalese has been publicized widely; it is no exaggeration. We have traveled comfortably throughout Nepal during the past 25 years and have found Nepal to be a truly remarkable country with a remarkable people.

How to use the book

This book is designed for quick reference in the field. The text for each species is on the page facing the illustration.

The first line in the description of a species, gives the English name (or names) and then the Latin designation. Scientific terminology and order follow, for the most part, that given by Ripley in THE SYNOPSIS OF THE BIRDS OF INDIA AND PAKISTAN. For the purposes of simplified identification, we have changed the sequential order of certain families. Thus we place cranes with storks, bustard-quail with quail, and swallows with swifts. Similarly, for ease of handling, we give family status to Timaliidae, Muscicapidae, Sylviidae and Turdidae rather than retaining them at subfamily level.

The second line of the description might read as follows:

3660-5490 m. (12,000-18,000') 53 cm. (21") R.

Abbreviations used here are: m. = meters; ' = feet; cm. = centimeters; " = inches. Thus the first two sets of figures refer to elevations above sea level in meters and feet. These are altitudes in Nepal between which the bird usually is found. One should remember, however, that birds are mobile creatures and occasionally may move out of their "normal" ranges. This is particularly true of young birds immediately after the nesting season. The high altitude Spotted Nutcracker was recently seen in the tropical forests of Dharan at 274 meters (900'), and a low elevation White-eye strayed to 3660 meters (12,000') among barberries on Ganesh Himal. In the main text we list 400 feet above sea level as Nepal's minimum altitude; revised data show this figure should be only 250 feet (76 meters).

The 53 cm. (21") in the second line refers to the total length of the bird, including tail. Size is a useful comparative identification tool. Judging size, though, is sometimes a bit difficult for the apparent size of the bird depends on its distance from the observer.

Thus if you misjudge distance, a correct assessment of size becomes difficult. This is especially true in cloud forests where a bird such as the Red-tailed Minla may look twice its size through the mist. Conversely, birds in the extremely clear air and vast expanses of the high Himalayas, look dwarfed. Those Tibetan Snow Cocks you judge to be about a hundred meters away and the size of partridges are, in reality, well over two hundred meters away and stand larger than some pheasants. Accurately judging size is a challenge to bird identifications.

The final letter of the second line gives the seasonal status of the bird in Nepal. Thus:

R = Resident   W = Winter
M = Migrant   S = Summer

Resident means that the bird is found in or near one location all year long. Some bird populations move slightly downhill in winter but these are still considered resident. *Migrant* birds pass through parts of Nepal on their way to and from nesting grounds. Spring migration begins about the end of February and continues into May, while autumn movements are from late August into November. *Winter* birds arrive in the locality from September to November and most have departed by late April. *Summer* birds arrive on their nesting grounds from late March to June and usually leave between September and November. If two capital letters appear at the end of the second line, it means that the population is divided (usually subspecifically). The Eurasian Kestrel is listed R., W. which indicates a resident population augmented in winter by birds from the north.

The third line begins with a comment on the abundance of the species in Nepal. Without actual censuses, these designations are approximations at best. They are based, in general, on what a person would be likely to see, given a full day's search in a favorable habitat at a suitable altitude and season. The terms are:

abundant = always seen in some numbers
common = usually seen
fairly common = chances are about 50%
occasional = usually not seen
scarce = very unlikely; only a few records for Nepal

Comments on pertinent field marks follow a reference to habitat. Birds, as all creatures, vary considerably from individual to individual even within the same species so that field identifications are partly a matter of elimination. One tries to find the illustration and description that *most* resembles the bird in the bush. Our paintings were taken from study specimens in good light whereas the bird before you may be singing in dull light and partly hidden by a branch covered with hanging moss. Several species, such as scimitar babblers, are secretive and rarely show themselves. All one sees, in the case of a scimitar babbler, is a dark form disappearing into a densely foliaged bush. To identify this bird you will need to use all possible clues including general shape, size, voice, behavior, habitat and altitude.

Following a description of a bird's vocal patterns, you may find a sentence beginning with a KV. This line gives specific data relevant to Kathmandu Valley. As half the birds in the book may be found at one time or another in Kathmandu Valley, we stress this particular section of Nepal.

The distribution of each species is given in the final line following a pipal leaf design ❦. Four Himalayan areas— Kashmir, Garhwal,

Nepal and Sikkim—are dealt with first. If the bird is found in any one or all of these regions it is so listed. For example, if you are in Srinagar, Kashmir, you may check quickly to see whether the bird occurs in Kashmir. Kashmir in this context refers to the Vale of Kashmir and side valleys which is essentially the upper Jhelum River watershed. Following these Himalayan areas and after a semi-colon, the world-wide range of the species is listed. This will help coordinate bird watching in Nepal with other geographical areas.

At the right hand edge of the final line is a number which refers the reader to subspecific material found in Ripley's SYNOPSIS and in Ali and Ripley's HANDBOOK OF THE BIRDS OF INDIA AND PAKISTAN. In this way you may supplement your field notes by cross-checking your data with information given in these important volumes. The symbol (AR) also refers the reader to these books.

The illustrations in our book feature adult birds, including females when different. Juvenile birds as well as breeding plumages are shown in some cases. Abbreviations used are: ad.=adult; juv.=juvenile plumage; breed.=breeding plumage; wint.= winter plumage; ♂=male; ♀=female. Birds on each page are proportional in size to others on the page except for two examples. On page 25 grebes form one section, the pelican a second and cormorants plus the anhinga a third. On page 109 the parakeets are all in proportion except the lorikeet which is twice proportional size. All species reported from Nepal within the last 100 years (except very late additions) are illustrated; Hodgson's unreconfirmed records of the early 1800's are included in the text but not illustrated.

Following the main text are two appendices. The first gives identifying field marks for 28 Kashmir (Vale of Kashmir) species not known from Nepal. Most of these are winter visitors from the north and are not likely to be found in Nepal. The second appendix lists 32 species from Sikkim that are not known yet from Nepal. As Sikkim and eastern Nepal are not only contiguous but also have very similar topography and biotope, we expect that many birds of the Sikkim appendix eventually will turn up in Nepal. Our data for Himalayan birds are still far from complete. Much among these great mountain ranges remains to be observed and recorded. We hope this book will stimulate an increased understanding and enjoyment of Nepal birds.

ACKNOWLEDGEMENTS

Several hundred people have contributed directly or indirectly to the production of this book; we wish we could adequately thank each person that has assisted us during our 25-year study of Nepal birds.

Officials of His Majesty's Government have been invariably helpful and we would like to thank members of the Foreign Ministry as well as the Home Ministry for permissions to live and travel in Nepal. General Singha Shumshere J. B. Rana, for example, was the Nepalese Ambassador to India through whom our initial permission to visit Nepal in 1949 was given. We wish to thank him again.

We are also most grateful to the Forest Department, H. M. G., for permission to study Nepalese birds. This department has been continually responsive to our work; Richard Willan, R. P. Pandey, M. B. Thapa and Emerald S.S.J.B. Rana are warmly remembered. As much of our work involved forested areas, we were assisted by many field officers of the Department; it is a pleasure to especially recognize Keshar Bajracharya, Kirthi Man Tamang, M. Haque, B. L. Das and Karna Sakya.

The Rudra Shumshere J. B. Rana family strongly supported our work from the very beginning and we express our great appreciation to members of this family: the late Field Marshal Rudra Shumshere J. B. Rana; his sons Col. Ishwar, former Governor Dhariya, Shri Bakti, Shri Shyam and Col. Gopal; and grandsons Sagar, Prabhat and Himanta. Sagar accompanied us on several later expeditions and developed into a first rate scientific collector and companion.

We would also like to thank the following for sending us specimens: J. S. Shah, Dinesh S.S.J.B. Rana, Lakshman Shah, Binode Shah, Dr. Ray Pendleton and Richard Mitchell. General Shushil S.S.J.B. Rana deserves special commendation for the unusual specimens he has obtained.

We appreciated our expedition companions for their enthusiasm and assistance in the field: Dr. Carl Taylor, Robert Bergsaker, Harold Bergsma, Dr. Carl Friedericks, Richard Parker, Ray Smith, Frank Stough, Nirmal Roberts, Dr. James Dick, Dr. Robert Berry, David Chesmore, Ronald O'Connor, Terrance O'Connor, Dr. Denis Roche, Richard Friedericks, Lawrence Thie, Lee Miller, Charles Baker, John Harris, Hari Sharan (Kazi) Nepali, Peter Petersen, Robert Waltner, John Blower, Michael Kellas, Keshar Bajracharya and Karna Sakya. John Propst located the Greater Flamingo as well as several other birds new to Nepal. A special word of thanks to Jeff Devitt, Mike Weeks and James White for arrangements in Bardiya district. Lal Bahadur Tamang not only organized porters and camping details for numerous field trips, but also found the first known Spiny

Babbler nest as well as a number of other "firsts"; grateful thanks go to him.

A great many people have assisted us during the course of our research expeditions. We would especially like to thank the Sherchan family of Tukche and Deva Nur Singh of Jomosom, K. D. Karki of Biratnagar, Swami Vivekananda Saraswati of Doti, K. T. Das in Ilam, B. P. Achariya in Jhapa, and John Coapman at Tiger Tops.

This book would not have been produced without the support of the Field Museum of Natural History, Chicago. The late Boardman Conover sponsored our first Nepal expedition and it has been through the encouragement of museum curators Austin L. Rand, Robert E. Blake and Melvin A. Traylor that we have continued working on Nepal birds.

Hari S. Nepali and G. B. Gurung very kindly loaned us specimens for paintings, as did the Field Museum, Bird Division, Mel Traylor, Curator, and also the Bombay Natural History Society where thanks goes to Zafar Futehally, Honorary Secretary and J. C. Daniel, Curator. In addition, we wish to acknowledge S. Christensen, B. P. Nielsen, R. F. Porter and I. Willis for information from their paper on Aquila Eagles included in a series of articles on flight identification of European raptors.

Artists Hem Poudyal and Hira Lal Dangol devoted three years to this project; we are extremely grateful for their perseverance. Thanks also to Margaret Fleming Waldron of Hawaii for doing the mountain plates and Linda Firth Fleming for assisting with shading as well as with branches and moss.

The ultimate impact of an illustrated bird book rests, in the final analysis, upon the quality of the color reproductions. In this regard, we feel ourselves extremely fortunate to be associated with G. U. Mehta, Arun Mehta, Katey Cooper and J. Nath of Vakil & Sons Limited, Bombay; we greatly appreciate their interest in the book and the unstinting effort they have given to produce high quality results.

The Methodist Mission Board in New York, through Mr. Henry Lacy, generously granted the senior author a year's leave of absence so that he could work under a Fulbright Fellowship for 1964-1965 as well as a two-year pre-retirement period to complete the manuscript.

Professor Emeritus George J. Wallace of Michigan State University and M. A. Traylor have gone through parts of the manuscript; we are most grateful for their corrections and suggestions. Thelma Fiorini greatly assisted by typing the final draft of the manuscript. For proof reading, thanks to Helen Fleming and Linda Firth Fleming.

CONTENTS

FOREWORD by ELVIS J. STAHR	7
INTRODUCTION	9
The Lowlands	9
The Midlands	11
The Highlands	12
Zoogeographical Considerations of Nepal Bird Life	14
Bird watching in Nepal	15
How to use the book	16
ACKNOWLEDGEMENTS	19
GREBES: Podicipedidae	24
PELICANS: Pelecanidae	24
CORMORANTS AND DARTER: Phalacrocoracidae	24
HERONS AND BITTERNS: Ardeidae	26
STORKS: Ciconiidae	30
CRANES: Gruidae	32
IBISES AND SPOONBILL: Threskiornithidae	34
FLAMINGO: Phoenicopteridae	34
GEESE AND DUCKS: Anatidae	36
KITES, HAWKS, EAGLES, VULTURES AND ALLIES: Accipitridae	44
FALCONS: Falconidae	62
PARTRIDGES, QUAIL AND PHEASANTS: Phasianidae	66
BUSTARD-QUAIL: Turnicidae	70
RAILS, CRAKES, GALLINULES AND ALLIES: Rallidae	76
BUSTARDS: Otididae	80
JACANAS: Jacanidae	80
OYSTERCATCHER: Haematopodidae	80
WADERS: Charadriidae	82
PAINTED SNIPE: Rostratulidae	92
AVOCET AND ALLIES: Recurvirostridae	92
THICK KNEES: Burhinidae	94
COURSER AND PRATINCOLES: Glareolidae	94

GULLS AND TERNS: Laridae	..	96
SANDGROUSE: Pteroclidae	..	100
PIGEONS AND DOVES: Columbidae	..	100
PARAKEETS: Psittacidae	..	108
CUCKOOS: Cuculidae	..	110
OWLS: Tytonidae and Strigidae	..	118
NIGHTJARS: Caprimulgidae	..	126
TROGONS: Trogonidae	..	128
ROLLERS: Coraciidae	..	128
HOOPOE: Upupidae	..	128
KINGFISHERS: Alcedinidae	..	130
BEE-EATERS: Meropidae	..	132
HORNBILLS: Bucerotidae	..	134
BARBETS: Capitonidae	..	136
HONEYGUIDE: Indicatoridae	..	138
WOODPECKERS: Picidae	..	138
BROADBILLS: Eurylaimidae	..	148
PITTAS: Pittidae	..	148
LARKS: Alaudidae	..	148
SWIFTS: Apodidae	..	152
SWALLOWS AND MARTINS: Hirundinidae	..	156
SHRIKES: Laniidae	..	158
ORIOLES: Oriolidae	..	160
DRONGOS: Dicruridae	..	162
WOOD-SWALLOWS: Artamidae	..	166
STARLINGS AND MYNAS: Sturnidae	..	166
CROWS AND ALLIES: Corvidae	..	170
MINIVETS AND ALLIES: Campephagidae	..	176
WAXWINGS: Bombycillidae	..	180
LEAF BIRDS AND ALLIES: Irenidae	..	180
BULBULS: Pycnonotidae	..	182
BABBLERS, LAUGHING-THRUSHES AND ALLIES: Timaliidae		186
FLYCATCHERS: Muscicapidae	..	214
WARBLERS: Sylviidae	..	226
THRUSHES, CHATS AND ALLIES: Turdidae	..	248
WREN: Troglodytidae	..	272
DIPPERS: Cinclidae	..	272
ACCENTORS: Prunellidae	..	272

TITMICE: Paridae	276
NUTHATCHES: Sittidae	282
TREE CREEPERS: Certhiidae	284
PIPITS AND WAGTAILS: Motacillidae	286
FLOWERPECKERS: Dicaeidae	292
SUNBIRDS: Nectariniidae	294
WHITE-EYE: Zosteropidae	296
SPARROWS AND WEAVER BIRDS: Ploceidae	298
FINCHES AND ALLIES: Fringillidae	304
BUNTINGS: Emberizidae	316
ADDITIONS	324
Possible New Records	328
Additional Sightings, Extensions and Corrections	328
BIBLIOGRAPHY	338
APPENDIX 1: KASHMIR BIRDS	343
APPENDIX 2: SIKKIM BIRDS	345
INDEX OF SCIENTIFIC NAMES	347
INDEX AND CHECK LIST OF ENGLISH NAMES	355

GREBES (Podicipedidae) are medium-sized, aquatic birds that ride low in the water. They appear plump with small wings and lobed toes. Most arrive in Nepal in November and depart by late March. Grebes shown are proportionate to grebes only and not to pelican or cormorants.

    Great Crested Grebe, *Podiceps cristatus.*
854-3050 m. (2,800-10,000') 46 cm. (18") W.

Occasional; on lakes in winter (Phewa Tal, Rara). Distinguished from other grebes by light color and large size; from ducks by long neck and long, sharp bill. No crest in winter. At mid-day in February, 85 sleeping together on Rara Lake. ♣ Kashmir, Nepal; Europe, Africa, Asia, Australia   **3**

    Black-necked Grebe, *Podiceps caspicus.*
854-3050 m. (2,800-10,000') 30 cm. (12") W.

Scarce; on Phewa Tal and Rara Lake. Only half the size of Great Crested Grebe and with comparatively short neck and bill. Larger than Little Grebe and neck paler. Note slight upturned bill that is thinner than any duck's. A dozen pairs on Rara Lake in February. ♣ Kashmir, Nepal; Europe, Africa, Asia, N. America   **4**

    Little Grebe, *Podiceps ruficollis.*
120-1372 m. (400-4,500') 25 cm. (10") R.

Fairly common; on reedy ponds and lakes of the *tarai*. A tiny duck-like bird with distinct two-toned bill. Note reddish neck which changes to pale rufous in winter. Quite tame; still bobbing around after ducks and others take flight. Slithers along, on fast wingbeats with legs dangling just above water. Call a repeated *klik* and a trill. ❋ KV: on Taudha Lake, and occasionally in rice fields in summer. ♣ Kashmir, Nepal; Europe, Africa, Asia, Australia   **5**

PELICANS (Pelecanidae) are large birds with broad wing spans, long, heavy beaks and ample throat pouches. Often glide at great height. Shown proportionately smaller than other birds.

    White Pelican, *Pelecanus onocrotalus.*
1372 m. (4,500') 180 cm. (71") S.

Scarce; a pair watched for thirty minutes soaring over Kathmandu Valley (J. V. Coapman, 1971). In flight, resembles White Stork but flies with head drawn in, not straight out. May occur anywhere in lowland Nepal. ♣ Nepal; Europe, Africa, Asia   **20**

    Spot-billed Pelican, *Pelecanus philippensis.*
120 m. (400') 152 cm. (60") S.

Scarce; on large expanses of water in the Kosi River. A *gray* and brown species, without black in wing (a good field mark in flight). Spots on bill seen only at close range. Only recently re-discovered in Nepal (thus no illustration) by J.F.S. Batson and Richard C. Gregory-Smith. Single birds noted at Kosi Barrage in April, June and July. ♣ Nepal; Africa, Asia   **22 (?)**

CORMORANTS and DARTER (Phalacrocoracidae). Cormorants are black, fish-eating birds, with long necks and serrated bills, hooked at tip. Fly and swim well. Darters have long, pointed bills used for spearing prey. Cormorants shown proportionate to Darter only.

    Large Cormorant, *Phalacrocorax carbo.*
152-1067 m. (500-3,500') 84 cm. (33") R.

Fairly common; on large rivers and lakes, occasionally at Pokhara and on rivers well into the mountains. Black with white throat in breeding season; a long, broad tail. Swims partly submerged with bill pointing upward. Flies with steady wingbeat and neck outstretched. Flocks fish together. Several hundred roosting near Devi Tal, Royal Chitwan National Park. Call a low, guttural *r-rah*. (Indian Shag, *Phalacrocorax fuscicollis*, Sikkim list, p. 336) ♣ Nepal; Europe, Africa, Asia, Australia, N. America   **26**

    Little Cormorant, *Phalacrocorax niger.*
120-244 m. (400-800') 48 cm. (19") R.

Scarce; haunts wooded streams and ponds of the *tarai*. Like Large Cormorant but only half size and lacks extensive white on throat. Usually single or in small, scattered groups on rivers—Mechi, Kosi. ♣ Nepal; Bangladesh to S.E. Asia   **28**

    Darter, *Anhinga rufa.*
120-305 m. (400-1,000') 91 cm. (36") R.

Fairly common; on lagoons, ponds and sluggish rivers. Long, thin, dark neck; back streaked with silver. Usually solitary. Often swims partly submerged with snake-like head and neck above water. Sits on stump in sun with wings outstretched. Noisy at nests. Call a rapid *chigi* (AR). ♣ Nepal; Africa to New Zealand   **29**

Great Crested Grebe

Black-necked Grebe

wint. sum.

Little Grebe

White Pelican (not to scale)

Large Cormorant

Little Cormorant

Darter

HERONS and BITTERNS (Ardeidae) are waders with long legs, necks and bills. Egrets are white herons. Herons fly leisurely on broad, rounded wings, their legs projecting well beyond short tails and necks drawn back in an S-curve (storks and cranes fly with necks outstretched). Shy bitterns are rarely seen for they crouch when disturbed or dash away in a short flight.

Great White-bellied Heron, *Ardea imperialis*. Last reported in 1846. Look along large rivers for a fairly uniform gray bird with a white belly (not gray as in the Gray Heron). 🍂 Nepal, Sikkim; Sikkim to Burma 33

Gray Heron, *Ardea cinerea*.
120-1280 m. (400-4,200') 96 cm. (38") R., M.
Occasional; on large rivers and lakes. A regular winter visitor near the Kosi Barrage in the eastern *tarai* where 20 or more may be seen standing together on sand bars. A silver-gray species with blue-gray wings and back; also a long, black occipital crest. Motionless most of the time; moves deliberately after prey. Voice a *quaaarnk* and a variety of harsh croaks (AR). ✲ KV: seen occasionally on the Bagmati below Chobar. (Giant Heron, *Ardea goliath*, see Sikkim list, p. 336.) 🍂 Kashmir, Nepal; Europe, Africa, Asia 35, 36

Purple Heron, *Ardea purpurea*.
120-305 m. (400-1,000') 79 cm. (31") R.
Occasional; in suitable lowland marshes. A large, darkish heron with rust-colored neck and underparts. Often single, skimming reed beds in deliberate flight. Hunts by standing quietly in shallow water amid reeds. Somewhat crepuscular, flying to roosting trees shortly after dark. Communal roosts except in breeding season. Call a conversational frog-like croak; loud *kaa-ka-row-ka-row-ka-row* when nesting. 🍂 Nepal; Europe, Madagascar to Philippines 37

Little Green Heron, *Butorides striatus*.
120-915 m. (400-3,000') 40 cm. (16") R.
Common; along overhanging banks of most lowland rivers and edges of ponds. Resident around Phewa Tal, Pokhara. A hunch-backed, heavily streaked bird with slow movements. Appears to be very dark in dim light. Retires under cover when alarmed or skims away close to the surface of the water. Call a croak. 🍂 Nepal; Africa, S. Asia to Australia, S. America 38

Pond Heron, *Ardeola grayii*.
120-1525 m. (400-5,000') 40 cm. (16") R.
Common; on mud flats and in wet fields. Diagnostic white wings in flight always distinguishes this bird from similar species—young Night Heron, Little Green Heron and Eurasian Bittern. Breeding plumage dramatically changes from obliterative winter form. Stalks prey slowly; often freezes with bill pointing down. Nests in colonies. Call a croak and other notes. ✲ KV: common in ponds, wet fields and along streams. 🍂 Kashmir, Nepal; Persian Gulf to Malaya 42

Night Heron, *Nycticorax nycticorax*.
274-1310 m. (900-4,300') 60 cm. (24") S.
Occasional; in reedy lagoons and near nesting sites in reeds or tall trees. A distinctive heron with long occipital crest. Young resemble adult Pond Heron but are darker and lack white wings. Illustration shows dark crown developing on young bird. May remain motionless for long periods. Flight is heavy and deliberate. Feeds mostly at night. Call a throaty *quawk* at several-second intervals; also a rapid *wuk-wuk-wuk-wuk*. ✲ KV: flies croaking over Kathmandu at dusk. Nests in tall trees of Kaiser Mahal and feeds at Rani Pokhari at night. Most leave the Valley for the winter; two seen mid-December. 🍂 Kashmir, Nepal; Europe, Africa, Asia, Americas 52

Cattle Egret, *Bubulcus ibis.*
120-1525 m. (400-5,000') 50 cm. (20") R.
Common; in scattered flocks feeding near cattle and buffaloes. Tan feathers in the breeding season and yellow bill without black tip distinguishes this species from other Nepal egrets. When pressed, stalks away; deliberate flight. At sunset, groups fly in irregular v-formations to their roosting places. May roost with other egrets (Rapti Dun) or with crows (Kathmandu). Call a croak. ✤ KV: a nesting colony in bougainvillea vine, Kaiser Mahal. ♠ Kashmir, Nepal; Europe, Africa, Asia, S. and N. America 44

Large Egret, *Egretta alba.*
120-305 m. (400-1,000') 90 cm. (35") R.
Occasional; in lagoons, reed beds and on banks of streams. Bill black in summer, yellowish in winter. Distinguished from Intermediate Egret by larger size and proportionately longer head and neck. In summer has plumes only on back (Intermediate Egret has plumes on back *and breast*). Rather shy and often solitary but sometimes near other water birds. Deliberate flight. It has a variety of guttural notes. ♠ Nepal; Europe, Asia to New Zealand, The Americas 46

Intermediate Egret, *Egretta intermedia.*
120-579 m. (400-1,900') 66 cm. (26") R.
Occasional; in the same habitat as other egrets. Very similar to Large Egret but has thinner neck and shorter bill. Diagnostic lacy *breast* and back plumes in summer. Bill black (breeding) and yellow tipped with black in winter. Leg joints faintly greenish-yellow (black in Large Egret) but this often hard to determine. Usually in small, scattered flocks. Often seen at edge of Royal Chitwan National Park on the Reu and Rapti Rivers. ♠ Nepal; Africa, S. Asia to Australia 47

Little Egret (Snowy Egret), *Egretta garzetta.*
244-1310 m. (800-4,300') 50 cm. (20") R.
Fairly common; at edges of rivers. Similar in size to Cattle Egret but black bill (not yellow as in the Cattle Egret) and *bright yellow feet* differentiate it from all other Nepal egrets. Drooping crest in breeding season; no tan feathers. Usually single or in loose pairs or small flocks in shallow water. Staggers about flushing and catching minnows and frogs. Congregates at roosts. ✤ KV: along Bagmati, Vishnumati, Manora. ♠ Nepal; Europe, Africa, S.Asia to Australia, N. and S. America 49

Chestnut Bittern, *Ixobrychus cinnamoneus.*
274-1372 m. (900-4,500') 38 cm. (15") S.
Occasional; in flooded rice fields. Look for a ruddy bittern with a dark crown. Female is buff and streaked below. Crepuscular, flies regularly across water at dusk (upper Bagmati). Often near Pond Herons. Call is a loud, repeated *goook* with notes in a descending scale. ✤ KV: in rice fields around Rani Bari and Gokarna. (In Kashmir, look for Little Bittern, *I. minutus*, see p. 334.) ♠ Nepal; S. Asia to Philippines 56

Yellow Bittern, *Ixobrychus sinensis.*
120 m. (400') 38 cm. (15") S.
Scarce; in reeds along Kosi River. A yellowish-buff bittern with contrasting *black flight feathers*. Similar Chestnut Bittern appears nearly uniform rusty in flight. Recently rediscovered in the Kosi Barrage area (thus no illustration) by R. C. Gregory-Smith and J.F.S. Batson. Apparently moves into Kosi reed beds in summer as one bird seen on 11 May, nine on 15 June and eight on 21 June 1975. ♠ Nepal; India to China and New Guinea 57

Black Bittern, *Dupetor flavicollis.*
152 m. (500') 58 cm. (23") R. (?)
Scarce; very dark, resembling no other bittern. Collected in 1937 in February from Bilauri Lake, Kanchanpur, S.W. *tarai* in dense reeds (Bailey). By 1974 this lake drained and land cultivated; this species may be elsewhere in the *tarai*. ♠ Nepal; S. Asia to Australia 58

Eurasian Bittern, *Botaurus stellaris.*
1372 m. (4,500') 76 cm. (30") M.
Scarce; found in November along the Manora River near Sankhu, KV (H. S. Nepali, 1970). Much larger than other bitterns; distinguished from a young Night Heron by larger size, neck pattern and fine, dark bars on back (not spotted). Solitary and largely nocturnal. General aspect — hunch-backed. ♠ Kashmir, Nepal; Europe, Africa, Asia 59

STORKS (Ciconiidae) are heavy birds with long legs and necks. Bills are much longer than length of head. In flight, head and neck are held straight out. Often seen soaring on updrafts and thermals. Mostly communal nesting. Hissing and clapping of mandibles are characteristic sounds.

Painted Stork, *Ibis leucocephalus*.
183 m. (600') 102 cm. (40") R.
Scarce; near water in fields and edges of streams. The only black and white stork with *pale pink* feathers ings. Also note black belly band. Often perches high in trees and sometimes seen soaring slowly in wide circles. It feeds by plowing through shallow water with bill immersed. Single, in pairs or small flocks. Found in Chitwan from April to June; also seen in Kailali District, S.W. *tarai* in winter. ♦ Nepal; Pakistan to S.E. Asia 60

Open-billed Stork, *Anastomus oscitans*.
120-305 m. (400-1,000') 64 cm. (25") R.
Fairly common; in small numbers around wooded ponds. Also noted in large flocks in open fields and mud flats above Kosi Barrage. A *pale gray* stork with black wings and tail; the open space between mandibles shows at close range. Eats snails with aid of specialized bill. Fairly shy. Slow flight. Stands erect, often on trees above water. Call said to be a moan (AR). ♦ Nepal; Pakistan to S.E. Asia 61

White-necked Stork (Woolly-necked Stork), *Ciconia episcopus*.
152-1372 m. (500-4,500') 90 cm. (35") R.
Fairly common; near water. The only black stork with a *white neck*. Single, in pairs or small parties with other water birds. The common stork in summer along mountain rivers up to about 915 m. (3,000'). Several along the Indrawati River, N.E. of Kathmandu in August. �֎ KV: in cutover grain fields; also high in trees, Chapagaon Forest. ♦ Nepal; Africa to Borneo 62

White Stork, *Ciconia ciconia*.
305 m. (1,000') 102 cm. (40") W.
Scarce; seen so far only near the Royal Chitwan National Park (P. Alden, 1972). An all-white bird with black flight feathers and dark trailing edge of wings. In underside view, might be confused with a White Pelican but stretches head straight out (not drawn in). The bright red bill and legs can be seen at considerable distance. Should be looked for in lowlands (western) in winter. ♦ Kashmir (?), Nepal; Europe, Africa, Asia 63

Black Stork, *Ciconia nigra*.
120-1525 m. (400-5,000') 96 cm. (38") W.
Occasional; along rivers and cutover rice fields. The only white-bellied stork with a black neck and coral-red bill (Black-necked Stork has black bill). Single or up to parties of twenty. Shy. Usually the only stork seen in valleys deep within the mountains on migration or in winter. Some remain in Pokhara Valley in winter. ✶ KV: passes over on migration. ♦ Kashmir, Nepal; Europe, Africa, Asia 65

Black-necked Stork, *Xenorhynchus asiaticus*.
152-305 m. (500-1,000') 122 cm. (48") R., M.
Occasional; selects open country along watercourses. Nepal's most spectacular stork. Note black neck and bill along with very long, conspicuous coral-red legs. Most often single and hard to approach. Wades through shallow water for food. Sometimes seen soaring during middle of day. ♦ Nepal· S Asia to Australia 66

Lesser Adjutant Stork, *Leptoptilos javanicus*.
120-274 m. (400-900') 122 cm. (48") R.

Occasional; along canal banks and reedy fields. A large, black and dirty white, chunky stork with naked-appearing head and no hanging pouch. Much darker than the Adjutant. Single or in small, scattered parties, standing on ground or perched bolt upright near top of tree with head pointing down. Not shy and often found near villages. Frequent in the E. *tarai*. Call a croak. ♠ Nepal; S. Asia to S.E. Asia   68

Adjutant Stork, *Leptoptilos dubius*.
213 m. (700') 152 cm. (60") S. (?)

Scarce; several sight records; most likely to occur in late monsoon period in open fields of the *tarai*. Said to occur along the Biratnagar-Dharan Road in summer. Resembles the Lesser Adjutant but the large pouch hanging from the neck of mature birds is diagnostic. Wing coverts almost silvery compared to the dark ones of the Lesser Adjutant. Eats fish from shallow pools and carrion. Its take off resembles that of a vulture's. ♠ Nepal; Pakistan to Malaysia   67

CRANES (Gruidae) are long-legged, long-necked birds with long, broad wings and short tails. They resemble storks but bills are no longer than length of head. They fly with outstretched neck, head and feet. Cranes call when flying (storks are usually silent); theirs is a powerful trumpet call.

Sarus Crane, *Grus antigone*.
120-213 m. (400-700') 152 cm. (5 feet tall) R.

Occasional; in damp, cultivated fields of the western *tarai*; scarce in central *tarai*. Very large, gray bird with gray cap and a diagnostic reddish face, nape and upper neck. In pairs or threes and quite tame. Sometimes kept as house guards. Flight slow and measured with audible wingbeat. Trumpeting similar to that of American Sandhill Crane. ♠ Nepal; Pakistan to S.E. Asia   323

Common Crane, *Grus grus*.
120-3050 m. (400-10,000') 140 cm. (54" tall) M.

Scarce; first reported in 1863. Very likely to occur with Demoiselle Cranes on migration. Look for a gray bird with a black throat and *gray breast* (not black as in the Demoiselle Crane). Reports persist that they occur in the Chitwan Dun as well as the Kali Gandaki Valley in October. ✥ KV: one at close range on Bagmati above Chobar, January 1974 (Gen: Shushil Rana). ♠ Kashmir (?), Nepal; Europe, Africa, Asia   320

Demoiselle Crane, *Anthropoides virgo*.
120-5185 m. (400-17,000') 76 cm. (30") M.

Fairly common; passing over Nepal in large groups in October and November and again in April-May (Col. R. Proud). Gray body with *black* throat and breast feathers elongated. They move south along large rivers in fall, passing over Jomosom and other points. Thousands reported resting briefly along the Narayani River. Also seen moving north above the Trisuli River (15th May). Settle unexpectedly when weather is bad. Migrate in a loose "V". Call a raucous goose-like *honk-honk*. ✥ KV: a large flock landed on the Tundikhel, Kathmandu, in May. ♠ Kashmir, Garhwal, Nepal, Sikkim; Europe, Africa, Asia   326

IBISES and SPOONBILL (Threskiornithidae). Ibises are much smaller than storks but often associate with them. Their bills are long and conspicuously decurved; that of the spoonbill, spatulate.

White Ibis, *Threskiornis melanocephala*.
120-274 m.   (400-900')   76 cm.   (30")   R.

Fairly common; feeding in shallow, muddy pools along with egrets, storks and waders. An unmistakable white bird with black head and long bill. In flocks up to 40; roost in colonies. Commonest in the eastern *tarai*, usually near water. Call an assortment of grunts. ♠ Nepal; India to Japan
69

Black Ibis, *Pseudibis papillosa*.
120-274 m.   (400-900')   74 cm.   (29")   R.

Occasional; on sandy river beds and in fallow fields. A plump, dark brown species with head reddish (adult) or brownish (young) and a diagnostic white shoulder patch best seen as bird takes flight. Solitary or in flocks up to 20. In flight may describe slow, wide circles in the air. Roosts in noisy groups in tops of trees. Sometimes feeds in meadows considerable distance from water. Voice a long, loud cry often heard at dusk. ♠ Nepal; Pakistan to Burma
70

Glossy Ibis, *Plegadis falcinellus*.
Not reported since 1846. Look for a dark bird about half the size of the Black Ibis, with a long, decurved bill and reddish-brown body. May occur in lowlands in winter. ♠ Nepal; Europe, Africa, Asia, Australia, N. America   71

Eurasian Spoonbill, *Platalea leucorodia*.
120 m.   (400')   84 cm.   (33")   W., M.

Scarce; seen in shallow water and on mud flats. A large, white bird with black legs. The much flattened, dark bill is evident at close range. Gathers in small parties. Rather shy; flies with strong, measured wingbeats and glides slowly in wide circles. In spring, to be found around the Kosi Barrage. ♠ Nepal; Europe, Africa, Asia
72

FLAMINGO (Phoenicopteridae). The Greater Flamingo has a very long neck and long legs and a large body. Breeding birds are pinkish but our wintering birds are mostly white. They prefer shallow water and mud flats.

Greater Flamingo, *Phoenicopterus roseus*.
120 m.   (400')   135 cm.   (53" tall)   M.

Scarce; migratory status uncertain. A small group seen on mud flats above Kosi Barrage in winter (John W. Propst, 1973). Probably occurs irregularly on major water systems of the Nepal *tarai*. ♠ Nepal; Europe, Africa, Asia
73

GEESE and DUCKS (Anatidae) are plump water birds with webbed feet. They swim and dive well and are swift fliers. Most ducks in Nepal are widely-known varieties, arriving from N. Eurasia in October-November and departing in March. Four species are non-migratory.

Graylag Goose, *Anser anser*.
120 m. (400') 76-90 cm. (30-35") M.
Occasional; on sand banks of large rivers. A large, gray-brown goose with pink bill and legs; in flight note white tail and vent. Migrates over Nepal in late February and early March, many not stopping here. Rarely seen on the autumn migration. Voice a fine honk on the wing; gurgles while feeding. (Lesser White-fronted Goose, *A. erythropus*, recorded in Kashmir, see p. 334.) ◆ Kashmir, Garhwal, Nepal; Europe, Asia   81

Bar-headed Goose, *Anser indicus*.
120-7625 m. (400-25,000') 76 cm. (30") M.
Common; on broad rivers of the *tarai* in spring. A small, light gray species with black primaries and two black bars on a white head. Numerous flocks in v-formation pass over Nepal on a wide front in spring and autumn migrations. Many apparently cross the Himalayas at night while others leave the lowlands at mid-morning and mid-day. Up to 1,000 in a flock on the Karnali late in March and early April. Seen at about 7625 m. (25,000') flying over a spur of Dhaulagiri in late March (T. Bech, 1973). ✵ KV: a regular visitor in small numbers October-November. ◆ Kashmir, Garhwal, Nepal, Sikkim; Asia   82

Whooper Swan, *Cygnus cygnus*. Not reported since 1846. An all-white bird with yellow and black bill. Possible but very unlikely, in winter. ◆ Kashmir, Nepal; Europe, Asia   86

Lesser Whistling Teal, *Dendrocygna javanica*.
120-305 m. (400-1,000') 43 cm. (17") R.
Occasional; around inlets and pools in wooded country. A tan-brown bird. Neck often outstretched when alarmed. Single or in flocks of 20-30; rests on banks of ponds and lakes or flies low over watercourses (Kosi Barrage). Call a wheezy *sea-sick* (AR). ◆ Nepal; Pakistan to Ryukyu Islands   88

Ruddy Shelduck (Brahminy Duck), *Tadorna ferruginea*.
120-4880 m. (400-16,000') 64 cm. (25") W., R.
Common; in pairs along sandy river banks. Size of a small goose; distinctive reddish-tan; white wing patch. Fairly wary. Strong fliers that migrate across the Himalayas in large numbers. Prior to spring migration, they feed ravenously in green fields of the *tarai* from about 6-9 A.M. then retire to river edge to rest during the day. A few possibly nest on northern Nepal lakes in Manang District. Call a rapid, trilled *k-k-k-k-k* and the familiar *chuk-a-wa*. ✵ KV: recorded passing over during migration. ◆ Kashmir, Garhwal, Nepal, Sikkim; Europe, Asia   90

Eurasian Shelduck, *Tadorna tadorna*.
120 m. (400') 60 cm. (24") M.
Scarce; seen in deep water at the Kosi Barrage in March (RLF, 1971). A distinctive white and black duck with a ruddy breast band. ◆ Nepal; Europe, Africa, Asia   91

Pintail, *Anas acuta*.
120-1372 m. (400-4,500') 55 cm. (22") M.
Common; in large flocks in spring. Perhaps the most numerous of ducks to cross Nepal. Pointed tail distinctive in both sexes. A surface feeder, it tips rump up when eating. Thousands, with strong flight, follow northward along the Kosi in spring. ◆ Kashmir, Garhwal, Nepal, Sikkim; Europe, Africa, Asia, N. America   93

Common Teal, *Anas crecca*.
120-1525 m. (400-5,000') 38 cm. (15") M.
Common; along rivers, reed beds and on ponds in winter. Note the small size and green speculum. Usually in pairs or small flocks with other ducks. A rapid, compact, wheeling flight. Call a *krit, krit* (AR). ❊ KV: a few pass over the Valley on migration. ❦ Kashmir, Nepal; Europe, Africa, Asia, N. America 94

Garganey, *Anas querquedula*.
120-1525 m. (400-5,000') 40 cm. (16") M.
Common; in rice fields and cultivations along streams. Small; both male and female have a green speculum edged with white bars, but in female the speculum largely obscured (in contrast to prominent speculum of female Common Teal). Male shows conspicuous eye-stripe; weak in female. Both sexes show a blue-gray forewing especially noticeable in flight. Moves in small compact flocks and feeds in grassy, wet rice fields. Call a harsh cackle, *krrrrr* (AR). ❊ KV: the first duck to arrive in fall—August. ❦ Kashmir, Nepal; Europe, Africa, Asia 104

Spotbill, *Anas poecilorhyncha*.
120-1280 m. (400-4,200') 60 cm. (24") R.
Occasional; in marshy areas and lakes with reeds. Due to habitat, frequently seen at close range. Conspicuous black and yellow bill tipped black, a good field mark; also note red spots base of forehead (absent in young). Usually in pairs or small parties of 4-6 birds in shallow water; a surface feeder. Call resembles that of a Mallard. ❊ KV: recorded on Taudha Lake. ❦ Kashmir, Nepal; India to E. Asia 97

Mallard, *Anas platyrhynchos*.
120-2897 m. (400-9,500') 58 cm. (23") M., R.
Occasional; on large rivers of the *tarai* in winter. Distinguished by dark green head of male and a blue-green speculum edged with white in both sexes. Thought to nest on Titi Lake (south of the Nilgiri peaks of Annapurna). Noted swimming on the Kali Gandaki at 2745 m. (9,000') in November. Small flocks up to thirty birds on Kosi, E. Nepal. Call a repeated *quack* becoming faster and softer. ❦ Kashmir, Nepal; nearly world-wide 100

Gadwall, *Anas strepera*.
120-1372 m. (400-4,500') 50 cm. (20") M.
Fairly common; small flocks in reedy marshes. Male has diagnostic rufous, black and white speculum and distinctive black undertail coverts. The black and white speculum of the female is unique among Nepal ducks. In flocks along rivers like the Kosi, in spring. Voice similar to a Mallard's. ❦ Kashmir, Nepal; nearly world-wide 101

Falcated Teal, *Anas falcata*.
120 m. (400') 48 cm. (19") W.
Scarce; in small parties of 4 to 8 birds along the Kosi River in March. The elegant male has a green and bronze head with long nape feathers. The female closely resembles a Eurasian Wigeon female but has a bright green (not dull green) speculum. A shallow water bird usually near reeds. ❦ Nepal; India to N.E. Asia 102

Eurasian Wigeon, *Anas penelope*.
120-4880 m. (400-16,000') 48 cm. (19") M.
Fairly common; among lowland spring migrants. Seen on a high altitude lake in Khumbu in May (B. Biswas). Smaller than a Mallard. Male has a pale forehead. Female resembles female Mallard but has green speculum (not blue-green) and bill is shorter and gray (not yellowish). In wet fields and on grassy lakes. Flies in compact flocks. Call a *whee-ooo* (AR). ❄ KV: along main rivers on spring migration. ◖ Kashmir, Nepal; Europe, Africa, Asia 103

Pink-headed Duck, *Rhodonessa caryophyllacea*.
120 m.(?) (400') 60 cm. (24") R.
Probably extinct; last birds in Nepal may have occurred in S.E. *tarai*. Male has bright pink head; female head is lightly washed pink. Should not be confused with Red-crested Pochard which has an orangy-red head. ◖ Nepal; India 106

Red-crested Pochard, *Netta rufina*.
120-3050 m. (400-10,000') 55 cm. (22") W., M.
Fairly common; on rivers and open lakes. Male has a large, distinctive orangy-red head. Female has brown head with white sides. Shy, usually in small flocks. Often near reeds. Dives deeper than Mallard. Winters as high as Rara Lake at 3050 m. (10,000'). ❄ KV: on Bagmati below Chobar; Taudha Lake in spring. ◖ Kashmir, Nepal; Mediterranean to Africa and India 107

Shoveler, *Anas clypeata*.
120-1525 m. (400-5,000') 50 cm. (20") M.
Fairly common; on large rivers of the *tarai* in spring. Male has wide bill, green head, white breast and flanks. Note rufous sides and blue wing patch. Female mottled throughout; has blue-gray wing patch. With many other species of ducks and water birds on the Kosi at the barrage in March. Swims with heavy bill pointed downward. Call a *quack*. ◖ Kashmir, Nepal; Old and New World 105

Common Pochard, *Aythya ferina*.
120-3050 m. (400-10,000') 46 cm. (18") W., M.
Occasional; on large lakes and many on large *tarai* rivers in spring. A plump species; head and neck darkish red in male; female has buff around the eyes and throat. Flocks of from 10 to 20 birds. Reported from Pokhara lakes in winter. ❄ KV: occasional on Taudha Lake in March. ◖ Kashmir, Nepal; Europe, Africa, Asia 108

White-eyed Pochard, *Aythya nyroca*.
120-1372 m. (400-4,500') 40 cm. (16") M.
Occasional; on lakes and often with other pochards. Male is very dark rufous-brown with white wing patch; female duller. Pale eye seen only at close range. Prefers large bodies of water but flies to marshes to feed. Call a harsh *kirr-kere-kirr* (Hume). ◖ Kashmir, Nepal; Europe, Africa, Asia 109

Tufted Pochard, *Aythya fuligula*.
120-4880 m. (400-16,000') 43 cm. (17") M.
Fairly common; in middle of lakes and large ponds. Male has diagnostic tufted head (tuft seen at close range). Note white at base of bill of the dark brown female. Swims low in water and dives after aquatic plants. Often seen in rather large flocks but also single or in pairs. One of the few ducks seen on small mountain lakes in highland Nepal. ❄ KV: one on Rani Pokhari in the heart of Kathmandu in spring. ◖ Kashmir, Nepal; Europe, Asia 111

Scaup, *Aythya marila*.
Not collected in Nepal since 1846. Male white underneath with a pale gray back (dark in Tufted Pochard), a dark greenish head, neck and breast. Should be looked for on large rivers and open lakes in winter. ◖ Kashmir, Nepal; Europe, Asia, N. America 112

Comb Duck (Nukhta), *Sarkidiornis melanotos.*
120-244 m. (400-800') 76 cm. (30") R.
Scarce; on ponds in wooded areas and large rivers. Size of a goose. Male is dark above, white with dark spots below and a knob on bill in breeding season. Female similar but without knob. A shallow water and ground feeder usually nesting in trees. Rather wary; is a strong flier. Twenty-five on a small pond east of Dhanghari, W. *tarai* (Dec.); 30 on Kosi in March. Voice a guttural sound and a loud *quack*. ♣ Nepal; Africa, S. and S.E. Asia, S. America 115

Cotton Teal (Pigmy Goose), *Nettapus coromandelianus.*
120-274 m. (400-900') 33 cm. (13") R.
Occasional; in shallow lakes and lagoons. A pint-sized black and white bird with the outline of a goose. Pairs or small flocks feed among aquatic vegetation with jacanas and gallinules. Not very shy; rapid wingbeat. Often seen in reed-lined ponds of Rapti Dun and the western *tarai*. ♣ Nepal; India to Australia 114

Goldeneye, *Bucephala clangula.*
915-3050 m. (3,000-10,000') 48 cm. (19") W.
Scarce; three birds noted on Rara Lake in February (RLF, 1971). Sight record from Pokhara (Ronald Brown, *et al*, 1972). Male has dark green head (looks black in the distance), with a prominent white spot between eye and bill. A deep water, diving duck. ♣ Nepal; Europe, Asia, N. America 118

Smew, *Mergus albellus*
183 m. (600') 46 cm. (18") W., M.
Scarce; Recorded in Jan. from Bilauri, S.W. *tarai* (Bailey, 1937) and rediscovered in Chitwan 1 Feb. 1983 (J. Ross and R. Wicks); both records from small, forest lakes but should also frequent rushing water where mountain rivers enter the plains. A small duck with distinctive white head (male) or reddish-brown head with white across face and down to lower neck (female). Dives frequently. ♣ Nepal; Europe, Asia, N. America 118

Merganser, *Mergus merganser.*
120-3050 m. (400-10,000') 64 cm. (25") W., M.
Fairly common; along large river courses. Male more white than black with narrow red bill. Female has tan head and neck. Sexes usually separate in winter. Small parties fish below rapids on mountain rivers such as Tila Karnali, Sunkosi, Trisuli. About 60 birds noted fishing in the Narayani River west of Tiger Tops; eleven on Rara Lake in February. ♣ Kashmir, Nepal, Sikkim; Europe, Africa, Asia, N. America 121

KITES, HAWKS, EAGLES, VULTURES and ALLIES (Accipitridae). Most of these birds of prey have strong bodies and powerful flight. Their food is largely animal matter including carrion. Many are winter visitors, arriving in Nepal from N. Eurasia in October-November and leaving in March-April. Females are usually larger than males and young darker than adults.

Black-crested Baza, *Aviceda leuphotes*.
244 m. (800') 33 cm. (13") R.
Scarce; collected once at edge of forest near Dharan in S.E. *tarai* (G. B. Gurung, 1959). A sleek, black and white hawk with a long black crest. Usually seen circling over forest and said to be somewhat crepuscular (AR). (Blyth's Baza, *Aviceda jerdoni*, see Sikkim list p. 336.)
🍂 Nepal; India, China, Malaya 128

Black-shouldered Kite, *Elanus caeruleus*.
120-1372 m. (400-4,500') 30 cm. (12") R.
Fairly common; perches at tops of acacia trees or on telephone wires in open country. Perhaps the least kite-like of the group, resembling a miniature harrier. Pale gray and white with black shoulder patch and primaries. Young bird is brown with distinct streaks and white-tipped tail. This trim little raptor often hovers, looking for prey, before plummeting to the ground. Flies across country rather slowly, its wingbeats interspersed with glides. Communal roosts. Call a shrill note. ❈ KV: occasionally on fence posts on Chapagaon road in summer.
🍂 Nepal; Africa to New Guinea 124

Brahminy Kite, *Haliastur indus*.
152-1372 m. (500-4,500') 48 cm. (19") R.
Occasional; over open grain fields and ponds. A beautiful chestnut and white kite. Young are streaked and told from Dark Kite by rounded tail. Solitary or in pairs, flying slowly over fields or perched at the edge of a pond looking for grasshoppers, frogs and fish. Call a squeal.
❈ KV: a few over rice fields in August-September. 🍂 Nepal; Pakistan to Australia 135

Honey Kite (Honey Buzzard), *Pernis ptilorhyncus*.
120-1525 m. (400-5,000') 53 cm. (21") R.
Fairly common; in trees bordering fields near water. Plumage extremely variable from very dark to almost white in young birds. Look for diagnostic barring on tail, a single dark bar towards tip and sometimes two bars toward base but non-conforming patterns occur and these exceptions hard to identify unless close at hand. Small, stiff feathers cover the face (seen only at close range) and presumably protect from bee stings. A rapid flier; also soars above trees. Communal roosts known. Eats honey and bees. Call a repeated high-pitched whistle (Baker). 🍂 Nepal; N. Asia to Celebes 130

Dark Kite (Pariah or Black Kite), *Milvus migrans*.
152-4880 m. (500-16,000') 60-66 cm. (24-26") R., M.
Common; around villages, cities and open fields. Brown with long tail v-shaped at end, used as a rudder in flight. The mountain race has extensive pale markings under wings. When perched, the *greenish cere* distinguishes it from other birds of prey. Single, or in pairs, also great numbers around garbage. A bold bird; will make off with domestic chicks. Sits upright in trees. Call a loud, interrupted squeal frequently heard during the heat of the day and when breeding. ❈ KV: a few pairs nest in the city and surrounding hills. 🍂 Kashmir, Garhwal, Nepal, Sikkim; Europe, Africa, Asia, Australia 133, 134

Sparrow Hawks (*Accipiter*) are strong, swift hawks that prey on other birds. They are usually seen soaring or perched on vantage points in trees. Adults much barred; young broadly streaked. Wings are rounded.

Goshawk, *Accipiter gentilis*.
1220-4880 m. (4,000-16,000') 48-60 cm. (19-24") R.

Occasional; above high altitude forests, scarce in midlands. A large accipiter. Look for extensive white undertail coverts that help distinguish it from the very similar but smaller Sparrow Hawk. Power dives to seize birds and mammals. Flies low above ground then glides into a tree with a quick upswing. Sometimes seen soaring near cliffs and above forests. Perches on lower branches of tall trees that command a wide view. The common accipiter of Khumbu where it attacks Snow Pigeons. ♠ Kashmir, Garhwal, Nepal, Sikkim; Europe, Africa, Asia, N. America   136

Crested Goshawk, *Accipiter trivirgatus*.
120-1372 m. (400-4,500') 40 cm. (16") R.

Occasional; in forests over streams. The only crested accipiter. It has a spotted and streaked breast above a barred abdomen. Note mesial throat stripe. Young bird has a broad tan eyebrow and the black mesial stripe. Secretive, it hunts by waiting quietly in a tree then suddenly strikes out at birds as large as pheasants. ✽ KV: a straggler in Valley forests. ♠ Kumaon, Nepal, Sikkim; India, S.E. Asia, China   144

Sparrow Hawk, *Accipiter nisus*.
610-1372 m. (2,000-4,500') 35 cm. (14") R.
2440-3965 m. (8,000-13,000') 35 cm. (14") W.

Occasional; along margins of lakes and near villages. Male very similar to the Shikra but paler with four bars on tail (not five). Also rufous wash on cheeks of male (not gray). Female resembles the Goshawk but smaller with white of the undertail coverts not as extensive as in the Goshawk. Young, spotted on breast and barred on abdomen; no mesial throat stripe. Single, often pursuing small herons, swallows and other birds. Flies low and fast. Voice two long notes followed by a short squeal. A light N. Eurasian race comes to Nepal in winter. ♠ Kashmir, Garhwal, Nepal, Sikkim; Europe, Asia   147, 148

Besra Sparrow Hawk, *Accipiter virgatus*.
244-2440 m. (800-8,000') about 33 cm. (13") R., M.

Fairly common; in tall trees in somewhat open country. A compact little accipiter with a white throat and black mesial stripe. Our only accipiter with *unbarred* rufous upper breast; abdomen barred. Illustration shows young bird with streaked upper breast and barred lower breast and abdomen. Often seen in pairs, perched with head drawn in and tail pointing down. Breeding pairs call back and forth to each other. Voice a squeal, louder than a kestrel's. ✽ KV: a pair often nest in the Royal Botanic Gardens, Godaveri. ♠ Kashmir, Garhwal, Nepal, Sikkim; Pakistan to Celebes   150

Shikra, *Accipiter badius*.
152-1525 m. (500-5,000') 33 cm. (13") R.

Fairly common; in forests of the *tarai*. Very similar to the male Sparrow Hawk but darker above and with a dark median throat stripe and *five* dark tail bands (not four). Note gray (not rufous) wash on cheeks of male; female larger and a little darker. Young Shikras have dark oval spots on breast and pale spots on a ruddy-brown back. They are difficult to distinguish in the field; note habitat, behaviour and throat stripe. Much smaller and slimmer than a Goshawk and much more distinctly marked on back than other young accipiters. Flies swiftly among bushes and low trees capturing small birds. Soars a great deal. Call a high, repeated double note. ♠ Nepal, Sikkim (?); Africa to S.E. Asia   138

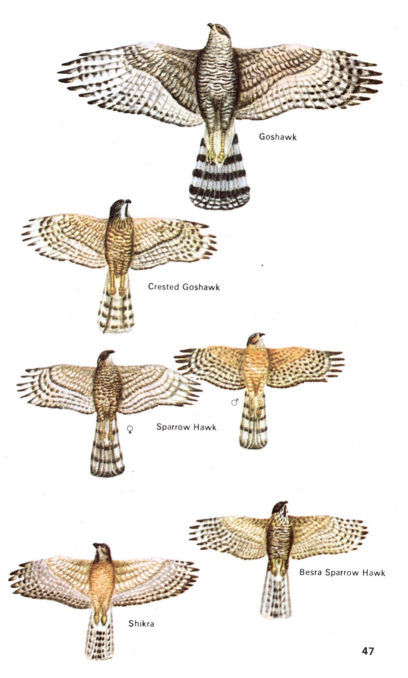

Buteo Hawks *(Buteo)*, also called "buzzards" in Europe, are medium-sized, chunky hawks with rounded wings and fan-shaped tails. They resemble eagles but are smaller. Field identification is extremely difficult as each species has up to four color phases as well as intermediate ones. An Upland Buteo, for example, in the semi-light phase, appears almost identical, except in size, with the light phase of the Eurasian Buteo.

Upland Buteo, *Buteo hemilasius*.
1372-4422 m. (4,500-14,500') 70 cm. (28") W., R. (?)
Uncommon; in open country. All of G. B. Gurung's specimens from Kathmandu (6) are pale with contrasting brownish abdomen and small, dark carpel (wrist) patches. The longish tail is finely barred. Very similar to light phase of Eurasian Buteo but larger; also paler on head and back. This species is said to nest in the vicinity of cliffs and feeds on birds and small mammals (Baker). ◐ Kashmir (?), Garhwal, Nepal, Sikkim (?), Asia 154

Long-legged Buteo, *Buteo rufinus*.
152-2440 m. (500-8,000') 55-60 cm. (22-24") W.
Occasional; along river courses and in adjacent fields. Look for the *pale rufous*, unbarred tail which is the commonest adult phase seen in Nepal. A number of birds, though, have tails with one dark subterminal band. (The Eurasian Buteo has several bars while the race *B. b. vulpinus* has a bright rufous tail, usually with a dark subterminal bar.) Usually single; flight measured and strong, spending hours circling high in the sky. When resting it resembles a Dark Kite but lacks green cere and forked tail. Call a loud *mew*. ❊ KV: often seen near Chobar Gorge along the Bagmati River. ◐ Kashmir, Garhwal, Nepal, Sikkim; Africa, Asia 153

Eurasian Buteo, *Buteo buteo*.
1220-2440 m. (4,000-8,000') 50-55 cm. (20-22") W.
Fairly common; in the same habitat as the Long-legged Buteo. Plumage variable; usually a brown to dark brown; throat to center of breast pale. Flight feathers paler than body and wing lining. Tail distinctly barred, often with *broad terminal bar*. The pale eastern race, *B. b. vulpinus* has a bright rufous tail (not pale rufous as in the Long-legged Buteo). Single, coasting above tree tops or over cultivations and at times rather high in the air. Perches for long periods in leafy trees; not very active; slow wingbeat. Silent in winter. ❊ KV: in tall pines, Indian Embassy; along Bagmati River. ◐ Kashmir, Garhwal, Nepal, Sikkim; Europe, Africa, Asia 155, 156

White-eyed Hawk (White-eyed Buzzard), *Butastur teesa*.
152-305 m. (500-1,000') 43 cm. (17") R.
Fairly common; in open country of the lowlands. Smaller and only half the weight of Eurasian Buteo. Note the rufous, barred tail best seen on dorsal aspect. Pale iris visible at close range. Acts much like the Indian Roller *(Coracias)*. Sits sluggishly on a post or branch, then drops to the ground for insects. It flies low over the ground with rapid wingbeats, then suddenly banks upward to a perch. Appears to be most common in the S.W. *tarai*. Call a *pit-weer* (Ali). ◐ Nepal; Pakistan to Burma 157

Crested Serpent Eagle, *Spilornis cheela*.
120-2135 m. (400-7,000') 68 cm. (27") R., M.
Fairly common; in wooded hills and along streams. A dark, chunky raptor with small white spots on lower breast. In flight, light band across wings and pale band on dark tail diagnostic. Single, or in pairs, describing slow, wide circles in the sky. Upon landing waggles tail sideways and adjusts wings. Sits bolt upright in leafy trees. Attacks jungle fowl, pheasants; snakes occasionally seen dangling from talons. Rarely seen above 915 m. (3,000') in winter. Decorates nest with large green leaves. Call a piercing *klik—kleeeeer-kleeeeer* as it circles high in the sky. ❊ KV: arrives in February; a nest above Anandaban Hospital. ◐ Kashmir (?), Garhwal, Nepal, Sikkim; Pakistan to Philippines 196

Mountain Hawk Eagle (Hodgson's), *Spizaetus nipalensis*.
120-2562 m. (400-8,400') 74 cm. (29") R.
Occasional; solitary, in forests. A dark brown bird with a prominent crest. In flight, broad wings and tail noticeably barred. Note black gular stripes and tan breast with oval spots. It is a strong flier, riding on air currents. Pairs are often very acrobatic, diving and "roller coastering" through the air. Usually hunts by perching patiently on a branch of a tall tree; strikes at whatever prey appears below. Pursues Kalij Pheasants, Red Jungle Fowl and other large birds. Voice is a shrill scream; also a quiet, repeated squeak resembling the sound of a rodent. ✤ KV: the common crested eagle of these forests. ◀ Kashmir, Garhwal, Nepal, Sikkim; India to Celebes 158

Changeable Hawk Eagle, *Spizaetus limnaeetus*.
120-1006 m. (400-3,300') 70 cm. (28") R.
Occasional; in *sal* and mixed forests. Plumage variable but often with a pale head, brown back; almost white below; older birds are quite dark. Fairly common in Rapti Dun where it builds a large platform for a nest in crotch of tall tree. When alert and hunting, the short few-feathered crest is erect. Rather wary. Effective hunting done in pairs. Call a drawn-out scream. ◀ Garhwal, Nepal, Sikkim (?); India to Philippines 160

Rufous-bellied Hawk Eagle, *Lophotriorchis kienerii*.
305 m. (1,000') 60 cm. (24") R.
Scarce; sight records from Chitwan (Ron Brown, *et al*, 1971). It should occur throughout forested areas of eastern *bhabar* and *tarai*. Differs from the Brahminy Kite in that white of underside extends only to upper breast. A bird of the forest (not open, wet fields). ◀ Nepal; India to Celebes 165

Bonelli's Eagle, *Hieraaetus fasciatus*.
1525-3050 m. (5,000-10,000') 68-74 cm. (27-29") R.
Occasional; in forests. Look for a large hawk eagle with a pale body, lightly streaked. Long tail has a distinctive broad, black subterminal band. Young are rufous with barred tails. The wing pattern of light-dark-light is helpful in identification of adult and young birds. Feeds on large birds such as crows, pheasants and waterfowl. Seen attacking chickens at edge of Dhunche Village, Rasuwa District. Sometimes seen soaring on updrafts near cliffs. Call a piercing *kie-kie-kikikiki* (AR). ✤ KV: in more open forests such as eastern Nagarjung. ◀ Kashmir, Garhwal, Nepal, Sikkim(?); Europe, Africa, Asia 163

Short-toed Eagle, *Circaetus gallicus*.
120-1830 m. (400-6,000') 64-68 cm. (25-27") R., M.
Scarce; in wooded and open areas. Looks like a white buteo hawk with a square, barred tail; slightly streaked. Some birds have a dark gray head and throat that contrasts with white breast. Hovers like a kestrel and may dive from considerable heights. Eats snakes. Voice a shrill cry like a Besra Sparrow Hawk's. ◀ Garhwal, Nepal, Sikkim(?); Europe, Africa, Asia 195

Booted Eagle, *Hieraaetus pennatus*.
305-2135 m. (1,000-7,000') 50-55 cm. (20-22") W.
Scarce; in forests and at edge of fields. A pale phase appears to be most frequent in Nepal. Pale brown above; below, all white except black primaries, gray head and long, unbarred gray tail. Flight resembles that of a kite. Similar to a phase of Long-legged Buteo but has a narrower, paler tail. Often hunts in pairs, striking down crows, small mammals and reptiles. It may carry off chickens and tame ducks. Call a clear cry, heard in April. ✤ KV: in forested areas like Nagarjung and Manichaur. ◀ Nepal; Europe, Africa, Asia 164

Eagles are large, powerful hunters with long, wide wings and rather short fan tails. Both curved bill and talons are extremely powerful. The head has a flat crown. In flight, Golden, Black and Serpent Eagles curve their wings upward in a wide "V" while the Greater and Lesser Spotted Eagles hold their wings in a slight down-curve. Others, as well as most vultures, hold their wings level.

Golden Eagle, *Aquila chrysaetos*.
2135-4575 m. (7,000-15,000') 90-102 cm. (35-40") R.

Occasional; single or in pairs in open, rocky country, usually well above the tree line. Large size; mature birds dark brown with tawny neck. First and second year birds have white on wings and at base of tail. Compared with younger ones, mature birds seldom seen. Pairs cavort in winds sweeping high altitude cliffs. Are often pursued by small accipiters and falcons. Aerial battle with a Lammergeier carrying food, seen in Khumbu in November. A near attack on full grown goat above Jomosom in December. Kills migrating Demoiselle Cranes in the air. Call a yelp. ♣ Kashmir, Garhwal, Nepal, Sikkim; Europe, Africa, Asia, N. America 166

Imperial Eagle, *Aquila heliaca*.
120-305 m. (400-1,000') 81-90 cm. (32-35") W.

Scarce; sight record in Kathmandu Valley (D. Proud, 1955). Look for a very large, dark eagle with whitish shoulders and pale head in adults. Young similar to young Steppe Eagle but not so white. Should not be confused with a dark immature Himalayan Griffon (see p. 56) and the young Black Vulture (see p. 58) which have different flight contours. May occur along lowland rivers in winter. ♣ Nepal; Europe, Asia 167

Tawny Eagle, *Aquila rapax*.
120 m. (400') 66-70 cm. (26-28") R.

Occasional; single or in loose pairs in tops of trees in open lowlands. Nearly uniform brown, paler on secondaries; tail quite short and rounded. Slow flight; non-migratory, not ascending into hills. Eats carrion. Often considered conspecific with Steppe Eagle but in Nepal these two species are quite distinct in size, plumage, behavior and distribution. Call a variety of loud notes. ♣ Nepal; Africa to Burma 168

Steppe Eagle, *Aquila nipalensis*.
305-7930 m. (1,000-26,000') 74-81 cm. (29-32") W.

Fairly common; in wooded, hilly areas. Usually brown with one or two conspicuous pale edges to wing coverts, both above and below; brightest in young. Completely dark brown adults most unusual in Nepal. A large eagle which often rests in middle of tree. A pirate and carrion eater. This species found dead at 7930 m. (26,000'), South Col, by Indian Mt. Everest Expedition, 1965. Migrates in late October and early November in strung-out "lines," using up drafts to move south then westward. Several birds (1-10) may pass observer every few minutes. ✼ KV: some sail over city; seen in trees on Nagarjung. ♣ Kashmir, Garhwal, Nepal, Sikkim; Europe, Africa, Asia 169

Greater Spotted Eagle, *Aquila clanga*.
1525 m. (5,000') 64-70 cm. (25-28") W.

Scarce; sight record from Godaveri (S. Madge, *et al*, 1973). A broad-winged eagle with short tail. Wings held in a slight down-curve. Spotted wing coverts only in young birds. A very dark, almost black eagle. ♣ Nepal; Europe, Africa, Asia 170

Lesser Spotted Eagle, *Aquila pomarina*.
183 m. (600') 58-66 cm. (23-26") W.

Occasional; in tall trees in open fields of the *tarai*. Very dark brown. Smaller and "thinner" than Greater Spotted Eagle. Young less spotted. Note down-curved wing line in flight. Upper breast faintly streaked and vent somewhat mottled. Said to feed largely on the ground. One perched on post above reedy ponds along Biratnagar-Dharan Road had eaten three frogs. Voice a high-pitched cackling laugh (Baker). ♣ Nepal; Europe, Africa, Asia 171

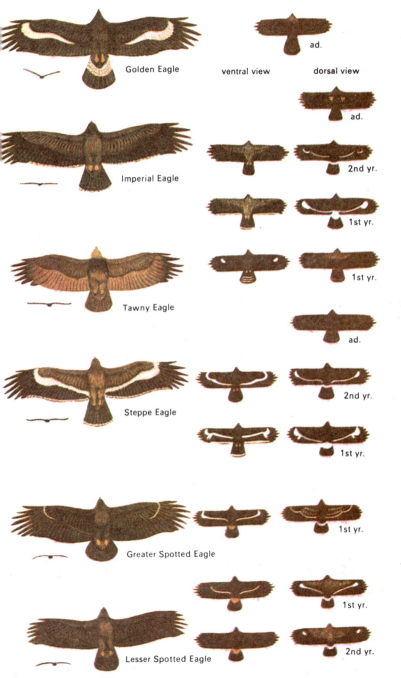

White-tailed Sea Eagle, *Haliaeetus albicilla*.
915 m. (3,000') 76-84 cm. (30-33") W.
Scarce; sight record in Pokhara, 1971 (Ron Brown, *et al*). Unmistakable, adult with *white* wedge-shaped tail. Wanders into Nepal in winter. 🦅 Nepal; Europe, Africa, Asia   172a

Black Eagle, *Ictinaetus malayensis*.
305-3355 m. (1,000-11,000') 66-70 cm. (26-28") R.
Fairly common; over forests and grassy mountain fields. An all-black, wide-winged eagle; wings held in upward "V". Inconspicuous pale rump rarely seen; yellow cere and feet noted only at close range. Skims silently and buoyantly just over tree tops manoeuvring back and forth to get a good look at trees and bushes. A noted nestling-snatcher. Glides for long distances; "roller coaster" display in breeding season. Call a moderate *klee-klee-klee*. ❋ KV: frequents the surrounding hills. 🦅 Kashmir(?), Garhwal, Nepal, Sikkim; Himalayas to Celebes
172

Pallas's Fishing Eagle, *Haliaeetus leucoryphus*.
120-305 m. (400-1,000') 76-84 cm. (30-33") R., M.
Occasional; along wooded rivers and small lakes. A large brown bird with pale head and neck, a white tail with a wide, dark terminal band. Young birds all brown and difficult to tell from other species. In appearance and flight, reminiscent of the closely related American Bald Eagle. Usually single or in breeding pairs. Call a repeated, unearthly, quavering, pre-dawn scream *chuck-kyuk-ca-w-w-w—cre-e-e-e* with variations. 🦅 Nepal; Asia   174

Gray-headed Fishing Eagle, *Icthyophaga ichthyaetus*.
152 m. (500') 74 cm. (29") R (?)
Scarce; forested streams and ponds of the Royal Chitwan National Park. Very similar to the Himalayan Gray-headed Fishing Eagle but basal half of tail almost pure white (vs. mottled gray). Thighs white in both birds so care should be taken to distinguish base of tail from thighs. Solitary; sluggish; often sits still for long periods so frequently overlooked. Rediscovered in Nepal in 1977 by Laurence Binford and Charles McDougal. 🦅 Nepal; India to Celebes
175

Himalayan Gray-headed Fishing Eagle, *Icthyophaga nana*.
120-3965 m. (400-13,000') 55 cm. (22") R.
Fairly common; along almost all forested rivers of the *duns* and *tarai*. A brown and gray eagle with white abdomen, thighs and basal two-thirds of tail mottled to look gray (not white) and rest of tail dark. Solitary, resting upright in large trees overhanging river banks. A steady, slow flight. Often present near Begnas Lake, Pokhara. Rarely seen above 915 m. (3,000'), noted by Biswas at 3965 m. (13,000'). Has a human-like cry. 🦅 Kashmir, Nepal, Sikkim (?); Himalayas to Sumatra
177

The Osprey is an active fish hawk noted for plummeting into water after its prey. Solitary. Beautiful wing movements. Soles of feet adapted to hold slippery fish.

Osprey, *Pandion haliaetus*.
120-1372 m. (400-4,500') 55 cm. (22") W.
Occasional; along wide rivers and large pools where it hovers on long graceful wings. In flight the white underwings and black wrist patches diagnostic. Almost always near water. Seven individuals counted along 15-mile stretch of Karnali River in April. Seen in *tarai* and *duns* as late as May but nesting in Nepal unconfirmed. ❋ KV: occurs sparingly along Bagmati in winter. 🦅 Kashmir, Garhwal, Nepal, Sikkim; nearly world-wide   203

Cinereous Vulture (European Black Vulture), *Aegypius monachus*.
   152-2287 m.   (500-7,500')   99-106 cm.   (39-42")   W.
Scarce; along river courses. A large, very dark vulture with no white on flanks; tail short and fan-shaped. Tufts of dark feathers on pale brown head can be seen at a surprising distance. Said to be the dominant vulture at a carcass. Often circles high in the sky usually below 2440 m. (8,000') in winter but should be seen at much higher altitudes during migration. Arrives in Nepal towards the end of October and leaves in March. ❋ KV: a winter visitor; three together on a terrace near Chobar. ❦ Kashmir, Garhwal, Nepal, Sikkim; Europe, Africa, Asia
179

Eurasian Griffon (Griffon Vulture), *Gyps fulvus*.
   120-1982 m.   (400-6,500')   102-122 cm.   (40-48")   R.(?)
Occasional; usually in the *tarai* and lowlands. A very large bird, similar to the paler Himalayan Griffon but altitude and habitat range rarely overlap. In flight, leading edge of wing appears pale but darker than the almost white of the Himalayan Griffon. In the *tarai* often with the Indian Griffon but is much larger and has a brown head and neck (not black). Has powerful wingbeat. One at Bigu, Chautara District, 1982 m. (6,500') in November was unusually high. ❦ Nepal; Europe, Africa, Asia
180

Himalayan Griffon, *Gyps himalayensis*.
   1525-6100 m.   (5,000-20,000')   122 cm.   (48")   R.
Occasional; on mountain ridges over the mid-Himalayas and fairly common at high altitudes. The heaviest Nepal breeding vulture. Wings in flight show an almost white leading edge and a dark trailing edge. Similar to Eurasian Griffon but more pale white to sandy-buff (not pale brown). Young bird dark and streaked, best distinguished from other young griffons by larger size, higher altitude and associated adults. Gracefully combs mountains for dead animals; lands and hops aggressively at carcass where fights may involve feathers flying. Frequent in Dolpo and Mustang; often over 5490 m. (18,000'); roosts and nests on cliffs.
❦ Kashmir, Garhwal, Nepal, Sikkim; Asia
181

Bearded Vulture (Lammergeier), *Gypaetus barbatus*.
   1220-7320 m.   (4,000-24,000')   122 cm.   (48")   R.
Occasional; around cliffs and near mountain villages. A grand bird with a wing span of up to nine feet. In flight, its long, wedge-shaped tail distinguishes it from all other large birds of prey. Adults have a brownish-golden head and body while juveniles are dark brown. Single or in pairs. Occasionally drops bones on rocks and eats shattered fragments. A large knuckle bone found in one stomach; frequents garbage heaps near habitation. May fly away clutching meat in its talons. One vigorously pursued a Himalayan Griffon at 4270 m. (14,000'). Will tackle griffons in the air but not on the ground. Usually occurs above 2440 m. (8,000'). Voice a guttural hiss. ❋ KV: only seldom seen gliding over the Valley. ❦ Kashmir, Garhwal, Nepal, Sikkim; Europe, Africa, Asia
188

Black Vulture (King Vulture), *Torgos calvus*.
120-2440 m. (400-8,000') 84 cm. (33") R., M.

Occasional; usually solitary or in pairs. The only vulture with red head and wattles. Body of adult, black with white oval patches on flanks; young, dark brown. Wings held high above back. A rather mobile bird, often the first to spot a carcass but timidly moves aside when other vultures crowd in. Voice a throaty scream. ❈ KV: occasionally around the western edge of the Valley. ◖ Kashmir(?), Garhwal, Nepal, Sikkim; Asia 178

White-backed Vulture, *Gyps bengalensis*.
120-2135 m. (400-7,000') 79 cm. (31") R., M.

Common; around villages of the *tarai;* uncommon above 915 m. (3,000'). A very dark brown species with a large white rump. Wings black and white from below. Young dark brown above and below, very similar to Indian Griffon but head and neck with dirty white down (not black). Usually several among a mixed group of vultures; dashes in on a carcass over the heads of competitors. The last to leave a carcass when closely approached by observers. Call a series of hisses and squeals. ❈ KV: usually several with Indian Griffons on Bagmati in summer. ◖ Garhwal, Nepal, Sikkim(?); Asia 185

Indian Griffon (Indian Long-billed Vulture), *Gyps indicus*.
152-1525 m. (500-5,000') 86 cm. (34") R., S.

Fairly common; around villages. A small, gray-brown griffon with a contrasting dark head and neck. Feathers pale-shafted and light-edged giving a streaked appearance. Much smaller and slightly paler than Eurasian Griffon and much paler than the very dark White-backed Vulture. In flight the leading edge of wings tannish (not white as in White-backed Vulture). A white rump, seen when banking, separates it from the Eurasian and Himalayan Griffons. Young, chocolate brown and much smaller than other two griffons. Feeds along the Bagmati River, Kathmandu; nests on tops of trees in the *tarai*. ❈ KV: common in summer; roosts in tall eucalyptus tree near Teku. Absent in winter. ◖ Kashmir, Garhwal, Nepal, Sikkim(?); Asia 184

Egyptian Vulture (Scavenger Vulture), *Neophron percnopterus*.
152-3050 m. (500-10,000') 60 cm. (24") R.

Fairly common; in open fields near villages and towns. The only white vulture in Nepal. Has a yellow head; flight feathers black. Young a dull brown. Tail wedge-shaped. Often single or in widely scattered parties. Circles on air currents over scavenging area; ambles about in open fields. Culls over garbage heaps with dogs, kites and crows. Stays on outer edge of a seething mass around a carcass, picking up small fragments of food. May wander well into the mountains; seen over Tukuche, Mustang District, in July. ❈ KV: occasionally noted gliding over the city. ◖ Kashmir, Garhwal, Nepal, Sikkim; Europe, Africa, Asia 187

Harriers are graceful hawks with comparatively long wings, legs and tails. Males usually gray; females larger, brown and streaked; young profusely streaked often with reddish-brown. All harriers in Nepal are migratory, most arriving in October and departing by late April.

Hen Harrier, *Circus cyaneus*.
274-4270 m. (900-14,000') 48-53 cm. (19-21") M., W.
Fairly common; over terraced fields and grassland. The ashy-gray throat and upper breast of male, along with more extensive white on rump, distinguishes it from the similar Pale Harrier; female difficult to separate (see under next species). In autumn often above tree line. One of the commonest harriers during migration along the main Himalayan range. Food consists of grasshoppers, rodents, lizards. ❊ KV: over terraced fields in spring and autumn. ⚜ Kashmir(?), Garhwal(?), Nepal, Sikkim(?); Europe, Asia, N. Africa   189

Pale Harrier, *Circus macrourus*.
305-1372 m. (1,000-4,500') 46-50 cm. (18-20") M.
Scarce; selects open, grassy country. Male similar to Hen Harrier but *throat and breast white* (not ashy), and very little white on rump. Body of female is slightly grayer than female Hen Harrier and with a lightly barred tail and a smaller white rump. Young faintly streaked above. Migrates in long, scattered lines and rests at night in fields. Nests in S. Russia and winters as far south as Sri Lanka. Flies low over fields, hovers and pounces on prey, eating it on the spot. Flies with a graceful, slow wingbeat. ⚜ Kashmir(?), Nepal; Europe, Africa, Asia   190

Montagu's Harrier, *Circus pygargus*.
244-1830 m. (800-6,000') 46-48 cm. (18-19") M.
Scarce; passing over open fields on migration. The only male harrier with narrow, black wingbar. Females have a tan throat and a small, white rump. Young, brown with light streaks on wings and tail. Flies with slow wingbeats and short glides, staying low over marshes and fields. Eats amphibians, rodents, insects. Seen most frequently in the eastern *tarai*. ⚜ Kashmir(?), Nepal; Europe, Africa, Asia   191

Pied Harrier, *Circus melanoleucos*.
152-915 m. (500-3,000') 46-48 cm. (18-19") W.
Occasional; over cultivated fields and ponds of the *tarai*. Male is a striking bird, our only black and white harrier. Illustration shows too much black on upper wing; black should be confined to narrow strip down center of wing. Black replaced by brown in female; pale fulvous below. Hovers and flies slowly over fields, more leisurely than other harriers. Wings blunter than other harriers (AR). Perches on clods of earth, often near water. Usually solitary. The common harrier near Begnas Tal, Pokhara, in February. ⚜ Nepal; Asia   192

Marsh Harrier, *Circus aeruginosus*.
120-1372 m. (400-4,500') 53-58 cm. (21-23") W.
Fairly common; sailing low over stream beds, reeds and marshland. Male distinctive brown and gray with large black wing tips. Pale forehead and shoulders of female easily seen and are diagnostic. Young entirely chocolate-brown except for pale throat and crown. Rests on mounds in cultivated fields. Investigates gunshots and makes off with game. ❊ KV: the common harrier over fields bordering Manora and other streams. ⚜ Kashmir, Nepal, Sikkim(?); Europe, Africa, Asia   193

FALCONS (Falconidae) are medium-sized or small raptors with long pointed wings. Flight is swift; rapid wingbeats often interrupted with a few glides. They are noted for their powerful dives after prey.

Red-thighed Falconet, *Microhierax caerulescens*.
120-762 m. (400-2,500') 18 cm. (7") R.

Fairly common; in open, grassy woodlands of the low hills. An unmistakable miniature falcon, black above with tan throat, thighs and undertail coverts. Note conspicuous white eyebrow. In flight, sometimes resembles a Gray-headed Myna. Perches on exposed branch looking this way and that and slowly pumps tail. Flies down to ground after insects. Two or three frequently seen together. Most prevalent in S.E. Nepal. ♣ Nepal, Sikkim; India to S.E. Asia 204

Laggar Falcon, *Falco jugger*.
120-1280 m. (400-4,200') 40-43 cm. (16-17") R., M.

Occasional; in open *tarai*. Similar to a Peregrine but smaller and more chunky, back *brown* (not gray or blackish); forehead and crown pale. Prominent black gular stripes. Single or in pairs, hunting above grassy fields. Said to have a breeding call *whee-ee-ee* (AR). ♣ Kashmir(?), Garhwal(?), Nepal; Europe, Africa, Asia 207, 208

Peregrine Falcon, *Falco peregrinus*.
120-2135 m. (400-7,000') 40-43 cm. (16-17") W., R.

Occasional; in forests and on rocky, steep mountainsides. A large, powerful falcon. Two forms (sometimes considered separate species) in Nepal. The wintering bird from N. Eurasia is typically *gray* with a white breast. The dark, oriental race (Shahin Falcon) is bright rufous below, streaked with black (the similar Oriental Hobby has clear rufous underparts without black spots). Both have strong, black gular stripes. Very swift in flight; usually power dives upon prey. Eurasian form often seen on sand bars of major rivers near many migrating ducks. The Shahin Falcon is a cliff and forest bird. May carry off domestic pigeons. Call a *chir-r-r-r* (AR). ❉ KV: in groves such as Gaucher Forest and Rani Bari. ♣ Kashmir, Garhwal, Nepal, Sikkim; almost world-wide 209, 211

Eurasian Hobby, *Falco subbuteo*.
1220-2135 m. (4,000-7,000') 30-33 cm. (12-13") W., R.

Occasional; in oak forests; perched in tall pine trees. Like a small Peregrine but with darker back, *rufous thighs*; below heavy dark lines of spots rather than gray bars (Oriental Hobby all rufous below). Young heavily spotted below; thighs pale. Strong and graceful flight, wheeling in wide circles after butterflies and small birds. Call a repeated *te-te-te*. ❉ KV: near Tokha Sanitarium on Sheopuri in May. ♣ Kashmir, Garhwal, Nepal; Europe, Africa, Asia 212

Oriental Hobby, *Falco severus*.
152-1525 m. (500-5,000') 30 cm. (12") R., S.

Occasional; in wooded groves. Looks like a small Shahin Falcon but is solid rufous below with no spots (Eurasian Hobby has rufous confined to thighs and lower abdomen). Most active after dawn and just before dusk; often catches bats. Haunts villages for chickens; seen eating a Robin Dayal. Remarkable power dives and a very rapid wing flutter. Voice shriller than the Eurasian Hobby, a *ki-ki-ki* (Proud). ❉ KV: a summer nester in the Indian Embassy pines. ♣ Kashmir, Garhwal, Nepal, Sikkim; India to New Guinea 214

Red-headed Merlin, *Falco chicquera*.
152-1372 m. (500-4,500') 30-35 cm. (12-14") R., M.
Occasional; in tall trees over rice fields near villages. A pale bird below with forehead to nape a distinctive chestnut. Often in pairs, flying in a straight line close to the ground. Pursues kites. Said to have a peculiar shrill, querulous scream (AR). ♣ Kashmir (?), Nepal; Africa to S.E. Asia   219

Merlin, *Falco columbarius*.
1372 m. (4,500') 28 cm. (11") W.
Scarce; a male seen at close range (Ron Brown, *et al*) in KV in winter. Look for a small gray-backed falcon with black-tipped tail (male). Female resembles small female kestrel but tail very short and much barred. Usually seen perched on a clod of mud or projection on the ground (AR). ♣ Kashmir (?), Nepal; Europe, Africa, Asia, N. America   218(?)

Red-legged Falcon, *Falco vespertinus*.
1372-4422 m. (4,500-14,500') 29 cm. (11$\frac{1}{4}$") M.
Scarce; in open country. Male distinctively black, dark gray and rufous below; female gray-brown with cream-colored throat and many black spots on breast. Status unclear in Nepal. Possibly a scarce passage migrant with a few birds remaining in N. Nepal during the summer. Female found dead on path in N. Dolpo at 4422 m. (14,500') in June (RLF, 1971). Male seen above Jomosom at 3660 m. (12,000') in July (RLF, 1973). ❉ KV: collected by H. S. Nepali, November 1965. ♣ Nepal; Europe, Africa, Asia   220

Lesser Kestrel, *Falco naumanni*.
610-2440 m. (2,000-8,000') 33 cm. (13") M.
Scarce; in flocks of about 15 on migration. Sight record (Ron Brown, *et al*) and along the Kali Gandaki River above Baglung in March (RLF). Look for the plain reddish back of male (not spotted); in illustration reddish should extend to wing coverts. Female is virtually identical to female Eurasian Kestrel but can be told at close range by *white claws* (not black). At Baglung this species noted in an acrobatic flock, hawking insects high above the river. Kestrels in flocks almost certainly this species. Migratory route, like the Red-legged Falcon, is from China to Africa and return. Specimen banded by the Arun Wildlife Expedition (T. Cronin, 1973). ♣ Nepal; Africa, Asia   221

Eurasian Kestrel, *Falco tinnunculus*.
152-4270 m. (500-14,000') 33-35 cm. (13-14") R., W.
Common; along cliffs above rivers; hovers over cultivations. Male has reddish back with dark spots; below, pale with dark spots; a long, gray tail with broad subterminal black band. Female reddish-brown marked throughout with dark bands and spots. The dark spotted back of male distinguishes it from the Lesser Kestrel. A rapid wingbeat and much hovering over feeding ground. One seen eating a snake; another a lizard. Call a shrill *kre-e-e-e-e*. The northern race, here in winter, is larger and lighter than the breeding form. ❉ KV: resident on rim of Valley as at Nagarkot. ♣ Kashmir, Garhwal, Nepal, Sikkim; Europe, Africa, Asia   222, 223

PARTRIDGES, QUAIL and PHEASANTS (Phasianidae) are well represented in the Himalayas. They have well-developed bills and legs for pecking and scratching on the ground. All have rounded wings; partridges and quail have short tails; those of the pheasant group are often much longer. Male plumages usually colorful, sometimes spectacular; females are mostly drab. They tend to be shy in places where hunted. They usually feed in morning and late afternoon; their crops allow them to store food between meals. The late H. B. Conover of the Field Museum, Chicago, commented on the large variety of this group found in a limited area of Thakola on the upper Kali Gandaki River.

Tibetan Snow Cock, *Tetraogallus tibetanus*.
3660-5490 m. (12,000-18,000') 53 cm. (21") R.

Occasional; on steep hillsides among tumbled boulders. A giant, gray partridge. Similar to the Himalayan Snow Cock but smaller, with gray sides of neck. Breast band is gray (not chestnut). Underparts white, streaked with black (not gray with flanks rufous streaked). Boldly streaked flanks a good field mark. Small parties of 4-15 birds feed on grassy slopes and near sheltering rocks. Quite shy. Escapes from humans by running uphill; also has extremely swift downward flight on set wings. May glide several miles after avoiding predators such as Golden Eagles. Inhabitant of Gorak Shep in Everest National Park. Calls early in morning *chuck-aa-chuck-aa-chuck-chuck-chaa-da-da-da;* also a *keep-kweep-kweep* from a crag. Alarm call a subdued *ko-ko.* ♦ Kashmir, Garhwal, Nepal, Sikkim; Pamirs to Sikkim
230

Himalayan Snow Cock, *Tetraogallus himalayensis*.
4270-5490 m. (14,000-18,000') 58 cm. (23") R.

Occasional; on open mountains among dwarf junipers. Similar to Tibetan Snow Cock but two rufous lines on sides of neck (not gray), with chestnut breast band. Lower breast and abdomen are dark gray (not streaked and pale). Digs in ground for tubers. Shy and usually escapes in typical snow cock manner by running uphill. Found as far east in Nepal as the N. Annapurna range. In Dolpo and Thakola, overlaps with the Tibetan Snow Cock but usually remains at a slightly higher altitude. Works the top of the grass line in summer, usually over 4880 m. (16,000'). Moves down in winter. Voice a cackle with a rising crescendo (Osmaston). ♦ Kashmir, Garhwal, Nepal; Turkestan to Himalayas
232

Chukor Partridge, *Alectoris graeca*.
2135-3660 m. (7,000-12,000') 38 cm. (15") R.

Fairly common; in Jumla and the western hills, on grassy slopes and steep hillsides, often near grain fields. Look for heavily barred sides and black "V" around pale throat; red bill and legs. Usually in pairs or small coveys. After calling in early morning from rock outposts, they feed in fields with a "guard" posted in a viewing position. Runs and flies well. Makes good pet and effective "watch dog," calling at the approach of strangers. Found as far east as Jiri in eastern Nepal. Call a loud, clear *chuck-chuck-chuck-chuck-koor-chuck-koor.* ♦ Kashmir, Garhwal, Nepal; Europe, Asia, recently N. America
236

Snow Partridge, *Lerwa lerwa*.
3050-5185 m. (10,000-17,000') 38 cm. (15") R.

Fairly common; on steep rocky or grassy slopes bordering alpine meadows. About the size of a Chukor Partridge but less plump and tail longer. Unmistakable; barred gray and white above; orange bill and legs. In flight, a narrow white trailing edge of wings quite conspicuous. In flocks of 5-20. Rather tame, often standing on a rock to watch you rather than flying away. Escape route is steeply downhill with speed. Roost together in caves and under overhanging rocks where they are very noisy as they assemble. Usually above 3965 m. (13,000') in summer. Has a series of shrill whistles, cackles and raspy notes. ♦ Kashmir, Garhwal, Nepal, Sikkim; Afghanistan to China
227

Black Partridge, *Francolinus francolinus.*
152-2135 m. (500-7,000') 30 cm. (12") R.
Fairly common; near cultivations and in grassy scrub jungle with bushes such as *ber (Zizyphus jujuba)*. Male dark with black head, white cheeks and chestnut collar. Female brown with pale throat and no white on cheeks (similar Gray Partridge is extensively barred). Single or in pairs. Roosts in low bushes. Calls from low branch or rock. When flushed flies straight away close to the ground. At maximum elevations in monsoon and post monsoon season. Call a raspy *chuck* (faint), *pawnbiri-cigaret* (loud). Nepalis render it *"theen thari theethri,"* meaning "three kinds of partridges." ❊ KV: in scrub jungle on surrounding hills at 1525-1830 m. (5,000-6,000'). ☛ Garhwal, Nepal, Sikkim (?); Cyprus to Assam 238, 239

Gray Partridge, *Francolinus pondicerianus.*
152-305 m. (500-1,000') 33 cm. (13") R.
Occasional; confined to grassy, dry country of the *tarai*. *Barred* light and dark brown above; paler below. Female has a rufous throat (not pale). When disturbed it runs, then rises with a fast wingbeat, glides in a straight line to the ground and runs again. Quite common in parts of the western *tarai*. Call a *ka-ti-tur-ti-tur-ti-tur;* also a high-pitched *klik*. ☛ Nepal; Iran to India and Sri Lanka 245

Swamp Partridge, *Francolinus gularis.*
213 m. (700') 38 cm. (15") R.
Scarce; in tall swamp grass of the S.W. *tarai*. Upperparts brown, barred rufous; a rusty throat; brown below, streaked with buff. Tail is chestnut. Noted only in restricted habitat of elephant grass and clumps of bamboo in the vicinity of little ponds or damp ground. Hard to flush. When alarmed gives a loud *kew-care*. Male is said to call *ko-ko-care* and the female responds with *kirr kirr kirr* (Sagar Rana). ☛ Nepal; U.P. *tarai* (India) to Bangladesh 247

Tibetan Partridge, *Perdix hodgsoniae.*
3660-4880 m. (12,000-16,000') 30 cm. (12") R.
Occasional; on dry hillsides associated with *Caragana* bushes and at times among dwarf juniper. Note chestnut collar and black patch in center of abdomen. A plump partridge in pairs in summer and coveys in winter. Picks over yak dung near sheds; eats green shoots. When disturbed, calls loudly and runs strongly uphill. If pressed, flock may scatter and plunge downhill. Habitat is Tibetan semi-desert. Voice a harsh, grating *chee-chee-chee* as if finger were run along a large comb. ☛ Nepal, Sikkim; C. Asia 249

Common Hill Partridge, *Arborophila torqueola.*
1830-2745 m. (6,000-9,000') 29 cm. (11½") R.
Fairly common; in deep forests damp with leaves, ferns and humus. Male has a rufous head and a black throat with white at base. Female has rufous head streaked with black, buffy-rufous chin and throat. The frontal band is dark tan (not white). Usually in pairs or small parties digging among leaves. When startled, may run, then fly a short distance with a whir of wings, to settle on a branch or on the ground. Roosts in trees in coveys. Alarm call a repeated *pir*. Also a mellow prolonged single whistle at intervals sometimes ending in a rising *bob-white—bob-white—bob-white*. ❊ KV: in the surrounding oak forests. ☛ Garhwal, Nepal, Sikkim; India to Yunnan and Tonkin 267

Rufous-throated Hill Partridge, *Arborophila rufogularis.*
305-1830 m. (1,000-6,000') 28 cm. (11") R.
Occasional; in dense undergrowth, keeping mostly to the ground. Similar to Common Hill Partridge but with a bright rufous throat (not black or buff) and a dark neck band. Female very similar to male but with a paler chin and throat and more white spots below. Single, in pairs, or small coveys. Usually at a lower elevation than the Common Hill Partridge. Digs in rich humus for animal and vegetable matter. Call a clear whistle heard morning and evening in spring. ❊ KV: chicks above fish ponds, Godaveri, in May, 1525 m. (5,000'). (Red-breasted Hill Partridge, *Arborophila mandellii,* Sikkim list, p. 336.) ☛ Nepal, Sikkim; Kumaon to S.E. Asia 270

Common Quail (Gray Quail), *Coturnix coturnix.*
213-1372 m. (700-4,500') 20 cm. (8") R., W.
Occasional; at edges of fields in the *tarai*. Male has black and white throat; a prominent eyebrow. Female similar but has creamy-buff throat and black spotted breast. Many migrate from the northwest in huge flocks in autumn, some spending the winter in lowland Nepal. When disturbed, bursts up from the ground, flies in an arc, then drops again to the ground. Its voice is a squeaky whistle *wet-mi-lips* (AR). ♠ Kashmir, Nepal; Europe, Africa, Asia   250

Blue-breasted Quail, *Coturnix chinensis.*
1280 m. (4,200') 14 cm. (5½") R.
Scarce; in scrub jungle at edges of marshland and tall grass of the *tarai*. Male grayish-brown above with diagnostic white gular patch, white neck and black bib. Upper breast and flanks blueish; lower parts dark rufous. Female brown with light bars above and dark bars below. A widespread resident species. Coveys are easily disturbed and disappear into vegetation. Its call said to be a soft *tir-tir-tir*, a piping whistle and a faint crow, *brain fever* (AR). ♠ Nepal; India to China and Malaya   253

Black-breasted Quail (Rain Quail), *Coturnix coromandelica.*
1342 m. (4,400') 18 cm. (7") R., M.
Scarce; noted in cultivations and cutover scrub. Male has a distinctive black throat and upper breast with white neck band; flanks streaked with black. Female has pale throat and spotted breast. Very like Common Quail female but outer web of primaries unbarred (not barred buff), seen only in the hand. Moves about on ground in small parties after insects and seeds. Calls early in morning or late afternoon, a repeated double *which-which* (AR). ♠ Nepal, India to Burma and Sri Lanka   252

Jungle Bush Quail, *Perdicula asiatica.* 16 cm. (6½"). No records since reported by Hodgson in 1846. Should occur in lowlands. Look for a fast-moving quail; male is darkish above with a distinct eyebrow and pale below (barred darker) with a distinctive *chestnut throat*. Female paler than male but retains the chestnut throat. ♠ Kashmir, Nepal; India and Sri Lanka   256

BUSTARD-QUAIL (Turnicidae) greatly resemble quail but lack hind toe. A sex reversal occurs in this family with females more colorful than males. Also, males incubate eggs and raise young. Placed here in the book because of similarity to quail. Phasianidae continues on next page.

Button-Quail, *Turnix tanki.*
305-1525 m. (1,000-5,000') 15 cm. (6") R.
Occasional; in grassy patches in fields or near water and forest. Male pale brown with white throat and black spots on wings and sides; no collar. Female is similar but has orangy-brown breast and collar. Both have yellow legs (Common Bustard-Quail has only a few black spots. Bill and legs are gray, not yellow). In small parties, feeding at the edge of forest and in thickets. Usually runs when frightened. If closely approached, it crouches then buzzes explosively into the air, completes a short arc, drops to the ground and runs again. Call said to be *off-off-off*, continuing for five seconds (Inglis). ♠ Nepal; Asia   314

Little Bustard-Quail, *Turnix sylvatica.* 14 cm. (5½"). No reports since 1846. The smallest of our bustard-quail; look for a barred "quail" (upperparts only) with a whitish coronal stripe. Also has a chestnut patch on either side of breast; underparts otherwise pale buff. Should still occur in lowland scrub. ♠ Nepal; Europe, Africa, Asia   313

Common Bustard-Quail, *Turnix suscitator.*
120-1372 m. (400-4,500') 15-16 cm. (6-6¼") R.
Fairly common; in weedy patches near villages. Male streaked dark and light brown with a pale, black-barred chin. Female tan and streaked above, a black or white throat, barred breast and tan abdomen. Both have slaty bills and legs (Button-Quail has yellow legs). Single or in pairs. Female often has white throat in winter. Runs on the ground and flies like the Button-Quail. A flushed bird was at once pursued by a hawk eagle, but zigzagged and escaped. ♠ Nepal, Nepal to Ryukyu Islands   316

Blood Pheasant, *Ithaginis cruentus*.
3355-4117 m.　(11,000-13,500')　38 cm.　(15").　R.

Fairly common; in heavy bamboo, juniper and rhododendron forests, often near water. Male pale gray, green and red. In dull light the almost white breast band and rump are conspicuous. Female a warm brown with red facial skin. Both sexes have coral-red legs and feet. Seen in pairs or small coveys, perching on rocks or working their way through bamboo or rhododendron thickets, feeding on berries and other vegetable matter. Quite tame near Buddhist monasteries such as Thangboche, Khumbu. Known to be as far west as the Annapurna Himal (G. Troth, 1973). Calls a repeated *chuk;* a loud grating alarm screech *kzeeuuk-cheeu-cheeu-chee;* a *pleet,* repeated by female with young; young when lost a *chip-chip-chip.* ● Nepal, Sikkim; Himalayas to China
281

Crimson Horned Pheasant, (Nepali—Monal), *Tragopan satyra*.
2592-3050 m.　(8,500-10,000')　60-68 cm.　(24-27").　R.

Occasional; in damp evergreen forests and bamboo groves. Male has magnificent, brilliant crimson underparts with white spots; dark, white-spotted back; blue facial skin. Female dull brown flecked with fulvous spots. Note proportionately long tail. Solitary or in small parties; spends much time on ground but roosts in trees. A crop full of fern pinnae of *Dryopteris wallichiana*. Seen feeding with White-throated Laughing-Thrushes. Calls, a loud, deep mammal-like *k-a-a-a-a* at dawn and dusk, repeated three or four times at about 20-second intervals, apparently a territorial call given by male. Also *wank-wank* and *w-a-a-o-o-k.* Alarm call a *ca-rook.* (Western Tragopan, *T. melanocephalus,* in Kashmir, see p. 334.)
● Garhwal, Nepal, Sikkim; E. Himalayas
286

Impeyan Pheasant, (Nepali—Danphe), *Lophophorus impejanus*.
2592-4575 m.　(8,500-15,000')　58-60 cm.　(23-24").　R.

Common; on steep, grassy slopes above the tree line; down into forests in winter. At a distance, male looks almost black with white rump and tan tail. Upperparts splendidly iridescent; space around eye blue, blue-black wings and black breast; the Nepali national bird of nine colors. Female light and dark brown with pale throat; blue around eye seen only at close range. Usually quite shy and will flush at a considerable distance. Digs for tubers with powerful bill, often remaining in one spot for half an hour or more. When alarmed, leaps screaming into the air and careens downward on set wings. A dozen cocks digging under fir trees in the early morning sunlight, an unforgettable sight. Call besides a loud *kleeee,* a number of subdued *kluks.* ❈ KV: heard once on top of Phulchowki; numbers S.E. on Narayanthan.
● Kashmir, Garhwal, Nepal, Sikkim; Himalayas
290

Kalij Pheasant, *Lophura leucomelana*.
305-3050 m.　(1,000-10,000')　50-55 cm.　(20-22").　R.

Occasional; in oak and mixed forests near water. Male a black pheasant with a long, arched tail, lower back barred white, pale breast and red facial skin. Crest does not stand erect as illustrated. Female is brown with arched tail and red around eye. Roosts in middle of trees; makes the same foraging circuit each day. Fast runners and swift fliers. Has favorite dusting spots. Male drums in spring. Call a loud, fast series of staccato notes; also a quiet clucking. A western Nepal race has a dirty white crest and a black and white barred back. In central Nepal the back is similar but the crest is black. In eastern Nepal both crest and back are black.
❈ KV: in most oak forests surrounding the Valley. ● Kashmir, Garhwal, Nepal, Sikkim; Pakistan to S. China
293, 294, 295

Koklas Pheasant, *Pucrasia macrolopha.*
2135-2745 m. (7,000-9,000') 50-60 cm. (20-24") R.
Occasional; in oak, conifer and bamboo forests from Annapurna westward. Male black head with white ear patch; its long crest is most noticeable. Female light brown and streaked; a short crest. Usually solitary or in pairs. When approached it often freezes on branch of tree or may fly up quickly into a tree. Chicks found the 2nd of June. Crows at first light of day and after a sudden noise such as thunder or gunshot. Voice a loud crow *kuk-kuk-kuk-kokas-kokas;* also has quiet conversational notes. ♪ Kashmir, Garhwal, Nepal; Afghanistan to W. China and S.E. Mongolia   306

Cheer Pheasant, *Catreus wellichii.*
2135-3050 m. (7,000-10,000') 58-91 cm. (23-36") R.
Scarce; on grassy, rocky slopes at edge of oak forests. Male mottled gray with red facial patch and long, barred tail. Female similar but pale brownish instead of gray. Crouches in grass until almost stepped on, then leaps up noisily and awkwardly with a great commotion and "dive bombs" down the steep slope. Numbers around Dhorpatan (C. Nepal); known from the Annapurna Himal westward. Noisy at dawn and dusk. Voice a gobble and a crow. ♪ Kashmir, Garhwal, Nepal; Himalayas   307

Common Peafowl, *Pavo cristatus.*
120-305 m. (400-1,000') wing 38-46 cm. (15-18") R.
Fairly common; in tall grass, thin *sal* forest and among tangled *Zizyphus* thorn bushes. Male absolutely magnificent—blue, black, gray, chestnut wings and a long, wide, ocellated tail. Female gray-brown, paler below. In small parties feeding in forest, thickets and fields. Drinks morning and evening from streams. When alarmed on ground, pulls down long neck and runs, eventually rising with labored flight. Commonly rests in tall trees such as *Bombax*. Call like a trumpet blast, *meeeee—aaooooo*. Also a rapid *kok-kok-ko-ko-ko* and a loud *ee-ha*. Quite vocal at night, especially in spring. ♪ Nepal; S. Asia   311

Red Jungle Fowl, *Gallus gallus.*
120-1067 m. (400-3,500') 43-58 cm. (17-23") R.
Abundant; in forests, at edges of fields, around villages. Cock like a large bantam rooster; hen like the bantam hen. Often feeds under fruiting trees or in grain fields. When disturbed it stretches its head forward and down and runs rapidly. Strong flier. The cock sounds like a domestic rooster only more tinny; hen like the domestic ones. Usually calls early in the morning and again at dusk near roosting places. ♪ Kashmir, Garhwal, Nepal; India to Java and introduced elsewhere   299

RAILS, CRAKES, GALLINULES and ALLIES (Rallidae). These are plump water birds with short, rounded wings, short, pointed tails (often cocked) and strong, long legs. They have well-developed bills. Usually shy and elusive; numbers are crepuscular, feeding at dusk. Short distance flight is heavy and weaves among reeds. After long migratory flights birds sometimes are found in exhausted condition.

Water Rail, *Rallus aquaticus*.
120 m. (400') 22 cm. (8¼") R.

Occasional; in marshy reed beds. Streaked light and dark brown above. The broad, pale eyebrow and dark eye line differentiate it from related Nepal species. It differs from the Blue-breasted Banded Rail which is blue-gray above and not brown. Similar to the Banded Crake but breast is gray not rufous. Abdomen and flanks broadly barred black and white. Look for the long, dull orange bill. Crepuscular, feeding at the edge of reed beds in shallow water. Reported from the S.E. *tarai* in November. ❊ KV: one found dead on Tribhuvan University campus (October 1973), by B. Brunner. ♠ Kashmir, Nepal; Europe, Asia   328

Blue-breasted Banded Rail, *Rallus striatus*.
120 m. (400') 20 cm. (8") R.

Scarce; secured by Bailey in Morang District, 16 Feb. 1938. Look for bird with ruddy head and mantle, pale throat and cheeks; flanks and abdomen *narrowly* barred olive-brown and white. ♠ Nepal; India to Philippines   329

Banded Crake, *Rallina eurizonoides*.
274 m. (900') 22 cm. (8½") R.

Scarce; among "elephant-ear" leaves at a spring just west of Hitaura, C. Nepal (June, RLF). Olive-brown above with rusty head, neck and breast, pale throat; abdomen broadly barred black and white. In female (illustrated here) rust replaces olive-brown. Call a deep "bull frog" croaking. ♠ Nepal; India to Ryukyu Islands and Celebes   332

Baillon's Crake, *Porzana pusilla*.
1372 m. (4,500') 18 cm. (7") M.

Occasional; on marshy bodies of water. A tiny rail, streaked above with dark brown; gray-brown below with white bars on lower abdomen. Quite confiding. In company with Little Grebe and other pond birds. During migration this species sometimes found exhausted on paths or in courtyards. ❊ KV: on Taudha Lake in spring. ♠ Kashmir, Garhwal, Nepal, Sikkim(?); Europe, Africa, Asia, Australia   337

Ruddy Crake, *Amaurornis fuscus*.
120-1280 m. (400-4,200') 22 cm. (8½") R., M.

Occasional; on clear streams lined with vegetation and in wet rice fields. A distinctive chestnut head, neck, upper breast and abdomen. Feeds early in morning. Flies with legs dangling; glides into shrubbery bordering stream. Found above Sunischari, Jhapa District. Said to have a low, repeated *chuk* and *tewk* (AR). ❊ KV: breeding birds here in rice fields in summer. ♠ Kashmir, Nepal; India to Japan and Celebes   339

Elwes's Crake, *Amaurornis bicolor*. Reported in 1894 but no definite data for Nepal. Look for the slaty head, neck and underparts. Back *olive-green* (not olive-brown as in Brown Crake). ♦ Nepal; Nepal to Laos   341

Brown Crake, *Amaurornis akool*.
152-305 m. (500-1,000') 28 cm. (11") R.
Occasional; among tufts of grass along streams and ponds of the *tarai* and *duns*. Mostly uniform olive-brown with pale chin, and gray below. Solitary along watercourses. Flies with apparent difficulty, keeping low over ground or surface of water. Tail cocked and constantly flipped, at about once per second. Feeds along surface of shallow pools; ducks head completely under water. Active early morning and late evening. Call a high rippling trill lasting three or four seconds. Others may join in. Also a repeated *thuk* while feeding.
♦ Kashmir, Nepal; India to Tonkin   342

White-breasted Waterhen, *Amaurornis phoenicurus*.
213-1372 m. (700-4,500') 30 cm. (12") R.
Fairly common; at edges of lakes, ponds and wet rice fields. Dark above with conspicuous white forehead, sides of head and underparts. Single or in pairs. Active early in the morning. Selects the same haunts year after year. Readily climbs into shrubbery. Often in company with other water birds. Voice a throaty *krr-kwak-kwak* and a repeated *kook* (Ali). ❊ KV: along the Vishnumati and in rice fields around Rani Bari. ♦ Nepal; India to S.E. Asia   343

Water Cock, *Gallicrex cinerea*.
120 m. (400') 35-43 cm. (14-17") S.
Scarce; in reedy swamps bordering the Kosi River. Male in summer very dark (black marked with gray) and large, fleshy *red horn* protruding above crown. Female and non-breeding male brownish, paler below with irregular bars; horny shield on forehead yellowish. In flight, appears slimmer than Purple Gallinule. First reported in Nepal by R.C. Gregory-Smith who saw six birds on 15 June and two on 21 June 1975. Apparently moves into area in summer.
♦ Nepal; India to Celebes   346

Indian Gallinule, *Gallinula chloropus*.
120-4575 m. (400-15,000') 30 cm. (12") R.
Common; in quiet lagoons and woodland ponds. Adult is gray with red bill tipped yellow and red frontal shield (greenish in young) and white edges to wings and white vent. A short, cocked tail has two large white "windows." Illustration shows brown juvenile. Scattered parties swim leisurely about in vegetation-choked pools. Constantly jerks head while walking among reeds, tail twitching. When disturbed, slithers across water with feet dangling. Voice a series of *kooks*. ♦ Kashmir, Nepal; Europe, Asia, N. America   347

Purple Gallinule, *Porphyrio porphyrio*.
120-305 m. (400-1,000') 40 cm. (16") R.
Occasional; in extensive reed beds bordering marshy ponds of the *tarai* and Chitwan Dun. Unmistakable—purplish with red bill and frontal shield; vent white. In loose parties of six to twelve birds clambering onto reed platforms. When confronted by a predator such as a Marsh Harrier, they form a circle with heads pointing outward and then squawk and shake their wings in unison. Flight slow and weak. Partial to sprouting rice. Voice a series of clucks and an alarm *kuk*. ♦ Kashmir(?), Nepal; Europe, Asia, Australia   349

Coot, *Fulica atra*.
305-3050 m. (1,000-10,000') 40 cm. (16") R., M.
Occasional; in quiet lagoons and open bodies of water. A plump, dark gray species with white frontal shield. Often with gallinules, jacanas and ducks. Forty to fifty spend the winter on Rara Lake. Swimming movements rather smoother than gallinules. Fairly strong fliers. Voice a *kluk* and a series of soft notes. ❊ KV: a pair in Rani Pokhari, December 1973.
♦ Kashmir, Nepal; Europe, Asia, Australia   350

BUSTARDS (Otididae). Members of the Bustard family are plump with long necks and legs, three toes, broad, rounded wings and short tails. Females are smaller and duller colored than males.

Great Indian Bustard, *Choriotis nigriceps.* Last reported in 1846 and apparently has long since disappeared from Nepal. A large, heavy bird with a golden back, black crown and breast band. (Little Bustard, *Otis tetrax,* rare in Kashmir, see p. 334.) 🌱 Nepal(?); Pakistan and India 354

Bengal Florican, *Eupodotis bengalensis.*
305 m. (1,000') 60 cm. (24") R.
Occasional; among clumps of tall grass in dry fields. Young male (illustrated) a large, mottled brown bird with diagnostic white wings (best seen in flight). Adult male is black with white wings and mottled brown back. Female is fawn and tan below. Active at dawn and dusk. Flight is strong and straight away from intruder. During the courting "dance" the cock repeatedly shoots several feet into the air. Occurs regularly in the western end of Rapti Dun. Call a repeated *chik* (AR). 🌱 Nepal; India to Cambodia 356

Lesser Florican, *Sypheotides indica.*
1310 m. (4,300') 46 cm. (18") S., M.
Scarce; in open fields not far from villages. Male differs from the Bengal Florican in having throat and lower sides of neck *white* (not black). Most peculiar "crest" sprouts from sides of face near bill. Female has dark lines at edges of throat. Runs along ground and flies like a lapwing, often covering considerable distance before settling. Voice varied croaks. ✲ KV: three in wet field in monsoon just S.E. of Patan parade ground. 🌱 Nepal; India 357

JACANAS (Jacanidae) are water birds with long legs and triple-length toes; associated with standing water and lily pads.

Pheasant-tailed Jacana, *Hydrophasianus chirurgus.*
1342 m. (4,400') 45 cm. (17½") S.
Scarce; on ponds with reeds and water plants. Breeding plumage unmistakable: blackish and white with yellow neck and very long, arched, thin tail; in non-breeding season, fawn and white with short, pointed tail. A lowland bird common around still ponds of northern India, but less frequent in Nepal. Voice a variety of calls; also a loud *klooo* (Bates). 🌱 Kashmir, Nepal; India to the Philippines 358

Bronze-winged Jacana, *Metopidius indicus.*
120-305 m. (400-1,000') 28-30 cm. (11-12") R.
Common; in still, shallow water of ponds in the *dun* and *tarai.* A blackish bird with bronze wings, rufous vent and tail; a long, white eye-stripe. Young, rufous head; dull whitish-rufous below with a black terminal bar on tail. In scattered groups in lagoons with other water birds. Rather shy, taking to cover at a moment's notice, flying low over the water with legs dangling. Its call a wheezy, repeated *seek* (AR). 🌱 Garhwal, Nepal, Sikkim; India to Sumatra 359

OYSTERCATCHER (Haematopodidae). Birds of coastal shorelines.

Oystercatcher, *Haematopus ostralegus.* A straggler last reported in 1846. Black and white with a long, red bill. 🌱 Kashmir, Nepal; Europe, Africa, Asia 360

WADERS (Charadriidae). Lapwings, plovers, sandpipers, stints and snipe represent a varied group of wading birds, often separated into two families. All have comparatively long legs and bills. Wings are pointed and flight strong; tails are rather short. They are usually found in groups and are mostly winter visitors in Nepal. Identification marks are patterns of wings, rump and tail. Sexes are alike.

Gray-headed Lapwing, *Vanellus cinereus.*
305 1310 m. (1,000-4,300') 37 cm. (14½") W.
Occasional; in cutover rice fields and on sand bars. Resembles White-tailed Lapwing but larger and has gray head (not brownish) and lacks white tail. Yellow bill seen at close range; no wattles. Often feeds with Red-wattled Lapwing; stands a head taller. Usually in small flocks of from 4-10 birds. A strong, deliberate flier. Call a hoarse *cha-ha-famous-meet.* ✻ KV: in winter in fields bordering the Manora River. ❦ Kashmir, Nepal; Asia 365

Yellow-wattled Lapwing, *Vanellus malabaricus.*
120-183 m. (400-600') 25 cm. (10") R., M.
Occasional; in meadows, on airstrips; farther away from water than most lapwings. Resembles Spur-winged Lapwing but lacks crest while sides of face and neck are brownish (not whitish). The only lapwing with yellow wattles. The bill is black, greenish at base (Gray-headed Lapwing has yellow bill). Single, in twos or threes. Not very shy. Runs evenly and flies with slow wingbeats. Call a slow *tee - - - air;* a rapid *wigwigwigwigwig.* ❦ Nepal; Pakistan to Bangladesh 370

Red-wattled Lapwing, *Vanellus indicus.*
120-1342 m. (400-4,400') 33 cm. (13") R.
Common; in open fields or at edges of streams. Note the black head, throat, breast and white abdomen. A red wattle in front of eyes. Fairly bold, running along the ground in spurts. Easily alarmed and calls loudly while circling overhead; frequently calls at night when disturbed. In pairs or small groups. Some seasonal altitudinal movement. Call a loud, repeated *did-you-do-it;* a quick *bid-bid-bid-bid.* ✻ KV: in open cultivations in summer and autumn. ❦ Kashmir, Garhwal, Nepal, Sikkim (?); Asia 366

White-tailed Lapwing, *Vanellus leucurus.*
120 m. (400') 25 cm. (10") W.
Scarce; around ponds of the W. *tarai;* found near Bilauri in winter. A pale lapwing with a white rump, tail and vent. Note black and white wings conspicuous in flight. Single birds near mud in small pools. Nests in the Middle East and rarely strays as far east as Nepal. Much like the Eurasian Lapwing in flight, food and actions (Baker). ❦ Nepal; Africa, Asia 362

Eurasian Lapwing (Peewit), *Vanellus vanellus.*
213-1310 m. (700-4,300') 30 cm. (12") W.
Occasional; on wide, grassy meadows, plowed fields and edges of marshland. Dark above with black breast, white abdomen and pointed crest. White tips to black wings noticeable at long distances when bird is in flight. Usually in small flocks of less than six birds; occasionally twenty or more (Pokhara). Very wary in Nepal; strong fliers with slow wing-beats. ✻ KV: on rivers of Valley during autumn migration. ❦ Kashmir, Nepal; Europe, Asia 364

Spur-winged Lapwing (Spur-winged Plover), *Vanellus spinosus.*
120-1280 m. (400-4,200') 29 cm. (11½") R.
Fairly common; in small scattered groups on rocky stream beds and adjoining fields. Similar to Red-wattled Lapwing but with black, pointed crest, gray breast (not black); no red near bill. The small spur on wing not a good field mark. Often assumes a hunched posture, head drawn in. Runs well; a deliberate flier. Bobs head while walking; raises crest and thrusts spurs at rival birds. Flies low over water. Mostly a *tarai* bird. Voice a spaced *pip;* on the wing a *pip-pip-pip-pip.* ✻ KV: above and below Chobar Gorge in spring; also in December. ❦ Kashmir, Garhwal, Nepal, Sikkim; Mediterranean to S.E. Asia 369

Black-bellied Plover (Gray Plover), *Pluvialis squatarola*.
76-152 m.   (250-500')   30 cm.   (12")   M.

Scarce; on sandbanks along rivers. In drab winter plumage, slightly paler than Eastern Golden Plover; *black axillaries* diagnostic and visible in flight. In breeding plumage, underparts black and upperparts gray (vs golden in Eastern Golden Plover). Rediscovered in Nepal (Rapti River, Chitwan) on 29 Nov. 1979 by Curry Lindahl and a flock of 20-30 birds in breeding plumage noted at the Kosi Barrage on 30 April 1982 (A. Cassels and S. LeClerq). ◆ Kashmir, Nepal; almost world-wide   371

Eastern Golden Plover, *Pluvialis dominica*.
120-2440 m.   (400-8,000')   24 cm.   (9½")   M.

Occasional; along watercourses and in cutover rice fields. A brownish bird with many "golden" spots; axillaries (under wings near body) *gray*. Parties of 6 to 20 move together in fast flight. Feeds in damp fields and usually first seen from quite a distance. ❉ KV: on the upper Bagmati during migration in October. ◆ Nepal; Asia, Americas   373

Greater Sand Plover, *Charadrius leschenaultii*. 22 cm.   (8½"),   No date since 1846. Look for a gray bird, white below with broken breast band and a white wing-stripe in flight. (See Lesser Sand Plover below.) ◆ Nepal; Africa, Asia, Australia   374

Little Ring Plover, *Charadrius dubius*.
244-1372 m.   (800-4,500')   15-18 cm.   (6-7")   R., W.

Fairly common; along margins of sandy islands in shallow rivers. Distinctive black upper breast band; also note head pattern. Young has incomplete brown breast band and resembles female Kentish Plover except the latter has a pale eyebrow and a darkish cheek patch. Chicks in Rapti Dun in May. Often in pairs or family groups, running in fast spurts along margins of mud flats. Flight a rapid whirr as they wheel in a compact group this way and that, close to the water. Voice a piping *peerp-peerp;* in flight, a twinkling *teeteetee-teetee* and a rapid *pirpirpirpirpir*. The large race *(C. d. curonicus)* found on Kosi in November; a winter visitor. ❉ KV: along rivers the year around. ◆ Kashmir, Garhwal, Nepal, Sikkim; Europe, Africa, Asia   379, 380

Long-billed Ring Plover, *Charadrius placidus*.
305-1372 m.   (1,000-4,500')   23 cm.   (9")   M., W.

Occasional; along flowing water. Winters in the *tarai* and *duns*. Similar to Little Ring Plover but a longer bill, a large gray patch (not white) in front and below eye; much less white in tail. Legs pale orange (not grayish-green). Often solitary, along pebbly beaches, streams and rivers. Food mostly flying insects and small beetles. Said to move rather slowly but is fast runner and swift flier. ❉ KV: occurs along Bagmati in April-May. ◆ Nepal, Sikkim; Asia   383

Kentish Plover (Snowy Plover), *Charadrius alexandrinus*.
244-1372 m.   (800-4,500')   16 cm.   (6½")   M., W.

Occasional; along sandy or pebbly stream beds of the *tarai*. Breeding male distinctive with rufous crown. In winter both sexes similar to young Little Ring Plover but a whitish eyebrow and dark cheek patches differentiate it. Legs dark (Little Ring legs greenish-gray). Solitary or in small parties often with other waders. During migration flocks up to 50 feed in open meadows of the *tarai*. Runs after insect with head drawn in and may suddenly tip whole body forward for the catch. A mellow *tee-tee-tee-tee* just before taking wing. ❉ KV: a few winter on the Bagmati. ◆ Kashmir, Nepal; almost world-wide   381

Lesser Sand Plover, *Charadrius mongolus*.
76-152 m.   (250-500')   19 cm.   (7½")   M.

Scarce; on sand banks of major rivers on migration. Most birds probably overfly Nepal. Very similar to Kentish Plover but lacks light collar. Except for size, virtually identical to Greater Sand Plover (see this page) but has slightly darker legs, comparatively slenderer bill and often shows a rather indistinct (vs. distinct) wing-stripe in flight. Extreme caution in identification advisable. Rediscovered in Nepal in Chitwan in Feb. 1981 by A. del-Nevo and P. Ewins and confirmed for Nepal by T. & C. Inskipp on 12, 14 March 1981 from the Kosi Barrage. ◆ Kashmir, Nepal, Sikkim, Africa, Asia, Australia   384

Whimbrel, *Numenius phaeopus.*
183 m. (600') 43 cm. (17") M.
Scarce; seen during migration on grassy stretches bordering streams. Told from Curlew by pale buff stripe over top of head as well as light-colored supercilia. Also smaller than Curlew. Re-discovered in Nepal in Sept. 1974 (thus no illustration) by RLF and Max Thompson; noted near Meghauli airfield, Chitwan, with Curlews. ♦ Nepal; Holarctic, wintering at tropical latitudes 385 (?)

Curlew, *Numenius arquata.*
213-5185 m. (700-17,000') 58 cm. (23") M., W.
Occasional; along river courses and damp *tarai* meadows. A pale brown bird (spots and markings very noticeable at close range) with a *long,* decurved bill. Could be confused with the Whimbrel but Curlew's head pattern rather *uniform,* not striped. Single or in small flocks, probing for food in mud. Wary; strong fliers. Six on mud flats of the Kosi near the barrage in March. Also on the Indrawati and Dudh Kosi on autumn migration. Call a loud, clear *cur-loo.* ✲ KV: passes through on fall migration in August. ♦ Kashmir (?), Nepal; Europe, Africa, Asia 388

Black-tailed Godwit, *Limosa limosa.*
78-1371 m. (250-4,500') 40-50 cm. (16-20") M.
Scarce; in shallow water near muddy banks. A distinctive bird with long, slightly *upcurved* bill, reddish at base. Black tail and white rump noted in flight. Single bird collected on 30 Aug. 1981 in Kathmandu by Hari S. Nepali and another seen along the Manhora River (K.V.) in Oct. 1983 (H. S. Nepali). About 55 seen on 21-24 April 1981 at the Kosi Barrage (M. Henriksen, O. Lou, N. Krabbe). ♦ Kashmir, Nepal; Europe, Africa, Asia, Australia 389

Greenshank, *Tringa nebularia.*
120-2440 m. (400-8,000') 33 cm. (13") W.
Common; on margins of lakes and rivers. Nepal's largest *Tringa* distinguished by slightly upturned bill. Quite pale with dull greenish-gray legs. Usually solitary or in scattered pairs often near other waders. A fast, wheeling flight. When disturbed, bobs up and down before taking off. Food includes insects, worms, crustaceans. Call a loud *ter-tur-----ter-tur-----tir-tirtirtir.* ✲ KV: along most streams; departs in May. ♦ Kashmir, Garhwal, Nepal, Sikkim; Europe, Africa, Asia to New Zealand 396

Ruff and Reeve, *Philomachus pugnax.*
1310 m. (4,300') 25-30 cm. (10-12") M.
Occasional, along river courses. Winter plumage of grays and dark brown, variable. Distinctive tail margined white and tipped black. Yellowish-black bill. Legs vary from brown to orangy-red. Strong flight showing white wingbar. Often with other species. Most appear in large flocks. Take off notes a low *chuck-chuck* (AR). ✲ KV: feeds in damp fields along upper Bagmati on migration. ♦ Kashmir, Nepal; Europe, Africa, Asia 426

Common Redshank, *Tringa totanus.*
120-3355 m. (400-11,000') 30 cm. (12") W.
Occasional; on mud flats and in shallow water. Told from Spotted Redshank by streaking and a conspicuous white bar along trailing edge of wing. Usually several in mixed flocks around Phewa Tal, Pokhara, in winter. With Spotted Redshanks in E. Nepal *tarai.* Solitary, on the Karnali in spring. Call a repeated, high-pitched *tiwee.* ✲ KV: occasionally along Bagmati and Manora in winter. ♦ Kashmir, Nepal; Europe, Africa, Asia 394

Spotted Redshank, *Tringa erythropus.*
152 m. (500') 28 cm. (11") W.
Occasional; in shallow ponds surrounded by swamp grass and along large rivers. Note red legs. Paler than Common Redshank and lacks white hind wingbar. Seen in winter when spots are not prominent. Usually with other waders such as the Greenshank and egrets. Seen in pools along Biratnagar-Dharan Road. Call a high-pitched *pe-wit.* ♦ Kashmir(?), Nepal; Europe, Africa, Asia 392

Marsh Sandpiper, *Tringa stagnatilis*.
152 m. (500') 25 cm. (10") W.

Scarce; sight records in Chitwan Dun along stream south of Meghauli airstrip in April (RLF). Should occur in wet areas all through south Nepal. Look for a slender, long-legged, very pale sandpiper. Usually several together, often with other waders. Alarm call is a *che-weep* (AR). ♦ Kashmir(?), Nepal; Europe, Africa, Asia, Australia 395

Wood Sandpiper, *Tringa glareola*.
120-2440 m. (400-8,000') 22 cm. (8½") W.

Occasional; at edge of pools and streams in open country. Very similar to the Green Sandpiper but paler with pale yellowish legs (not greenish). Pale marks on back stand out on the dark background whereas marks of Green Sandpiper inconspicuous. Single or in pairs but migrates in fairly large flocks. Food includes minnows. Call a shrill *pee-pee-pee* (AR). ♦ Kashmir (?), Nepal; Europe, Africa, Asia, Australia 398

Green Sandpiper, *Tringa ochropus*.
120-3873 m. (400-12,700') 25 cm. (10") W.

Fairly common; along pools and margins of streams. A dark sandpiper with pale throat and upper breast, extensive white rump and heavily barred tail. Told from the Wood Sandpiper by its darker appearance and dark legs. The white rump showy in flight. Usually solitary; sometimes in widely scattered groups on migration. Call a *cheer-weet-weet* and a rapid *pree* in flight. ❊ KV: the commonest medium-sized *Tringa* of the Valley. ♦ Kashmir, Garhwal, Nepal, Sikkim; Europe, Africa, Asia 397

Common Sandpiper, *Tringa hypoleucos*.
120-3812 m. (400-12,500') 20 cm. (8") R., W.

Fairly common; on soggy ground, around little streams and puddles. Similar to Green Sandpiper but smaller, paler and has brownish upper breast (not pale), a dark rump and conspicuous white wing-stripe seen in flight. Often associates with wagtails on sand bars. Single birds sometimes flush from tiny trickles of water between cultivated fields. Jerky head and tail movements. Call a high-pitched *tee-tee-tee-tee-tee*. ❊ KV: a common sandpiper in winter. ♦ Kashmir, Garhwal, Nepal, Sikkim; Europe, Africa, Asia, Australia 401

Long-toed Stint, *Calidris subminutus*.
1280 m. (4,200') 15 cm. (6") M.

Scarce; on shallow sand bars with many other small water birds. Similar to Temminck's Stint but distinctly darker with blotched appearance above (not uniform brown) and yellowish legs (not greenish); outer tail feathers brownish. Throat and breast often lightly streaked. It runs this way and that for insects, bobbing a tiny tail as it picks up food. Often with Temminck's Stint. Voice a single shrill note. ♦ Nepal; Europe, Asia to Philippines 418

Little Stint, *Calidris minutus*.
120-1372 m. (400-4,500') 15 cm. (6") M., W.

Scarce; on shallow mud flats of large rivers. A very small, pale sandpiper. Told from Temminck's Stint by its *black legs* (not greenish-yellow) and distinctly mottled back. Note, in flight, the brownish (not pure white) outer tail feathers. Usually in company with other small waders. Darts here and there after insects and worms. Call a *whit-wit-wit* and in flight a low *trrrrrrr* (AR). ❊ KV: look for them along the Bagmati River. ♦ Kashmir (?), Nepal; Europe, Africa, Asia 416

Temminck's Stint, *Calidris temminckii*.
213-1372 m. (700-4,500') 15 cm. (6") W.

Common; on sand bars and mud flats of lowland and foothill streams. Similar to the Little Stint but fairly uniform above; legs greenish (not black). Leg color determination sometimes difficult because of caked mud. Outer tail feathers *white* (not brownish). In scattered parties, usually with wagtails and other waders. A group flies in compact formation, calling, weaving this way and that as they swiftly skim the water. It has a thin, high-pitched, twinkling twitter— *tititititititititit*. ❊ KV: on rivers and sand bars all winter. ♦ Kashmir, Nepal, Sikkim; Europe, Africa, Asia 417

Dunlin, *Calidris alpinus*.
1372 m. (4,500') 18 cm. (7") W.

Scarce; on sand bars with other sandpipers. Note bill decurved at tip as well as dark center to rump (seen in flight). After Hodgson's days, recorded again in 1973 (H. S. Nepali, RLF), in Kathmandu Valley. Not illustrated as re-discovered in Nepal after plate completed. ♦ Kashmir, Nepal; Europe, Asia, Africa, Americas 420

Wood Snipe, *Capella nemoricola.*
1280-3965 m.   (4,200-13,000')   30 cm.   (12")   R., M.

Scarce; found in wooded areas; habitat is important clue to identification. A large snipe similar to Solitary Snipe but is black above with buffy streaks (not spots). The pale neck and breast are barred (not spotted). Also completely barred abdomen like a Woodcock but marks on crown are long stripes (not bars). Rather slow flight described as "bat-like" with bill pointing down (AR). Sometimes a low *tok-tok* when taking wing (AR). Noted by Ted Cronin as nesting at tree line in E. Nepal in summer, 1973. ◖ Garhwal, Nepal, Sikkim (?); India to Burma   405

Jack Snipe, *Capella minima.*
610-1372 m.   (2,000-4,500')   22 cm.   (8½")   W.

Occasional; in damp areas with other snipe. Small; *two* light stripes *over crown*, no bars on flanks, tail brown; the only snipe with no bars on tail. Usually solitary; often under shrubbery at edges of fields. The escape flight is slow and in a nearly straightaway direction. Covers a short distance then drops to the ground. Usually silent when flushed. ✤ KV: here with other snipe in winter.   ◖ Kashmir (?), Nepal; Europe, Asia   410

Pintail Snipe, *Capella stenura.*
120-1280 m.   (400-4,200')   27 cm.   (10½")   W.

Fairly common; in damp cutover rice fields. Smaller and a bit paler than the Wood Snipe. Darker than the Fantail Snipe below. When on the ground it squats and appears to sink out of sight as do other snipe, but usually with one eye visible over a clod of earth. On take off it gives a *quoik* and flies in quick zigzag movements. Once aloft it may describe wide circles uttering an occasional *vitch*. ✤ KV: in damp, flooded rice fields in winter. ◖ Kashmir, Nepal; Asia   406

Fantail Snipe, *Capella gallinago.*
120-2745 m.   (400-9,000')   27 cm.   (10½")   W.

Fairly common; in wet fields bordering streams. Darker above and paler below than Pintail Snipe. Hard to distinguish in field but in flight, note *white trailing edge of wing* (tips of secondaries). A comparatively long bill. Sometimes with other species of snipe in same field but usually prefers damper areas; stands in water in small streams. Flight is a strong zigzag pattern but the take off call is longer than that of the Pintail—a harsh *preech*. ✤ KV: in winter usually at edges of streams. ◖ Kashmir, Nepal; Europe, Africa, Asia   409

Solitary Snipe, *Capella solitaria.*
1220-2745 m.   (4,000-9,000')   30 cm.   R.(?), M.

Scarce; seen for a few days during migration, around open ponds and among reed beds. A large snipe, dark brown with much spotting above and on neck and breast; white eye-stripe and white edges to scapulars. Rises suddenly with a *pench*. Zigzag movements much slower than most snipe. ✤ KV: Godaveri along stream flowing into Royal Botanic Gardens. ◖ Kashmir, Nepal, Sikkim; Asia   404

Woodcock, *Scolopax rusticola.*
1372-3660 m.   (4,500-12,000')   34 cm.   (13½")   R., M.

Occasional; haunts wooded ravines of foothills (winter) and mountain forests (summer). A large, dark "snipe" with a long, heavy bill and *dark bars* (not stripes) on head. Solitary or in separated pairs. When disturbed it bursts into a short, zigzag flight and on alighting, crouches behind protection. In April-May, flies back and forth at dawn and dusk over breeding ground, usually between 3050-3660 m. (10,000-12,000'), calling a repeated *seek*. Has a croaking noise in spring. ✤ KV: in places like Godaveri under vegetation along streams in winter. ◖ Kashmir, Garhwal, Nepal, Sikkim; Europe, Asia   411

99

PAINTED SNIPE (Rostratulidae).

Painted Snipe, *Rostratula benghalensis*.
152-1310 m. (500-4,300') 25-28 cm. (10-11") R., M.

Occasional; in flooded fields and along grassy, muddy stream banks bordered with reeds, grass and bushes. A colorfully mottled snipe. Female larger than male with rufous throat and neck, tan line through crown and broad, white eye-stripe. Male smaller and duller, lacking rufous; attends to nesting duties. Single or twos and threes. Bobs like a sandpiper when probing in mud for food; active in dull light. Squats when alarmed and hard to flush. When nearly trod upon, rises suddenly with rather slow wingbeat and fairly straight flight. Male tending young in May. Usually silent when taking wing but has an assortment of notes during breeding season. ✲ KV: in wet field in Kupandol; also flooded fields along rivers.
♦ Kashmir, Nepal; Africa, Asia, Australia429

AVOCET and ALLIES (Recurvirostridae). The three species in Nepal are fairly large waders with long upcurved, decurved or straight bills and double-length legs. Only one nests here.

Black-winged Stilt, *Himantopus himantopus*.
120-1310 m. (400-4,300') 25 cm. (10") W., M.

Scarce; in shallows along large rivers. Males black and white; females brown and white. Flies with long pink legs extending beyond tail. Often solitary, walking about in quiet water. Noted along the Kosi in March and the Karnali in April. ✲ KV: found along the Manora in October (G. B. Gurung, 1965). ♦ Kashmir, Nepal; nearly world-wide430

Avocet, *Recurvirostra avosetta*.
120 m. (400') 46 cm. (18") M.

Scarce; in small parties along the Kosi River in March (RLF, 1969). Unmistakable—a black and white bird with a long, black, upcurved bill. Feeds in shallow water and also in deep water "where it up-ends like a duck" (AR). Strong flight. Noted resting on sand bars. Call a clear *klooit* (AR). ♦ Nepal; Europe, Africa, Asia432

Ibisbill, *Ibidorhyncha struthersii*.
183-3965 m. (600-13,000') 39 cm. (15½") R., W.

Occasional; in small flocks on stony and sandy river beds. Gray with a prominent decurved bill. Note black forehead and face; a wide white band at base of gray neck. Bill adapted for securing food underneath small stones in the water. Bobs head and wags tail. Shy; a strong flier. Hides like a snipe. Nests in old glaciated valleys such as the upper Langtang Valley usually above 3050 m. (10,000') in summer. Look for them in winter at the base of foothills where mountain rivers spill onto the plains. Also in stony areas along major rivers. The call resembles a Greenshank's but is more penetrating—a *teew-teew*. ✲ KV: a few pass through in Sept.-Oct. (General Sushil Rana). ♦ Kashmir, Garhwal, Nepal, Sikkim; C. Asia433

THICK KNEES (Stone Plovers; Stone Curlews), (Burhinidae). These two species have long legs, fairly long, heavy bills, large heads and chunky bodies. Eyes are exceptionally large. Terrestrial.

Eurasian Thick Knee (Stone Plover), *Burhinus oedicnemus*.
120-1310 m. (400-4,300') 40 cm. (16") R.

Fairly common; in open cultivated fields, meadows and along stony river bottoms. A conspicuously streaked bird. Two narrow white wingbars and a white wing patch noticeable in flight. Usually in pairs; active at dawn and dusk. May be seen at night in headlights of a car. Holds large head in steady balance when running. Has a strong, slow wingbeat and runs upon alighting. After dark one often hears its call from cultivated fields *parr——eeeeeek*.
♦ Nepal; Europe, Africa, Asia 436

Great Thick Knee (Great Stone Plover), *Esacus magnirostris*.
120-244 m. (400-800') 50 cm. (20") R.

Occasional; on wide, sandy or stony river banks. Much larger than the Eurasian Thick Knee and rarely found away from large river banks such as the Kosi, Narayani and Karnali. The large black and yellow bill and the black face pattern are diagnostic. Illustrated eye comparatively too small. In pairs. Active during the day as well as at dawn and dusk. When approached, crouches obliteratively among stones. A fast runner and a strong flier with deliberate wingbeat. Usually silent but when alarmed gives a harsh *see-eek*. Five on one Narayani sand bank in May (Corbett). ♦ Nepal; Pakistan to Australia 437

COURSER and PRATINCOLES (Glareolidae). The Courser is a tidy-appearing bird resembling a lapwing. Usually seen running across fields. The Pratincoles are reminiscent of large swallows. They fly back and forth over stony river beds morning and evening and rest among the river pebbles at mid-day.

Indian Courser, *Cursorius coromandelicus*.
244 m. (800') 22 cm. (8½") R.

Scarce; inhabits open, cultivated fields north of Dhanghari in far western *tarai*. A compact little bird with long legs and colorful rusty head and breast; a white rump seen in flight. In small parties in dry country. Runs like a lapwing with white legs moving rapidly. Flies low over the ground on fast, steady wingbeats. Gives a single note when flushed. ♦ Nepal; S. Asia 440

Collared Pratincole, *Glareola pratincola*.
1280 m. (4,200') 23 cm. (9") M.

Scarce; apparently young birds wander into Nepal in the late monsoon. Look for a buff throat bordered with black. Also note, in flight, rufous underwing linings. Not illustrated as discovered in Nepal after plate completed. May occur along large rivers of the western *tarai* in winter. ❈ KV: a single bird collected by H. S. Nepali on a sand bar in the Manora River, Sept. 1973. ♦ Nepal; Africa, Asia, Australia 443

Small Pratincole, *Glareola lactea*.
213-305 m. (700-1,000') 16 cm. (6¼") R.

Occasional; along wide, stony river beds. Only two-thirds the size of the Collared Pratincole and very much paler. Grayish with long, pointed black primaries and white tail with black tip. The prominent black underwing linings (not rufous of Collared Pratincole) seen in flight. Rests among pebbles, facing the wind with wings held close to body. Fly up one after another and cruise 20 or 30 feet above the river bed, catching insects. Very active just before dusk. Also found in plowed fields near rivers. Voice a shrill warble. ♦ Kashmir, Nepal; Pakistan to S.E. Asia 444

GULLS and TERNS (Laridae). Gulls are gray and white with long, broad wings and fan tails. The young are often brownish. They scavenge near water and nest in colonies. Terns are slim, graceful birds with long, pointed wings and most have long, v-shaped tails. Usually gray and white, several have black caps and red bills. They feed by swooping down to the surface of the water or actually diving into it

Herring Gull, *Larus argentatus*.
120-3050 m. (400-10,000') 58 cm. (23") M.

Scarce; on rivers and lakes of the Nepal midlands. A large, pale gull with white head, pearl-gray back; the black primaries have white tips. Young are streaked brown and white. Usually single or in pairs. Flies with a strong, slow wingbeat. Seen in Pokhara and on Rara Lake. A large, light-colored gull at high altitudes likely to be this species. Rides high on the water. Voice a loud *kee-au*. ✿ KV: along the Bagmati during the rainy season. ◢ Kashmir (?), Nepal; Europe, Asia, N. America   450

Great Black-headed Gull, *Larus ichthyaetus*.
120-1280 m. (400-4,200') 74 cm. (29") M., W.

Scarce; on large rivers of Nepal. Pale head with some darkish markings (winter). Primaries white with terminal black patches. Immature bird has white tail with broad black band. Large size, massive yellow bill with black band and red tip, most noticeable. Rides high on the water. Single or in pairs, flying repeatedly up and down a favorite stretch of water. Occasionally on the Karnali in April; noted on the Kamala by late October. ✿ KV: one resting on Bagmati in April. ◢ Nepal; Mediterranean to Burma   453

Black-headed Gull, *Larus ridibundus*.
152 m. (500') 40 cm. (16") W.

Occasional; on rivers of the *tarai*. Lacks black head in winter plumage and is like the Brown-headed Gull but *primary tips are entirely black*. Young brown but with adult wing pattern; end of tail barred black. A scavenger, often associated with other gulls such as the Brown-headed Gull. Call a harsh *kwu-rip*. ◢ Nepal; Europe, Asia   455

Brown-headed Gull, *Larus brunnicephalus*.
120-1280 m. (400-4,200') 46 cm. (18") W.

Occasional; on large rivers often with other gulls, terns and kites. Medium size. Head in winter a mottled brown, becoming darker in spring; a dark ear patch. Look for white patches near tips of black primaries. Young brownish with black band at end of tail; wing pattern similar to adult and this differentiates it from closely related Black-headed Gull. Many rest on sand bars of the Kosi River near the barrage. ✿ KV: occasionally on the Bagmati. ◢ Kashmir, Nepal; Asia   454

Slender-billed Gull, *Larus genei*.
120 m. (400') 43 cm. (17") W.

Scarce; on sand bars of Kosi River. In winter, very similar to Black-headed Gull but stands higher, with a longer neck and smaller head. Breeding plumage (seen once in Nepal): a white head and distinctive *pinkish* body. Sight records of single birds; first reported by Stephen Madge and party (7 Feb. 1974) and confirmed by J.F.S. Batson on 9 Feb. 1975 (thus no illustration). ◢ Nepal; Black Sea to India   456

Caspian Tern, *Hydroprogne caspia*.
120 m. (400') 53 cm. (21") W.

Scarce; at the Kosi Barrage in March (RLF). A very large tern with a strong orange-red bill. Rather heavy flight; dark under-surfaces of primaries conspicuous in flight. Frequents edges of sand bars. Usually solitary here but as many as 20 scattered individuals (Madge, February 1974) on Kosi. ◢ Kashmir(?), Nepal; Europe, Africa, Asia, Australia, N. America   462

Whiskered Tern, *Chlidonias hybrida.*
183 m. (600') 25 cm. (10") W.
Occasional; along flooded fields of the eastern *tarai;* seen only in winter. A small, light-colored tern with blackish bill (red only in summer) and *short, slightly forked tail.* Crown, flecked with black; dark behind eye. Dark breeding plumage not seen here. Young, streaked brown and white. Along the Chatra Canal, S.E. *tarai* in March. Flies back and forth over shallow pools; usually solitary. Said to have a note like a shrike. ♣ Kashmir, Nepal; Europe, Africa, Asia, Australia
458

Gull-billed Tern, *Gelochelidon nilotica.*
120 m. (400') 38 cm. (15") W.
Fairly scarce; on sand bars of Kosi near barrage. A white tern; gray back, with a *black* stubby bill like that of a gull. The size of the Indian River Tern, long black legs and a white, forked tail. A flock of 20-30 with gulls and terns. Feeds on insects, rarely dipping into water. Observed by Stephen Madge, *et al*, February 1974. ♣ Kashmir, Nepal; Europe, Africa, Asia, N. and S. America
460

Indian River Tern, *Sterna aurantia.*
120-610 m. (400-2,000') 38-46 cm. (15-18") R.
Common; patrolling rivers, streams and marshy lakes. Head, black in summer, streaked in winter, otherwise all gray above and white below; a swallow-like tail; *bill bright yellow* (summer) or dingy yellow, black tipped (winter). The smaller Black-bellied Tern similar in winter but has orangy-yellow bill and legs. Turns with spread tail as it plunges into the water. Covers hunting course on slow, regular wingbeats. Several in the same area; rest together on sand bars. Has harsh notes. ♣ Nepal; Pakistan to Laos
463

Common Tern, *Sterna hirundo.*
1310 m. (4,300') 35 cm. (14") M., W.
Occasional; along rivers in Nepal. Gray above and white below; the only Nepal tern with reddish base to the black bill (Caspian has heavy, orange-red bill). Often a late monsoon visitor. To be expected on rivers of the *tarai* in winter. ✣ KV: first recorded in autumn (Proud). Noted along the Bagmati and Manora Rivers (RLF). ♣ Kashmir, Nepal; Europe, Africa, Asia, Americas
465

Black-bellied Tern, *Sterna acuticauda.*
120-732 m. (400-2,400') 33 cm. (13") R.
Fairly common; over watercourses of the lowlands. Slightly smaller than the Indian River Tern; the only Nepal tern with a *black* belly in summer. In winter, belly usually white but some are black and this aids in identification. A few patrol sections of lakes and rivers with other terns. Flies with bill turned down, skimming the water. Numbers gather together on sand bars for the night. Has a repeated high note. ♣ Nepal; Pakistan to Laos
470

Little Tern, *Sterna albifrons.*
120-1280 m. (400-4,200') 23 cm. (9") M., W.
Occasional; along large *tarai* rivers in spring. A tiny tern with white forehead and black line from eye to around nape; tail squarish. Fishes with other terns, gulls and kites at the Kosi Barrage in spring. Very active, wheeling this way and that in rapid, graceful flight. Plunges from a considerable height. Voice a high-pitched *jer-reek.* ✣ KV: recorded on Bagmati in late monsoon (Sept. 1973) by General Sushil Rana and RLF. ♣ Nepal; nearly world-wide
477

Indian Skimmer, *Rynchops albicollis.*
120 m. (400') 42 cm. (16½") R.
Scarce; only noted on Kosi River. A large, pied "tern" with outstanding orangy-yellow bill, the lower mandible protruding beyond the upper. The white collar and white underparts seen at long range. Skimming behavior, often in pairs or small parties, diagnostic. Recently discovered in Nepal (thus no illustration) by RLF and Harvey Gilston who watched three birds at the Kosi Barrage on 11 April 1975. ♣ Nepal; Pakistan to Indochina
484

SANDGROUSE (Pteroclidae) are dry country birds with obliterative coloring.

Indian Sandgrouse, *Pterocles exustus*. 32 cm. (12½"). Last reported in 1846. Tail feathers long and pointed; abdomen rufous. (Tibetan Sandgrouse, *Syrrhaptes tibetanus*, reported from Sikkim, p.336.) ♠ Kashmir, Nepal; Africa, Asia 487

Imperial Sandgrouse, *Pterocles orientalis*. 33 cm. (13"). No data since 1846. Male has black belly and rufous throat. Female has dark v-shaped bars above and also a black belly. ♠ Nepal; Europe, Africa, Asia 489

Close-barred Sandgrouse, *Pterocles indicus*. 27 cm. (10½"). In Hodgson's 1846 collection. A small sandgrouse with black and white forehead. The male has a wide tan breast band divided from the abdomen by a dark brown line. ♠ Nepal; Africa, Asia 492

PIGEONS and DOVES (Columbidae) are plump, fast-flying birds that feed on grain and fruit. Although large birds in this family are termed "pigeons," and small ones "doves," there is really no scientific distinction. Except for the green pigeons, sexes are usually alike.

Pintail Green Pigeon, *Treron apicauda*.
152-305 m. (500-1,000') 42 cm. (16½") R.
Occasional; in forests of the *tarai*. The only green pigeon with a long, pointed tail. Also note the gray neck and two yellow wingbars. Congregate in fig trees in small flocks in deep forest. Rather sluggish but wingbeat is strong. A fruit-eater. Drinks regularly at streams. Call a varied, mellow whistle. ♠ Nepal, Sikkim; Kumaon to S.E. Asia 493

Wedge-tailed Green Pigeon, *Treron sphenura*.
152-2440 m. (500-8,000') 33 cm. (13") R.
Fairly common; in mixed forests. The only green pigeon in oak forests of the hills above 1525 m. (5,000'). Male has a maroon mantle, upper back and scapulars; breast a pale orangy-pink. Female lacks maroon and is duller green. Blue bill outstanding at close range. Usually single or in pairs in heavy forest. Several may congregate in a fruiting tree. Sits silently for long periods and feeds quietly, reaching into awkward positions to secure fruit. Call a pleasant, mellow whistle *hoo-huhuhu-hoo-eee-hu*. ❊ KV: Godaveri, Sheopuri and surrounding hills. ♠ Kashmir, Garhwal, Nepal, Sikkim; Kashmir to S.E. China 494

Thick-billed Green Pigeon, *Treron curvirostra*.
120-457 m. (400-1,500') 27 cm. (10½") R.
Occasional; usually in heavy *sal* and mixed forests of the *tarai*. Similar to Wedge-tailed Green Pigeon but much smaller; head gray, not yellowish; black on the tail. Female has *green and white undertail coverts*, not green and buff as the former species. Rather shy. Flies off with a clapping of wings as do other pigeons. Voice a subdued whistle. ♠ Nepal, Sikkim; Nepal to the Philippines 495

Orange-breasted Green Pigeon, *Treron bicincta*.
183-305 m. (600-1,000') 29 cm. (11½") R.
Scarce; seen in quite open country as well as in forests. Has lilac and orange breast brighter than other green pigeons. Also look for yellow vent and a blackish tail, broadly tipped with gray. Female like the male but breast is green. Found in trees near airstrips such as Simra and Meghauli; also in *sal* forests. Feeds early and late in the day. Unripe figs are frequently eaten. ♠ Nepal; India to S.E. China 501

Gray-fronted Green Pigeon (Pompadour), *Treron pompadora*.
120-213 m. (400-700') 28 cm. (11") R.
Fairly common; in forests of the *tarai* not far from streams. Has a gray head with an orange throat and breast. Also note the yellow pattern on dark wings. Cinnamon undertail coverts a good field mark when male is perched directly overhead. Female has tan undertail coverts, mottled with gray-green. Moves deliberately in tree tops, sometimes clinging to undersides of branches. Flocks sun themselves in leafless trees in winter. Many may assemble in fruiting trees and also visit fruiting bushes near ground. Call a whistle of soft, warbling notes. ♠ Nepal; India to Celebes 498

Bengal Green Pigeon, *Treron phoenicoptera.*
120-1310 m. (400-4,300') 33 cm. (13") R.

Fairly common; in villages, *pipal* trees and roadsides of the foothills. A large light gray-green pigeon with a lilac shoulder patch. *Yellow legs* (not red), a good field mark. Much less of a forest bird than other green pigeons. Clumsy; a voracious feeder. Partial to fruiting *pipal* (fig) trees, usually below 1220 m. (4,000'). ❋ KV: scarce, in city groves, Pashupati, Rani Bari. ❦ Nepal, Sikkim(?); India to S.E. Asia 503

Imperial Pigeon, *Ducula badia.*
152 m. (500') 50 cm. (20") R., M.

Scarce; in heavy evergreen forests of the *tarai.* A very large bird with gray head and white throat. Difficult to see as it sits concealed among leaves. Noisy in nesting season. During courtship, male will shoot into the air well above the tops of trees. Call a distinctive, deep, booming *uk-ook——ook.* ❦ Nepal; Nepal to S.E. Asia 510

Snow Pigeon, *Columba leuconota.*
1525-4880 m. (5,000-16,000') 34 cm. (13½") R., W.

Fairly common; in high cliff country. A very pale pigeon; note how dark head contrasts with pale neck. Feeds in open fields; remains active even in snowstorms. Considerable altitudinal movement; some descend in large flocks as low as 1525 m. (5,000') in winter. In pairs or small flocks in summer. Often feeds with Blue Rock Pigeons. Along the Suli Gad, W. Nepal at 2745 m. (9,000') in June but usually above 3660 m. (12,000') at that time. It has a repeated croak (AR); usually silent in winter. ❦ Kashmir, Garhwal, Nepal, Sikkim; Afghanistan to W. China 513

Hill Pigeon, *Columba rupestris.*
1982-5490 m. (6,500-18,000') 33 cm. (13") R., W.

Common; in Dolpo and the Trans-Himalayan parts of Nepal. Both in villages and well away in *Caragana* scrub. Similar to Blue Rock Pigeon but paler; rump white; tail feathers white at base with dark terminal band. Very tame in Dolpo and may approach within five yards of observer. Nests in Shey Gompa and other buildings as well as cliffs. Occasionally moves south in winter (Kodari, Jumla, Rara). Voice a cooing gurgle, softer and higher-pitched than that of Blue Rock Pigeon's. ❦ Kashmir, Nepal, Sikkim; C. Asia 515

Blue Rock Pigeon, *Columba livia.*
120-3965 m. (400-13,000') 33 cm. (13") R., M.

Abundant; in cities and less frequent along river gorges. Similar to the Hill Pigeon but a dark blue-gray with no white on rump or in tail. Gather in large flocks around temple domes and in public squares in Kathmandu. Many forage in cutover grain fields. In winter, mixes freely with Snow Pigeons around Jomosom. Breeds throughout the year; males are ardent wooers. Abroad in very coldest weather. Voices issue from under eaves of houses. ❦ Kashmir, Garhwal, Nepal, Sikkim; introduced nearly world-wide 517

Wood Pigeon, *Columba palumbus.*
   2135 m.   (7,000')   43 cm.   (17")   W., M.

Scarce; in hill forests. A large gray-brown bird with a pinkish half-collar, and large white band on the wing. Winter birds here in large, noisy flocks, feeding greedily on fruit of forest trees. Body movements clumsy. Some feed on the ground. Voice said to have five notes with accent on the second (AR). ✲ KV: migratory movements little understood. Many in the Tin Pani Bhangjang forest at 2135 m. (7,000') in February. ◐ Kashmir, Garhwal, Nepal, Sikkim; Europe, Africa, Asia
519

Speckled Wood Pigeon, *Columba hodgsonii.*
   1525-2745 m.   (5,000-9,000')   38 cm.   (15")   R., M.

Occasional; both in dense jungle and in somewhat open country. A dark pigeon with speckled wings and back, and dark spots on vinous breast. Resembles a small crow in the distance. Often perches in exposed positions on dead branches. Fruit-eater that may hang upside-down to reach a berry. Will descend to small bushes *(Coriaria)* for food. Fairly bold; strong flight. Usually in small parties. Irregular migration and wandering movements which are not well understood. Call a deep *whock—whr-o-o—whroo* (AR). ✲ KV: on Nagarjung, Sheopuri and surrounding hills. ◐ Kashmir, Garhwal, Nepal, Sikkim; India to W. China   520

Ashy Wood Pigeon, *Columba pulchricollis.*
   610-2440 m.   (2,000-8,000')   35 cm.   (14")   W.

Occasional; in fairly dense forest groves. Similar to Speckled Wood Pigeon but lacks spots and head is pale (not dark). A black and buff collar; also breast gray (not vinous). Rather sluggish. Usually pairs in high forest trees, sometimes in moderate-sized groups. Often sits quietly in leafy canopy and at this time hard to detect. Behavior not as exposed as that of Speckled Wood Pigeons. As high as 2287 m. (7,500') in January. ✲ KV: nests in Chapagaon Forest. Pursued by hunters in Rani Bari. ◐ Nepal, Sikkim; Nepal to Formosa   523

Long-tailed Cuckoo Dove, *Macropygia unchall.*
   305-2745 m.   (1,000-9,000')   40 cm.   (16")   R.

Scarce; in dense forests not far from water. Brown and barred. The very long tail, longer than the body, is most distinctive feature. Spends much time sitting quietly in leafy trees and hard to detect. When several feed in a fruiting tree, then easy to see as they clamber about. Quiet flight. Resembles a barred cuckoo but head and bill small and dove-like. After short flights between branches, tail is widely fanned on alighting. Voice a repeated booming *croo-uuuumm* (AR). ✲ KV: along stream on west side of Nagarjung. ◐ Kashmir, Garhwal, Nepal, Sikkim; Kashmir to S.E. China
526

Rufous Turtle Dove, *Streptopelia orientalis.*
   152-3660 m.   (500-12,000')   33 cm.   (13")   R., M.

Common; a forest bird frequenting streams and edges of cultivation. The only dove with distinctive rufous back and gray breast. Dark tail with broad gray terminal band very noticeable in flight. Usually in pairs but scattered flocks sometimes assemble in fallow fields, especially in winter. Thirty or more may sun on top of leafless trees on an early winter morning. Three races in Nepal. *S.o. meena* has undertail feathers white; *S.o. agricola* and *S.o. orientalis* gray. The first and second races are common; the third scarce. ✲ KV: *S.o. meena* resident; *S.o. orientalis* autumn visitor from Tibet. ◐ Kashmir, Garhwal, Nepal, Sikkim; Asia   530, 531, 532

Red Turtle Dove, *Streptopelia tranquebarica*.
183-1372 m. (600-4,500') 23 cm. (9") R., S.

Occasional; affecting bare branches of tall forest trees at edges of fields. The little male is reddish above with black collar on hind neck. Female is a pint-sized, darkish edition of the Indian Ring Dove. Attractive birds, often in pairs. As the male calls, he pumps up and down on a horizontal limb. During breeding season, male flies into the air with a flapping of wings and spreading of tail. Some altitudinal movement. Feeds on the ground. Voice a loud, high-pitched *crew-cru-cru-crook*. ✽ KV: arrives in March-April, Rani Bari, Nagarjung. ♣ Nepal, Sikkim; E. and S.E. Asia 535, 536

Indian Ring Dove, *Streptopelia decaocto*.
120-2440 m. (400-8,000') 32 cm. (12½") R.

Fairly common; especially in western Nepal around villages and in acacia groves in dry country. Pale brownish-gray with black half-collar on hind neck. Resembles female Red Turtle Dove but much larger and slightly paler. Rapid wingbeat like a pigeon's. Found in Jumla at 2440 m. (8,000') in mid-winter. Call *kuk-a-rooooook*. ✽ KV: a few visit here in spring and autumn eating wheat and rice. ♣ Kashmir, Garhwal, Nepal; Europe, Asia 534

Little Brown Dove (Laughing Dove), *Streptopelia senegalensis*.
610-2440 m. (2,000-8,000') 27 cm. (10½") R., M.

Scarce; in fields along rivers and around villages. A small gray-brown dove with black marks on sides of neck (do not show well in illustration) and pinkish breast. Outer tail feathers are black and white. Often associated with other species in grain fields. Movements in Nepal not well understood. A small flock along Trisuli River in spring. Some apparently winter around Jumla town at 2440 m. (8,000'). Voice a soft, pleasant *coo-roo-roo--roo-roo* (AR). ✽ KV: a party of four on the upper Vishnumati. ♣ Kashmir (?), Nepal; Africa, Asia 541

Spotted Dove, *Streptopelia chinensis*.
120-3965 m. (400-13,000') 30 cm. (12") R.

Common; around towns, villages and fields. The common dove in most of Nepal. Pale with spots above. Also look for dark half-collar and gray tail tipped white, conspicuously flared when settling. Somewhat shy. Single, in pairs or scattered flocks. A fast, irregular flight, alighting awkwardly in trees. Nest a very flimsy affair with two eggs laid on a twig platform. Numbers around Jumla town at 2440 m. (8,000') but rarely above this height. One seen on roof of Everest View Hotel at 3873 m. (12,700'), October. Call a *kuk-kuk-krrruuuuuuu-kru-kru-kru* and variations, seemingly for hours on end. ✽ KV: a familiar resident. ♣ Kashmir(?), Garhwal, Nepal, Sikkim; Pakistan to S.E. China 537

Emerald Dove, *Chalcophaps indica*.
120-1372 m. (400-4,500') 27 cm. (10½") R.

Common; in damp forests. Male unmistakable. A dark dove with a pale gray head, greenish-bronze back and wings. Female has brown, not gray, crown. Solitary or in pairs on forest roads. Arrows its rapid flight below forest trees and how it manages to avoid branches, vines and tree trunks is remarkable. Rests in shaded, watered ravines. Common in Chitwan Dun forests. Voice a low, mournful and prolonged *ooooooooooo*, repeated at intervals. ♣ Kashmir, Garhwal, Nepal, Sikkim; Kashmir to Australia 542

PARAKEETS (Psittacidae). Nepalese parakeets are fairly large, bright green birds with long, thin tails. They have hooked beaks and short feet. Many call loudly from "roosting" trees as they gather in noisy flocks. Raids are common on rice, wheat and other grain fields.

Rose-ringed Parakeet, *Psittacula krameri*.
120-305 m. (400-1,000') 40 cm. (16") R.

Abundant; in and around villages, mango groves, fields and forests. Very similar sex for sex to Large Parakeet but lack of maroon shoulder patch and presence of black lower mandible (not red) distinguish this species. Also note in male the rose collar is narrow (not wide). Tail blue-green above and yellow below. Pairs quite attentive, mating a dozen times a day over five or six weeks (McDonald). Apparently quite destructive to grain crops where great flocks have to be frightened away. Voice a rapid, tinny *kee-et*. ✲ KV: a few around the city may be escapees from pet dealers. ◖ Nepal; Africa, Asia 549

Large Parakeet, *Psittacula eupatria*.
120-915 m. (400-3,000') 50 cm. (20") R.

Common; in *sal* and mixed forests of the *duns* and *tarai*. Our largest parakeet. Size and a *distinct maroon shoulder patch* distinguish this species from the Rose-ringed Parakeet. Female lacks black throat and pink collar of male. Small parties of 6-16 climb about in high, fruiting trees. Heavy wingbeat. Ascends foothills in Jhapa, E. Nepal, to a level higher than other lowland parakeets. Easily told by its low-pitched, clangy notes. Call a slow, deep *klak-klak-klak-klak*. ◖ Nepal; Pakistan to S.E. Asia 545

Rose-breasted Parakeet, *Psittacula alexandri*.
120-1372 m. (400-4,500') 35 cm. (14") R.

Fairly common; in groves and light forests bordering fields. The only species with a rosy breast; head violet-gray with black gular stripe. Female has a green head and a darker reddish breast. Seen in parties from 15 to several hundred, often in semi-open country with mango groves and other trees. Rarely above 610 m. (2,000'). Less noisy than other species but voice is a penetrating, deep, rapid *kak-kak-kak-kak-kak*. ◖ Nepal; Kumaon to S.E. China 551

Blossom-headed Parakeet, *Psittacula cyanocephala*.
120-1525 m. (400-5,000') 34 cm. (13¼") R.

Common; occupying *sal* forests and trees at the edge of fields. Male a slim bird with a brilliant blueish-red head and a slender blue tail tipped white (tails of other low-level parakeets not distinctively tipped white). Mandibles red and black. Female has a gray head like the Slaty-headed Parakeet but is much slimmer and with black (not orangy-red) mandibles. Parties of ten to several score fly in close formation, twisting rapidly this way and that. Many in Rapti Dun eating fruit and seeds. Calls a repeated, shrill *kooy* and a rapid *pe-pe-pe-pe-pe* and a chattering *twee—eet*. ◖ Nepal; Pakistan, India, Sri Lanka 557

Slaty-headed Parakeet, *Psittacula himalayana*.
213-2135 m. (700-7,000') 40 cm. (16") R.

Occasional; usually in oak and mixed forests, confined to the hills (rare exceptions in winter). Look for dark gray head and maroon shoulder patch of male. Tail is bright blue with a *long yellow tip*. Female has pale gray head and no shoulder patch. Flies in close flocks wheeling in and out and flashing the yellow-tipped tail, gliding upward into a tree at the end of the flight. Rather noisy and somewhat shy. Winter flocks often of one sex. Haunt flowering Silk Cotton trees. Call a loud, rapid, repeated *koi*; also a tinny *trrrreeeee-trreee*. ✲ KV: in spring, in flowering Silk Cotton trees on Nagarjung. ◖ Kashmir, Garhwal, Nepal, Sikkim; Kashmir to S.E. Asia 562

Indian Lorikeet, *Loriculus vernalis*.
274 m. (900') 14 cm. (5½") R. (?)

Scarce; found by H. S. Nepali in the eastern *tarai*. Look for a small, green bird with a short, squarish tail and a conspicuous red rump and bill. Bird illustrated is proportionately 2x normal size, compared to other parakeets shown. Inhabits forest. Call a *chi-chi—chee* (AR). ◖ Nepal; Nepal to S.E. Asia 566

CUCKOOS (Cuculidae) are slim birds with loud voices. Fourteen species in Nepal are "social parasites," laying their eggs in the nests of "host birds;" four others are non-parasitic. Colors are generally drab; sexes usually alike. Most have an upward altitudinal movement in spring. Their voices are distinctive, some calling at night. Their hawk-like flight and form often provoke small birds into giving alarm calls.

Pied Crested Cuckoo, *Clamator jacobinus*.
305-3873 m. (1,000-12,700') 33 cm. (13") S., M.

Occasional; in *sal* forests of the foothills. A small, thin black and white edition of the Red-winged Crested Cuckoo. White wing patches noticeable in flight, also outer tail feathers tipped white. Known to parasitize laughing-thrushes. Sometimes strays as high as 3660 m. (12,000') in such areas as Everest but rarely above 1525 m. (5,000'). Has a repeated single note and also a loud *piu-piu-pee-pee-pin* (AR). ♠ Kashmir, Garhwal, Nepal, Sikkim(?); Africa, Asia   570

Red-winged Crested Cuckoo, *Clamator coromandus*.
305-1372 m. (1,000-4,500') 46 cm. (18") S., M.

Occasional; in cutover jungle and along rivers and streams. A handsome, long, slender bird; the dark head and upperparts contrasting with reddish-brown wings and fawn throat and breast. Young, brown and rufous above. Solitary, in pairs and small parties. Rather shy, keeping a tree or two away from observer. Said to parasitize necklaced laughing-thrushes and similar species. Voice a shrill double whistle. ❄ KV: a few pass through from April to June. ♠ Garhwal, Nepal, Sikkim; Garhwal to Philippines   569

Large Hawk Cuckoo, *Cuculus sparverioides*.
305-2897 m. (1,000-9,500') 38 cm. (15") R., M.

Fairly common; in oak-rhododendron forests, spring and summer. A very hawk-like bird, dark above and mottled or barred brown and rufous below. Told from hawks by shape of bill and also slender appearance. Never soars. Very similar to low elevation Common Hawk Cuckoo but look for black chin (not pale gray) and darkish (vs. pale) throat. Posterior flanks barred (not pure white) but wings usually obscure this field mark. Told from other gray cuckoos by rufous on breast. Shy, keeps to leafy trees. In summer, rarely below 1830 m. (6,000'). Parasitizes Red-headed and other laughing-thrushes. Call *beer-frever*, which begins slowly, gains momentum and ends with a *bee-frever* on a slightly higher pitch. ❄ KV: noisy in the hills from March to May. ♠ Kashmir, Garhwal, Nepal, Sikkim; Kashmir to Philippines   572

Common Hawk Cuckoo, *Cuculus varius*.
120-1372 m. (400-4,500') 34 cm. (13¼") R., M.

Common; in mango groves and open country of the *tarai*. Similar to Large Hawk Cuckoo but chin is gray (not black) and throat is gray (not dark gray). Rarely above 915 m. (3,000'). Very noisy, the monotonous scream often repeated far into the night. Silent in winter. Lays eggs in nests of Jungle Babbler and allied species. Call a strident series of *brain fever* notes accelerating to a high pitch. ♠ Nepal; India, Bangladesh, Sri Lanka   573

Hodgson's Hawk Cuckoo, *Cuculus fugax*. 29 cm. (11½"). Not reported since 1846.
A gray cuckoo with *unbarred, rufous* breast and abdomen, though some show considerable white (other hawk cuckoos have barred breasts and abdomens). May occur in subtropical or oak forests, 610-1830 m. (2,000-6,000'). ♠ Nepal, Sikkim; India to Japan   575

Eurasian Cuckoo, *Cuculus canorus.*
305-3812 m. (1,000-12,500') 33 cm. (13") R., M.
Common; in rather open hill country. Similar to Indian Cuckoo but lacks black band on tail. Like Himalayan Cuckoo but has white bend in wing barred with brown (not pure white). Female, a brownish tinge on upper breast, brown and black abdominal crossbars. Hepatic females occur infrequently. A distinct juvenile plumage (dark above with whitish bars) is hard to tell from juvenile Himalayan Cuckoo except often a white nuchal patch present. Strong flight. Assumes ungainly drooping posture when it calls. Europeans feel at home in the Himalayas when they hear its familiar sound. Lays eggs in nests of small birds such as warblers, pipits, shrikes and bush chats. Voice a loud *cuk---koo* sometimes accompanied by a bubbling noise. ❉ KV: heard in spring and summer. ♠ Kashmir, Garhwal, Nepal, Sikkim; Europe, Africa, Asia, Australia
578

Indian Cuckoo, *Cuculus micropterus.*
305-2135 m. (1,000-7,000') 33 cm. (13") S.
Fairly common; throughout the foothills. Gray and brown above with *throat* to *breast gray*; barred black and white abdomen. Look carefully at tail which is white-tipped with a *subterminal dark band* best seen on dorsal aspect (the very similar Eurasian and Himalayan Cuckoos lack this band). Parasitizes drongos. Winter movements not well known. Call *kaiphal pakkyo* sounds like "one more bottle." Also a bubbling noise. ❉ KV: arrives for the summer in early April. ♠ Kashmir, Garhwal, Nepal, Sikkim; Pakistan to S.E. Asia
576

Himalayan Cuckoo, *Cuculus saturatus.*
305-3355 m. (1,000-11,000') 33 cm. (13") S.
Fairly common; in oak-rhododendron forests, descending to the foothills and plains in winter. Like the Eurasian Cuckoo but has *white at bend of wing* (not barred with brown) and broader gray bars on the abdomen. Also lacks black tail band. Hepatic females known. Young birds progress through two plumage stages: (1) from upperparts nearly black to (2) slaty. Both stages with narrow, faint, white bars on back. White nuchal patch usually lacking (present in Eurasian Cuckoo young). Strong flight. The call is a mellow, musical, repeated *oo--poo-poo-poo.* ❉ KV: a familiar call in the surrounding hills. ♠ Kashmir, Garhwal, Nepal, Sikkim; S. Asia to Australia
580

Small Cuckoo, *Cuculus poliocephalus.*
1220-3355 m. (4,000-11,000') 25 cm. (10") S.
Fairly common; on migration and summering in high altitude oak forests. Very similar to the Himalayan Cuckoo but much smaller; buffy underneath; bend in wing is gray (neither white nor barred brown and white). Sexes alike but young birds progress through three distinct plumages: (1) very dark above with faint white bars; (2) bars less distinct and white nuchal spot present; (3) bright chestnut barred black. Flares out its tail when calling. One chased by a Gray-headed Warbler. Parasitizes leaf warblers and small babblers. Often calls at night. Voice a scratchy, rapid *pretty-peel-lay-ka-beet* repeated about five or more times. ❉ KV: common on Sheopuri in spring; heard on Pharping Road in August. ♠ Kashmir, Garhwal, Nepal, Sikkim; Afghanistan to Japan
581

Banded Bay Cuckoo, *Cacomantis sonneratii*.
152-2440 m. (500-8,000') 24 cm. (9¼") S.
Scarce; in heavy forest and scrub jungle of the *duns* and *tarai*. Distinctively banded throughout; dark brown and rufous. Resembles hepatic Plaintive Cuckoo but look for tail feathers that narrow toward ends. Sits among leaves at top of tall trees. Usually solitary. Parasitizes babblers and bulbuls. Voice a four-note whistle *wee-ti-tee-ti* (AR). ♣ Garhwal, Nepal, Sikkim; India to S.E. Asia 582

Plaintive Cuckoo, *Cacomantis merulinus*.
305-2135 m. (1,000-7,000') 23 cm. (9") S.
Fairly common; in relatively open country and in groves near villages. Resembles the Dark Gray Cuckoo-Shrike (also shown for comparison) but graduated tail feathers have narrow white bars (not white spots). Hepatic phase very similar to Banded Bay Cuckoo but tail feathers retain base width throughout (not narrowing towards tips). Solitary, calling from a perch in a bush or tree. Rather shy, often flies quite a distance between resting places. Parasitizes small birds such as tailor birds and wren babblers. Voice a mournful *ka----teer*, repeated after one-second intervals. Also an ascending series of notes *please-don't-do-it*. ❊ KV: in cutover scrub jungle around the Valley. ♣ Garhwal, Nepal, Sikkim; Kashmir to Celebes 584

Drongo Cuckoo, *Surniculus lugubris*.
213-1830 m. (700-6,000') 25 cm. (10") R., S.
Fairly common; in open groves at the top of tall trees. Appears all black with a forked tail, resembling the Bronzed Drongo, but *vent* and *outer tail feathers faintly barred with white*. Gape red. Young, black flecked with white. Perches with wings held loosely and tail drooped. Parasitizes drongos and minivets. Voice a rapid and repeated ascending scale of six notes. ❊ KV: commonly heard in spring (March-May), Royal Botanic Gardens, Godaveri, Tokha, Nagarjung. ♣ Garhwal, Nepal, Sikkim; India to Celebes 588

Emerald Cuckoo, *Chalcites maculatus*.
1280 m. (4,200') 18 cm. (7") R.(?)
Scarce; recorded by G. B. Gurung along the Vishnumati River, KV, in May. A tiny, brilliant green bird with barred black and white breast and abdomen. Female duller. Active. Call three ascending notes. ❊ KV: single birds noted along Vishnumati. ♣ Garhwal, Nepal, Sikkim; Garhwal to S. China and Sumatra 586

Large Green-billed Malkoha, *Rhopodytes tristis.*
120-1830 m. (400-6,000') 58 cm. (23") R.
Fairly common; in dense tangles of vegetation and among leafy trees. A striking gray-green bird with red facial patch and extremely long tail. When feeding, graduated tail is tilted up and flared out, disclosing white tips to feathers. Disturbed, it slips quietly up branches near trunk of tree to fly out the top; flight is in jerky flaps. Solitary or in pairs. Constructs its own nest. Calls a loud *cow* at three or four-second intervals, a low *k-o-o-o* like a distant barking deer and an alarm *kluk*. ❊ KV: Godaveri, Nagarjung and lower hills. ♠ Garhwal, Nepal, Sikkim; India to Sumatra 593

Koel Cuckoo, *Eudynamys scolopacea.*
120-1372 m. (400-4,500') 43 cm. (17") R., S.
Common; in orchards and leafy groves near habitation. Male resembles a black crow but much slimmer and the tail proportionately longer. Red eye noticeable at short distance. Female is startlingly marked with bold white bars and spots. Young, barred. Pairs chase each other with much flapping through leafy trees. Parasitizes crows. Call *ko---el*, the source for both local and English names. Also has a rapid *kukukukukukuk* and a *whoop* when excited. ❊ KV: usual calling period March-July, often far into the night. ♠ Garhwal(?), Nepal, Sikkim(?); Pakistan to Australia 590

Sirkeer Cuckoo, *Taccocua leschenaultii.*
120-1372 m. (400-4,500') 43 cm. (17") R.
Occasional; in bushy, rocky places among thorn shrubs and acacia trees. A pale grayish-brown bird with long, graduated, white-tipped tail. Bill a bright red, tipped yellow. Young are streaked with black. Single or in pairs. Often terrestrial but also high in trees such as acacias. Somewhat shy, moving quietly away from observer. Call like the chatter of a parakeet; an increasingly rapid *wit-wit-wit-tit-tititirrrr*. ♠ Garhwal, Nepal; S. Asia 597

Small Coucal, *Centropus toulou.*
274 m. (900') 33-37 cm. (13-14½") R.
Occasional; in wide stretches of tall grass in dry ravines and in wet reed beds. Very similar to Large Coucal but smaller, with tail tipped pale rufous (not uniformly black). Young birds streaked brown with pale tip to tail (illustrated). Solitary; perches on a stalk of grass or reed, often near water. Flight several hurried wingbeats then a glide. Moves deliberately among bushes on ground. Food mostly grasshoppers. Call a hollow *kuk-kuk-kuk-tullapa-tullapatullapa*. ♠ Nepal; Madagascar to Philippines 605

Large Coucal (Crow Pheasant), *Centropus sinensis.*
120-305 m. (400-1,000') 48 cm. (19") R.
Fairly common; at edge of tall marsh grass, thorn bushes, in reeds and cultivated fields. Size of a crow with black body and chestnut wings. Told from Small Coucal by entirely black tail (not tipped pale rufous). Ambles through grass, up bamboos and reeds. Robs nests, eats birds, small mammals and some vegetation. Usually in pairs. Voice a hollow, resounding *w-o-o-o-p*, a repeated *co-oo-oo-oo* about every ten seconds. ♠ Kashmir, Garhwal, Nepal; Pakistan to Philippines 600

OWLS (Families Tytonidae and Strigidae) are nocturnal predators equipped with large, curved beaks and strong talons, large eyes, enormous ears and a noiseless flight which assists in nighttime hunting. Nepalese folklore relates owls as lazy birds that bring ill fortune to those who see them.

Grass Owl, *Tyto capensis*.
274 m. (900') 35 cm. (14") R.

Occasional; in tall grass along rivers in the vicinity of Tiger Tops. Similar to Barn Owl but dark brown above (not fulvous-gray). A nocturnal and crepuscular hunter that may be seen in the day when flushed by elephants working in tall grass. Once air-borne, note uneven wingbeats and a semicircle flight path before soon dropping again into the grass. Nests found on ground in late October. A villager selling young in November to medicine men in Narayanghat. ♣ Garhwal, Nepal; Africa, Asia, Australasia 608

Barn Owl, *Tyto alba*.
1280 m. (4,200') 35 cm. (14") R.

Occasional; under eaves of large, old buildings. A very pale owl with whitish facial discs and whitish beneath; finely stippled with white and dark spots. Single or in family parties; seldom seen in the day. Snaps bill when disturbed. Food mostly rodents. Hovers over fields like a kestrel. Voice an assortment of sounds. ❊ KV: lives under the roofs of some old palace buildings. ♣ Nepal; nearly world-wide 606

Bay Owl, *Phodilus badius*. 29 cm. (11¼"). No data since 1846. A bright rust-colored owl with ear tufts and pale facial disc. May occur in dense forests of S.E. Nepal. ♣ Nepal, Sikkim; Nepal to S.E. Asia 609

Scops Owl, *Otus scops*.
120-1525 m. (400-5,000') 19 cm. (7¼") R.

Common; in secondary jungle and forests of the *tarai*. Similar to the Spotted Scops but streaked (not spotted) with fewer marks on head; ruff more prominent. Also note the two pale wingbars. Varying phases of grayish-brown and reddish-brown. Usually solitary; sometimes seen in open places such as on a fence post from where it hunts. When calling from leafy trees, very hard to see. Voice a *puck-poo-puck* sometimes repeated two to three hundred times without a pause. ♣ Garhwal, Nepal; Europe, Africa, Asia 616

Spotted Scops Owl, *Otus cpilocephalus*.
1525-2745 m. (5,000-9,000') 18-20 cm. (7-8") R.

Fairly common; in leafy ravines in oak forests. A light brown owl with dark spots and faint bars. Illustration shows the bright rusty phase (especially frequent in E. Nepal). Rather shy, usually single and entirely nocturnal. Twists head around 180 degrees when calling, thus "throwing its voice" and making the bird difficult to locate. Male aggressive in spring; will challenge anyone whistling his call in his territory. Seeks refuge in clefts in tree trunks, banks or rock cliffs during the day. Call *pew-pew*, a double whistle at three-second intervals, a hundred or more at a stretch. Several may be heard calling from different places in an oak forest. ❊ KV: in the surrounding hills above 1525 m. (5,000'). ♣ Kashmir, Garhwal, Nepal, Sikkim; Himalayas to Formosa 611, 612

Collared Scops Owl, *Otus bakkamoena*.
183-1525 m. (600-5,000') 23-25 cm. (9-10") R.

Fairly common; in the foothills in open forests and near villages. Differs from other scops owls in the *pale collar edged with black*. Single or in pairs in mango groves, *sal* and oak forests. Emerges at dusk and may sit conspicuously on a telephone wire or a branch of a dead tree over fields. Not very shy. Call a questioning *wuuuuuuuk*. ♣ Kashmir, Garhwal, Nepal, Sikkim; Himalayas to Philippines 621, 624

Great Horned Owl (Eagle Owl), *Bubo bubo*.
915-1830 m. (3,000-6,000') 55 cm. (22") R.

Fairly common; emerges at dusk from shelter (often a hole in a rocky cliff), calls and flies off to hunt near villages and in fields. A very large, horned bird, broadly streaked. Iris, orangy-yellow. Roosts also in deep gorges such as the Seti River Gorge in Pokhara town. Flight, a slow flapping followed by glides. Takes a similar route night after night. The common large owl of Nepal. Voice, at intervals, a chilling, prolonged *whoooooo-whooooo*. Young sold for medicine. ❉ KV: south face of Nagarjung; above Anandaban Hospital. ❦ Kashmir, Garhwal, Nepal, Sikkim; Europe, Africa, Asia   627

Forest Eagle Owl, *Bubo nipalensis*.
305-1982 m. (1,000-6,500') 64 cm. (25") R.

Scarce; in heavy forest, near water. A large, *dark brown* owl with dark ear tufts. Face is pale and upper breast barred. Look for dark "V"s on lower breast and abdomen. Young, pale with dark marks. Sometimes feeds during the day on birds coming to drink at a forest pool. At night, seizes large birds from their roosts and small mammals on the ground. Voice a *boom* at three-second intervals. ❉ KV: Nagarjung cliffs. ❦ Nepal, Sikkim; Kumaon to S.E. Asia   628

Dusky Horned Owl, *Bubo coromandus*. 58 cm. (23"). No records since 1846. Look for a large, grayish owl with twin "ears" that stand nearly erect, almost paralleling each other. Should occur in *tarai* groves. Call a loud, accelerating *wo---wo--wo-wo-o-ooo*, decreasing in volume towards end (AR). ❦ Nepal; S. to S.E. Asia   630

Tawny Fish Owl, *Bubo flavipes*.
305 m. (1,000') 60 cm. (24") R.

Scarce; in deep, wooded ravines with water. Similar to Brown Fish Owl but tawny above (not dark brown) and brighter orange-rufous below. Iris, pale yellow (not deep yellow). Feeds on fish, rodents and birds. May swoop down from trees, even during the day, in the manner of fish eagles (AR). Call a loud, double hoot, sharply accented, *bu-ku* (Smythies). ❦ Kashmir, Garhwal, Nepal, Sikkim; Kashmir to Formosa   633

Brown Fish Owl, *Bubo zeylonensis*.
120-1525 m. (400-5,000') 55 cm. (22") R.

Fairly common; in thick forest almost always near water. Tufted; a large white throat patch. Similar Tawny Fish Owl also has a whitish throat but is warm rufous (not brownish) below. Also note thin, dark shafts and fine bars of underparts in contrast to wide streaks of the Great Horned Owl and "V"s of the Forest Eagle Owl. Iris, deep yellow. Single or in pairs; a slow, strong flight. An upright stance while waiting for prey; seen on leafless limbs and stumps. Fond of fish. Voice a muted, hollow *hoo-hoo-hoo—hoo-hoo-hoo—hoo-hoo-hoo* "like old men talking together." ❉ KV: haunts government fish pools at Godaveri. ❦ Nepal; Asia   631

Barred Owlet, *Glaucidium cuculoides*.
244-2440 m. (800-8,000') 23 cm. (9") R.
Common; in *sal*, pine and oak forests. Similar to Jungle Owlet but noticeably larger and darker with wider gray-brown and white barring and *middle of abdomen white*. Frequently seen in daytime, sitting upright with tail swaying from side to side when alarmed. Often "attacked" by small birds. Eats mice, insects, birds. Voice a prolonged, musical ripple; also a *keek*. ❊ KV: occasionally in surrounding hills. ◆ Kashmir, Garhwal, Nepal, Sikkim; India to Bali 639

Jungle Owlet, *Glaucidium radiatum*.
120-915 m. (400-3,000') 20 cm. (8") R.
Common; in scrub and thin forests of the *dun* and *tarai*. Above, uniformly finely barred brown and *rufous*-brown; below, wide, brown bars. Very similar to Barred Owlet but look for *rufous* primaries (not dark brown) and the *entirely barred abdomen* with no white in the center. Appears most active at dusk and just after dawn. Seen flying from one leafy tree to another with rapid wingbeats and glides. Squats on branch with head pulled in; sometimes mobbed by birds. The call begins slowly, then accelerates *piu---piu---piutuk-piutuk-piutuk-piutak*. ◆ Garhwal, Nepal, Sikkim(?); S. Asia 636

Collared Pigmy Owlet, *Glaucidium brodiei*.
610-3050 m. (2,000-10,000') 16 cm. (6½") R.
Fairly common; in mixed temperate oak forests. A tiny species, lightly barred above and streaked below. No ear tufts. A dark half-collar. Single, in leafy tree tops. Active day and night. Often mobbed by small birds. Diet insects, skinks, possibly small birds. Call a four syllable *hooo--hoo-hoo--hooo* on same pitch, beginning and ending weakly; mellow and repeated at intervals. ❊ KV: in the forests of surrounding hills. ◆ Kashmir, Garhwal, Nepal, Sikkim; Himalayas to Borneo 635

Spotted Owlet, *Athene brama*.
120-1525 m. (400-5,000') 20 cm. (8") R.
Common; in open fields, around villages and in cities. Brownish-gray with many diagnostic white spots above. Often in family groups; roosts in chimneys, under roofs and in hollow trees. In cold weather suns at entrance of nest. Perches on wire or dead tree at dusk. Several may congregate while hunting for insects near an electric light at night. Call sudden screeches and catcalls that resemble a "clan feud." ❊ KV: our most common owlet. (Tibet Owlet, *Athene noctua*, reported from N. Sikkim, see p. 336.) ◆ Nepal; S. and S.E. Asia 650

Brown Hawk Owl, *Ninox scutulata.*
120-1310 m. (400-4,300') 32 cm. (12½") R.

Fairly common; single or in pairs in leafy groves and heavy *sal* forests. Long tail gives this owl a most un-owlish appearance. Uniform brown above; paler and spotted with fulvous below. Sits immobile in a leafy tree during the day; active at dusk and often quite vocal. Flies out after insects, returning to same perch. Uses same branch night after night. Diet also includes small rodents and frogs. Voice a slow, questioning *ho--wek*. ❋ KV: a few in dense groves such as Rani Ban. ◾ Garhwal, Nepal, Sikkim; India to Japan and Philippines 642

Brown Wood Owl, *Strix leptogrammica.*
762-2623 m. (2,500-8,600') 53 cm. (21") R.

Occasional; in heavy subtropical or oak-rhododendron forests. A dark brown owl, heavily barred; throat is pale. Facial discs prominent. Single, or in pairs, rests sluggishly during day in heavily leafed trees. Feeds on rats and other animals. A flying squirrel much alarmed by its presence. Voice a hollow, drawn out *hoo---hooooo* at two or three minute intervals but is silent after three or four hoots. A loud, nerve-tingling *weeeeee--ooohhh* heard in winter and spring. ❋ KV: in Chapagaon Forest and surrounding hills. ◾ Garhwal, Nepal, Sikkim; India to Formosa 658

Tawny Wood Owl, *Strix aluco.*
2287-3965 m. (7,500-13,000') 45 cm. (17½") R.

Fairly common; in rhododendron-juniper-hemlock forests. A medium-sized owl with a light facial disc. Blotchy appearing above with streaks, bars and white spots below. Nocturnal and difficult to see. If call is imitated, may come immediately to investigate. A forest species independent of human habitation. Call a mellow *hoo----hoo*, the second syllable lower than the first, at 15-20-second intervals. Also a soft *hoo-hoo-hoo* in flight as well as a raucous *kaw-chi---kaw-chi----kaw-chi.* ◾ Kashmir, Garhwal, Nepal, Sikkim; Europe, Africa, Asia 662

Long-eared Owl, *Asio otus.* 37 cm. (14½"). No data since 1846. Look for a long "eared" owl hunting over grassy slopes and open fields. Starts flying at dusk. Should occur over grassy hills of W. Nepal. ◾ Kashmir, Garhwal, Nepal; Europe, Africa, Asia, N. America 663

Short-eared Owl, *Asio flammeus.*
244-2287 m. (800-7,500') 38 cm. (15") W.

Occasional; in open, grassy fields. Light facial disc and small dark ear tufts. Streaked. In flight, noticeable dark wingbars and dark-tipped wings. A ground bird. Arrives in winter in small flocks. When flushed from a grassy patch, flies with slow-moving roll then drops again into the grass. Hunts during day as well as night. Iris is a bright lemon-yellow. ◾ Kashmir (?), Garhwal, Nepal; Europe, Africa, Asia, Americas 664

NIGHTJARS (Caprimulgidae), like American nighthawks, are birds with small bodies, large mouths, flat heads, long wings and long, rounded tails. Their hunting flight is irregular, reminiscent of a giant moth. At night they often rest in the middle of forest roads and along edge of East-West Highway in the *tarai*. Their red eyes reflect in headlights of a car as bright as a tiger's. At a distance, nightjar told from tiger by one eye showing (vs. two in tiger). Loud calls are diagnostic.

Long-tailed Nightjar, *Caprimulgus macrurus*.
213-1525 m. (700-5,000') 32 cm. (12½") R.

Common; usually at edge of forest. Darker above than Jungle Nightjar; wings dark with white spots on secondaries and white wing patch. Sleeps among leaves on forest floor. Can be caught in daylight, it is said, in a butterfly net. Begins feeding at dusk. Parent bird catches a mouthful of beetles and other insects, disgorging them into the mouths of young huddled on ground in flimsy nest. Call a *chunk* repeated slowly from 1 to 15 times; sounds like a heavy axe hitting a hollow log. Men sometimes bet on number of notes in the next series. Largely confined to foothill forests. ♦ Garhwal, Nepal, Sikkim; Pakistan to Australia   675

Jungle Nightjar, *Caprimulgus indicus*.
610-2745 m. (2,000-9,000') 29 cm. (11½") R.

Common; over grassy forest glades or cultivated fields. Paler than similar Long-tailed Nightjar, with *pale rufous* (not white) wing patch seen in flight. Single or in family groups. Flight amazingly irregular. Active just at dusk when beetles and other insects emerge from ground. Sits lengthwise on branch from where it launches hunting sorties. Call a rapid *chunk-chunk-chunk*, about five per second for several seconds. ❋ KV: calls in spring on Sheopuri and places like Gokarna. (In Kashmir listen for Eurasian Nightjar, *Caprimulgus europaeus*, see p. 334.) ♦ Kashmir, Garhwal, Nepal, Sikkim; Pakistan to Japan   670

Little Nightjar (Indian Nightjar), *Caprimulgus asiaticus*.
152 m. (500') 24 cm. (9½") R.

Scarce; in the Nepal *tarai* (very common farther south in India). *Much smaller and somewhat paler* than other nightjars. Selects dry fields of short grass and dusty roads near cultivation; also sandy river banks. More on the ground than other nightjars. Eggs placed on bare ground with little protection. Noted near the Simra airport. Call like sound of a ping-pong ball bouncing on a marble floor *tuk---tuk--tuk-tu-r-rrrr*. ♦ Nepal; Pakistan to S.E. Asia   680

Franklin's Nightjar, *Caprimulgus affinis*.
120-305 m. (400-1,000') 25 cm. (10") R.

Occasional; along rivers and neighboring meadows. The darkest Nepal nightjar. Look for a buffy "V" on its back. Spends the day on the ground among boulders in shade along river courses. At dusk, sits on a rock before starting to hunt. Patrols a limited area briefly, then moves on. Usually flies low over boulder-strewn banks near water but also over fields. Call a single, piercing *chait* at about one per second. ♦ Nepal; Pakistan to Formosa   682

(Hodgson's Frogmouth, *Batrachostomus hodgsoni*, family Podargidae, resembles a large nightjar. See Sikkim list, p. 336.)

TROGONS (Trogonidae) are highly-colored forest birds. Their graduated tail feathers are long and square with pale blotches at the ends. Feathers are extremely soft and fluffy. Trogons' movements are rather sluggish.

Red-headed Trogon, *Harpactes erythrocephalus.*
152-1525 m.　(500-5,000')　34 cm.　(13½")　R.

Occasional; in light forests of the foothills. Unmistakable; red breasted; female lacks red head of the male. Found singly or in pairs in dense tropical and subtropical forests. Flares tail as it eats. Insects, bamboo culms and fruit make up main diet. Call *cu-cu-cu* and a low *krrr-r-r* (AR). ❊ KV: D. Proud reported a pair nesting at Godaveri. ◀ Nepal, Sikkim; Kumaon to S. China and Sumatra　　　　　　　　　　　　　　　　　　　　　　　713

ROLLERS (Coraciidae) are conspicuous birds with large bills, slow wingbeats and raucous voices. During the breeding season, males spend considerable time dive bombing and somersaulting in the air. Sometimes miscalled "Blue Jays."

Dark Roller (Broad-billed Roller), *Eurystomus orientalis.*
120-305 m.　(400-1,000')　28 cm.　(11")　S.

Fairly common; in forests of Chitwan Dun. A dark greenish-purple bird with a white wing patch seen in flight. Bright coral-red bill cne of the most conspicuous features. Looks like a short crow as it sits in the top of a tall tree. Shy, keeping high in branches. Arrives in Chitwan Dun in May and spends much time wheeling above the tree tops. Fifty seen in one large, open field in June hawking flying termites after a rain. Voice a loud, piercing *whek-whek-kakakakaka.* ◀ Nepal, Sikkim; Kumaon to Manchuria and Australia　　　　　　758

Indian Roller, *Coracias benghalensis.*
120-1372 m.　(400-4,500')　28 cm.　(11")　R.

Common; over fields of the *tarai* and in groves or open forests. Conspicuous in flight with brilliant two-toned blue wings. When resting, blue is less noticeable; bird appears brownish. Slow, measured, crow-like flight. Swoops upward when alighting on post or branch. Often descends to ground for insects. Single or in loose, noisy pairs. Somewhat shy. Voice unpleasant screeches and a raucous, quick *ka-ka-ka-ka* prolonged for several seconds. ❊ KV: two reports (near National Museum and beyond Bhadgaon). (Eurasian Roller, *C. garrulus*, breeds in Kashmir, see p. 334.) ◀ Nepal, Sikkim; Iran to S.E. Asia　　　　　755

HOOPOE (Upupidae). The Hoopoe is mentioned in ancient Egyptian hieroglyphics as well as the Old Testament. Common in the Mediterranean region. It could well be called a "Ground Pecker" for it extracts segmented worms and grubs from the earth with a long, curved bill.

Hoopoe, *Upupa epops.*
120-5795 m.　(400-19,000')　29 cm.　(11½")　R., M.

Common; on lawns in cities as well as on grassy alpine slopes. Many near *tarai* villages in winter. A striking fawn-colored bird with "zebra stripes" on wings; a crest flares up upon alighting or when startled. The breast of the Tibetan race is lightly streaked while that of the Indian race is unmarked and pinkish. Tame. Has a strong, undulating flight. Nests in holes in walls. Smell from these sites offensive. Crows seen devouring nestlings as they emerge. Dolpo Nepalis look forward to the arrival of this species in rainy season (C. Jest). Call a mellow *poo-poo-poo* given at short intervals. ❊ KV: nests here in summer. ◀ Kashmir, Garhwal, Nepal, Sikkim; Europe, Africa, Asia　　　　　　　　　　　　　　　　764, 765

KINGFISHERS (Alcedinidae) are stout-billed, small-legged birds. Blue is a common color; some are dark gray and white. They nest in sand banks.

Large Pied Kingfisher, *Ceryle lugubris*.
274-1525 m. (900-5,000') 35 cm. (14") R.

Occasional; single or in pairs along large rivers. A distinctive gray and white kingfisher with a large crest. Flies low over water; rarely hovers. Perches on tree or rock above water. Moves tail up and down when excited. Call a nasal *klik*. ♠ Kashmir, Garhwal, Nepal, Sikkim; Himalayas to Japan   717

Small Pied Kingfisher, *Ceryle rudis*.
152-915 m. (500-3,000') 28 cm. (11") R.

Common; on large rivers of the *tarai*. Smaller than the Large Pied Kingfisher; lacks an erect crest and markings are different. Hunts by hovering high above water, then plunging straight down. One of the most active kingfishers, usually over large expanses of still water. Ascends mountain rivers as high as Pokhara and Trisuli Reservoir. Call a repeated *chik-kur* (AR). ♠ Kashmir, Nepal; Africa, Asia   719

Eurasian Kingfisher, *Alcedo atthis*.
120-2287 m. (400-7,500') 16 cm. (6½") R.

Fairly common; along the edges of streams and rivers. A brilliant little bird. Very similar to Blue-eared Kingfisher but rusty-tan (not blue) below the ear. Single, along flowing water usually in open parts of the country. Very rapid wingbeat, skimming over the water. Sits patiently on exposed roots or dead branches just above the water, then plunges down for minnows. Voice a high-pitched *chit*. ❄ KV: at Balaju reservoir and along river banks. ♠ Kashmir, Garhwal, Nepal, Sikkim (?); Europe, Asia, Australia   723

Blue-eared Kingfisher, *Alcedo meninting*.
244-305 m. (800-1,000') 15 cm. (6") R.

Scarce; along forest streams or at the edge of jungle grass in the *tarai* and *duns*. Very similar to the Eurasian Kingfisher but darker blue above and *blue* rather than tan *below ear*. Faint green bars over crown. Most frequently seen along dimly lit streams running through the forest. Often darts among branches and plants bordering wooded brooks. Hunts from perches above water. (Great Blue Kingfisher, *Alcedo hercules*, in Sikkim, see p. 336.) ♠ Nepal, Sikkim; Nepal to Sula Islands   725

Three-toed Kingfisher, *Ceyx erithacus*. 13 cm. (5"). No recent information. Look for a small, orange kingfisher with purple back and wings. May still occur along forest streams of the *tarai*. ♠ Nepal, Sikkim; India to Philippines   727

Stork-billed Kingfisher, *Pelargopsis capensis*.
120-762 m. (400-2,500') 35 cm. (14") R.

Occasional; over lagoons, reed-fringed ponds and more open forest streams. A large, swollen, dull red bill and brown head diagnostic. The blue-green back and wings and bright blue rump conspicuous in flight. Solitary; rather sluggish with a slow wingbeat. Bobs head. Eats fish, lizards, mice. Call a loud *krrr-ley-you-koo*. ♠ Nepal; India to Sula Islands   730

White-breasted Kingfisher, *Halcyon smyrnensis*.
120-2745 m. (400-9,000') 25 cm. (10") R.

Common; along water and over grain fields. Brilliant blue back, maroon mantle; white throat and breast diagnostic. Eats fish but often catches grasshoppers and other insects. Perches motionlessly in trees or on electric wires for long periods. Wanders up remote valleys; found as high as Jomosom at 2745 m. (9,000') at edge of the Trans-Himalayan zone (Daleep Nur Singh). Call a loud *klik* a loud, long *pitpitpitpitpitpit*. ❄ KV: common on Valley floor. ♠ Kashmir, Garhwal, Nepal, Sikkim(?); Middle East to Philippines   736

Ruddy Kingfisher, *Halcyon coromanda*.
305 m. (1,000') 25 cm. (10") R.

Scarce; along small streams in dense forests of Rapti Dun. Striking brownish-purple and tan with white rump and bright red bill and legs. Young darker with blackish bill. Eats fish and a variety of insects. Shy. More often heard than seen. Voice a distinct, mellow *ki-ki ki-ki-ki*. ♠ Nepal, Sikkim; Nepal to Sula Islands   733

Black-capped Kingfisher, *Halcyon pileata*.
183 m. (600') 30 cm. (12") S.

Scarce; noted only along banks of Reu-Rapti Rivers, Chitwan, C. Nepal. A distinctive kingfisher, the dark crown separated from mantle by a white collar. Large white patch in wing noticeable in flight. Appears darker than somewhat similar White-breasted Kingfisher. Recently discovered in Nepal (Sept. 1974) by RLF, Max Thompson and Charles McDougal. ♠ Nepal; India to Celebes   739

BEE-EATERS (Meropidae) in Nepal are bright green or blue, with long bills, wings and tails. They fly in deliberate, graceful arcs as they snap insects out of the air.

Chestnut-headed Bee-eater, *Merops leschenaulti*.
120-1677 m. (400-5,500') 20 cm. (8") R., M.
Fairly common; in scrub as well as edges of dense jungle. The only bee-eater with a chestnut head and upper back. Also look for a pale, yellowish-tan throat with a chestnut and black neck band and a pale blue rump. Usually in small, loose parties, fairly high in trees. Flight is a series of strong wingbeats followed by a glide. Often returns to same perch after pursuing an insect. Bores a tunnel into a sand bank for nesting purposes. In non-breeding season, roosts in huddles. Not very shy. The only bee-eater to penetrate far up Himalayan river valleys. Call a short series of mellow notes repeated at intervals. ❈ KV: some in forests of Nagarjung, Gokarna in summer. ☾ Nepal, Sikkim(?); India to Bali 744

Blue-tailed Bee-eater, *Merops philippinus*.
120-1525 m. (400-5,000') 28 cm. (11") R., M.
Occasional; over streams and open places of the *tarai* and lower hills. Only bee-eater with blue rump and tail; middle feathers of tail have wire-like extensions. Gregarious, several skim back and forth over running water. Most common in W. *tarai*. Seen catching orange butterflies over gram field. During heat of day, often sit with bills open. Quite bold; noisy at nesting banks. Voice a sharp trill. (Eurasian Bee-eater, *Merops apiaster*, breeds in Kashmir, see p. 334.)
☾ Nepal; India to Celebes 748

Blue-bearded Bee-eater, *Nyctyornis athertoni*.
152-1525 m. (500-5,000') 33 cm. (13") R., M.
Occasional; in pairs or solitary in thin forests bordering fields. A distinctive bird, blue-green with a prominent blue "beard" protruding from the throat. Abdomen streaked. Rests hunched forward with tail drooping vertically. Puffs out beard when calling. Two seen feeding at entrance to a beehive in a tree, picking off bees as they emerged from hole. Voice a repeated *cha-a-a* and *lay-key-tik*. ❈ KV: in summer at beehives of Father Saubolle, Godaveri. ☾ Garhwal, Nepal, Sikkim; India to S. China 753

Green Bee-eater, *Merops orientalis*.
120-1280 m. (400-4,200') 23 cm. (9") R.
Common; on fences, wires, in mango groves of the *tarai*. Golden-green above with a long, pointed tail. The only Nepal bee-eater with a bright *green throat* (note dark line between throat and breast). Sunlight bouncing off green feathers at just the right angle makes them appear iridescent gold. Small, scattered parties, unafraid of humans. May form a noisy group in the evening. Voice a musical twitter; also a *tik*. ❈ KV: seen once by E. Forster and C. Harrop near former Hotel Royal. ☾ Nepal; Africa, Asia 750

HORNBILLS (Bucerotidae) are awkward-appearing creatures with prominent casques and broad, curved bills. Wings are rounded and in flight the long tails look somewhat disjointed. During the nesting season, the female is plastered inside a nest cavity in a hollow tree and is fed, along with the young, by the male.

Gray Hornbill, *Tockus birostris*.
120-305 m. (400-1,000') 40 cm. (16") R.

Fairly common; in semi-open parts of the country where there are fruiting trees. The smallest and most awkward moving of the Nepal hornbills; uniformly gray with a small casque. Often in pairs or small groups. Flight is undulating with body held horizontally; proceeds with a few wingbeats and then a glide. Alights in a tree after a terminal upward swerve. Noisy and sociable. Plucks fruit with end of bill and by a backward jerk, drops the morsel into the throat. Voice high and tinny, a repeated *cheeeeee-eye; ka-seeeeer; kleer-kleer-kleer* in flight. ◖ Nepal; S. Asia 767

Pied Hornbill, *Anthracoceros malabaricus*.
120-305 m. (400-1,000') 70 cm. (28") R.

Fairly common; a noisy bird of the *tarai* and lower foothill forests. Black and white with large yellow bill. The casque has a black frontal patch. Look for *black neck*. In small parties in upper half of fruiting trees. Flight, a follow-the-leader fashion; slow, strong wingbeats with glides. Rather wary. Tail hangs straight down when bird is resting on a branch. Food, fruit and small animals. Fighting males are determined; may fall to the ground and lie there grasping and "chewing" each other with their huge beaks. Voice heard at a great distance, a piercing, tinny, repeated cackle *kaa-kaa-klaak-klaak* and also a *ku-ku-klaaaaask-klaaask*. ◖ Nepal; India to S. China 774

Rufous-necked Hornbill, *Aceros nipalensis*.
122 cm. (48"). No reports since 1846. Survival in Nepal doubtful as suitable habitat destroyed. A large bird with underparts entirely rufous. Fairly common in Assam and points east. ◖ Nepal, Sikkim; Nepal to S.E. Asia 771

Giant Hornbill, *Buceros bicornis*.
120-274 m. (400-900') about 112 cm. (44") R.

Scarce; in heavy forests of the *tarai* and *duns*. A great black and white bird with a huge beak topped by a large, yellow, flattened casque. Neck is white (not black) and bird is much heavier than the Pied Hornbill. The amount of yellow on the casque varies for it is an oil stain that comes from the rump gland. Concentrated oil produces an orange color; when more dilute, it is yellow. In pairs, threes and fours in leafy, fruiting trees. Fig trees favored. Roosts more or less in the same area each night. At dawn, regularly flies across broad rivers and low over tree tops to feeding places. In flight, sounds like puffing engines as air moves between splayed wing feathers. Quite shy and frequently hunted by villagers who claim its oil will restore falling hair. Voice a low-pitched, hollow moan of two notes; also noisy syllables. ◖ Nepal, Sikkim; India to Sumatra 776

BARBETS (Capitonidae). Nepal barbets are green birds with plump bodies and swollen bills. Wings are rounded; tails moderately long. They are arboreal fruit eaters with loud and monotonous voices; more often heard than seen. Sexes alike. Nest in holes in trees.

Great Himalayan Barbet, *Megalaima virens*.
305-3050 m. (1,000-10,000') 32 cm. (12½") R.

Common; in oak and mixed temperate forests. Large, yellow bill contrasts with dark head. The only Nepal barbet with a red vent, the red easily seen from below. Single or in pairs in leafy trees. Several may gather at fruiting tree. Rather sluggish; a labored, undulating flight with head stretched forward. Fairly shy except during breeding season. Usually above 1525 m. (5,000'). One of the few birds with a "duet" call: male, a *pir-ao* once a second for long periods while female answers simultaneously with a trilled *pur*, about three per second. ✿ KV: common in the surrounding hills. ◆ Kashmir, Garhwal, Nepal, Sikkim; Himalayas to S. China
777, 778

Green Barbet, *Megalaima zeylanica*.
183-305 m. (600-1,000') 25 cm. (10") R.

Fairly common; around villages and in groves in cities as well as *tarai* forests of W. Nepal. A pale brown and green bird with yellow facial skin. Large bill pale yellow. Very similar to Lineated Barbet but irregular brown mottling extends down only to upper breast (not upper belly). Also note heavier bill. From side view, look for green feathers of shoulder region which are usually lightly tipped pale buff. A variable brown stain may occur on head, neck and throat feathers of both species (illustration shows dark stain on throat). Call a loud, slowly repeated *ka-roo*. ◆ Nepal; India and Sri Lanka
780

Lineated Barbet, *Megalaima lineata*.
183-915 m. (600-3,000') 28 cm. (11") R.

Common; in the *sal* forests of central and eastern *tarai*. Very similar to the Green Barbet but irregular brown mottling extends down beyond the upper breast and bill not as heavy. Feathers of shoulder region uniform bright green. Individual without brown stain illustrated. Flight noisy and undulating. Call a *go-paul* at two-second intervals for several minutes; also a *kroop-kroo-kroop* and a *k-r-r-r-r-rud-du-da*. ◆ Nepal, Sikkim; Nepal to Bali
783, 784

Golden-throated Barbet, *Megalaima franklinii*.
305-2745 m. (1,000-9,000') 20 cm. (8") R.

Fairly common; in dense hill forests. A colorful bird with diagnostic golden crown and throat. Rather hard to see among the leafy trees. Single, in the middle of a tree on low branches. One nest hole only six feet from the ground. Sits quietly for fairly long periods. Not very shy. Silent in winter; found as high as 2287 m. (7,500') in January. Call three notes, the first subdued and the other two loud and tinny: *tuk--whoe--welp*, repeated once every two seconds. ✿ KV: call is a dominating sound of Valley forests in April-May. ◆ Nepal, Sikkim; Nepal to S. China and Malaysia
787

Blue-throated Barbet, *Megalaima asiatica*.
120-1830 m. (400-6,000') 22 cm. (8½") R.

Common; in small scattered parties in forests and groves. A bright-colored green bird with a red forehead and a blue throat and sides of face. Color of young duller than in adults. Sits fairly erect with head pulled in and bent forward. Basks in winter sun, high in leafless trees. Collects in numbers in fruiting trees. Voice a loud *chuperup*, seven in five seconds for several minutes. Also a *trrrrrrr-trrrrrrr-t-ra-t-ra-t-ra*, and a subdued *pook*. ✿ KV: common in wooded groves. ◆ Kashmir, Garhwal, Nepal, Sikkim; India to S. China and Borneo
788

Blue-eared Barbet, *Megalaima australis*.
120-244 m. (400-800') 16 cm. (6¼") R.

Scarce; in tall forest trees of the E. *tarai*. A miniature green bird, with diagnostic blue-black forehead. Also has blue throat, hind crown and ear patch. Young has a green head. Solitary, in high trees at edge of forest. Hunches over and sits quietly for long periods. Calls regularly early in the morning and late in the day. Voice *tuk-tuk-rrrrrrrrrrr; prr-r-r-r-r* and a faint whistle-trill *trrrr-trrrr*. ◆ Nepal, Sikkim; Nepal to S.E. Asia
789

Crimson-breasted Barbet, *Megalaima haemacephala*.
120-1525 m. (400-5,000') 14 cm. (5½") R.

Common; around fig trees in dryish country. A mottled green bird with a distinctive red breast patch below a yellowish throat. Single, or in small, scattered parties, feeding on fruit or sitting motionlessly in top of tree. Call sounds like someone tapping on metal or the slow whistle of a rice mill, an endlessly repeated *took* on the same pitch. ✿ KV: nests in groves in summer. ◆ Nepal; Pakistan to Philippines
792

HONEYGUIDE (Indicatoridae). The Himalayan Honeyguide in Nepal is a small chunky bird with a slightly swollen bill. It is not known to "guide" men to honey. Its behavior only recently studied in detail in E. Nepal by Ted Cronin.

Himalayan Honeyguide, *Indicator xanthonotus.*
610-3050 m. (2,000-10,000')   15 cm.   (6")   R., M.

Scarce; near cliffs above streams and rivers in forests. In size and shape, resembles a sparrow but is gray-green with a *yellow rump* and *forehead*. Rests hunched over like a small barbet. Solitary or in small, loose parties in remote gorges of the Himalayas. Feeds on bee combs attached to perpendicular cliffs; often clings upside-down when feeding. Also sallies forth like a flycatcher, frequently returning to favorite perch. Sits motionlessly for long periods. One stomach examined was crammed with wax. Seasonal movements unknown. Seen in Dec. at 610 m. (2,000'). Social parasitism not confirmed; possibly may build its own nest. Voice *tzt*. ◆ Kashmir, Garhwal, Nepal, Sikkim; Pakistan to N. Burma   794

WOODPECKERS (Picidae). Wrynecks, piculets and woodpeckers are arboreal insectivorous birds. Wrynecks are slim birds with stout, pointed bills, pointed wings and rather long, soft, squarish tails; superficially they do not resemble woodpeckers. Piculets, on the other hand, do resemble pigmy woodpeckers except for their short, "soft" tails. Woodpeckers, as they hitch up and down trees, piercing the bark for insects, are easily identified. They have long tongues, stiff tails and strong feet.

Wryneck, *Jynx torquilla.*
120-1372 m.   (400-4,500')   18 cm.   (7")   W.

Occasional; in low branches of trees or down among grasses and shrubbery. Gray-brown with dark blotches above and bars and spots below. If held in the hand, the bird twists its head this way and that at curious angles, hence its English name. Single or in loose pairs. In flight the head is thrust forward while the tail wobbles loosely behind. Winters in wet marshlands of the *tarai*. Voice a loud, repeated squeak (Baker). ✲ KV: passes through on migration. ◆ Kashmir, Garhwal, Nepal, Sikkim (?); Europe, Africa, Asia   796, 797

Rufous Piculet, *Sasia ochracea.*
274-701 m.   (900-2,300')   10 cm.   (4")   R.

Occasional; among bamboo groves of the eastern *tarai* and foothills. Olive-rufous above and below with a golden forehead, pale eye-stripe and a short, black tail. Female has no yellow on forehead. Usually solitary, clambering along curved bamboos like a tit. Swift, slightly undulating flight. Associates with leaf warblers, nuthatches and tits. Fond of ants. Descends to the ground among damp leaves, picking up these insects. ◆ Garhwal, Nepal, Sikkim; Garhwal to S. China   800

Spotted Piculet, *Picumnus innominatus.*
274-1830 m.   (900-6,000')   10 cm.   (4")   R.

Fairly common; in bamboo and mixed forests. Yellowish-green; underparts pale with dark specks. Look for white line on cheek and white outer tail feathers. Single, or in pairs, often with other species. Usually on the lower third of a tree or in small bushes quite close to the ground. Found in clusters of bamboos. Twists around small branches in typical woodpecker style. Not very shy. The tapping is light and rapid, four or five taps per second. Call a high, rapid squeak *sik-sik-sik*, repeated at short intervals. ✲ KV: in light forests of Godaveri, Nagarjung. ◆ Kashmir, Garhwal, Nepal, Sikkim; Pakistan to S. China   798

Gray-crowned Pigmy Woodpecker, *Dendrocopos canicapillus.*
120-1372 m.   (400-4,500')   14 cm.   (5½")   R.

Fairly common; in mango groves, bamboo, *sal* and mixed forest. A miniature "ladder-back" with black upper back. Very similar to the Brown-crowned Pigmy Woodpecker but has *blackish* crown. Also look for black tail. Below, streaked with black. Often in pairs, moving actively along with mixed hunting parties of small birds. Eats insects and fruit. Usually fairly high in a tree. Bamboos are a favorite area of operation. Tapping is very rapid. Voice a high, quickly repeated *tit-tit-errrrrrr*. Also a spaced *tzit*. ◆ Kashmir, Garhwal, Nepal, Sikkim; Pakistan to Korea and Formosa   848, 849

Brown-crowned Pigmy Woodpecker, *Dendrocopos nanus.*
152-274 m.   (500-900')   13 cm.   (5")   R.

Occasional; in light forests at the edge of fields in the lowlands. Very similar to the Gray-crowned bird but crown brown and tail spotted (not black). Beneath, streaked brown (not black). Usually with other species feeding on topmost twigs of a tree where it acts like a tit, circling around, underneath and above branches. Call a high-pitched, squeaky, repeated note. ◆ Nepal; Pakistan to Lesser Sunda Islands   851

Large Scaly-bellied Woodpecker, *Picus squamatus*.
1982-3660 m. (6,500-12,000') 35 cm. (14") R.

Scarce; usually on conifer trees often above rhododendron thickets. A large, dull greenish bird with white eyebrow bordered in black. Male has crimson crown and crest. Scaly-appearing below. Resembles Small Scaly-bellied Woodpecker but habitat and elevation never overlap. Also note differences in cheek stripes. Often in pairs hitching up trees in jerky spurts. May feed on ground. Some altitudinal movement in winter. Usually calls from top of dead tree. A noisy, rising and descending *kleeeee-you;* a raspy *tech-tech-tech* and a rapid *tektektektektek*. Drums in spring. ♣ Kashmir, Garhwal, Nepal, Sikkim; Transcaspia to Sikkim
807

Small Scaly-bellied Woodpecker, *Picus xanthopygaeus*.
120-305 m. (400-1,000') 25 cm. (10") R.

Occasional; in dry scrub land of the *tarai*. A dark green and gray bird, scaly-appearing below. Similar to the larger species but altitudinal range does not overlap. Often seen in mixed hunting parties of wood-shrikes, minivets and drongos. Sometimes feeds on ground on ants and other insects. Single or in pairs. Partial to acacia trees. Voice a repeated, mellow *teek*.
♣ Garhwal, Nepal; India to S.E. Asia
808

Black-naped Woodpecker, *Picus canus*.
152-2440 m. (500-8,000') 30 cm. (12") R.

Common; in oak forests and also among groves near water in the *tarai*. The only green woodpecker with a *black nape*. Male has red on crown; female, black. Somewhat shy; edges up and down a tree trunk on side away from observer. Often on ground where it may hop about stiff-legged. Sometimes with laughing-thrushes. Occasionally perches atop a large boulder on steep hillside. Usually solitary. Partial to ants; eats beetles, berries and nectar. Voice a rapid *kep-kep-kep-kep* and also a *kekekekekekeke*. ❋ KV: in hills surrounding the Valley. ♣ Garhwal, Nepal, Sikkim; Europe, Asia
809, 810

Large Yellow-naped Woodpecker, *Picus flavinucha*.
213-2135 m. (700-7,000') 33 cm. (13") R.

Fairly common; in *sal* and mixed forests. A large gray-green species with a conspicuous *yellow nape*. Told from the Small Yellow-naped species by its larger size, heavier bill, brown wings and conspicuous *throat markings*. Chin and upper throat yellow in male; rufous in female. Seen in scattered pairs or family groups. Partial to larvae of beetles such as *sal* borers. May descend to ground for food. Often in mixed hunting parties with other woodpeckers, babblers and drongos. Call a loud *ku-ret*. ❋ KV: Godaveri, Nagarjung, Gaucher forests.
♣ Garhwal, Nepal, Sikkim; Garhwal to S. China and Sumatra
813

Small Yellow-naped Woodpecker, *Picus chlorolophus*.
120-2135 m. (400-7,000') 25 cm. (10") R.

Fairly common; in thin scrub jungle, pine or mixed forests. A medium-sized bird with a yellow nape. Similar to larger species but lower throat is brown and gray (not black with white markings); barred below. Male has red crown; female, gray. Young, barred olive and white below. Often with other species such as laughing-thrushes. Fairly bold. A weak tapping about five or six times a second. Call a loud *skrreeeeeaaa*, like a raptor, at about fifteen-second intervals.
❋ KV: seen among pines on Nagarjung above Balaju, Godaveri. ♣ Garhwal, Nepal, Sikkim; Himachal Pradesh to S. China and Sumatra
814, 815

Lesser Golden-backed Woodpecker, *Dinopium benghalense.*
120-274 m. (400-900') 25 cm. (10") R.

Fairly common; in open *sal* forests, dry scrub land and mango groves of the *tarai*. The only golden-backed woodpecker with a *black rump*. Fairly bold, often working among trees at the edge of villages. An insect-eater but also takes berries. In small parties, often with other species. Noisy. Call a clatter of rapid notes given when flying or spiraling up a tree.
🕭 Garhwal, Nepal; S. Asia 819

Three-toed Golden-backed Woodpecker, *Dinopium shorii.*
120-274 m. (400-900') 28 cm. (11") R.

Occasional; in forests of the *tarai*. Male a brilliant bird with a red head, yellow-orange back and crimson rump. Look for the white neck with broad black stripes. Neck pattern a key to identification. Associates with other woodpeckers and small birds but keeps to forests. Voice a rapid, repeated, tin-panny *klak-klak-klak-klak-klak* slower and softer than the Large Golden-backed Woodpecker with which it associates. 🕭 Garhwal, Nepal, Sikkim; India to Burma 824

Large Golden-backed Woodpecker, *Chrysocolaptes lucidus.*
120-1525 m. (400-5,000') 33 cm. (13") R.

Common; in cultivated groves as well as forests of the *tarai*. Much larger and noticeably "heavier" than the other two "golden-backs." Has a scarlet rump like the Three-toed Goldenback but the *throat* and *breast* are heavily *spotted* (not narrowly streaked). Black lines of face from eye and bill run only to the nape, not down sides of neck as in the Three-toed bird. Single or in loose pairs, working on boles of trees and onto high branches. Rather shy and usually hides to watch one from the opposite side of the branch. Commonest in *sal* forests. Associates with other woodpeckers, racquet-tailed drongos and small birds. Call, the loudest of the "golden-backs," a piercing, raucous and rapid *klakklakklakklak* given mostly on the wing. 🕭 Garhwal, Nepal, Sikkim; India to the Philippines 860, 861

Black-backed Woodpecker, *Chrysocolaptes festivus.*
244 m. (800') 32 cm. (12½") R.

Scarce; in light forests and along the borders of cultivations in the western *tarai*. Unmistakable. A black-backed woodpecker with a large white heart in center of back; golden wings. Male, a red crest and female, golden. Single or in pairs and small family parties. Fairly bold, often working well down on tree trunks. Flies to higher branches when disturbed. Often remains in a selected territory even when closely followed. Seen near Dhanghari and as far east as the Karnali River in acacia-shisham forest. Voice a rapid babbler-like chatter. 🕭 Nepal; India and Sri Lanka 858

Himalayan Pied Woodpecker, *Dendrocopos himalayensis*.
1830-3050 m. (6,000-10,000') 24 cm. (9½") R.

Fairly common; in pine, oak and rhododendron forests of western Nepal. Back and tail all black; white wing patch conspicuous. Very similar to Darjeeling Pied Woodpecker but has white around eye and a black gular stripe and no orangy-yellow ear patch. Female, head all black. Usually in pairs, working along the boles and branches of trees. Descends to fallen logs on forest floor. Heavy, dipping flight. Eats kernels of pine seeds as well as insects. Like the sapsucker, said to bore rows of holes in trees. Fairly common around Rara Lake east to Dhaulagiri. Call a loud, repeated *tri-tri-tri*. (Kashmir, Garhwal, Nepal; Afghanistan to Nepal   837

Darjeeling Pied Woodpecker, *Dendrocopos darjellensis*.
1830-3751 m. (6,000-12,300') 25 cm. (10") R.

Fairly common; in oak-rhododendron and hemlock forests. Has a solid black back; scapulars form a conspicuous white patch. Like the Himalayan Pied Woodpecker but with distinctive orangy-yellow patch near ear (not black and white); breast and abdomen heavily streaked with black (not uniform). Usually in pairs in the upper half of a tree. Not shy. Fairly strong flight. Often with small birds and the Rufous-bellied Sapsucker. Food is beetle larvae and other insects. Call a *zik-zik;* a mellow whistle *whe-ee-uu;* alarm a rapid *titititi*. ❊ KV: around the upper rim of the Valley. (Nepal, Sikkim; Nepal to W. China   838

Brown-fronted Pied Woodpecker, *Dendrocopos auriceps*.
1067-2897 m. (3,500-9,500') 19 cm. (7½") R.

Fairly common; in oak forests. Pale "ladder-back" bird with diagnostic brown forecrown, red and yellow nape in male; greenish-yellow in female. Also look for heavily spotted wings and streaked breast and abdomen. In pairs or scattered parties. Moves restlessly from one tree to another in undulating flight. Most common between 1830-2440 m. (6,000-8,000') and partial to Ban Oak (*Quercus leutrichophora*). Call a high *cheek-cheek-cheek-krrrr*, a tinny *peeeeeep-prprprprprprpr* and a subdued *tu-twit*. ❊ KV: regularly seen above 1830 m. (6,000'). (Kashmir, Garhwal, Nepal; Afghanistan to Nepal   842, 843

Fulvous-breasted Pied Woodpecker, *Dendrocopos macei*.
152-2440 m. (500-8,000') 19 cm. (7½") R.

Common; in mixed forests. Male resembles Brown-fronted Pied Woodpecker except for crown which is red and black (not brown). Female has black and brown underparts smudged with buffy-gray and not heavily streaked as in the Brown-fronted species. Single or in loose pairs, often with other birds such as tits and nuthatches. Prefers main trunks of trees and high branches. Restless and much on the move. Eats fruit, seeds, insects. Loud tapping often reveals its presence. Sometimes drums. Call a *peek-peek-trrrrrrrrrrrr*. ❊ KV: the common woodpecker on the Valley floor. (Kashmir(?), Garhwal, Nepal, Sikkim; Pakistan to Bali   845

Yellow-fronted Pied Woodpecker, *Dendrocopos mahrattensis*.
244-274 m. (800-900') 18 cm. (7") R.

Occasional; in dry country of the *tarai*. A very pale "ladder-back," the male with a red nape and female with a golden-brown crown. Much streaked below; abdomen orangy. Single or in pairs in tall trees along edges of rivers, in mango groves and sometimes in tall Silk Cotton and fig trees. Searches lower parts of tree like a piculet, before spiraling upward. Eats insects, fruit, nectar. Nests fairly near the ground. Voice a sharp *click—click—click—clickrrrr* (AR). (Nepal; Pakistan to Laos   847

Small Crimson-breasted Pied Woodpecker, *Dendrocopos cathpharius*.
915-3050 m. (3,000-10,000') 18 cm. (7") R.

Occasional; in pine and oak-rhododendron forests. A small replica of the Darjeeling Pied Woodpecker except sides of neck in male *red* (not orangy) and in female, tan and pink. These colors do not show too well in illustration. Both have red patches on breast but usually these are hard to see. Single, or in pairs, working fairly low on trees and in bushes. Much on the move from one feeding site to the next. Eats insects and nectar. Voice a loud, repeated *chip*, a soft *pivik* (Lister), also a *dee-deep-dee-di-di-di-di-di*. ❊ KV: Godaveri and Tin Pani Bhangjang at about 2135 m. (7,000'). (Nepal, Sikkim; Nepal to W. China   840

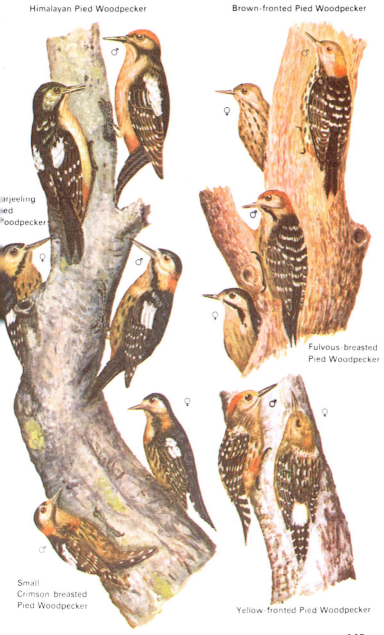

Red-eared Rufous Woodpecker, *Blythipicus pyrrhotis*.
1525-2135 m. (5,000-7,000') 29 cm. (11½") R.

Occasional; in dense, mixed forests of the mid-Himalayas. Similar to the Brown Woodpecker but larger and more heavily barred with black (not brown). Bill, a conspicuous yellow. Male has a red patch on neck. Young has dark head streaked with chestnut. Single or in pairs; keeps low in dense thickets and often on the ground. Shy and difficult to see except when it occasionally moves up a tall tree. Noisy when disturbed. More often heard than seen. Associates with laughing-thrushes. Call, an occasional, loud, rapidly descending *kak-kak-kak-kak-kak;* also frequently gives a sound like the chugging of a small steam engine. ❀ KV: in groves around the Valley; Godaveri. ● Nepal, Sikkim; Nepal to S. China 857

Pale-headed Woodpecker, *Gecinulus grantia*.
274 m. (900') 25 cm. (10") R.

Scarce; at the edge of large bamboo clumps. Look for rufous back, olive-green breast and yellowish head with red crown. Female lacks red crown. Two birds watched 4 miles north of Sunischari, Jhapa District, at the edge of groves of bamboos, Feb. 1 and 3, 1974 (Stephen Madge). Taps rather slowly on bamboo. Located in Nepal after plate was completed, thus no illustration shown. ● Nepal, Sikkim; Nepal to S. China 827

Brown Woodpecker (Rufous Woodpecker), *Micropternus brachyurus*.
120-1525 m. (400-5,000') 25 cm. (10") R.

Fairly common; in *sal*, acacia and pine groves and forests. The only entirely *light rufous-brown* woodpecker. Resembles the Red-eared Rufous Woodpecker but is paler and is not barred black. The bill is *dark* (not yellow). Single, or in pairs, spiraling around boles and branches of trees. Undulating flight. Said to build nest in large red ant's nest. Has small, thick feathers around head something like those on a Honey Kite's face. Call a high *ka--aa-ki-ki-ki-ki-ki*. ● Nepal; India to S. China 803

Rufous-bellied Sapsucker, *Hypopicus hyperythrus*.
1830-3202 m. (6,000-10,500') 23 cm. (9") R.

Fairly common; in oak-rhododendron forests. The only "ladder-back" (back barred black and white) woodpecker with rufous underparts. Head of male, red; female, black. Single or in pairs on boles and branches of large trees. Bores rows of holes in bark of oaks (*Quercus semecarpifolia*) and returns to drink the flowing sap, pokes bill into "sap holes" and may work at one tree for as long as half an hour, repeatedly visiting productive openings. At least a dozen other species, especially sibias, drink this sap. Fairly tame and can be watched at close range. Voice a rapid, high *tik-tik-tik-tik*, and an alarm call *titi-r-r-r-r-r*. ❀ KV: on Phulchowki and surrounding hills above 2135 m. (7,000'). ● Kashmir, Garhwal, Nepal, Sikkim; Kashmir to Korea 833

Great Slaty Woodpecker, *Mulleripicus pulverulentus*.
152-244 m. (500-800') 50 cm. (20") R.

Scarce; in belts of mature forests of the *tarai*. Unmistakable; the only gray woodpecker; huge size. In pairs or small, scattered parties, loudly banging on dead trees. Somewhat shy, sliding around to the back side of a tree when approached. Slow movements and awkward flight. Nests high in hollow trees; found only where there are many mature and aged trees. Voice a loud *we-kuk-kuk-kuk;* a softly repeated *shan* and a low note rising on the second syllable, *mow-ah*. ● Nepal, Sikkim; India to Palawan and Balabac Islands 828

Red-eared Rufous Woodpecker

Brown Woodpecker

Rufous-bellied Sapsucker

Great Slaty Woodpecker

BROADBILLS (Eurylaimidae) are gregarious forest birds. The base of the bill is enlarged, hence the name. Behavior is sluggish and quiet.

Hodgson's Broadbill, *Serilophus lunatus*. 19 cm. (7½"). No records since 1846. Look for a small flock of lethargic, gray birds with chestnut backs and white-tipped black tails. May still occur in S.E. Nepal forests. 864

Long-tailed Broadbill, *Psarisomus dalhousiae*.
274-1342 m. (900-4,400') 27 cm. (10½") R.
Fairly common; in foothill forests. A beautiful bird. Cannot be confused with any other species. Usually in parties up to fifteen birds, moving rather slowly from tree to tree; often in company with other species. Not very wary. Voice a loud, piercing screech resembling that of a hawk. Also a repeated *tseeay*. ♠ Garhwal, Nepal, Sikkim; Himalayas to Borneo 865

PITTAS (Pittidae) are plump birds with strong legs, short tails and often brilliant plumage. They are sometimes called "jewel thrushes." They fly well. Migratory habits of some species are erratic.

Blue-naped Pitta, *Pitta nipalensis*.
1525 m. (5,000') 25 cm. (10") M.
Scarce; in leafy forests where humus soil is prevalent. Male blue and tan with *blue* on hind neck. Female similar but hind neck is green. Small scattered parties comb the forest floor for insects, worms and other little animals. As they bounce along, they flick aside dead leaves with their bills much in the manner of babblers. Rather bold; undisturbed by passing woodcutters. Song a fairly loud, double whistle. ❋ KV: at Godaveri, Nagarjung for a day or two in spring. ♠ Nepal, Sikkim (?); Nepal to Tonkin 866

Indian Pitta, *Pitta brachyura*.
244 m. (800') 19 cm. (7½") S.
Occasional; in wooded *duns* and foothills. Paler than Green-breasted Pitta; breast uniform fulvous (not blueish-green) and a conspicuous black coronal stripe. Arrives in Chitwan Dun in May. Somewhat shy; usually on ground but flushes into low trees. Calls from a branch, throwing its head back like a jungle cock. A loud, clear *whee-teeyou* repeated from one ⌣ more than 30 times at two-second intervals. Other pittas in the vicinity respond. ♠ Garhwal, Nepal, Sikkim; India, Bangladesh, Sri Lanka 867

Green-breasted Pitta, *Pitta sordida*.
120-305 m. (400-1,000') 19 cm. (7½") R., M.
Occasional; in evergreen forests near water. A beautiful green bird with top of head rich maroon-brown, the rump and shoulder patch bright blue; a black neck and collar. Young are duller. Single or in pairs on the ground or among low parts of trees. Spends much time feeding on the ground. Voice kingfisher-like notes at spaced intervals. Found near Hitaura. ♠ Garhwal (?), Nepal, Sikkim; India to Philippines 869

LARKS (Alaudidae) are small, brown or sandy-colored ground birds, often streaked. Their wings and tails are somewhat rounded (pipits, which are similar, have longer tails). When approached by humans, larks tend to crouch, then spring up with a little chirp. Courting birds sing as they flutter high in the air. Sexes alike.

Bush Lark, *Mirafra assamica*.
120-274 m. (400-900') 15 cm. (6") R.
Common; in open, dry country among short grass clumps and plowed fields. A brown lark, streaked above and spotted on breast. Look for diagnostic *rufous on wings*. Usually runs, but when pressed it flutters upward for a short distance, then drops to the ground to run again. Call a rapid *vic---vic---vic*, or a light *tee-tee-tee* on the ground and a sweet melody sung on the wing. ♠ Nepal; India to S.E. Asia 873

Ashy-crowned Finch Lark, *Eremopterix grisea*.
120-305 m. (400-1,000') 13 cm. (5") R.
Fairly common; creeping on dusty paths and in cultivated fields of the *tarai*. A small, thick-billed lark; the male's black eye line and black underparts distinctive. The brown female is pale and drab but at close range the thick finch-like bill is conspicuous. In pairs or loose flocks up to fifteen birds. Fairly tame. When pressed, tends to squat and blend with the soil. Has a long, sustained song in flight. ♠ Nepal; S. Asia 878

Short-toed Lark, *Calandrella cinerea*.
1310-4575 m.   (4,300-15,000')   15 cm.   (6")   R., M.

Occasional; a winter visitor south of the main Himalayan range. A *tawny* lark, slightly larger than pale Hume's Short-toed Lark. Whitish outer tail feathers. Young are more fulvous above and more heavily streaked below than adults. Large flocks, sometimes up to 200 birds, in winter. Said to have a sweet song sung on the ground and in the air (Baker). (Long-billed Calandra Lark, *Melanocorypha maxima*, in N. Sikkim, see p. 336.) ♦ Kashmir, Garhwal, Nepal, Sikkim; Africa, Asia   886

Hume's Short-toed Lark, *Calandrella acutirostris*.
3660-4575 m.   (12,000-15,000')   14 cm.   (5½")   R., M.

Common; in semi-desert of northern Dolpo near scattered *Caragana* bushes and other xerophytic plants. Paler and smaller than similar Short-toed Lark and without fulvous wash. Single or in pairs energetically running about on the ground searching for seeds and insects. Overturns small stones with a quick sideways flick of the bill; also digs vigorously in the hard earth. Moves down slightly in winter. Has a fine courting flight and song display but does not match that of the Skylark. Courtship song a mellow, moderately strong *tee-leu-ee-lew* with many variations. Flies up with a typical lark *chirp*.(Eastern Calandra Lark, *Melanocorypha bimaculata*, Kashmir, see p.334.) ♦ Kashmir, Nepal, Sikkim; Iran to E. Tibet   888

Horned Lark, *Eremophila alpestris*.
3965-5490 m.   (13,000-18,000')   18 cm.   (7")   R.

Fairly common; on bare, stony hillsides. Unmistakable. Male, black face, ear patch and fore-crown ending in "horns." Fulvous to pale pink above. Also look for broad black upper breast band. Female lacks black on head but has similar band. Very high altitude bird almost always found on grassy slopes above last bushes [usually above 4880 m. (16,000')]. In Dolpo, birds descend to 4117 m. (13,500') in desert biotope. Tame and easily approached. In mid-June many young just out of the nest and able to run after parents. Sings mostly from rocks (not in flight). Song a short, gurgling *pee-su-seet* and *pew-seep* with variations.
♦ Kashmir, Garhwal (?), Nepal, Sikkim; Europe, Africa, Asia, N. America   897

Crested Lark, *Galerida cristata*.
120-274 m.   (400-900')   18 cm.   (7")   R.

Fairly common; in river beds and fields of the lowlands. The only Nepal lark with a prominent, pointed *crest*. Grayish-brown and heavily streaked above; fulvous below with streaked breast. Single or in pairs working slowly over the ground. When disturbed it flies 30 or 40 feet then drops to the ground in the next field. A good runner. Voice is a weak *ti-tee-tee-ook;* also *pew-pip* in flight.   ♦ Nepal; Europe, Africa, Asia   899

Little Skylark, *Alauda gulgula*.
120-3050 m.   (400-10,000')   16 cm.   (6½")   R., W.

Fairly common; in fallow and plowed fields. Light brown above with a pale rump noticeable in flight. Very pale below with white abdomen. Three races in Nepal, the northern ones visiting Nepal in winter. Congregate in flocks of 15 to 50. They fly up slowly with a chirp, circle widely in a loose flock, then drop down to spread out over a field. After sitting immobile for awhile they begin to hunt between clods of earth and through short grass. Voice a *chink* in flight, like a wagtail; flight contact note *bzzzweet* and also a *chirrrrrrrt-it*. Courtship song, noted in Dhorpatan Valley, is a prolonged, bubbling series of warbles and shorter notes sung as bird flutters in circles high above grassy plain.   ♦ Kashmir, Garhwal, Nepal, Sikkim; India to Philippines   905, 906, 907

Sand Lark, *Calandrella raytal*.
120-305 m.   (400-1,000')   14 cm.   (5½")   R.

Fairly common; along sandy river beds. A very pale lark with paler cheeks and eyebrow and a few fine lines on breast. Outer tail feathers whitish. When motionless, almost impossible to distinguish from sandy surroundings. Not very shy; crouches when approached. A weak flight. In pairs or single near the vicinity of quiet water. Often nests on sand in direct sunlight. A typical lark-like *trr-trr* when flushed. Also a few musical notes (Baker).   ♦ Nepal; Iran to Burma   891

SWIFTS (Apodidae) are small, dark birds; their long, pointed wings extend well beyond their tails. They capture insects in the air in large mouths. They resemble swallows but flight is a fast fluttering rather than graceful, deep wingbeats. They never perch on wires. Roosting in colonies, there is some migration but movements are not well known. The large swifts may range a great distance in a single day.

White-rumped Needletail (Spinetail), *Chaetura sylvatica*.
213 m. (700') 11 cm. (4½") R. (?)

Scarce; noted in small flock in Nawalpur District (RLF, 1972). A small swift with white rump and *underparts white below breast*. Seen circling over forest and descending to dart between trees lining the East-West Highway (Mahendra Rajmarg). Amazingly agile as it speeds between trees. Seen on 16 March; movements and status in Nepal unknown. Flock retains contact through typical swift-like twitterings. 🌢 Garhwal, Nepal, Sikkim; India to Bangladesh   692

Black Swift, *Apus apus*.
3355 m. (11,000') 16 cm. (6½") R. (?)

Scarce; four birds seen hawking insects in mountain gorge at 3355 m. (11,000') in Dolpo in June 1971 (RLF). A large, dark swift with *black* body and *slightly* pale throat. Birds disappeared flying north towards Ringmo Lake. Movement and status in Nepal not known. 🌢 Kashmir, Nepal; Europe, Africa, Asia   696

Khasi Hills Swift, *Apus acuticaudus*. 16 cm. (6½"). No recent data. Look for a dark swift, underparts flecked with white; also has white throat and dark rump. Most likely to occur in E. Nepal. 🌢 Nepal; Nepal to Assam   698

Large White-rumped Swift, *Apus pacificus*.
1372-3355 m. (4,500-11,000') 18 cm. (7") R.

Fairly common; usually in flocks over ridges. Black with large white rump and deeply forked tail best seen when bird banks sharply. A pale throat; flecks of white feathers below. Often with Alpine Swift and Nepal House Martin. Usually some distance from human habitation; frequently high in mountain gorge. ✤ KV: over Kakani Ridge in February. 🌢 Kashmir, Garhwal, Nepal, Sikkim; Kashmir to Japan and Australia   700

House Swift, *Apus affinis*.
120-2135 m. (400-7,000') 15 cm. (6") R., M.

Common; above city buildings and over grassy ridges during day. Similar to Large White-rumped Swift but has less white on rump; shorter tail less deeply forked; dark below, except throat, with no white edges to feathers. Communal roosting and nesting under eaves of houses. Forages during the day to return to nest holes in scattered groups. Early evening, flies around and around nesting site before quickly diving in. Much initial conversation in their sleeping quarters. Most leave Kathmandu in December; return in early February. Call a series of tinkling notes in flight and a subdued *churrrrrrr* in their nests. ✤ KV: nests in buildings around city. 🌢 Garhwal, Nepal, Sikkim; Africa, Asia   703, 705

Crested Swift, *Hemiprocne longipennis*.
120-305 m. (400-1,000') 23 cm. (9") R.

Fairly common; almost always over or near forests. A gray bird with a long, wire-like tail. An unmistakable crest, erect when perched. Overhead, the thin wings and long tail look like an aircraft of modern design. Scattered parties of 10-20 catch insects over rivers and above tall trees. When resting, sits motionlessly on bare branch high in a tree. Flight is slow and graceful for a swift. Nest most unusual—a tiny, shallow saucer built on a horizontal branch into which the egg is glued! Call a *clee-chee: teek-teek* and a nasal *zaaaa* on the wing. 🌢 Nepal; India to Celebes   709

Edible Nest Swiftlet, *Collocalia brevirostris*.
152-4575 m. (500-15,000') 14 cm. (5½") R.

Fairly common; in deep mountain valleys. Small size and fairly uniform color; a pale rump sometimes visible in flight. Similar to Crag Martin (a swallow) which is also brown but martin is heavier with broader wings and a white patch in tail. Palm Swift much thinner with narrower wings. Flocks of 10-50 (rarely up to 300) seen hawking insects just above the water of Himalayan rivers; also over ridges. When almost dark, they suddenly disappear from feeding areas and presumably go to their nesting-roosting sites in high rock caves. In winter, often with martins and swallows and usually below 2440 m. (8,000'). Voice a high-pitched twitter. ♦ Garhwal, Nepal, Sikkim; Himalayas to C. China 683

Palm Swift, *Cypsiurus parvus*.
120 m. (400') 13 cm. (5") R.

Occasional; associated with Palmyra Palms along the Indian border at places like Biratnagar and Birganj. Resembles an Edible Nest Swiftlet but much thinner and lacks pale rump. Tail very narrow and forked. Wingbeat a rapid flutter. Twists and turns covering the same area for a number of minutes. Many noted at Raxaul, Bihar, India, but very few seen two or three miles farther north in Birganj. One nesting tree (palm) also occupied by old weaver bird nests currently being used by White-throated Munias. Voice a *titititieeee* (AR). ♦ Nepal; Africa, Asia 707

Alpine Swift, *Apus melba*.
120-3050 m. (400-10,000') 22 cm. (8½") R.

Occasional; over rugged mountain slopes and in low altitude river gorges. White underneath except for diagnostic breast band. Usually seen in small flocks, twisting and turning together high in the air; sometimes will shoot down low over a ridge. Fast fliers; eat winged insects. Communal nesting. Noted as high as 1830 m. (6,000') on 1 July but daily and seasonal movements not well known. Call *chee-chee* in flight; a twittering at the roosting site (AR). ♦ Kashmir, Garhwal, Nepal, Sikkim; Europe, Africa, Asia 694

White-throated Needletail (Spinetail), *Chaetura caudacuta*.
152-2257 m. (500-7,400') 24 cm. (9½") R.

Occasional; skimming over surfaces of water (Chitwan) or over mountain ridges. A very large, black swift with white throat and pale mid-back. Spines on tail not seen except at extremely close range. Usually pairs or parties up to 20, flying back and forth over a ridge or a section of flowing water. Beetles and winged insects found in stomach. Very swift flier, thought to cover record distances in a short time. Wind whistles through its wings as bird shoots past the observer. Roosts in colonies. Voice a high twitter similar to that of a House Swift. ♦ Kashmir, Garhwal, Nepal, Sikkim; Asia to Australia 688, 689

SWALLOWS and MARTINS (Hirundinidae). Swallows are graceful birds with long wings and long, forked tails. They fly, banking and twisting with effortless beauty, as they catch insects in their wide mouths (flight of similar swifts is a fluttering considerably faster than swallows). Sexes are alike. Martins are small swallows with short tails.

Sand Martin, *Riparia paludicola*.
274-1372 m. (900-4,500') 11 cm. (4½") R.

Common; over river courses in the shadows of steep sand banks. Light brown above, a pale rump sometimes noticeable in flight. Look for slightly pale throat, ashy breast and white abdomen. Loose parties of 20 to 200 birds hawk insects over fields adjoining streams and rivers. Rest on telephone wires, dead branches or projecting rocks. Nest in cavities in sand banks. Call a high-pitched *tsimp* given at intervals. ❄ KV: fairly common over rivers of the Valley. (Collared Sand Martin, *R. riparia*, see p. 321.) ◀ Nepal; Africa, Asia   912

Crag Martin, *Hirundo rupestris*.
915-4575 m. (3,000-15,000') 15 cm. (6") R., M.

Fairly common; near cliffs and over steep, grassy slopes. Uniform brown above with wings reaching beyond squarish tail; pale throat and pale brown below. Look for white patches on tail as bird turns in flight. In winter, parties of 30-40 birds cover favorite route several times before moving on. Pairs or small colonies nest on cliffs, usually just above a mountain stream. Rarely below 3050 m. (10,000') in summer. Contact note a high *teet*. ◀ Kashmir, Garhwal, Nepal, Sikkim; Europe, Africa, Asia   913

Barn Swallow, *Hirundo rustica*.
152-1830 m. (500-6,000') 18 cm. (7") R., M.

Common; over cultivated fields as well as city streets. The uniform dark upperparts distinguish this swallow from the similar Striated Swallow that has a pale rump. A graceful flier, skimming closely over fields and paved roads alike. Voice a rapid, constant twitter *vik*. ❄ KV: some build nests in stores, considered good luck to owners. ◀ Kashmir, Garhwal, Nepal, Sikkim (?); nearly world-wide   916, 917

Wire-tailed Swallow, *Hirundo smithii*.
120 m. (400') 14 cm. (5½") R.

Scarce; first reported in 1885. Recently seen in Bhairhawa and Nepalganj. In flight, may look almost black and white with very long wire-like tail feathers. The Crested Swift also has a similar tail but is gray and usually over forest whereas the Wire-tailed Swallow is in open country almost always near water; often on bridge abutments. ◀ Nepal; Africa, Asia   921

Indian Cliff Swallow, *Hirundo fluvicola*.
120 m. (400') 11 cm. (4½") R.(?)

Scarce; along Kosi River. Look for chestnut from forehead to crown; short tail and boldly streaked underparts. No other swallow has this combination. Discovered along the Kosi on 10 April 1975 by RLF and Harvey Gilston. ◀ Kashmir, Garhwal, Nepal; Afghanistan to India   922

Striated Swallow, *Hirundo daurica*.
274-2745 m. (900-9,000') 19 cm. (7½") R., M.

Common; over hills and fields as well as cultivated terraces near habitation. Similar to Barn Swallow but has *pale, tan rump*. Also a tan throat and breast finely streaked with dark brown. Loose parties of 10 to 50 glide over rice fields and above streams on agile wings. A bit more rural than the Barn Swallow. Gathers clay from mud holes along village paths. Voice a quiet twitter and a loud *cha--reeeee*. ❄ KV: most leave in winter to return in March; nest in houses. ◀ Kashmir, Garhwal, Nepal, Sikkim; Europe, Africa, Asia   923, 925, 926

Eurasian House Martin, *Delichon urbica*.
305-4575 m. (1,000-15,000') 14 cm. (5½") S., M.

Occasional; in flocks over the mid-Himalayas and foothills in winter; among cliffs, usually above 3050 m. (10,000'), in summer. Told from Nepal House Martin by *white* (not black) undertail coverts, chin and throat. A strong glider; prefers hunting over ridges rather than streams. During winter they mix in large flocks with Nepal House Martins. Colonial nesters on cliffs. A sharp twittering in flight. ◀ Kashmir, Garhwal, Nepal, Sikkim; Europe, Africa, Asia
930, 931

Nepal House Martin, *Delichon nipalensis*.
305-2745 m. (1,000-9,000') 13 cm. (5") R., M.

Fairly common; over grassy ridges, villages and mountain streams. Tail not as deeply forked as in Eurasian House Martin and the *throat* and *undertail coverts black* (not white). Usually seen in large flocks (40-100) fluttering through the air over wooded ravines. Large groups rest in leafless trees in winter in early morning sun. Often with Barn and Striated Swallows. Nests in loose colonies on cliffs. Quite tame. Moves downhill in winter. Voice a faint twitter.
◀ Garhwal, Nepal, Sikkim; Garhwal to Burma   932

SHRIKES (Laniidae) are birds with comparatively large heads, dark lines through eyes, hooked bills and long tails. They perch atop shrubs, small trees and telephone wires, descending to the ground for prey. Solitary or in pairs in open country. Young are barred. Sexes alike.

Bay-backed Shrike, *Lanius vittatus*.
120-335 m. (400-1,100') 18 cm. (7") R.
Occasional; in dryish acacia groves of the *tarai*. A small shrike with a dark red back and a distinctive white rump. Underparts white. White wing patch conspicuous in flight. Usually single or in pairs near cultivations where grasshoppers abound. Seen at the edge of grass fires. Not very shy. Nests made of grass; placed in bushes. Voice a harsh, hoarse *cha-a-a-a-a*. 🍀 Garhwal, Nepal; Transcaspia to S. Asia   940

Gray Shrike, *Lanius excubitor*.
137 m. (450') 24 cm. (9½") W.
Scarce; noted in December near Nepalganj by H.S. Nepali. All gray and white except for black mask. Single bird in open country. Call a repeated *kwi-rick* (AR). 🍀 Nepal; Eurasia, Africa   933

Black-headed or Rufous-backed Shrike, *Lanius schach*.
152-2745 m. (500-9,000') 24 cm. (9½") R.
Common; in open country or hedges of towns. Two subspecies in Nepal. Black-headed variety (in C. and E. Nepal) unmistakable. Rufous-backed (of W. Nepal) very similar to Gray-backed but former has white spot in wing and back paler gray. Solitary or in pairs, perched conspicuously on bush tops. Feeds on insects, small reptiles and young birds. Sometimes impales prey on thorns so it can be ripped apart with strong bill. Mandibles are used in Nepali "rice feeding ceremony" for six-month-old children, said to assure wisdom. Song a hoarse warble, rasping chirps and *vic-vic-vic* for half a minute or more. At dusk one hears a rapidly repeated, raspy *cha-dit*. ❋ KV: conspicuous bird in city suburbs. 🍀 Kashmir, Garhwal, Nepal, Sikkim; Transcaspia to S.E. Asia   946, 948

Gray-backed Shrike, *Lanius tephronotus*.
274-4575 m. (900-15,000') 25 cm. (10") R., M.
Occasional; in open country and cutover jungle. Very similar to Rufous-backed Shrike but look for darker gray on back; fulvous breast and flanks. Also note lack of white wing patch. Heavy wingbeat; straight flight with a terminal upward glide to a perch. Nests above 2745 m. (9,000') in the Himalayas and Trans-Himalayan region. Eats insects and small animals. Seen catching a skink at 4270 m. (14,000'). Call a harsh *ktcht-ktcht-ktcht* at dusk or when alarmed. ❋ KV: arrives in October, departs in March. 🍀 Kashmir, Garhwal, Nepal, Sikkim; Kashmir to S. China   945

Brown Shrike, *Lanius cristatus*.
120-1830 m. (400-6,000') 19 cm. (7½") W.
Occasional; in the same habitat as other shrikes but more often seen in light forests than on electric wires. A pale brown bird with a pale eyebrow above a dark eye line (does not show well in illustration). Many birds here are faintly barred on breast and abdomen. Single or in loose pairs in bushes and at forest edge. Rests with head bent forward and tail down. Wingbeat is heavy and quick. Birds active at dusk. Call a harsh, repeated *je-je-je-je-je-jeeeet*. ❋ KV: winter on hedges along roads to Godaveri, Chobar, Sankhu. 🍀 Nepal, Sikkim; Asia   949

ORIOLES (Oriolidae) are beautiful yellow and black or maroon birds. Females duller-colored than males; young are streaked. Orioles have strong, pointed bills and stout legs. Flight is undulating. They are partial to leafy trees.

Golden Oriole, *Oriolus oriolus*.
152-1830 m.   (500-6,000')   24 cm.   ($9\frac{1}{2}$")   R., S.

Occasional; in village groves and trees at edges of fields. Male an unmistakable golden with black eye line, wings and tail. Female dull yellowish-brown and streaked. Single or in pairs and sometimes small family parties. Often shy, flying a long distance when disturbed. Usually near the tops of leafy trees, often along streams. Feeds on insects and fruit. Song a full, mellow *who-he-heer* or *he-too-roo*. Also a nasal hiss *ka-a-lee-aa* and a rapid *tur-tur-tur-tur*. ❊ KV: here in spring, some nest in the Valley. ● Kashmir, Garhwal, Nepal; Europe, Africa, Asia   953

Black-naped Oriole, *Oriolus chinensis*.
152-2287 m.   (500-7,500')   27 cm.   ($10\frac{1}{2}$")   R. (?), M.

Scarce; high in leafy trees in open country as well as in forest groves. Male very similar to male Golden Oriole but the prominent black eye line continues around the nape. Also note yellow (not black) secondaries and scapulars. Female has suggestion of dark nape. Residential status unclear. Seen in Nepal only a few times, mostly in the *tarai*. Call a single loud note. ❊ KV: once seen in April east of Thankot. ● Nepal, Sikkim; E. Asia   955

Black-headed Oriole, *Oriolus xanthornus*.
120-1372 m.   (400-4,500')   24 cm.   ($9\frac{1}{2}$")   R.

Common; in open foothill forests as well as in village groves. A striking, bright yellow bird with black head. The darkish head of the female separates it from other female orioles. Found in tops of tall leafy *sal* trees, often in pairs. Strong, undulating flight. Feeds on fruit and insects. Nests suspended from forked branches as are New World "oriole" nests. Some upward migration in summer. Call a penetrating *chew* or *tee-you* and also a *kew-ko-kolti-lee*. ❊ KV: an unusual summer visitor. ● Garhwal, Nepal, Sikkim; India to Borneo   958

Maroon Oriole, *Oriolus traillii*.
305-2440 m.   (1,000-8,000')   27 cm.   ($10\frac{1}{2}$")   R., W.

Fairly common; in heavy mixed forests of the mid-Himalayas. Distinctive maroon of male looks black in many lights. Light maroon tail often best field mark, especially as it flares when bird lands on branch. Striking pattern of female unmistakable; heavily spotted and shows very little maroon except on tail. Usually single or in pairs in heavy oak forest. Keeps well within the upper half of leafy trees. Often associated with thrushes and leaf birds. Quite shy. Usually above 1525 m. (5,000') in both summer and winter although some birds descend in cold weather. More often heard than seen. A song with several warbling notes; also a loud *j-a-a-a-ay*, a *ko-lay-wa* and a *mew* like that of an American Catbird. ❊ KV: common in oak forests all the year around. ● Garhwal, Nepal, Sikkim; Himalayas to S.E. Asia   961

DRONGOS (Dicruridae) are black birds with long, forked tails. They inhabit both forests and open country where they perch on exposed points looking for insect prey. Drongos are rather noisy and often solitary.

White-bellied Drongo, *Dicrurus caerulescens*.
152-305 m. (500-1,000') 24 cm. (9½") R.

Occasional; in cutover jungles and forests of the *tarai*. Similar to Ashy Drongo or young Black Drongo but has a *white abdomen*, neither barred nor flecked. Young are brown; pale below. Single or pairs in low or middle parts of trees in open forest, often near cultivation. Less active and noisy than most drongos but has same strong flight. Near the nest will attack species much larger than itself. Often in mixed parties with small birds. Song a ringing *whee-deal-whee-del*. ♣ Garhwal, Nepal; S. Asia   967

Small Racquet-tailed Drongo, *Dicrurus remifer*.
274-2440 m. (900-8,000') 50 cm. (20") R.

Occasional; in mixed tropical and subtropical forests. A most interesting tail: long and wire-like, conspicuously spatulate at end. Similar to Large Racquet-tailed Drongo but smaller and *lacks crest*. Undulating flight; often with other birds. Active but somewhat shy. One of the best mimics among Nepal birds. Quite common in Chitwan Dun north of the Churia Range. Call a sharp *why-tu-tu-why* and a number of high notes. ❊ KV. nests in forests at edge of Valley. ♣ Garhwal, Nepal, Sikkim; India to W. China   972

Large Racquet-tailed Drongo, *Dicrurus paradiseus*.
120-1372 m. (400-4,500') about 58 cm. (23") R.

Fairly common; in the *tarai* forests south of the Churia Range. A striking, large-sized drongo with long, thin outer tail feathers sporting black spatulae. This tail combined with the prominent curved crest, diagnostic. Usually solitary, frequently at low and middle forest levels. A "self-appointed" watchman of mixed groups of woodpeckers, nuthatches and laughing-thrushes. Calls loudly at the sight of danger and causes flock of birds to disappear into vegetation. Much on the move and somewhat shy. Has an extensive vocabulary. A loud *see-pretty-bird* in descending notes sung at the break of dawn. Alarm *kit-kaat-kaat-kaat*. Also whistles a *jay-pe-preeeee* along with *here-you-are-ja-ja-ja*. ❊ KV: once noted in Rani Bari temple grove. ♣ Nepal, Sikkim (?); India to S. China   976

Hair-crested Drongo, *Dicrurus hottentottus*.
213-4117 m. (700-13,500') 29 cm. (11¼") R.

Common; in the *tarai* especially around flowering Silk Cotton trees. A heavy drongo with bright greenish gloss on neck, wings and breast. Look for conspicuously upturned distal corners on tail. "Hairs" in crest practically invisible except at very close range. Small, loose groups forage at the edge of forest. Strong flight. In winter, up to 40 birds may congregate and fly from one tree top to another. Rarely seen above 915 m. (3,000') but one vagrant found at 4117 m. (13,500') in June (Dolpo). Noisy; a great variety of notes: a loud, metallic *chee-pur-weep*, a repeated *cheef-fert* or *wheet-to-reet*, also a *tsip* in flight. ♣ Garhwal, Nepal, Sikkim; Pakistan to Australia   973

Ashy Drongo, *Dicrurus leucophaeus*.

120-2745 m. (400-9,000') 27 cm. (10½") R., S.

Common; perching on bare branches at tops of forest trees. Similar to Black Drongo but smaller with *dark gray underparts* (not shiny black) and proportionately shorter tail. Single or in small groups. Looks from side to side like a flycatcher, then darts out swiftly and returns to same perch. Quite active into early twilight. A few wander high up the mountains. Very much a forest bird [Black Drongo is in open country usually below 1830 m. (6,000')]. Call a bright *chee-bee-chew; cha-cha-chipper-reet; chipper-tz-ert-tze-ert; tuk-cheer-cheer.* ✣ KV: in Godaveri forests, Rani Bari; fewer in winter. ♠ Kashmir, Garhwal, Nepal, Sikkim; Afghanistan to S. China   965

Black Drongo, *Dicrurus adsimilis*.

274-1830 m. (900-6,000') 30 cm. (12") R.

Abundant; in open fields, villages and in suburbs of cities. All black (glossy in right light) with a long, deeply forked tail. At close range a white dot at base of bill is visible. Young have bellies barred or flecked black and white. Take care not to confuse these with White-bellied Drongo which is much whiter below besides residing in or near forests (not open country). Swoops after insects in the air, returns to perch and bobs tail. May feed at dusk on emerging termites. Deliberate flight. Bold and noisy in nesting season. Call a loud *chi-bee* and a slow *weeper--weep-----weep---weeper.* ✣ KV: the common drongo on the Valley floor; starts singing before dawn (about 3:45 A.M.) in early summer. ♠ Kashmir, Garhwal, Nepal, Sikkim; Africa to Formosa   962

Little Bronzed Drongo, *Dicrurus aeneus*.

274-1982 m. (900-6,500') 23 cm. (9") R.

Fairly common; in upper half of forest trees. Somewhat similar to Black Drongo but smaller and with shorter tail. The most glistening of the drongos. Single or in scattered groups, hawking insects from high, bare branches. At dusk may fly about with others over a river bank catching morsels (such as Evening Brown butterflies) at nearly ground level. Some altitudinal movement and usually below 1220 m. (4,000') in winter. Song a rapidly descending *chew-chew-chew-didititii.* ✣ KV: a few resident at Nagarjung and Godaveri. ♠ Garhwal, Nepal, Sikkim; India to Formosa   971

Crow-billed Drongo, *Dicrurus annectans*.

152-457 m. (500-1,500') 27 cm. (10½") S?, R?

Scarce; in sal and mixed forest of the *tarai* and *duns*, almost always near water. Good identification pointers are a bill especially thick at the base and a comparatively short tail fork. The tips of tail feathers "greatly upturned" as previously reported is not supported by current specimen examination. Very similar to Black Drongo but thick bill, relatively short tail, lack of white dot at base of lower mandible, and dense forest habitat different. Crow-billed habitat overlaps that of Ashy but the latter is dark ashy not steely blue-black, has a deeper tail fork and a red eye conspicuous at short range. Considerable confusion in identification has led to erroneous reports of Crow-billed Drongos. Summer specimens from Chitwan and Bara Districts indicate the birds nest in Nepal but movements uncertain. Somewhat shy but energetic and active while feeding; usually haunts lower half of forest canopy. Call a high but fairly mellow *wik-a-wik.* ♠ Nepal, Sikkim; Nepal to S.E. Asia   970

WOOD-SWALLOWS (Artamidae) are plump birds with large, sharp drongo-like bills. Their wings are long, legs small and tails short. Sexes are alike and young are barred.

Ashy Wood-Swallow (Ashy Swallow-Shrike), *Artamus fuscus*.
120-2440 m. (400-8,000') 18 cm. (7") R., S.

Occasional and local; around open fields of the *tarai* and grassy ridges of the foothills. Ashy above, paler below with *stout blue bill*. In small flocks. A slow wingbeat, then glide, sometimes circling with legs dangling. In winter 20 or 30 squeeze together on branch like skein of gray pearls. Up into hills in spring. Often rests in pines, two or three touching each other; much body-shifting and tail-wagging. In flight a harsh *chaaaa;* also a slow repeated *k-e-r-r-a*. ♣ Garhwal, Nepal, Sikkim; India to S. China 982

STARLINGS and MYNAS (Sturnidae). The Starling family in Nepal includes a starling, six mynas, one stare, the Rosy Pastor and the Talking Myna. They are all noisy, gregarious birds with heavy flight and strong legs. Most show a white or pale wing patch in flight. Sexes alike except for the stare.

Spot-winged Stare, *Saroglossa spiloptera*.
120-1830 m. (400-6,000') 16 cm. (6½") R.

Fairly common; in open *tarai* and low river valleys. Gray above with feathers edged black. Throat of male dark chestnut, breast rufescent and abdomen white. A white wing patch. Female is brown with gray abdomen. Eyes paler than shown. Young like female, only streaked. Usually in large, noisy flocks near villages. Partial to flowering Silk Cotton trees. Associated with mynas and drongos in flowering and fruiting trees; only rarely on the ground. Moves into low foothills in warm weather. Voice is a mellow whistle with chipping contact notes, also a *churrr*. ♣ Garhwal, Nepal, Sikkim; India to Burma 984

Brahminy Myna, *Sturnus pagodarum*.
213-366 m. (700-1,200') 19 cm. (7½") R.

Fairly common; with parties of stares and Gray-headed Mynas in the western *tarai*. The only crested myna in Nepal. A trim bird. Scarce in the hills but a few nesting birds seen along the Indrawati River, east of Kathmandu. Usually very tame, spending much time on the ground; also in leafy trees with other mynas. Voice less harsh than other mynas, almost approaching a song (Baker). ♣ Kashmir, Garhwal, Nepal; Afghanistan to S. Asia 994

Gray-headed Myna, *Sturnus malabaricus*.
120-1372 m. (400-4,500') 18 cm. (7") R.

Common; in fruiting trees and village groves. A slim, trim, light-colored myna, pale gray above and reddish-brown below with an orange-tipped bill best seen at close range. No white in wing. Large flocks congregate in the *tarai* in flowering trees and descend to flowering bushes. Often in company with other birds. Flight groups are compact, all birds wheeling and turning together. Clambers along branches and rests on tops of high, bare trees. Voice a clatter, more subdued and higher-pitched than most mynas. Contact note a quick *treet* repeated every few seconds. ❋ KV: early spring to fall; a few in January. ♣ Garhwal, Nepal, Sikkim; India to S. China 987

Rosy Pastor, *Sturnus roseus*. 23 cm. (9"). Scarce; reported in Hodgson's collections. Diagnostic pale pink body. Should be looked for in S.W. *tarai* during spring migration and possibly on N.W. Nepal-Tibetan frontier in summer. 996

Eurasian Starling, *Sturnus vulgaris*.
244-1280 m. (800-4,200') 22 cm. (8½") M.

Scarce; in cultivated fields and leafy trees near water. Dark purple with a green gloss and many tan marks above; whitish spots below (amount of marks and spots varies from bird to bird). Single or in small parties. Spends much time on ground eating insects, worms, fruit and grain. A rural bird, rarely in towns. It has a variety of noisy, chattering notes. ❋ KV: the race *S. v. poltaratskyi* is here in winter and spring. ♣ Kashmir, Nepal; Europe, Africa, Asia, N. America 997, 999, 1001

Pied Myna, *Sturnus contra.*
120-305 m.   (400-1,000')   23 cm.   (9")   R.
Common; in lowlands near villages and in fields in vicinity of cattle. The only black and white myna; note the orange patch around eye and the orange bill. Females and young are duller than males. In pairs or small parties around cattle sheds or at the margins of ponds and slow flowing streams. An open country bird. Flight strong. Not as bold as the Common Myna. Call a harsh *sri-chu-chu-chu,* more grating than some mynas. 🍀 Nepal; India to S.E. Asia
1002

Common Myna, *Acridotheres tristis.*
120-2440 m.   (400-8,000')   24 cm.   (9¼")   R.
Abundant; scattered everywhere around houses, gardens and fields. The only *brown* myna with *yellow bare patch around eye.* Look for white wing patch and white tips to tail best seen in flight. Bill yellow. Often on ground but also strong fliers. Omnivorous. Regularly combs hedges and flowers for insects. Contests for nesting sites in walls, buildings, often battling one another. Congregates in noisy crowds at evening. Common as high as Jumla town, 2440 m. (8,000'). Voice a variety of mews, gurgles, chirps as *kiki-kiki---chuk-chuk-chuk------konkkonkkonk.* ✲ KV: always much in evidence. 🍀 Kashmir, Garhwal, Nepal, Sikkim; Asia and introduced elsewhere
1006

Bank Myna, *Acridotheres ginginianus.*
120-1220 m.   (400-4,000')   20 cm.   (8")   R.
Fairly common; around villages and in open fields near animals. A dark gray myna with an *orange* patch around eye (not yellow) and a *tan* wing patch. Found in pairs or small parties. Closely associated with cattle and buffaloes grazing in fields. Several noted on backs of rhinoceroses wallowing in a muddy pool in Chitwan Dun. A rural bird in Nepal; not common in towns. Call a variety of notes like *klikky-klak-tsu-tsu,* with variations. 🍀 Nepal; S. Asia
1008

Jungle Myna, *Acridotheres fuscus.*
274-1525 m.   (900-5,000')   23 cm.   (9")   R.
Common; at outskirts of cities and villages, in fields and forest. A dark *gray* myna similar to the Bank Myna but paler below and has *no bare eye patch.* Bill partly orange. A distinctive *tuft* of short erect feathers on the forehead just behind the beak. Seen in pairs or family groups in summer but collect in large flocks up to 100 birds or more during winter. Several hundred seen on a sand bar of a *tarai* river. Has a variety of clucks, gurgles and a loud *cheep-er, cheep-er.* ✲ KV: scattered throughout the Valley. 🍀 Kashmir, Garhwal, Nepal, Sikkim; Pakistan to Sumatra
1009

Talking Myna (Hill Grackle), *Gracula religiosa.*
152-457 m.   (500-1,500')   38 cm.   (15")   R.
Fairly common; among tall trees of the *tarai* and *dun* forests. A large, plump, black bird with yellow wattles, orangy-yellow bill and bright yellow legs. Also has white wing patch, typical of mynas. Moves about in pairs or small parties among fruiting trees. Fond of figs; also eats insects. Caged pets eat fruit, grass, clover and bread. One of the bird world's best imitators of the human voice. Does not appear to "talk" until almost a year old. In the wild, has a variety of loud, metallic notes. 🍀 Nepal, Sikkim; Kumaon to Palawan Island 1015

CROWS and ALLIES (Corvidae). Jays, pies, Nutcracker, choughs, Ground Pecker, crows and Raven are mostly medium-sized, noisy birds, eating animal and vegetable matter. Their beaks and legs are strong, wings rounded and tails moderate to long. Crows, the Raven and choughs are black; jays largely tan, gray and blue; pies are colorful with long, graduated tails; the Nutcracker is speckled white and the Ground Pecker is a sandy color. Flight is strong and measured. Sexes are alike in these gregarious birds.

Eurasian Jay (Himalayan Jay), *Garrulus glandarius*.
915-2745 m. (3,000-9,000') 30 cm. (12") R.
Fairly common; in temperate forests. Tan with dark wings and tail; a white rump conspicuous in flight. In scattered parties up to ten birds. Somewhat shy. Eats viburnum berries, fruit and small mammals. Often sits parallel to the branch keeping mostly to the middle of leafy trees. Rarely below 1830 m. (6,000'). Call a loud *cu-cr-blink-blink*, similar to that of the Red-billed Blue Magpie. Also in chorus a *kler--keee* and an alarm *jay-jay-jay*, plus conversational notes. ✣ KV: in oak forests surrounding the Valley. ♠ Kashmir, Garhwal, Nepal, Sikkim; Europe to Asia   1020, 1021

Black-throated Jay, *Garrulus lanceolatus*.
1067-2287 m. (3,500-7,500') 23 cm. (9") R.
Occasional; mostly in oak forests. Blue-gray with a black semi-crest. Moves in loose parties, often with other species. A strong flier. Feeds in trees but frequently descends to ground for fruit and insects. A fledgling in stomach of a Himalayan Pit Viper. Rare as far east as Kathmandu. Voice a gentle *kra-a-a-a* and a harsh *jay-jay-jay*. ✣ KV: a few in Nagarjung forest. ♠ Kashmir, Garhwal, Nepal; Afghanistan to Nepal   1022

Green Magpie, *Cissa chinensis*.
152-1830 m. (500-6,000') 35 cm. (14") R.
Fairly common; in dense streamside thickets of the foothills usually below 915 m. (3,000'). Bright green; an unmistakable bird. Bright rufous wings most conspicuous feature as bird dashes to cover amid green foliage. Noisy, usually with two or three others. Popular zoo bird in U.S.A. but is kept isolated because of its cannibalistic tendencies. In study skins the feathers fade from green to turquoise. Somewhat shy, keeping to leafy cover. Calls *kik-wee*, mews and whistles (AR). ♠ Garhwal, Nepal, Sikkim; Himalayas to S.E. Asia   1023

Red-billed Blue Magpie, *Cissa erythrorhyncha*.
274-1525 m. (900-5,000') 67 cm. (26½") R.
Fairly common; in mixed subtropical and temperate forests, the low altitude blue magpie. Note coral-red or orange bill. Similar in habits to the Yellow-billed bird but more frequently seen near villages and at edges of fields. Feeds on carrion as well as vegetable matter. Quickly spots a panther kill and tugs at the flesh. Very aggressive when near its nest. Robs other birds' nests and is fond of fledglings and eggs. They follow one another through trees and across valleys. A piercing call *quiv-pig-pig* and a softer, repeated *beeee--trik*, also a subdued *kluk* and a sharp *chwenk-chwenk*. ✣ KV: often in Royal Botanic Gardens, Godaveri. ♠ Garhwal, Nepal, Sikkim; Himalayas to S. China   1027

Yellow-billed Blue Magpie, *Cissa flavirostris*.
2135-3660 m. (7,000-12,000') 64 cm. (25") R.
Fairly common; in oak-rhododendron and coniferous forests. The high altitude blue magpie. Note *yellow bill*. Follow-the-leader flight across ravines; strong, heavy wingbeats, interspersed with glides. Feeds in trees and on ground, cocking up the conspicuous, long tail. Usually above 2440 m. (8,000'). Shy, keeping trees between itself and the observer. Voice a wheezy *bu-zeep-peck-peck-peck; pop-upclea; pu-pu-weer* and a high *clear-clear*. ✣ KV: on the upper rim of the Valley. (Pied Magpie, *Pica pica*, in both Kashmir and Sikkim, see p. 334.) ♠ Kashmir, Garhwal, Nepal, Sikkim; Pakistan to S. China   1025, 1026

Indian Tree Pie, *Dendrocitta vagabunda*.
152-1372 m. (500-4,500') 43 cm. (17") R.
Common; in low foothills. Tan with black head and breast; a long, graduated tail. Himalayan Tree Pie is gray (not tan). In scattered pairs or small parties. Forages on low branches, in bushes and on the ground. Omnivorous; may pick over feces. Heavy wingbeats interspersed with glides. Voice a loud *kok-aye-leep ter-ko-ko, quay-ka-ka-ka-ka-ka.* ♦ Garhwal, Nepal, Sikkim; Pakistan to S.E. Asia   1032

Black-browed Tree Pie, *Dendrocitta frontalis*.
25 cm. (10"). Survival in Nepal doubtful; not recorded since 1854. Look for a tree pie with a *black face*, white nape and a *brown lower back* (Himalayan Tree Pie has gray back). ♦ Nepal, Sikkim; Nepal to Tonkin   1035

Himalayan Tree Pie, *Dendrocitta formosae*.
610-2592 m. (2,000-8,500') 40 cm. (16") R.
Common; in scrub, thick forests and village orchards. Similar to Indian Tree Pie but *body is dark gray* (not tan) with dark wings and tail. In flight, look for white wing patch and rufous vent. Spends much time in tops of trees. Flight is jerky with floppy tail movements. Feeds in scattered parties; a dozen birds eating insects on the ground. Preys on other birds' eggs and young. Noisy, heard from quite a distance. Voice *ko-ku-la*, its Nepali name. Also a spaced *tiddly-aye-kok*. ❅ KV: in foothills around Valley. ♦ Kashmir, Garhwal, Nepal, Sikkim; Pakistan to Formosa   1037, 1038

Nutcracker, *Nucifraga caryocatactes*.
305-3660 m. (1,000-12,000') 37 cm. (14½") R.
Fairly common; in conifer stands, usually above 2745 m. (9,000'). A large, dark bird with conspicuous white patches on sides of tail. Solitary or in small, scattered flocks. Usually seen rather high in trees although it also forages on the ground. Beetles a favorite food. Moves restlessly among trees; continuously flicks tail revealing white sides. Straggler seen at 305 m. (1,000') in Dharan, E. Nepal (Oct.). Voice a harsh, slow *kra-a-a-a* which can be heard half a mile or more away, repeated at short intervals. ♦ Kashmir, Garhwal, Nepal, Sikkim; Europe to Asia   1043

Hume's Ground Pecker (Ground Chough), *Podoces humilis*.
3965-4270 m. (13,000-14,000') 16 cm. (6½") R.
Occasional; in Trans-Himalayan desert biotope. Unmistakable. A small sandy-colored bird with a strong, decurved bill; white tail feathers conspicuous in flight. A lark-like flutter; skims over the surface of the ground for quite long distances. Pecks vigorously into the earth. Usually solitary but up to four noted in one flock. Perches on stones or raised hummocks to rest. Little altitudinal movement in winter. Nests in Dolpo and Mustang Districts. Call a high-pitched *p-z-e-e-e*. ♦ Nepal, Sikkim; Tibet   1041

Red-billed Chough, *Pyrrhocorax pyrrhocorax.*
2440-5490 m. (8,000-18,000') 46 cm. (18") R.
Common; large flocks among cliffs and feeding in cultivated fields. Similar to the Yellow-billed Chough except larger with a *red bill* (not yellow) and redder legs. Young birds have yellowish bill (this bill much longer than that of next species). Very playful, cavorting in the air. A favorite game, noted near Dhaulagiri, is to descend slowly down a narrow gully, supported by a strong updraft. Once at the bottom, birds whisk up quickly and wait in turn for next descent. A bold bird, coming into villages; often found in fields. In pairs (spring) and large flocks (winter). Voice a sharp cry *kau* or *kew*, echoing through the mountains. ♣ Kashmir, Garhwal, Nepal, Sikkim; Europe, Africa, Asia 1047

Yellow-billed Chough, *Pyrrhocorax graculus.*
3660-8235 m. (12,000-27,000') 40 cm. (16") R.
Fairly common; among cliffs and near high altitude villages. A thin, black "crow" with a *yellow bill.* Immature has a blackish-yellow bill. Gregarious in winter, crowds riding air currents at great heights. Juniper fruit a favorite food in winter; flocks of over 100 birds "flowing" from one bush to the next. In Dolpo, steals sticks from village house tops for nest. Recorded high on Mount Everest, entering tents for food. Sometimes mingles with the Red-billed Chough but usually at a higher altitude. Voice a high, rolling *krrrrr*. ♣ Kashmir, Garhwal, Nepal, Sikkim; Europe, Asia 1045

House Crow, *Corvus splendens.*
120-1525 m. (400-5,000') 43 cm. (17") R.
Abundant; in both cities and open country. Black with gray neck, back and breast. Colonial roosters. Scatters over chosen areas to forage. Mischievous, may steal eyeglasses from houses and golf balls from the greens. Omnivorous. Nest, a lined cup on a platform of sticks. Parasitized by Koel Cuckoos. An injured crow draws a noisy crowd of crows which flick wings over their backs in agitation. Young make untidy pets. Voice a raucous *caw-caw*, falsetto notes and gurgles. ✱ KV: rookeries near Royal Palace and mouth of Vishnumati. (Similar Jackdaw, *C. monedula*, common in Kashmir, see p. 334.) ♣ Kashmir, Garhwal, Nepal, Sikkim; Pakistan to S.E. Asia 1049

Jungle Crow, *Corvus macrorhynchos.*
120-4880 m. (400-16,000') 43-50 cm. (17-20") R.
Common; completely black. Two *tarai* races are village and field birds. The mountain or third race is in forest or open country above the tree line. Has a somewhat wedge-shaped tail and often confused with a Raven but is smaller and has relatively smooth (not shaggy) throat feathers. Flocks ride air currents. Omnivorous. Shier than House Crow. Call a *caw, kaala* and croaks. ✱ KV: congregates around temple groves, picnickers, in rookeries. (In Kashmir look for the Rook, *C. frugilegus* and Carrion Crow, *C. corone*, see p. 334.)
♣ Kashmir, Garhwal, Nepal, Sikkim; Afghanistan to Japan 1054, 1055, 1057

Raven, *Corvus corax.*
2745-8235 m. (9,000-27,000') About 66 cm. (26") R.
Fairly common; in Trans-Himalayan parts of Nepal. A huge black "crow" with big bill and long wedge-shaped tail. The "Gorax" of the Sherpas. Quite tame around villages above 3660 m. (12,000'). Attacked food packets of expeditioners on Everest at 8235 m. (27,000'), 1971. Waddles under ground; usually single until food draws a crowd. On Annapurna I climb, Major G. F. Owens saw 20 at 6405 m. (21,000') and two at 7167 m. (23,500') Rare on southern Himalayan slopes, even at high altitudes. Call a deep, hoarse *c-r-o-o-a-a-k*.
♣ Kashmir, Nepal, Sikkim; Europe, Asia, N. America 1060

MINIVETS and ALLIES (Campephagidae). Minivets are bright-colored, long-tailed, arboreal birds. Wood-Shrikes are mostly drab brown; in active, small flocks. Cuckoo-Shrikes are gray and found in pairs.

Lesser Wood-Shrike (Indian Wood-Shrike), *Tephrodornis pondicerianus*.
152-457 m.   (500-1,500')   16 cm.   (6½")   R.

Fairly common; in open, dry forests of the *tarai*. A small edition of the female Large Wood-Shrike but with a white supercilium, and *white* in tail. In mixed flocks; sometimes with Large Wood-Shrikes. Moves slowly through low and middle parts of trees. Takes insects in trees, in the air and on the ground. Perches after an upward glide; remains immobile for a bit then looks around and starts moving again. Not shy. Call a repeated, moderately loud *chaa---chaa*, also a soft *tik*. ◆ Nepal; India to S.E. Asia   1070

Large Wood-Shrike (Nepal Wood-Shrike), *Tephrodornis gularis*.
244-1433 m.   (800-4,700')   23 cm.   (9")   R.

Fairly common; in *sal* and tropical forests of the foothills. Male has forehead to nape gray, a black mask with no pale eyebrow. Female very like Lesser Wood-Shrike but outer tail feathers brown and also lacks white eyebrow. Nests on horizontal branch fairly close to the ground. Pairs or small, noisy groups with mixed species; follow-the-leader route through the trees. Calls a mellow *thul-thul*, a *chup---chup*, a harsh *tra-a-a-a* and a loud, sharp *pew-ti-ti-te-te-tew* like a woodpecker's notes. ✳ KV: on Nagarjung, Godaveri. ◆ Nepal, Sikkim; Nepal to S.E. Asia   1067

Pied Wood-Shrike, *Hemipus picatus*.
152-1830 m.   (500-6,000')   14 cm.   (5½")   R.

Common; in thin forests and edges of glades in the foothills. Note the broad white wingbar on these confiding birds. Sits bolt upright. Small, scattered parties work leisurely through the trees, sometimes darting after insects like flycatchers. Wingbeat slow with a final glide upward into a tree. Often with tits, warblers and minivets. Call a buzzing *cu-ziz-ziz-ziz-zip*. ✳ KV: occasionally at Godaveri, Nagarjung. ◆ Garhwal, Nepal, Sikkim; India to Sumatra   1064

Large Cuckoo-Shrike, *Coracina novaehollandiae*.
244-2135 m.   (800-7,000')   28 cm.   (11")   R.

Fairly common; in tree tops in fairly open country and in groves. A large, pearly-gray bird with broad, dark eye-stripe. Primaries and tail darker. Single or flying in scattered pairs with deliberate wingbeats. Descends to the ground for insects. When perching lifts one wing, then the other, giving a slow, repeated *perl-lee*. Also calls on the wing and frequently is noticed first in flight. ✳ KV: in temple groves of Rani Bari, Gaucher. ◆ Garhwal, Nepal, Sikkim; India to Australia   1073

Dark Cuckoo-Shrike, *Coracina melaschistos*.
152-1830 m.   (500-6,000')   23 cm.   (9")   R.

Fairly common; in wooded parts of the *tarai* and foothills. Dark gray; long, graduated tail feathers tipped with *round*, white spots (The similar Plaintive Cuckoo has white *bars* on tail). Young birds paler with brown spots. Usually single, sometimes in pairs, often with other species. Partial to dense, leafy trees; eats caterpillars. Call three clear, descending notes on three-blind-mice scale. ✳ KV: begins calling on Nagarjung early in March. ◆ Kashmir, Garhwal, Nepal, Sikkim; India to S. China   1077

Black-headed Cuckoo-Shrike, *Coracina melanoptera*.
120-274 m.   (400-900')   19 cm.   (7½")   R.

Scarce; in light forests, scrub jungle, mango groves. Male gray with black head and throat; dark wings and tail edged with white. Female and young grayish-brown, may be lightly barred below. Some migratory movement at the beginning and end of rains. Collected by Biswas in May 1947, at Hetaura, 274 m. (900'). Single or in pairs, usually feeding with other species. Food: fruit and insects. Call a *whit-whit-wheet-wheet-wheet-wheet* (Henry). ◆ Nepal; S. Asia   1079

Short-billed Minivet, *Pericrocotus brevirostris.*
152-2440 m. (500-8,000') 18 cm. (7") R.

Occasional; in forests; also in trees bordering roadsides and fields. Closely resembles Scarlet Minivet but lacks "drops" on secondaries. Male nearly identical with male Long-tailed Minivet but *lacks red edging to secondaries* and black bib descends farther on breast. Female has bright yellow forehead back to level of eyes (not the pale yellowish-gray forehead of female Long-tailed species). In winter, mixed species of minivets may flock together. Undulating flight; bird calls as it goes. A high-pitched, squeaky *zeeeeeee*, of rising notes. ❉ KV: scarce, at Balaju in pines near water reservoir. ◖ Nepal, Sikkim; Nepal to W. China
1084

Long-tailed Minivet, *Pericrocotus ethologus.*
305-3812 m. (1,000-12,500') 20 cm. (8") R.

Common; in oak and pine forests, descending to foothills in winter. Male nearly identical to Short-billed Minivet but has red edging to secondaries and a less extensive black bib. Female has grayish forehead, sometimes with a yellowish wash, and pale yellowish throat (not bright yellow). Sexes often segregate in winter. The high altitude minivet; in summer as high as pines around Ringmo Lake at 3812 m. (12,500'). Usually the only minivet above 2440 m. (8,000'). Compact nest studded with lichens. Song a mellow, repeated *to-weet,* a flight note *tik-tik-tik.* Female gives a squeak on leaving nest. ❉ KV: the common species on surrounding hills. ◖ Kashmir, Garhwal, Nepal, Sikkim; Afghanistan to N.E. China
1085, 1086

Scarlet Minivet, *Pericrocotus flammeus.*
152-1830 m. (500-6,000') 23 cm. (9") R.

Common; in gardens and tropical and subtropical forests. Partial to pines. Male *orangy-red* and black; *orangy-red "drops" on outer secondaries.* Female gray and yellow; *outer secondaries with yellow "drops."* Young males orangy-yellow (illustrated head shows color). Seen in small groups in summer and up to 20-30 birds in winter. It keeps on the move, sidling along branches, hovering or dropping to the ground for insects. Song a mellow *tweet-tweet;* also *ti-tits-vie-see-sweet* as well as a sharp *chip-prit-preechy-prit.* ❉ KV: in gardens and among pines. ◖ Garhwal, Nepal, Sikkim; India to Philippines
1080

Yellow-throated Minivet, *Pericrocotus solaris.*
1342-1830 m. (4,400-6,000') 18 cm. (7") R.

Scarce; in mixed subtropical and oak forests. Male, a *dark gray head, pale yellow throat,* pale gray cheeks. Female largely pale gray with olive back and lower parts yellow. Single or in small parties; perches upright on tall trees but descends to lower branches to feed. Usually not with other species. Movements poorly known. Rather noisy; call a high-pitched, buzzy *tsee-tsee.* ❉ KV: above St. Xavier's School, Godaveri; Chapagaon Forest. ◖ Nepal, Sikkim; Nepal to S. China
1088

Rosy Minivet, *Pericrocotus roseus.*
244-1372 m. (800-4,500') 19 cm. (7½") R.

Occasional; in thin forests near streams. The only *pale pink* minivet; gray above with pale throat. In the female, yellow replaces pink on wings and tail. Pairs or small parties hunt through *tarai* forests, often with other species. Most frequent in W. Nepal. Some upward migration during spring. Hawks insects from middle or lower branches of trees. Not very shy. Call a mellow *teep-teep.* ◖ Kashmir, Garhwal, Nepal, Sikkim; Afghanistan to S. China
1089

Small Minivet, *Pericrocotus cinnamomeus.*
137-290 m. (450-950') 15 cm. (6") R.

Fairly common; in *sal* forests, orchards and trees bordering fields. Male gray above with orange breast and rump. Golden on wings and tail. Female paler, orange-yellow replaces orange in wing and on rump. Flocks from five to twenty accompany other species. Attracted to mistletoe flowers; often in acacia trees bordering sandy stream beds. Actively on the move. Call a high-pitched *twe-twe.* ◖ Garhwal, Nepal, Sikkim; Pakistan to Flores Island 1091, 1092

WAXWINGS (Bombycillidae) are trim, brown birds with jaunty crests. Their winter movements are erratic. Birds seldom reported from the Indian sub-continent. They are found in winter around fruiting trees and bushes.

Bohemian Waxwing, *Bombycilla garrulus*.
3660 m.   (12,000')   18 cm.   (7")   W.
Scarce; four birds noted in a leafless tree in snow in Helumbu, December at 3660 m. (12,000'). When wintering in Nepal they apparently eat juniper berries. A strong flight. Call a thin *zi-zi-zi-zi* when about to fly. ♣ Nepal; Europe, Asia, N. America   1062

LEAF BIRDS and ALLIES (Irenidae). In Nepal this group includes an Iora, two leaf birds and the Fairy Bluebird, all dissimilar. The Iora is something like a lethargic tit, the leaf birds are reminiscent of bulbuls and the Fairy Bluebird resembles a thrush. They have well-developed bills and fairly long wings and tails and are birds of groves or forests.

Iora, *Aegithina tiphia*.
213-1677 m.   (700-5,500')   13 cm.   (5")   R.
Common; among leafy trees. Male greenish above and bright yellow below. Wings, black and white. Female duller yellow with green and white wings. In pairs or loose parties. Ioras sometimes hang upside-down on branches in search of insects. Often in acacia and mango groves with other species. Not shy. Song a clear, slow *che-e-e-tooooor*, repeated after a couple of seconds. Also a *chee-chit-chit-chit-chit*, like a Tailor Bird. ❋ KV: nests in Gaucher Forest; here April to December. ♣ Garhwal, Nepal, Sikkim; India to Borneo   1098

Golden-fronted Leaf Bird, *Chloropsis aurifrons*.
274-2287 m.   (900-7,500')   19 cm.   (7½")   R.
Common; in forest trees with mistletoe. A bright green bird; the orange forehead and green abdomen distinguish it from the Orange-bellied Leaf Bird. Eats fruit and insects and is especially partial to fig trees. Upward movement in summer. Rarely above 915 m. (3,000'). Caged by local people. A good mimic; a great variety of notes; a frequent *chup-chaw*, a sweet *zi-zi*, a metallic *kaa-chip* and a strong *tzik* like a Streaked Spiderhunter's note. ❋ KV: sometimes visits the back side of Nagarjung. ♣ Garhwal, Nepal, Sikkim; India to Sumatra   1103

Orange-bellied Leaf Bird, *Chloropsis hardwickii*.
915-2440 m.   (3,000-8,000')   18 cm.   (7")   R.
Fairly common; among forest trees. Male a bright green with an orange belly and purplish-black throat, wings and tail. Female paler; young nearly all green. Single or in scattered pairs. Quite active, sometimes flying above trees after insects like a flycatcher. Chase one another and perch with great agitation on tree tops. Often with tits, warblers and woodpeckers. Calls a *klipper-klipper-klipper-che-aye-yar-bing*; *peer-chee-poot-pee-chip*. ❋ KV: on forest road from Godaveri to Phulchowki. ♣ Garhwal, Nepal, Sikkim; Himalayas to Malaya   1106

Fairy Bluebird, *Irena puella*.
152-762 m.   (500-2,500')   25 cm.   (10")   R.
Scarce; in heavy forest near streams. Male rich cobalt-blue above and velvety-black below. When sun reflects a blueish tinge, the Hair-crested Drongo can be mistaken for a Fairy Bluebird but confusion ends as bird shifts position. Female dull blueish-green with dark brown wings and tail. Single or in small parties. Partial to flowering trees and figs, usually at top of tree. Quite active and separate from other species. Constantly flips tail (on one count 33 times in 30 seconds). Found in *tarai* and low hills of Ilam and Morang Districts. Call a loud *pee---wit* and a rapid, melodic, rising *do-re-me-hew-hew-hew* like the sound of a Striated Laughing-Thrush. ♣ Nepal, Sikkim; India to S.E. Asia   1110

BULBULS (Pycnonotidae) are medium-sized, crested birds with strong bills, legs and fairly long tails. They are arboreal fruit and insect eaters. They perch conspicuously on hedges and trees and their affectionate stance, in paired birds, is often mentioned in oriental love poetry. Nests are placed in bushes and in forks of trees. Sexes alike.

Black-headed Yellow Bulbul, *Pycnonotus melanicterus*.
120-1525 m. (400-5,000') 19 cm. (7½") R.

Occasional; in cutover and evergreen forests of the lowlands and in tangled undergrowth bordering streams, usually below 610 m. (2,000'). The jaunty black crest and head contrasts with the olive-yellow body. In pairs or small, scattered parties. Somewhat shy, but will allow a quiet approach. Song a bubbling *seet-tre-trippy-wit* (Baker); alarm call a metallic *t-r-r-r-r*. ❋ KV: seen twice along stream in Godaveri forest. ♪ Garhwal, Nepal, Sikkim; India to S.E. Asia   1115

Red-whiskered Bulbul, *Pycnonotus jocosus*.
120-457 m. (400-1,500') 19 cm. (7½") R.

Common; in gardens, fields and scrub jungles of the lowlands. A trim bird with an erect black crest; red cheek (in adult) diagnostic. Often in company with other species of bulbuls. Actively flying about and perching on tops of small bushes with much chattering and tail flipping. Noisy around nest when threatened by predators. A favorite zoo bird. Introduced in 1960 to Florida. Song a series of mellow warbles. ♪ Nepal; India to Hong Kong   1118

White-cheeked Bulbul, *Pycnonotus leucogenys*.
274-3050 m. (900-10,000') 20 cm. (8") R.

Common; in hedgerows and cutover jungle. Dark crest cocked forward; *white* cheeks and underparts; *yellow* vent. Flocks crowd into fruiting trees. Scolds noisily, flicking tail and moving head this way and that. Fairly bold. Most common between 1220-1830 m. (4,000-6,000'). Songs: *we-did-de-dear-up; whet-what; who-lik-lik-leer; three-thirty; take-it-eber;* on the wing, *plee-plee-plee*. Alarm *wik-wik-wik-wiker*. ❋ KV: Tokha, Godaveri, Balaju and at bases of surrounding hills. ♪ Kashmir, Garhwal, Nepal, Sikkim; Arabia to Assam 1125

Striated Bulbul, *Pycnonotus striatus*.
1525-2592 m. (5,000-8,500') 23 cm. (9") R.

Occasional; in tops of leafy forest trees, often near streams. Yellow and olive-green with *heavily streaked breast*, erect crest and a *bright yellow throat*. Usually found in areas of heavy rainfall. Among leaves, it is much on the move; shy, and less talkative than other bulbuls. Species usually alone. Some altitudinal movement. Known as far west as Annapurna. When alarmed, a flock perches on exposed branches near tops of trees to scold. Calls a quick *whe-wheet; all-leet-trik; klu-bert; tree-kur*. ❋ KV: in oak-rhododendron forests of surrounding hills. ♪ Nepal, Sikkim; Nepal to S. China   1133

Red-vented Bulbul, *Pycnonotus cafer*.
120-2135 m. (400-7,000') 23 cm. (9") R.

Common; in gardens, orchards, scrub jungle. A dark bird with a semi-crest, pale rump and a white-tipped tail conspicuous in flight. Note *deep red vent*. Noisy and somewhat quarrelsome. Eats garden produce as well as insects. Flight strong and direct. Flocks together in winter. Nests in wayside hedges; pitiful cries when crow devours young. Songs, rapidly repeated *wheet-wheet-ear; pritly-pararae-oh; wheet-wheet-dheetttttt*. Alarm a repeated *whit*. ❋ KV: in city gardens; often perches on arching bamboos. ♪ Garhwal, Nepal, Sikkim; Pakistan to Java   1131

White-throated Bulbul, *Criniger flaveolus*.
120-457 m. (400-1,500') 23 cm. (9") R.

Occasional; in hilly ravines and tangled bushes along streams in the *tarai* and foothills. Light greenish-brown above; pale yellow below with a pale throat and a floppy, olive-brown crest. In small parties fairly close to the ground or among entwining vines. Rather shy, it is heard more often than seen. Its call is a sharp, whip-like and oft repeated *teek-da-teek-da-teek*.
🍂 Nepal, Sikkim; Himalayas to Bali   1140

Rufous-bellied Bulbul, *Hypsipetes virescens*.
915-2287 m. (3,000-7,500') 23 cm. (9") R.

Fairly common; in heavy forests of the foothills. Olive-brown with an unruly crest elevated when bird is alarmed. Paler and streaked below. Pale, nearly white throat, a conspicuous field mark. Works noisily in small parties through shaded ravines, eating fruit and berries. Active but rather shy. A strong, slightly dipping flight. Call a sharp, repeated *tzip*, also a *tha-sik* and *cheep-har-lee*. ❉ KV: along forest roads at Godaveri, Nagarjung, Sheopuri.
🍂 Garhwal, Nepal, Sikkim; Himalayas to S.E. Asia   1146

Gray Bulbul (Black Bulbul), *Hypsipetes madagascariensis*.
120-2592 m. (400-8,500') 24 cm. (9½") R.

Common; in tops of forest trees. Gray with black head and semi-crest, bright coral-red bill and legs. Small scattered flocks in summer; up to 80 birds together in winter. Keeps up a constant, excited chatter; quiet during nesting period. Somewhat shy; strong flight. Common around flowering rhododendrons in spring. Has a variety of loud calls, *pa-chit-chit,* a repeated *kra-a-a-a* and a quick *tut*. ❉ KV: abundant at Godaveri and in similar forests. 🍂 Kashmir, Garhwal, Nepal, Sikkim; Madagascar to Formosa   1148

Brown-eared Bulbul, *Hypsipetes flavalus*.
305-1525 m. (1,000-5,000') 20 cm. (8") R.

Fairly common; among tall trees of the foothills. A gray bulbul with white throat and bright greenish-yellow on wings. Often in groups up to twenty birds in fruiting trees. Fairly bold and quite active, movements accompanied by musical phrases. The most melodic of Nepal bulbuls. Songs include five rapidly descending notes, *do-la-te-so-la*, a mellow *dik-dik* and *dig-er-deep* and on the wing, *wheat-tent-peeper-rut*. 🍂 Garhwal, Nepal, Sikkim; Himalayas to Burma   1147

BABBLERS, LAUGHING-THRUSHES and ALLIES (Timaliidae). This is one of the largest and most fascinating families in Nepal, both in diversity of species and numbers of individuals. Generally they have short, rounded wings, long tails, strong legs and bills. Some are arboreal, while many spend much time foraging on the ground. Almost all are gregarious, rather drab-colored and secretive. They eat insects, fruit and other vegetable and animal matter. Most nests are hidden low in vegetation and in moss on trees. Amazingly vocal, they are heard more often than seen. This group often is treated as a subfamily of Muscicapidae.

Spotted Babbler, *Pellorneum ruficeps*.
120-1525 m. (400-5,000') 16 cm. (6¼") R.
Fairly common; in *tarai* and foothill ravines and forests near water. Usually hard to see but in good light note the rufous crown and streaked breast and flanks. Pairs or small, scattered flocks flick through leaves on the forest floor; also in bamboos and other low bushes. Often near other species. Rather shy. Call a *beat-you, he'll-beat-you* and a song in spring. ✲ KV: very occasionally on northern face of Nagarjung. ♠ Garhwal, Nepal, Sikkim; India to S.E. Asia 1153

Slaty-headed Scimitar Babbler, *Pomatorhinus schisticeps*.
274-1982 m. (900-6,500') 27 cm. (10¾") R.
Occasional; in evergreen and bamboo thickets. Brown above; a gray head, white eyebrow and a large, curved *yellow bill;* white below, with chestnut flanks. Shy. Often in company with other babblers and laughing-thrushes. Spends much time on the ground eating insects and vegetable matter. Rarely above 915 m. (3,000'). Has a fine, mellow whistle by which the bird may be decoyed. Pairs call in duet. Alarm call guttural, loud and prolonged.
♠ Garhwal, Nepal, Sikkim; India to Formosa 1169

Rufous-necked Scimitar Babbler, *Pomatorhinus ruficollis*.
274-2592 m. (900-8,500') 20 cm. (8") R.
Fairly common; in bracken and scrub jungle. Similar to Slaty-headed species but much smaller and white on underparts limited to throat. Usually in pairs under heavy cover near the ground thus hard to see. Occasionally ascends high in tree and flies out the side opposite observer. Varying combinations of three clear notes disclose its presence: a mellow *poo-koo-poth,* a *pra-pre-deed, pit-pit-pit, whert-whert-zzzzzz, per-per-per* and *twai-du-doot.* ✲ KV: in scrub jungle at about 1830 m. (6,000'). ♠ Nepal, Sikkim; Nepal to Formosa
1178, 1179

Rusty-cheeked Scimitar Babbler, *Pomatorhinus erythrogenys*.
305-2440 m. (1,000-8,000') 25 cm. (10") R.
Common; in secondary growth bordering fields. A rusty-brown bird with a long, curved bill and no eyebrow; dirty white below. Single and in pairs or small parties. Bounces over ground between bushes; flight short and floppy. Sits on branch jerking tail with each head movement. May stretch forward, almost tipping over, to seize a ripe fruit. A duet call: male, *turk-turk,* female replies with a high-pitched *teek.* Also a *que---irk* and an alarm, a fast rattling *wheat-jig-jig-jig-jig.* ✲ KV: frequent in scrub land around the Valley. ♠ Kashmir, Garhwal, Nepal, Sikkim; Himalayas to Thailand 1182, 1183

Slender-billed Scimitar Babbler, *Xiphirhynchus superciliaris*.
2287-3507 m. (7,500-11,500') 18 cm. (7") R.
Occasional; in bamboo thickets and rhododendron groves. Brown with a very *long, thin, decurved bill* and a narrow, white supercilium. Usually solitary or in pairs; rather shy. Clambers into rhododendron trees to pierce flowers with long bill. Bounces about on ground among bamboos. Known from as far west as Annapurna Himal. Song like the mellow ripple of a Barred Owlet; birds easily decoyed. Also a squeaky *doo------whee-whee-whee-whee,* each "whee" lower. ✲ KV: unusual, on north face of Sheopuri among bamboos. ♠ Nepal, Sikkim; Himalayas to S.E. Asia 1191

Coral-billed Scimitar Babbler, *Pomatorhinus ferruginosus*.
2745-3660 m. (9,000-12,000') 23 cm. (9") R.
Scarce; in bamboo thickets of far eastern Nepal. Told from other scimitar babblers by ferruginous throat and breast combined with a bright *coral-red bill.* Recently re-discovered (thus no illustration) in Nepal by Ted Cronin who reported a dozen sight records in the Arun Valley. ♠ Nepal, Sikkim; Nepal to Indochina 1186

Wren Babblers (Genera *Pnoepyga* and *Spelaeornis*) are tiny denizens of wet forests. Wings are small and rounded, legs stout and tails very short.

Scaly-breasted Wren Babbler, *Pnoepyga albiventer*.
610-3660 m. (2,000-12,000') 9 cm. (3½") R.

Fairly common; in deep ravines with boulders, brushwood and bamboos. Dark brown above with pale, scaly-patterned breast; one phase is tan, the other white. In the field appears identical to the Lesser Scaly-breasted Wren Babbler. Best separated by distinctive calls and summer ranges which rarely overlap. Usually above 2440 m. (8,000') in summer. Single or in separated pairs, creeping over moss and under roots. Very hard to see in deep shadows. Flicks wings constantly. Well hidden nest noted at 3660 m. (12,000'). Alarm a high-pitched, repeated *tzit*. Song a fine, strong warble: *tzee-tze-zit-tzu-stu-tzit*, rising and ending abruptly. ❊ KV: in winter on Sheopuri and Phulchowki at 2440 m. (8,000'). (Long-billed Wren Babbler, *Rimator malacoptilus* and Wedge-billed Tree Babbler, *Sphenocichla humei*, in Sikkim, see p. 336.) ☙ Garhwal, Nepal, Sikkim; Himalayas to Formosa   1197, 1198

Lesser Scaly-breasted Wren Babbler, *Pnoepyga pusilla*.
274-2592 m. (900-8,500') 8 cm. (3") R.

Fairly common; among rocks and wet debris. Appears identical to the Scaly-breasted Babbler, also with two color phases, but nests at a lower elevation. Call is diagnostic. Not shy as it pokes in and out of rotting branches, flicking its wings as it moves. Song a loud, slowly squeezed out *see------saw*, a second long with two-second intervals, repeated up to thirty times. Alarm a *tzit; tzook*. ❊ KV: nests near rim of Sheopuri. ☙ Nepal, Sikkim; Nepal to S.E. Asia   1199

Tailed Wren Babbler, *Spelaeornis caudatus*.
2135-2440 m. (7,000-8,000') 10 cm. (4") R.

Scarce; in wet forests among moss-covered rocks and roots. Similar to the two above species but has only one color phase. Differs from the other wren babblers in that underparts are distinctively two-toned: a scaly-patterned rufous breast and a pale abdomen. Partial to areas thickly covered with green, terrestrial ferns. Moves slowly on the forest floor; may hop up on a dead branch of fallen tree to view intruder. Flies readily but only short distances. Alarm call *tzit*, louder and higher-pitched than that of the other wren babblers. In Nepal, known only from Ilam District. (Spotted Wren Babbler, *Spelaeornis formosus*, see Sikkim list, p. 336.) ☙ Nepal, Sikkim; Nepal to Bhutan   1200

Stachyris and allied Babblers are small, dull-colored birds with sharp bills. Groups are often heard in dense, low vegetation, where they are hard to see.

Golden-headed Babbler, *Stachyris chrysaea*.
1830-2440 m. (6,000-8,000') 10 cm. (4") R.

Scarce; in bamboo and mixed shrubbery from Machapuchare eastwards. Look for a bright yellow bird with black streaks on head. Very active and sprightly. Hovers near golden rod and other terrestrial flowers. Often with other species. Call a constant, soft, low twittering, a *chirik-chirik* and a rising *tzu-tzu-tzu* (AR). ☙ Nepal, Sikkim; India to Burma, Malaya and Sumatra   1212

Red-headed Babbler, *Stachyris ruficeps*.
1220-2745 m. (4,000-9,000') 11 cm. (4¼") R.

Fairly common; in dense scrub jungle, forest and bamboo thickets of far eastern Nepal. An active olive-brown bird with a rufous forehead; yellowish below. In pairs in spring and in mixed hunting parties in cool weather. Keeps to low bushes but seldom on the ground except when nesting. Peers at spectators. Call a mellow whistle on one note, *we-we-we-we-we-we*. (Red-fronted Babbler, *Stachyris rufifrons*, see Sikkim list, p. 336.) ☙ Nepal, Sikkim; Nepal to Formosa   1210

Yellow-breasted Babbler, *Macronous gularis*.
152-762 m. (500-2,500') 13 cm. (5") R.

Common; in forest undergrowth at low elevations. Olive-green above; yellow throat and breast, finely streaked with black. In scattered flocks with tits and warblers foraging among trees. Bolder than most babblers; keeps on the move. Easily located by a loud, monotonous *chunk-chunk-chunk* up to fifteen times at the rate of two per second. Also an alarm *bizz----chir-chur*. ☙ Nepal, Sikkim; Nepal to S.E. Asia   1228

Black-chinned Babbler (Red-billed Babbler), *Stachyris pyrrhops*.
305-2440 m. (1,000-8,000') 13 cm. (5") R.
Fairly common; in cutover scrub and at edges of light forest. A small, light brown babbler with black on chin and in front of eye. Moves, follow-the-leader fashion, in loose parties of up to eight; often with other species. Usually confined to low shrubbery; rarely in trees. Curious, it can be coaxed to the edge of a bush with squeaks. A mellow song on one note in spring, *dur-dur-dur-dur-dur*. Alarm a *pee-a-wee* and *peer-vee-vee*. ❈ KV: around Valley below oak belt. ❧ Kashmir, Garhwal, Nepal; Himalayas
1211

Black-throated Babbler, *Stachyris nigriceps*.
610-1830 m. (2,000-6,000') 14 cm. (5½") R.
Occasional; in foothill forests and bamboo groves. Head and throat a black and white pattern, body brown. Keeps well under cover but can be seen flitting across forest trails or small ravines. Can be watched foraging on ground if observer is on opposite bank. Weak flight in follow-the-leader fashion. A spring song of quiet, mellow notes; also a loud repeated *churrrr*. ❈ KV: regularly found in ravines behind Godaveri School. ❧ Nepal, Sikkim; Nepal to S.E. Asia
1214

Rufous-bellied Babbler, *Dumetia hyperythra*.
137-274 m. (450-900') 14 cm. (5½") R.
Occasional; in scrub forests and grassy areas of the *tarai*. Slightly streaked, reddish-brown forehead; olive-brown back; paler below. Loose flocks up to ten birds follow each other through high grass and low bushes, using a high-pitched, chirping contact note *see*. Habits something like Jungle Babblers. Not shy; flies with jerky tail motion. Nest is built just off the ground. A clear, whistling song of seven notes (*Lister*). ❧ Nepal; India, Sri Lanka
1222

Yellow-eyed Babbler, *Chrysomma sinensis*.
213-305 m. (700-1,000') 16 cm. (6½") R.
Fairly common; in thickets, tall grass, bamboos and reeds near water. Yellow eye only seen at close range. Reddish-brown above, a bright eye-ring; white below and a long, graduated tail. Occurs in scattered flocks, often in bushes with other species. Partial to sugar cane fields and acacia trees. Rather shy; weak flight. Disappears into undergrowth when disturbed. A faint *tip-tip* contact note; alarm a rasping *churrrrrr* and a *whit-tit-tit-tit*. ❧ Nepal; Pakistan to S. China
1231

Red-capped Babbler, *Timalia pileata*.
120-305 m. (400-1,000') 15 cm. (6") R.
Fairly common; in open scrub jungle mixed with tall grass and damp reed beds. Look for distinctive black bill, white face and dark rufous crown. Small groups frequent *Zizyphus* bushes. Curious, it clambers up on an exposed grass stem to have a better look. Usually near water and often with Yellow-eyed Babblers. Song a *bizz-bizz-bee-chur-bee-churchur*. Contact note *tzt* and alarm call *pic-pic-pic*. ❧ Nepal, Sikkim; India to S.E. Asia
1229

Parrotbills are unique bamboo and grass-haunting species. Scattered birds follow each other through dense cover; a running conversation keeps the flock together. Most are shades of brown with pug-shaped bills.

Great Parrotbill, *Conostoma aemodium*.
2745-3660 m. (9,000-12,000') 27 cm. (10½") R.

Fairly common; in high altitude *ringal* bamboos. Pale brown with a swollen, pale orange bill and a whitish forehead. Usually in undergrowth but will mount tall maples and conifers. In company with laughing-thrushes. The most arboreal of Nepal parrotbills, searching mossy tree branches for morsels. Periodically clambers up on arched bamboos. Found as high as 3355 m. (11,000') in late January. Little altitudinal movement. Song a loud, mellow whistle *tek-tek--whrrew;* alarm a *churrrrrrr*. ♣ Garhwal, Nepal, Sikkim; India to S.W. China   1236

Brown Parrotbill, *Paradoxornis unicolor*.
2592-3050 m. (8,500-10,000') 19 cm. (7½") R.

Scarce; in bamboo stands on Machapuchàre (C. Nepal) and in E. Nepal. A small edition of the Great Parrotbill but with a dark forehead and eyebrow; small bill dull yellow. Parties steal through dense bamboos and are seldom seen. Sometimes with Great Parrotbills. Nesting behavior unknown. Female with enlarged ovaries 19 May at 2928 m. (9,600'). Call a *chirrup* and also a loud alarm *churrrr---churrrrr*. ♣ Nepal, Sikkim; Nepal to S. China   1237

Nepal Parrotbill, *Paradoxornis nipalensis*.
1982-3050 m. (6,500-10,000') 11 cm. (4¼") R.

Fairly common; among bamboos in oak forests. Orangy-brown above, pale below with white cheeks (E. Nepal race, illustrated, has rufous cheeks) and a long black eyebrow. Found in flocks up to 20 birds. Resembles the Red-headed Tit (See p. 280) with which it sometimes consorts, clinging upside-down on twigs. Nervous movements, lingering in one spot for but a moment. Keep together with a constant high twitter. ❋ KV: on northern faces of Sheopuri, Phulchowki at 2135-2745 m. (7,000-9,000'). ♣ Garhwal, Nepal, Sikkim; Garhwal to Yunnan   1240, 1241

Gould's Parrotbill, *Paradoxornis flavirostris*.
Recorded by Gould in 1836. Noted in bamboo groves and among damp reeds and grass in forests about 1525 m. (5,000'). Tan above, fulvous below with black and white face and throat. May occur in E. Nepal. (Black-browed Parrotbill, *P. atrosuperciliaris,* Red-headed Parrotbill, *P. ruficeps,* and Gray-headed Parrotbill, *P. gularis,* all in Sikkim, see pp 336, 337.) ♣ Nepal, Sikkim; Nepal to China   1251

Fulvous-fronted Parrotbill, *Paradoxornis fulvifrons*.
2592-3507 m. (8,500-11,500') 13 cm. (5") R.

Fairly common; in bamboos. Grayish-brown back; forehead and eyebrow fulvous-orange and longish tail. Below, tan; pale abdomen. Continually on the move, passing near the ground, through bamboo, viburnum and other shrubs; pauses for an instant on bamboo, sometimes hanging upside-down while examining stalk. Parties up to 30 seen several times on the Gosainkund trail at 3507 m. (11,500') in May. Nest still unknown. Call a soft, musical *pee-pee-pee*, a contact chirp and a *tik-tik-tik*. ♣ Nepal, Sikkim; Nepal to Yunnan   1238

Common Babbler, *Turdoides caudatus*.
120 m. (400') 23 cm. (9") R.

Fairly common; in extremely limited area near Nepalganj airport. Smaller and paler than Jungle Babbler. First collected by John A. Propst (1973). Gregarious, in dry, scrubby habitat. Often on ground. Contact call a *which-which-which* and a *ri-ri-ri-ri-ri*(AR) as well as squeaky alarm notes higher-pitched than that of Jungle Babbler. ♦ Nepal; Iraq to India   1254

Large Gray Babbler, *Turdoides malcolmi*.
91 m. (300') 28 cm. (11") R (?)

Scarce; noted in patch of scrub forest in central *tarai*. Resembles the Jungle Babbler, *Turdoides striatus* but rump and lateral tail feathers very pale buff (almost white). This mark best seen in flight and when bird alights. Discovered in Nepal by Jack Cox, Jr. when he found a flock of about 10 birds 4 km. (3 mi.) N, of the Indian border on the main India-Taulihawa road; 10 Aug. 1978. Call, a loud, abrasive *zaa-zaa-zaa-zaa* that carries well. ♦ Nepal; India   1258

Jungle Babbler ("Seven Sisters"), *Turdoides striatus*.
76-1220 m. (250-4,000') 25 cm. (10") R.

Common; in city gardens, fields and cutover jungles of the *tarai*. Earthy-brown; bulkier and darker than the Striated Babbler. In noisy parties up to 15, feeding much on the ground and bouncing along with tail aflop. Flies with wing flutter, then a glide. Nests in close communities. Very excitable when a cat or snake is sighted. Alarm call a harsh *twe-twe-twe-twe*, also subdued chirps. ♦ Garhwal, Nepal; Pakistan to Bangladesh   1265

Spiny Babbler, *Turdoides nipalensis*.
915-1982 m. (3,000-6,500') 24 cm. (9½") R.

Fairly common; in cutover scrub at the edge of fields. Grayish-brown with some white on face and chin; streaked and pale below. Single or in small, scattered parties. Shy, escaping into tangled thickets along streams. Nests in clumps of grass or crotches of small, leafy trees in the same vicinity year after year. Mounts branches of bushes or small pine trees to sing, bill pointed upward and tail down. A good mimic with squeaks, chuckles and chirps. Call has a descending *tee-tar--tee-tar--tee-tar--tee-tar--tee-tar*, preceded and concluded with a *preep--pip-pip-pip*. Largely silent in winter. Alarm note, a buzzing *churrrrrr*. ❋ KV: in scrub jungle surrounding the Valley. ♦ Nepal from Doti to Taplejung District.   1269

Striated Babbler, *Turdoides earlei*.
76-305 m. (250-1,000') 24 cm. (9½") R.

Common; in marshes and tall grass of the *tarai* and *duns*. A slim, streaked, brown bird with floppy wings and tail. A rufous wash especially noticeable on throat and neck. Moves follow-the-leader fashion through reeds where it roosts and nests. Noisy and restless, clambering up tall grass stems for a better view. Alarm call a harsh, chittering, repeated *prew*. ♦ Nepal; Pakistan to Burma   1256

Streaked Laughing-Thrush, *Garrulax lineatus*.
1067-3904 m. (3,500-12,800') 18 cm. (7") R.

Fairly common; along roads, edges of forests and in scrub jungle. Earthy-brown; tail with black subterminal band tipped gray. In pairs or small parties, scurrying across a path or creeping through vegetation like a rat. Mounts roadside walls, flicking tail and wings as it calls. Most common above 2440 m. (8,000'). Rather bold; usually the only laughing-thrush near houses. Nests low in bushes; eggs, sky blue. Song a squeaky *sweet-pea-pea-pea*, and alarm, a sharp, repeated *seek*. ❋ KV: uncommon; between 1830-2287 m. (6,000-7,500') on Chandragiri, Phulchowki. ♦ Kashmir, Garhwal, Nepal, Sikkim; S. Russia to Bhutan

1314, 1315

Slender-billed Babbler, *Turdoides longirostris*.
152 m. (500') 23 cm. (9") R.

Scarce; in grassland of Chitwan National Park. Bird is conspicuous reddish-brown but shy and hard to see as it clings to thick grass clumps. Has a variety of notes (AR). Presence in Nepal confirmed by T. and C. Inskipp. ♦ Nepal; Nepal to Burma   1257

Common Babbler

Large Gray Babbler

ngle Babbler

riated Babbler

Spiny Babbler

Streaked Laughing-Thrush

Slender-billed Babbler

Laughing-Thrushes average larger than babblers. Some gather in groups of thirty or more while others are in small parties. They often forage on the ground. Their alarm calls, the "laughing" one hears, carry quite a distance through their forest hideaways.

White-throated Laughing-Thrush, *Garrulax albogularis*.
762-3355 m. (2,500-11,000') 28 cm. (11") R.

Common; in evergreen forests. Olive-brown with a large, white throat; in flight the white-edged tail usually flared and easily seen. Found in loose flocks up to 50 or more. Flicks aside dead leaves with powerful strokes of its bill. A "wheezy" call when following each other through bushes and middle of trees. Fairly tame. Alarm call *tzzzzzzzzz* which brings a flock off the ground into low bushes. A warning, *koil-tzeee* and a contact note while feeding, a gentle *teer-teer*. ❉ KV: in oak and mixed forests around the Valley. ♠ Kashmir, Garhwal, Nepal, Sikkim; Himalayas to Tonkin   1274

Lesser Necklaced Laughing-Thrush, *Garrulax moniligerus*.
152-915 m. (500-3,000') 30 cm. (12") R.

Fairly common; in mixed *sal* forests and bamboo groves near fields. Earthy-brown above, white below with a black necklace *narrowing* towards the center of the breast. White-tipped tail noticeable in flight. Often with other species such as the Large Racquet-tailed Drongo. Quite wary. When disturbed, may hide high in a leafy tree. Small, scattered flocks feed on ground among dead leaves. Song a loud, mellow *tee-too-ka-kew-kew-kew;* contact note a subdued *turrrrr* and a *kaaaaaa*. ♠ Nepal (largely south of the Churia Range), Sikkim; Nepal to Thailand   1275

Large Necklaced Laughing-Thrush, *Garrulax pectoralis*.
152-1220 m. (500-4,000') 33 cm. (13") R.

Fairly common; in heavy evergreen and *sal* forests. Similar to the previous species but the prominent black necklace on white breast broadens toward center or retains same width. In C. Nepal this species is largely north of the Churia Range. In Jhapa District it exploits an unusual ecological niche—flicking bill through humus and leaf litter at base of ferns growing on tree branches. Can be traced by periodic showers of debris falling sixty feet or more from tall tree. Song a loud *what-what-who-who* and an alarm, *pukreeeeeee; pa-kak-kak-kak*. ♠ Nepal, Sikkim; Nepal to S. China   1277

Striated Laughing-Thrush, *Garrulax striatus*.
610-2745 m. (2,000-9,000') 28 cm. (11") R.

Common; in shady forest ravines near water. Rich cinnamon, narrowly streaked with white; a large, dark, floppy crest. Single or in pairs. Most arboreal of the laughing-thrushes; searches mossy branches in tall trees. When disturbed near the ground, hops up branch after branch near the middle of a tree and flies out the top. As many as six birds gather in one flowering tree *(Leucoseptrum)*. Has a wide vocabulary: a prolonged "wolf whistle" *hoo-wee---chew-chew*, also a *hooooooo-weeeeee-chew*, a gurgling *which-we-we-heet-chuuu, per-far-rigger* and a soft *poor-poor*. ❉ KV: in surrounding forests from 1525-2440 m. (5,000-8,000'). ♠ Garhwal, Nepal, Sikkim; Himalayas to N. Burma   1280, 1281

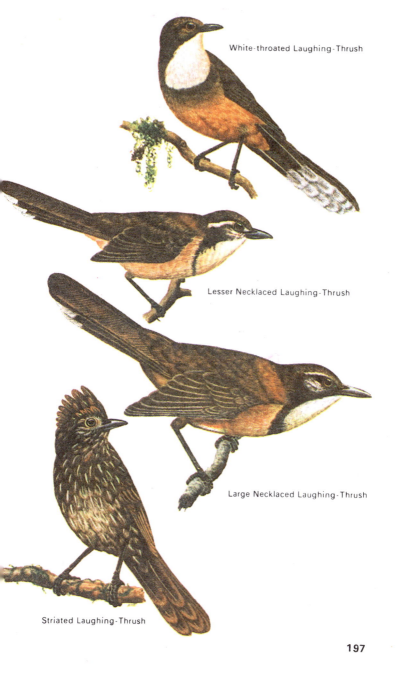

White-crested Laughing-Thrush, *Garrulax leucolophus*.
244-1525 m. (800-5,000') 33 cm. (13") R.
Common; in open scrub land and shady, evergreen forest. Brown and rufous with a full, white crest and white down to the breast; a broad, dark line through the eye. "Bird with a white turban" (Chepang saying). In compact flocks of 8 to 10 or more. Spends much time on ground but is shy and moves off when a guard gives the signal. Short, heavy flight. Sudden bursts of sound, like cheers after a score at a football match, *baba's shirt tail's out--chow-chow-chow!* ♠ Garhwal, Nepal, Sikkim; Himalayas to S.E. Asia   1283

Variegated Laughing-Thrush, *Garrulax variegatum*.
2440-3812 m. (8,000-12,500') 28 cm. (11") R.
Fairly common; in conifer, oak and bamboo forests and in bushes around fields. Grayish-brown; note broad white and tan mustachial streak and black throat. Noisy pairs or small parties. Feeds on ground or in low bushes. When disturbed, branch-hops up center of tall tree and flies out top. The only high altitude *Garrulax* in N.W. Nepal around Jumla, Mugu and Rara. Extends as far east as Jugal Himal. Keeps up a running conversation. Song a clear, mellow *tu-tiiu-we*, often repeated. A rasping alarm call. ♠ Kashmir, Garhwal, Nepal; Himalayas   1290

White-spotted Laughing-Thrush, *Garrulax ocellatus*.
2135-3660 m. (7,000-12,000') 33 cm. (13") R.
Fairly common; in mixed forests of conifers, maples, rhododendrons and bamboo. A large bird with long, white-tipped tail. The only *Garrulax* profusely spotted white. In small parties foraging over the forest floor in damp moss. Rather shy but may be approached when singing. Partial to edges of alpine meadows; often associated with Black-faced Laughing-Thrushes. Through early morning mist comes its clear, whip-like call *pooreep-whoee-weer-----whoeee-weer-poo--ee-ooo* which sets off a second bird *per--war-----pee-wee----per-roo*, repeated two or three times. Also a subdued, repeated *pie*. ♠ Garhwal, Nepal, Sikkim; Himalayas to Szechuan   1298, 1299

Rufous-chinned Laughing-Thrush, *Garrulax rufogularis*.
610-2135 m. (2,000-7,000') 28 cm. (11") R.
Occasional; in dense undergrowth of subtropical forests. Brown with black head, rufous cheeks and a *rufous-tipped tail*. Dark flecks above and below. In pairs or small parties; a weak flight; secretive. Partial to stands of *Gleichenia* ferns. Usually below 1677 m. (5,500'). Often in mixed hunting parties with babblers and laughing-thrushes. Calls a *t-r-r-r, ru-ur-ur-ur-rutek, turp-turp-turp-tur-what-tak*. A short, mellow song like a Blue-headed Rock Thrush's. ✿ KV: on wooded hills in summer; Godaveri ravines in winter. ♠ Kashmir, Garhwal, Nepal, Sikkim; Himalayas to Tonkin   1293, 1294

Gray-sided Laughing-Thrush, *Garrulax caerulatus*.
1372-2745 m. (4,500-9,000') 25 cm. (10") R.
Occasional; in oak-rhododendron forests of midland Nepal. Brown above, head dark brown, faint white patch below ear; whitish below with dusky gray flanks. Single or in small parties; short flight, and keeps much to underbrush. Inquisitive and investigates strange sounds. Quiet in winter but has a great vocabulary in spring. Nests at 2287 m. (7,500') on Sheopuri in May. Calls a hawk-like squeai, *klee-loo*, a jovial *ovik-chor-r-r*, a loud *joy-to-weep, poo-ka-ree, new-jeriko*, an alarm, *chik-chik-chik*. ✿ KV: in the surrounding oak forests. ♠ Nepal, Sikkim; Nepal to S. China   1300

Rufous-necked Laughing-Thrush, *Garrulax ruficollis*.
274 m. (900') 23 cm. (9") R.

Scarce; several sight records from bamboo forests around Tiger Tops, Chitwan (J. V. Coapman, RLF). Very dark rufous-brown, a black head and throat. In poor light, looks black. In small, noisy groups, among bushes and low shrubbery in mixed forests. Contact notes and a sharp alarm call *teek*. ♠ Nepal, Sikkim; Nepal to Burma 1303

Blue-winged Laughing-Thrush, *Garrulax squamatus*.
1220-2440 m. (4,000-8,000') 25 cm. (10") R.

Scarce; in heavy undergrowth of subtropical and oak-rhododendron forests. Black eyebrow and a dark, scalloped feather pattern; a tan-tipped tail conspicuous in short flight. Blue on wing hard to see in field. In pairs or small family groups. Young beginning to fly in mid-June. Clumsy flight; shy. Perches with head bent forward and constantly flicks and lowers tail. Song a *cur-white-to-go* and alarm a scratchy *seek*. ✿ KV: south face of Sheopuri at 2348 m. (7,700'); Thankot forest. ♠ Nepal, Sikkim; Nepal to Tonkin 1319

Plain-colored Laughing-Thrush, *Garrulax subunicolor*.
1677-3050 m. (5,500-10,000') 23 cm. (9") R.

Fairly common; in tangled thickets, especially in eastern Nepal. Similar to the Blue-winged Laughing-Thrush but has a gray head, darker breast and outer tail feathers tipped white (not tan). Also, in good light, note the golden-edged primaries. Quite bold but usually gives loud alarm on first seeing a person. Moves noisily about when feeding. Westernmost record is from Machapuchare, central Nepal. Song a four-note whistle (Smythies). Alarm a harsh *bzzz-bzzz-bzzz-bzzz* and a *trr-trr-trr*. ♠ Nepal, Sikkim; Nepal to Tonkin 1320

Red-headed Laughing-Thrush, *Garrulax erythrocephalus*.
1525-3355 m. (5,000-11,000') 25 cm. (10") R.

Common; in oak forest and at edges of fields. Dark brown with chestnut over top of head (chestnut hard to see in dim light). Eastern race has silvery ear patch. Wings flash a dull golden as bird disappears into bush. In pairs or small parties working through leaf litter; bounces over forest floor. Shy but quite vocal when disturbed. Stares momentarily at intruder with wings flicking above back. Downward movement in winter. Song a loud *to-reet* (male) and *pe---err* (female), also a repeated *to-ree-a-rear* and alarm *m-u-r-r*. ✿ KV: on rim of Valley in summer; ravines in winter. ♠ Garhwal, Nepal, Sikkim; Pakistan to Vietnam
1325, 1326

Black-faced Laughing-Thrush, *Garrulax affinis*.
1830-4270 m. (6,000-14,000') 28 cm. (11") R.

Common; in oak-rhododendron and coniferous forests. Olive-brown above, brown below. A darkish laughing-thrush with a white mustachial streak and a gray-tipped tail. In dim light, white on face most conspicuous feature. Gregarious and fairly bold. Digs in moss and under rocks. Partial to maples and rhododendrons. Large nest studded with moss, usually placed about halfway up a tree. Flops tail and wings as it calls, a loud *tew-wee-to-whee-to-whee-you-whee*. Alarm a repeated, rapid *dze*. The race *G. a. bethelae*, named for Dr. Bethel Harris Fleming. ♠ Nepal, Sikkim; Nepal to Tonkin 1322, 1323

Crimson-winged Laughing-Thrush, *Garrulax phoeniceus*. 23 cm. (9"). Not reported since 1846. Olive-brown with crimson sides of head and wings; orange-tipped tail. Look for it in E. Nepal at about 1220 m. (4,000'). ♠ Nepal, Sikkim; Nepal to Yunnan 1331

Silver-eared Mesia, *Leiothrix argentauris.*
305-1830 m.   (1,000-6,000')   18 cm.   (7")   R.
Occasional; along edges of cultivations in bamboos and trees in shaded ravines. A colorful bird with dark head and silver ear patches. Colors only seen in good light; looks brownish with pale cheeks in dim light of thick, small bush. Flocks constantly on the move through tree tops and undergrowth. Strong fliers and easily alarmed. Mixed hunting parties feed on insects and fruit. Kept as a caged bird. Has a clear song of several syllables. ♠ Garhwal, Nepal, Sikkim; Himalayas to S.E. Asia   1333

Fire-tailed Myzornis, *Myzornis pyrrhoura.*
2135-3812 m.   (7,000-12,500')   13 cm.   (5")   R.
Occasional; a bird of dense moss-covered forest and bamboo scrub. A trim green bird with deep red tail tipped black. Male is illustrated; less rufous on breast of female. Usually single and close to ground. In spring, several may gather in one rhododendron tree. Drinks sap from boles of oaks. Climbs vertically up moss-covered rocks like a Wall Creeper. Teeters on bush top when alarmed, moving this way and that like a sunbird. Has unusual bristled tongue adapted for nectar feeding. Flight swift and direct. Call a *trrrr-trrrr-trrr* preceded by a high squeak; alarm a repeated *tzip*. ♠ Nepal, Sikkim; Nepal to Burma   1338

Red-billed Leiothrix (Pekin Robin), *Leiothrix lutea.*
1220-2745 m.   (4,000-9,000')   15 cm.   (6")   R.
Fairly common; in thick scrub undergrowth of subtropical and oak forests. A beautiful species. The golden throat and breast are brightest features as birds work their way through the shrubbery. Small, compact flocks forage in dense bushes and among fallen leaves. One will peer out for an instant then scurry on. Fairly vocal even in winter; presence often first detected from bubbling contact notes. Often with Black-chinned Babbler. Introduced and flourishes in Hawaii. Song a lilting melody beginning slowly and ending quickly ❉ KV: on Valley rim in summer, sheltered ravines in winter. ♠ Kashmir(?), Garhwal, Nepal, Sikkim; Himalayas to Tonkin   1337

Nepal Cutia, *Cutia nipalensis.*
2135-2745 m.   (7,000-9,000')   18 cm.   (7")   R.
Occasional; in dense oak forests. Male rufous above with dark eye band. Look for barred flanks. Female is brown above streaked with black. In pairs and small parties, often with barwings and shrike babblers. Clings to boles of oaks for sap, feeds well out on branches among ferns, moss and lichens. May spend considerable time investigating underneath and around one branch. Nest remains undiscovered. Song a loud, repeated two-note whistle; alarm a harsh *dzzzz-dzzzz-dzzzz;* in flight a *peet-peet-peet*. ❉ KV: at 2287 m. (7,500') in surrounding oak forests. ♠ Nepal, Sikkim; Himalayas to Malaya   1339

Rufous-bellied Shrike Babbler, *Pteruthius rufiventer.*
2440 m. (8,000')   18 cm.   (7")   R.

Scarce; known from Machapuchare (C. Nepal) eastward. A lethargic bird with shiny black head, chestnut back, gray throat and dark wings and tail (male). Female less colorful than male. Rests motionlessly for periods in middle of a tree. Also works fairly close to the ground in bamboo stands. Apparently partial to very wet areas. Song is a bright *pew-pew-peee-tu,* repeated without much variation; often heard well into the day. ♣ Nepal, Sikkim; Nepal to Tonkin   1340

Red-winged Shrike Babbler, *Pteruthius flaviscapis.*
305-2745 m. (1,000-9,000')   18 cm.   (7")   R.

Fairly common; in oak and mixed forests. Male white below with black head and a broad white stripe behind eye. Bright fulvous secondaries easily seen if viewing angle is good. Female has greenish-brown inner secondaries. Often in pairs hunting through the topmost tree branches in mixed companies of drongos and barwings. Rather sluggish and shy; a weak flight. Usually first detected by white underparts and a clear, double whistle *due---deeeee.* Also a repeated *cheep.* ❀ KV: partial to oak forests of surrounding hills. ♣ Garhwal, Nepal, Sikkim; Himalayas to S.E. Asia   1341

Green Shrike Babbler, *Pteruthius xanthochloris.*
2135-3355 m. (7,000-11,000')   14 cm.   (5½")   R.

Occasional; in oak and coniferous forests. Drab olive-green with gray head, pale throat and black wing patch. Wing patch does not show in illustration. Pairs or small parties accompany leaf warblers, tits and sibias. May be overlooked amid active tits and warblers among which it appears bulky and lethargic. Runs along horizontal branches. Song of six rapid syllables on same key, *whee-tee--whee-tee--whee-tee*; resembles song of a tit. Alarm a grating, repeated *chaa.* ❀ KV: on sides of Valley about 2135 m. (7,000') and up. ♣ Garhwal, Nepal, Sikkim; Himalayas to Yunnan   1342, 1343

Chestnut-throated Shrike Babbler, *Pteruthius melanotis.*
1525-2135 m. (5,000-7,000')   11 cm.   (4¼")   R.

Occasional; in mixed forests. A strikingly patterned bird. Male has conspicuous white wing-bars and eye-ring. These combined with chestnut throat and upper breast diagnostic. Female somewhat duller with chestnut confined to throat. Scattered pairs in lower half of forest canopy often with yuhinas, tits and sunbirds. Only occasionally in bushes. Sluggish; investigates curious sounds. Song a bright *tew--wee---tew--wee---tew-wee;* also a *dz---wee---tik* and a rasping alarm note. ❀ KV: in light forests like Suriya Banayak and Godaveri. ♣ Nepal, Sikkim; Himalayas to S.E. Asia   1345

White-headed Shrike Babbler, *Gampsorhynchus rufulus.*
120 m. (400')   23 cm.   (9")   R.(?)

Scarce; seen in *sal* forest in Jhapa District (RLF) in December. Unmistakable. Brown with a striking white head and breast. More data needed for Nepal. Usually several birds together. Call a weird *kaw-ka-yawk* (Smythies). ♣ Nepal, Sikkim; Nepal to Malaya   1347

Spectacled Barwing, *Actinodura egertoni.*
1830-2257 m. (6,000-7,400') 22 cm. (8½") R.
Fairly common; in dense forests and tangled thickets of E. Nepal. Grayish-brown with floppy crest, barred wings and a long, brown, graduated tail tipped with white. Rufous around face and eyes forms a faint spectacle but this does not show well in illustration. In small parties, working among large, horizontal branches of tall trees. Found among *Gleichenia* ferns on steep hillsides. Actions sometimes resemble those of parrotbills; may move in follow-the-leader fashion. A *pi-pi-pi-pi-pi* on the wing and a chattering alarm call. ♠ Nepal, Sikkim; Nepal to Burma
1348

Hoary Barwing, *Actinodura nipalensis.*
1982-3050 m. (6,500-10,000') 19 cm. (7½") R.
Fairly common; in oak-rhododendron forests. A stumpy edition of the Spectacled Barwing but *gray* and *black* on *face* (not rufous). Also note comparatively short tail. Only very rarely are both species found in same tree; Hoary Barwing is usually at a higher elevation. Pairs or small parties peck through moss and ferns on oaks, often hanging upside-down like a tit. Nests, large balls of moss affixed to tree trunks as high as thirty feet from ground. Deliberate movements; quite noisy. Associated with cutias and sibias. Calls in spring, *whee-you---dee-dee---whee-you*, a monotonous *kreeuu* and an alarm note, *jay*. ✣ KV: frequent at 2440 m. (8,000') on Sheopuri and Phulchowki. ♠ Nepal, Sikkim; Nepal to Burma
1352, 1353

Red-tailed Minla, *Minla ignotincta.*
762-3385 m. (2,500-11,100') 14 cm. (5¼") R.
Fairly common; in oak forests as well as scrub land near fields. Colorful with black head and white eyebrow extending around the nape. Look for red in tail and the yellowish wash below. Often sits for a time hunched over with tail lowered. Not as active as tits, warblers and yuhinas with which it associates. Most common in E. Nepal between 1830-2440 m. (6,000-8,000'). Song a *twe-de-dew*, repeated about every five seconds. ✣ KV: in mixed hunting parties near top of Sheopuri. ♠ Nepal, Sikkim; Nepal to Tonkin
1357

Bar-throated Minla, *Minla strigula.*
1830-3202 m. (6,000-10,500') 16 cm. (6¼") R.
Common; among oaks and bamboos. A brightly-colored bird with a jaunty, floppy crest. Dark tail edged with yellow, conspicuous in flight. Bars on throat seen in good light. Small, noisy parties with other species, constantly on the move through trees and underbrush. Partial to flowering rhododendrons. Not shy; a weak flight. Nests among bamboos. Rarely below 2440 m. (8,000') in summer. Song three descending notes *tee-der-do* (three blind mice scale). Alarm, a harsh chatter. ✣ KV: nests on Sheopuri, Phulchowki. ♠ Garhwal, Nepal, Sikkim; Himalayas to Malaya
1358, 1359

Blue-winged Minla, *Minla cyanouroptera.*
1067-2440 m. (3,500-8,000') 15 cm. (6") R.
Fairly common; in heavy, mixed forests. A trim bird with longish, squared tail. Blue on head, wings and tail easily noted in good light. Scattered parties hunt through center of trees and bushes with babblers, flycatchers and warblers. Partial to berries in tangled thickets. Fairly strong fliers. Call a mellow *par---ree;* song a short, bright *plee-*(soft) *teer-teer.* ✣ KV: Phulchowki iron mine area in summer; Godaveri in winter. ♠ Nepal, Sikkim; Himalayas to Malaya
1362

Chestnut-headed Yuhina, *Yuhina bakeri*.
915-1525 m. (3,000-5,000') 13 cm. (5") R.
Fairly common; in a very limited range on Hans Pokhari Danda, E. Nepal. Chestnut head and crest combined with silvery cheeks are diagnostic field marks. In parties up to 20 with other species and very much on the move. Eats insects and berries in tall trees and low vegetation; a bird of wet forests. Quite vocal, a ringing, forktail-like *zee-zee* or *zeuu--zuee* as well as high-pitched alarm notes. (White-browed Yuhina, *Y. castaniceps*, in Sikkim, see p. 337.)
♦ Nepal, Sikkim; Himalayas to Yunnan   1366

Yellow-naped Yuhina, *Yuhina flavicollis*.
915-2745 m. (3,000-9,000') 13 cm. (5") R.
Common; in trees and underbrush of subtropical and oak forests. The buffy-yellow collar not very outstanding; look for dark mustachial stripe. Bird illustrated is in fluffy, cold weather position. An active, sociable species in flocks up to 40, often associated with other yuhinas, tits and leaf warblers. Not shy; responds to squeaky notes. Partial to raspberries. Nests on Sheopuri at 2287 m. (7,500') in May. Noisy chattering; sounds an alarm--*gigi*-----*zigg* at the slightest provocation. Also a *du-du-du-du*. ❈ KV: on the surrounding rim of hills.
♦ Garhwal, Nepal, Sikkim; Himalayas to Yunnan   1367, 1368

Stripe-throated Yuhina, *Yuhina gularis*.
1830-3355 m. (6,000-11,000') 14 cm. (5½") R.
Common; in oak and rhododendron forests. A fairly uniform grayish-brown. Note the chestnut-edged wing and slightly streaked throat. The crest is quite variable; when alarmed, crest is erected and curved slightly forward. Small scattered parties with other species. A bird may suddenly flutter up above bush tops after an insect. Partial to flowering rhododendrons and *Leucoseptrum* flowers. As many as 20 seen in one tree. Clings to boles of oaks, drinking sap. Nest a compact structure in a ball of moss underneath horizontal oak branch. Quite bold. Scolds with a nasal *chaaaaaaa*. ❈ KV: in surrounding oak forests. ♦ Garhwal, Nepal, Sikkim; Himalayas to Laos   1372

White-bellied Yuhina, *Yuhina zantholeuca*.
183-2287 m. (600-7,500') 11 cm. (4½") R.
Occasional; in tropical and mixed subtropical forests. Yellowish-green above, white below. The semi-crest often depressed and not very noticeable but raised and easily seen when alarmed. Single or in small parties in low branches of trees and bushes along streams. Often with tits, warblers, nuthatches and flycatchers. In flowering rhododendrons with minlas. Uncommon above 1525 m. (5,000'). Not shy but rather quiet and easily overlooked. Call a high, subdued, metallic *chit*; alarm, *cheaan*. ❈ KV: Nagarjung, Chapagaon, Suriya Banayak.
♦ Nepal, Sikkim; Himalayas to Sumatra   1375

Rufous-vented Yuhina, *Yuhina occipitalis*.
1830-3507 m. (6,000-11,500') 13 cm. (5") R.
Fairly common; in oak-rhododendron forests. Rufous-brown with grayish head and crest, chestnut band on lower part of crest; *bright chestnut vent*. The common yuhina at 3050-3355 m. (10,000-11,000') in summer. Flocks up to 15 along with babblers, tits and leaf warblers congregate around flowering *Leucoseptrum* trees. Leaps out, flycatcher fashion, after insects. Carries on a constant chittering. Song a high-pitched, strong *zee-zu-drrrrr*, *tsip-che-e-e-e-e*; alarm, *z-e-e----zit*. ❈ KV: in oak forests in winter above 2135 m. (7,000'); Kakani. ♦ Nepal, Sikkim; Nepal to Yunnan   1373

Black-chinned Yuhina, *Yuhina nigrimenta*.
610-1372 m. (2,000-4,500') 11 cm. (4½") R.
Occasional; in tangled thickets of the low foothills. Gray and black crest, blackish face. Black of chin not extensive and somewhat hard to see in field. Small parties up to a dozen birds hunt with other species among vines and ferns quite close to the ground. Shy, disappearing at a moment's notice. Active, the party is held together by a constant twittering and buzzing. Also a high *de-de-de-de*, a *zee-zoe-zeu*. Song a soft, dreamy *whee-to-whee-de-der-n-whee-yer*. ♦ Garhwal, Nepal, Sikkim; Himalayas to Laos   1374

Tit Babblers are confiding, small, active birds.

Golden-breasted Tit Babbler, *Alcippe chrysotis*.
2440-2745 m. (8,000-9,000') 11 cm. (4½") R.
Scarce; among bamboos. Grayish-green with golden-yellow breast, yellow abdomen, white ear patch, gray throat flecked with white. In groups up to 30 birds feeding low in bamboos like parrotbills. Seen in company with White-browed Tit Babblers. Recorded by Stevens from the Mai Valley, Ilam District, in spring. Also from Machapuchare, C. Nepal, in December 1973 (RLF). Alarm call a high-pitched buzz. ♣ Nepal, Sikkim; Himalayas to Tonkin   1376

Dusky-green Tit Babbler, *Alcippe cinerea*.
1037-2135 m. (3,400-7,000') 11 cm. (4½") R. (?)
Scarce; in evergreen forest. Dull green and pale below. Note eyebrow. Reported by D. Proud from Godaveri, Kathmandu Valley, otherwise no record since 1845. Confirmation of present status desirable. ♣ Nepal, Sikkim; Himalayas to Tonkin   1378

Chestnut-headed Tit Babbler, *Alcippe castaneceps*.
1525-2745 m. (5,000-9,000') 11 cm. (4½") R.
Common; in mixed subtropical and oak forests. Chestnut of head with pale streaks easily noted in field. In pairs in spring; flocks up to 30 in winter. Not very shy; actively twittering in oaks and low shrubbery. Usually in homogeneous group. Drinks sap from boles of oaks. Nests found above 2287 m. (7,500') in May in clumps of moss near ground or in low bushes. Song a weak, lisping *tz-tu-tzee----tzu--ee-tzuu*. ❊ KV: on the surrounding hills. ♣ Nepal, Sikkim; Himalayas to Yunnan   1379

White-browed Tit Babbler, *Alcippe vinipectus*.
1525-3965 m. (5,000-13,000') 13 cm. (5") R.
Common; in bushes and bamboos. Chocolate-brown above, extended white eyebrow; white below. Remains close to the ground. Bold, watches observer from ten feet without alarm. Restless, flicking tail and thrusting head forward when calling. Often the highest elevation timaliid. In Langtang Valley and around Jumla town with night temperatures--5 degrees C. Nests in late May, mostly above 2592 m. (8,500'). Song a rapid *chit-it-it-it-or-key* and *tew-tu-tu-wheeee;* alarm a *vek----vek---vek* and a faint *czzzzzz*. ❊ KV: common around rim of Valley. ♣ Garhwal, Nepal, Sikkim; Himalayas to Tonkin   1381, 1382

Abbott's Babbler, *Trichastoma abbotti*.
120-274 m. (400-900') 15 cm. (6") R.

Fairly common; in dry, tangled thickets at the edge of *sal* forests. A dumpy, earthy-brown bird, paler below with gray throat and upper breast. Usually in pairs or up to four in number; on ground or near it. Territories appear limited as birds are in the same area day after day. Known only from the eastern lowlands. Squats and flicks tail while calling. Pairs call in duet: male, *poor-ol-bear;* female, *dear-dear*. Alarm notes *duzzt-bzzp-duzzt-bzzp-duzzt*. ❦ Nepal, Sikkim; Nepal to Thailand   1167

Nepal Babbler (Quaker Babbler), *Alcippe nipalensis*.
610-2287 m. (2,000-7,500') 13 cm. (5") R.

Common; in bushes of mixed forest and cutover jungle. A pale gray and light brown bird with distinctive white eye-ring, seen even in dimly lit bushes. In small parties with other babblers, yuhinas and warblers. Restless and shy, rarely affording a clear view. May work up into small trees but soon flies down to neighboring bushes. Keeps up a constant chitter. Nests on Sheopuri; common at 2135 m. (7,000'). Call a quiet *wich-wich-wich;* and a sharp alarm *p-p-p-p-p-jet*. ❉ KV: in thickets and forests of surrounding hills. ❦ Nepal, Sikkim; Himalayas to Malaya   1392

Black-capped Sibia, *Heterophasia capistrata*.
915-3355 m. (3,000-11,000') 23 cm. (9") R.

Common; in oak-rhododendron forests. A conspicuous light rufous ("orangy") bird with black head and semi-crest. When alarmed the crest is fully raised (as illustrated), otherwise it is depressed and may be hard to see. Jerks tail up and down as it perches; quite acrobatic when searching for food. Usually well up in trees; hops up branches and works through epiphytic mosses and ferns. Its clear whistle is as much a part of oak forests as the hanging moss. Song a loud, ringing whistle (notes of scale *do,la,do,fa,la*) *te-te-tu-ra-lee; tir-tir-ta-prit-a-lee*. ❉ KV: everywhere on surrounding hills. ❦ Kashmir, Garhwal, Nepal, Sikkim; Himalayas   1396, 1397, 1398

Long-tailed Sibia, *Heterophasia picaoides*.
274 m. (900') 30 cm. (12") R. (?)

Scarce; recorded by Scully about 100 years ago from the central *tarai*. Should still occur in lowlands of E. Nepal. Grayish-brown with long, graduated tail tipped gray. (Chestnut-backed Sibia, *H. annectens*, in Sikkim, see p. 322.) ❦ Nepal, Sikkim; Nepal to S.E. Asia   1401

FLYCATCHERS (Muscicapidae) are small birds, many with varied shades of blue; others are brown, yellow, black or white. Females are generally brown; young are spotted. Some catch insects from exposed perches while others work below the tree canopy. They perch fairly erect with heads moving this way and that, flicking their tails. All have altitudinal migration, nesting at the highest levels of their ranges.

Sooty Flycatcher, *Muscicapa sibirica*.
274-3355 m. (900-11,000') 13 cm. (5") S.
Fairly common; on leafless branches among high trees at edges of glades. A dull grayish-brown bird. Look for the whitish eye-ring as well as white on throat and center of abdomen. Young streaked and mottled. Single, or in small scattered family groups. Active in late afternoon and at dusk, flying out after an insect and returning to same dead branch. Absent in highest part of its range in winter; returns in April. Common above 2440 m. (8,000') in summer. Call a high, thin squeak. ✹ KV: nests on north face of Sheopuri. (In Kashmir, look for Spotted Flycatcher, *M. striata*, see p. 335.) ♣ Kashmir, Garhwal, Nepal, Sikkim; Asia   1406

Brown Flycatcher, *Muscicapa latirostris*.
274-1372 m. (900-4,500') 14 cm. (5½") R.
Occasional; in open forest groves. Larger and paler than Sooty Flycatcher. Underparts pale brown (not dark brown). Single or in pairs on low branches at edge of fields and forests. Rather bold; hovers and flits through mango groves of the *tarai* in winter, descending to the ground for insects. Nests up to about 1220 m. (4,000') in summer. May be seen within village limits hunting from *pipal* or other fig trees. Courtship includes much "shivering" and leaping into air (April). Song a wispy *tzeu----ti--ti*. ✹ KV: nests May-June in Gaucher Forest. ♣ Kashmir, Garhwal, Nepal; Asia   1407

Rufous-tailed Flycatcher, *Muscicapa ruficauda*.
762-3355 m. (2,500-11,000') 13 cm. (5") S.
Occasional; in tops of bushes or in low branches of oaks. The only flycatcher with uniform brown underparts and a bright rufous tail. A shy bird, single or in small groups. Forages among branches of rhododendrons and the tops of fir trees in its breeding range. Is in S. India in winter. Song is a strong warble, resembling that of a small thrush; also has a single contact note. ✹ KV: passes through during May migration. ♣ Kashmir, Garhwal, Nepal; Afghanistan to India   1409

Ferruginous Flycatcher, *Muscicapa ferruginea*.
1982-3294 m. (6,500-10,800') 13 cm. (5") S.
Fairly common; in oak-chestnut forests of E. Nepal. A distinctly rufous flycatcher, brightest on flanks and rump. Also note the pale throat. Single or in pairs in ravines of damp, dense forest. Works from branches of fallen trees. Active, jerking left and right · usually near ground but occasionally on top of standing dead tree in open ravine. Alarm call a high, thin *zeeeeeee*. ✹ KV: north face of Sheopuri (Proud). ♣ Nepal, Sikkim; Himalayas to S.E. Asia   1410

Red-breasted Flycatcher, *Muscicapa parva*.
244-1830 m. (800-6,000') 13 cm. (5") W.
Fairly common; in hedges bordering fields. A small brownish flycatcher. Look for black and white tail. Wintering males may not have the orangy-tan chin and throat of the breeding season; the size of the orangy patch extremely variable, picture shows orange only moderately developed. Tail often cocked and wings drooped like an English Robin. Single or in pairs; a bit shy. Works in low canopy, descending to ground for food. Contact note a *clik--clik*. ✹ KV: winters near Indian Embassy and Rani Bari. ♣ Kashmir, Garhwal, Nepal, Sikkim; Europe, Africa, Asia   1412

Kashmir Red-breasted Flycatcher, *Muscicapa subrubra*.
213-1372 m. (700-4,500') 13 cm. (5") W.
Scarce; an open forest bird. Male resembles male Red-breasted Flycatcher but orangy-red a deeper shade and bordered by black. Orangy-red extends onto abdomen often more profusely than illustrated. Female is difficult to tell from female Red-breasted species but is slightly darker above and may have some suggestion of orangy-red on breast. Tail often cocked. Status in Nepal poorly known. Alarm call a *weet-weet-trtrtrtr*. ✹ KV: noted here in winter (D. Proud). ♣ Kashmir, Garhwal, Nepal; Pakistan, India   1413

Orange-gorgetted Flycatcher, *Muscicapa strophiata*.
915-3965 m. (3,000-13,000') 15 cm. (6") R.

Fairly common; in forests and at edge of clearings. A dark bird with a black and white tail. Also note white forehead and pale eyebrow. Orange throat patch often inconspicuous. The tail pattern catches the eye as bird darts between hanging moss of its forest haunts. Less active than most flycatchers; raises and flicks tail. Single or in pairs not far above forest floor in stands of hemlock, rhododendron or oak. May remain as high as 2135 m. (7,000') all winter. Calls a thin *zreet-creet-creet-chirt-chirt;* a *pee-tweet* at 5-8-second intervals and a weak *tick*. ❀ KV: in ravines of forests in winter. ♠ Kashmir, Garhwal, Nepal, Sikkim; Himalayas to S.E. Asia
1414

White-gorgetted Flycatcher, *Muscicapa moniliger*.
1525-2440 m. (5,000-8,000') 11 cm. (4½") R.

Scarce; in dense underbrush or in small trees in mixed forests. Grayish-brown above, paler below; a conspicuous white bib bordered with black. Spends much time near and on ground; also flies through the air after insects. Shy and keeps under cover for the most part. Call, chattering notes (Ludlow). ❀ KV: once on Sheopuri ridge; once in damp ravine at Godaveri. ♠ Nepal, Sikkim; Nepal to Sumatra
1415

Little Pied Flycatcher, *Muscicapa westermanni*.
274-2684 m. (900-8,800') 11 cm. (4¼") S.

Occasional; in tall oaks. Male the only small black and white flycatcher. Female has reddish-brown rump and tail. Resembles female Slaty Blue Flycatcher but white undertail coverts (not pale brown) contrast strongly with the rump. In pairs or small parties feeding on insects at the top of oaks. Rarely near the ground (Slaty Blue usually near ground). Actively shifts from tree to tree throughout the day. In lowland forests in winter. Behavior sometimes reminiscent of American Black-and-White Warbler. Song a weak *tz-trrrrrrrr-ti-ti-ti; tz-ti-ti-ti-ti* and a high squeaky *ti-ti-ti-ti*. ❀ KV: Godaveri-Phulchowki road at 1982 m. (6,500'). ♠ Nepal, Sikkim; Himalayas to Australia
1419

White-browed Blue Flycatcher, *Muscicapa superciliaris*.
244-3202 m. (800-10,500') 10 cm. (4") R.

Common; in mixed and oak forests. Male dark blue and white. Blue extends to sides of white breast to form a wide "vest." White eyebrow often lacking in eastern race. Female is gray-brown above (other similar female flycatchers are darker), gray below with white throat, breast and abdomen. Single or in pairs. Hovers and clings to boles of trees. Only rarely descends to the ground for insects. Nests high in holes in dead branches. Song a faint trilling *ti-ti-ti-ti;* call note a soft *tik*. ❀ KV: in oak forest above 2135 m. (7,000') in summer. ♠ Kashmir, Garhwal, Nepal, Sikkim; Himalayas to Burma
1421, 1422

Slaty Blue Flycatcher, *Muscicapa leucomelanura*.
244-3660 m. (800-12,000') 11 cm. (4¼") R.

Occasional; in dense vegetation close to the ground. Male blue-gray above and gray and white below. Look for white on basal part of blue tail. Female very similar to female Little Pied Flycatcher but undertail coverts pale brown (not white) which do not contrast as strongly with rump (also habitat dissimilar—bushes vs. trees). Secretive, acts like a chat or robin, droops wings. Single or in pairs, much on the move. Summer in rose and spirea bushes above 3050 m. (10,000'). Winter in reed beds, sugar cane fields and tall lowland grass. Spends much time on ground. Song a soft *see-see-zik; cheep-cha-cha;* alarm a lisping, repeated *zik*. ❀ KV: among bushes and scrub jungle in March. ♠ Kashmir, Garhwal, Nepal, Sikkim; Himalayas to Yunnan
1423, 1424

Rufous-breasted Blue Flycatcher, *Muscicapa hyperythra*.
274-2287 m. (900-7,500') 11 cm. (4¼") R.

Occasional; in bamboos and below dense forest crown. Male the only rufous and blue flycatcher with a *white eyebrow*. Color pattern of male resembles some male chats (see p. 250) but size, summering altitudes and behavior different. Female is brown above and dull rufous or brown below. Note short supercilium ending at eye. Often solitary and rather quiet and unobtrusive. Nests above 1525 m. (5,000'). Most common in E. Nepal in damp ravines of oak-chestnut forests. Song of four notes (Smythies). ♪ Nepal, Sikkim; India to Philippines   1417

Rusty-breasted Blue Flycatcher, *Muscicapa hodgsonii*.
274-1830 m. (900-6,000') 14 cm. (5½") R., W.

Scarce; in undergrowth of oak forests (summer) and mixed woodlands of the *tarai* (winter). The only reddish-breasted blue flycatcher with white at base of tail. Female similar to female Rufous-breasted but lacks supercilium; it is also larger and duller with dark rufous on rump and tail. Usually solitary. Works low branches, flying towards outer parts of trees in pursuit of insects. Stance fairly vertical. Returns to same territory year after year. Song rippling notes (Ludlow). ❋ KV: in cold weather, near pool at Godaveri (D. Proud). ♪ Nepal, Sikkim; Nepal to S.E. Asia   1418

Blue-throated Flycatcher, *Muscicapa rubeculoides*.
274-2135 m. (900-7,000') 15 cm. (6") R.

Fairly common; above open forest floor in groves and foothill forests. Male is blue and orangy with *a blue throat* and white abdomen. Female the only flycatcher with a rufous forehead and rump. Also note the rusty breast and white abdomen. Flits from place to place among branches a few feet from the ground. Shyly hides behind a branch when disturbed. Spotted young just out of the nest in early June. Song a musical warble of a dozen thin notes. ❋ KV: nests in Rani Bari near Indian Embassy. ♪ Kashmir, Garhwal, Nepal, Sikkim; Himalayas to S.E. Asia   1440

Large-billed Blue Flycatcher, *Muscicapa banyumas*.
2592 m. (8,500') 14 cm. (5½") S.

Scarce; in damp ravines with tangled vegetation. Male a blue and light chestnut bird. Note the orange-rufous breast and white from abdomen to vent. Male very similar to Tickell's Blue Flycatcher but with little black on face. Female very similar to Brook's Flycatcher (see page 222) but throat is fulvous (not white). Reported by Lowndes from Marsyandi River Valley in summer. ♪ Nepal, Sikkim; Nepal to Palawan   1441

Tickell's Blue Flycatcher, *Muscicapa tickelliae*.
305 m. (1,000') 15 cm. (6") R.

Occasional; in ravines bordering dry, open *sal* forests. A western and *tarai* version of the Large-billed Blue Flycatcher but with a *black face*, paler breast and white flanks (not rusty). Female, *dull blue above*, pale below. Young, streaked and spotted. Recorded from the western *tarai*. Not very shy; moves about a great deal. Pursues insects from low branches in the gathering dusk. Short song in spring (Baker); *tik,tik,tik;* alarm a *churrrrr*. ♪ Nepal; India to Celebes   1442

Pigmy Blue Flycatcher, *Muscicapella hodgsoni*.
1525-2989 m. (5,000-9,800') 10 cm. (4") R.

Scarce; in mixed and oak-rhododendron forests. Very small male dark blue above, orange below, paler on forehead and abdomen. Female rufous-brown above, golden below, paler on lower abdomen and vent. Single or in pairs both in tops of trees or among undergrowth on steep, shaded ravines. Hovers before flowers like a warbler. Will drop to the ground for insects and to drink water. Song a short, weak *tzzit-che-che-che-heeee* and also a *tzit* and *tsimp*. ❋ KV: Phulchowki in summer; Godaveri ravines in winter. ♪ Nepal, Sikkim; Nepal to S.E. Asia   1447

Sapphire-headed Flycatcher, *Muscicapa sapphira*.
152-2135 m. (500-7,000')   11 cm.   (4¼")   R.

Scarce; in vegetation and trees bordering fields and streams. Older males are blue above and orange with an incomplete blue breast band; these are rarely seen in Nepal. Young males (illustrated) have blue confined to lower back and rump (this is the color phase usually seen in Nepal), while female has an orangy throat and lacks pale eyebrow (present in similar female Rufous-breasted Blue Flycatcher). Single or in small parties low in trees. Acts much like a Gray-headed Flycatcher often pursuing insects some distance before returning to same perch. Head and tail move while looking for prey. Found in the Mai Khola Valley, E. Nepal. Contact note a *tik*. ♠ Nepal, Sikkim; Nepal to Laos   1426

Large Niltava, *Muscicapa grandis*.
1525-2745 m. (5,000-9,000')   20 cm.   (8")   R.

Fairly common; in damp oak-chestnut forests of Annapurna east to E. Nepal. Male appears nearly black in forest light. Female brown with blue neck patch (lacks pale throat of female Beautiful Niltava and rufous rump of female Small Niltava). Single or in pairs under dense forest canopies, descending to the ground for insects and berries. Fairly tame, resting in one place for long periods but flicking wings and bobbing tail. Song a soft *more-time-to-eat; right-here*. Alarm a buzzing *t-t-z-z-z* and *ha-ha-ha-ha-ha*. ❋ KV: Godaveri, rare in autumn and winter.
♠ Nepal, Sikkim; Nepal to S.E. Asia   1428

Small Niltava, *Muscicapa macgrigoriae*.
274-1982 m.   (900-6,500')   13 cm. (5")   R.

Fairly common; in shrubbery above streams. Male small edition of the Large Niltava but *abdomen* and *vent dark gray* (not black). Female olive-brown, *rufous rump* (does not show well in illustration), blue neck patch. In ones and twos, perched in shady places ready to dart after insects. Rather shy and quickly disappears. Secretive during nesting season but can be located by its distinctive call, a buzzing lisp of five notes; alarm, *t---zzz---t---zzzz*. ❋ KV: near stream above Godaveri School; Nagarjung. ♠ Garhwal, Nepal, Sikkim; Himalayas to S. China   1429

Beautiful Niltava, *Muscicapa sundara*.
274-3050 m.   (900-10,000')   16 cm.   (6¼")   R.

Common; in forests and shady ravines and hedgerows near water. Male blue above, crown brighter, bright rufous below. Female brown with chestnut tail, blue neck patch and a *pale throat* (other niltava females have dark throats). Sits quietly on a branch near a stream; quite shy. Single or in pairs, not with other species. Nests in rhododendron and oak forests above 2135 m. (7,000'). Silent most of the year but vocal when near nest. Alarm a raspy *z-i-i-i-f-cha-chuk;* contact note a thin *see*. ❋ KV: in the surrounding hills and ravines.
♠ Kashmir, Garhwal, Nepal, Sikkim; Himalayas to S.E. Asia   1432

Pale Blue Flycatcher, *Muscicapa unicolor.*
274-610 m. (900-2,000') 15 cm. (6") R.
Scarce; in dense, damp forests. Male like the Verditer Flycatcher but paler blue with *gray abdomen* (not blue); lacks black in front of eye. Female brown above with brighter brown wings and tail. Single and pairs in high trees and also near the ground. When resting, cocks tail like a Robin Dayal. Said to ascend to 1830 m. (6,000') in Sikkim, breeding commonly at 1494 m. (4,900') (Ali). It has a good song (Baker) and an alarm *tr-r-r* (Ali). ♣ Garhwal, Nepal, Sikkim; India to Indochina 1439

Verditer Flycatcher, *Muscicapa thalassina.*
152-2623 m. (500-8,600') 15 cm. (6") R.
Common; in tree tops of open forest glades. Male nearly uniform bright greenish-blue with broad black line in front of eye. Female duller. Migrates in spring in scattered flocks from India into the Nepal hills. Usually feeds at top of tree though may be seen disappearing to its nest among roots of a loose earth overhang. Fairly tame; constantly moves its head. Returns to the same place year after year. Likes to feed from telephone wires above a forest. Song a fine, cheery warble, repeated at intervals. ❀ KV: April-October on ridges around the Valley. ♣ Kashmir, Garhwal, Nepal, Sikkim; Himalayas to S.E. Asia 1445

Black-naped Flycatcher, *Monarcha azurea.*
120-1,000 m. (400-1,200') 15 cm. (6½") R.
Occasional; in sheltered ravines and thin forests of the *tarai*. Male bright blue with black nape and breast line. Female has head and neck blue (no black), back brown, pale below. Quite active and fairly bold. Single or in pairs. Sidles along branch to a different position. Less sidew as motion though, than in fantail flycatchers. Often near water. Has metallic note, softer than that of the Paradise Flycatcher. ♣ Nepal; India to Philippines 1465

Brooks Flycatcher, *Muscicapa poliogenys.*
152-457 m. (500-1,500') 15 cm. (6") R.
Fairly common; in bushes and undergrowth of relatively open *tarai* forests. A plump, pale brown bird with a grayish head, white throat, buffy-orange breast and fulvous tail. Single or in pairs in *sal* forests. Actively working in vegetation quite near the ground where it resembles a small babbler. More in the open in winter. Song a clear, mellow *do-do-chi-cha; su-rani-so-sweet.* Alarm a repeated *tik*. ♣ Nepal, Sikkim; Nepal to Burma 1436

Paradise Flycatcher, *Terpsiphone paradisi.*
274-1525 m. (900-5,000') Male to 43 cm. (17") S.
Occasional; in gardens, mango groves, edges of ravines in thin forest. An unmistakable bird. First-year male resembles rusty female; second-year male adds long rusty tail; third-year male white and black. Single or in small scattered groups. Long undulating tail spectacular in flight (often called "Ribbon Bird"). Returns to same place year after year. Nest sometimes in tall trees but more often nearer the ground. Palm squirrels seen eating the bird's eggs. Pair attacked Crested Serpent Eagle at flycatcher's nest site. Call a loud, metallic *klik.* ✤ KV: arrives in April; Chapagaon and Suriya Banayak forests. ♠ Kashmir, Garhwal, Nepal, Sikkim; Africa, Asia 1460

Yellow-bellied Fantail Flycatcher, *Rhipidura hypoxantha.*
762-3965 m. (2,500-13,000') 10 cm. (4") R.
Fairly common; in thin forests bordering paths as well as dense stands. Gray above, bright yellow below, black eye line, fanned tail tipped white. Resembles Black-faced Warbler (see p. 46) but latter has white abdomen (not yellow), and behavior not fantail-like. Turns whole body this side and that; very active. In pairs in tall trees working thoroughly before passing on. Just below the tree line in summer where it nests near the Slaty Blue species. Our highest altitude flycatcher. Call a high, repeated *tzip*, two a second at short intervals. ✤ KV: in winter; also passing through on migration. ♠ Garhwal, Nepal, Sikkim; Himalayas to S.E. Asia 1450

White-throated Fantail Flycatcher, *Rhipidura albicollis.*
120-2440 m. (400-8,000') 19 cm. (7½") R.
Fairly common; in forest ravines. A dark fantail with a white eyebrow and throat. Behavior very similar to White-breasted species. Often near babblers and other flycatchers. Swings from a vine or grass stalk with tail flared. Little altitudinal movement; found up to 2135 m. (7,000') in February. Sometimes seen working up grassy cliffs, perching momentarily on outcropping bushes. Song a short series of silvery descending quarter tone notes—a melody which seems incomplete. Alarm note a metallic, repeated *pek.* ✤ KV: in ravines of the surrounding hills. ♠ Kashmir, Garhwal, Nepal, Sikkim; Pakistan to S.E. Asia 1454, 1455

White-breasted Fantail Flycatcher, *Rhipidura aureola.*
152-274 m. (500-900') 18 cm. (7") R.
Occasional; in underbrush in ravines. Dark gray above, white forehead, eyebrow, breast and abdomen. Moves body from side to side and flares tail widely as it snaps up insects. Rather shy and retires behind vegetation when disturbed. Constantly on the move. Sometimes high in forest trees associating with other birds in a mixed flock. Song a musical series of thin ascending notes with the last one lower: *toot-toot-teet-wert.* Also a *har-up-----har-reep.* ♠ Garhwal, Nepal, Sikkim (?); Pakistan and India 1451

Gray-headed Flycatcher, *Culicicapa ceylonensis.*
152-2867 m. (500-9,400') 11 cm. (4¼") R.
Common; in wayside groves and forests. Green and yellow with a gray head, breast and semi-crest. Usually in pairs and small, scattered parties with tits and warblers; among low branches. Sits upright on looping vine, vigorously flipping tail and moving head. Rarely descends to the ground. Song a mellow whistle *whip-chur-chur-reeeeeee.* Contact note a *flik.* ✤ KV: in forests of the Valley floor. ♠ Kashmir, Garhwal, Nepal, Sikkim; Himalayas to Flores 1448

WARBLERS (Sylviidae) in Nepal are a greatly varied group of 61 species. Most are small and dull-colored. Many are near the ground in grass, bushes and reeds; others are arboreal. Some species are best identified by their songs. Most have altitudinal movement, breeding in their upper ranges. Nests are placed on the ground, in low bushes or in balls of moss on branches of trees. Sexes are alike; young resemble adults.

Slaty-bellied Ground Warbler, *Tesia cyaniventer*.
120-2440 m. (400-8,000') 10 cm. (4") R.

Occasional; in damp areas. A small species, olive-green above, gray below; strong, long legs. Solitary or in loose pairs, bobbing underneath decaying logs and wet ferns. When disturbed, bounces back and forth sideways on a low perch. Flight, short, weak. Usually above 1525 m. (5,000') in summer; in the *tarai* in winter. Almost always near water. Song a bright descending whistle *pee-tee-pit-to-to-critt* with a terminal rise. Also *ti-ti-whee-two-two-whee*. (Similar Olive Ground Warbler, *Tesia olivea*, in Sikkim, see p. 337.) ♠ Garhwal, Nepal, Sikkim; Himalayas to Java   1471

Chestnut-headed Ground Warbler, *Tesia castaneo-coronata*.
915-3965 m. (3,000-13,000') 10 cm. (4") R.

Fairly common; under brush or on rocky slopes beneath vegetation. Unmistakable; a tiny mite with a bright yellow breast and chestnut head. A pale yellow spot just behind eye stands out in dim forest light. Found among debris in damp ravines; almost stepped upon before rising in a weak, short flight. When disturbed stares at intruder, bobbing up and down. Above 2135 m. (7,000') in summer. Song a bright warble *cheep-could-you-do* and an alarm *psit*, every two seconds. ❉ KV: in Godaveri ravines 1830 m. (6,000') and up, in winter. ♠ Garhwal, Nepal, Sikkim; Himalayas to S.E. Asia   1473

Bush Warblers are dull-colored, secretive birds near ground. A loud song in spring.

Blanford's Bush Warbler, *Cettia pallidipes*.
152-1830 m. (500-6,000') 11 cm. (4¼") R.

Occasional; at edge of forest bordering grassy river courses. Very similar to Strong-footed Bush Warbler but pale below (not light brown) and pale yellowish legs (not brown). Very shy and usually single. When disturbed, flutters close to the ground to next clump of grass. In spring, its song may suddenly explode near one's feet: *rip------rip-chi-a-chuk*; also a rapid *paree-choop* and *riti-jee*. ♠ Garhwal, Nepal, Sikkim; Himalayas to S.E. Asia   1474

Strong-footed Bush Warbler, *Cettia fortipes*.
1830-2440 m. (6,000-8,000') 11 cm. (4½") R.

Occasional; in tangled vegetation around ponds and shaded ravines. Similar to Blanford's Bush Warbler but wings and tail edged with *buff* (not rufous-brown), breast buffy-brown (not pale tan). Also note dark legs. Solitary, creeping through bushes near ground. When flushed, hurries off with a weak flight. Most common in Ilam District at the edges of forest clearings between 1982-2440 m. (6,500-8,000') in spring. Song an explosive *perrrrrrr------tee-you----whee-you*, sometimes sung from a small tree. First syllable drawn out, then a pause before the succeeding couplets. ♠ Kashmir, Garhwal, Nepal, Sikkim; Himalayas to S. China   1477, 1478

Aberrant Bush Warbler, *Cettia flavolivaceus*.
915-2745 m. (3,000-9,000') 10 cm. (4") R.

Fairly common; in hedges bordering fields and scrub vegetation. Told from other bush warblers by the yellowish eyebrow and underparts buffy-*yellow*. A long, graduated tail distinguishes it from yellowish leaf warblers. Constantly on the move, keeping near the ground; flicks wings and tail. Scolds from interior of bush. Call *dik;* a drawn out *ä-r-r-r*. ❉ KV: winter, on southern slopes of surrounding hills. ♠ Garhwal, Nepal, Sikkim; Himalayas to Yunnan   1481

Hume's Bush Warbler, *Cettia acanthizoides*.
2592-3660 m. (8,500-12,000') 10 cm. (4") R.

Occasional; in *ringal* bamboo usually on northern slopes. A rather nondescript bird. Rufous tinge to wings and a pale yellow abdomen and flanks differentiate it from other bush warblers. Solitary or in pairs always associated with bamboos. Shy and keeps well out of sight. Begins calling in March; traced by unique song of five slow, ascending notes not to scale. The last is so high it is only heard at close range. These are followed by a rapid, repeated *whee--de--dew*, loudly sung. ❉ KV: in bamboo scrub, northern slopes of Sheopuri. ♠ Garhwal, Nepal, Sikkim; Himalayas to Fukien   1484

Large Bush Warbler, *Cettia major.*
120-4117 (?) m. (400-13,500') 13 cm. (5") R.

Scarce; in reed beds of *tarai* in winter. Said to prefer rhododendron and silver fir forests in summer (Ludlow). A small brown bird with top of head chestnut-brown and broad, tan eyebrow. Like a Rufous-capped Bush Warbler but larger and plumper; whole top of head chestnut, not just the forehead. Two birds bounded into a mist net among reeds near the Kosi Barrage at 120 m. (400') in March. Apparently a wide altitudinal migration with summer status uncertain. Obtained in Sikkim in September at 4117 m. (13,500') (Ali). Call unrecorded.
🌓 Garhwal, Nepal, Sikkim; Himalayas to Szechuan 1479

Rufous-capped Bush Warbler, *Cettia brunnifrons.*
213-3660 m. (700-12,000') 11 cm. (4¼") R.

Common; in tall *tarai* grass in winter; among rhododendrons and barberries in summer above 2745 m. (9,000'). Similar to Large Bush Warbler but slenderer and with chestnut restricted to *forehead*, gray (not white) throat. Often in pairs, one pursuing the other with great vigor. Frequently mounts a small bush to look around. Bold; sings in the rain. Nest a ball of grass lined with feathers placed in a bush near ground. Song a burry, rapid *chee-wheeta*, also a jolly *spit-ziggy-ziggy-zigger;* alarm, *chuck*. ✻ KV: spring passage and in winter on Nagarjung, Kakani. 🌓 Kashmir, Garhwal, Nepal, Sikkim; Himalayas to S. China 1486

Spotted Bush Warbler, *Bradypterus thoracicus.*
457 m. (1,500') 13 cm. (5") R.

Scarce; in cutover waste lands and reeds in winter; above tree line in summer. Dark brown above; gray below. *Black spots on throat and upper breast;* amount of spotting variable. Rather shy, keeping close to the ground under low vegetation and bracken where it nests. Call said to be a loud *tchik tchik* (Ali). (In Kashmir, look for Long-billed Bush Warbler, *B. major*, see p. 335.) 🌓 Kashmir, Garhwal, Nepal, Sikkim; Russia to Thailand 1490

Chinese Bush Warbler, *Bradypterus tacsanowskius.*
244 m. (800') 11 cm. (4½") W.

Scarce; in reed beds in January, Sunischari, Jhapa District. Similar to Spotted Bush Warbler but lacks profuse spotting on throat; underparts buff (not pale gray). In Nepal probably only in winter. Summers among vegetation of fir forests about 3050-3507 m. (10,000-11,500') (Ali). 🌓 Nepal; C. Asia to S.E. Asia 1492

Brown Bush Warbler, *Bradypterus luteoventris.* 13 cm. (5"). Scarce; no data since 1846. Similar to Chinese Bush Warbler but more reddish-brown above, usually no markings on throat. Also more ruddy on upper breast, flanks and vent. Long, graduated, cross-rayed tail. May occur in far eastern Nepal. 🌓 Nepal, Sikkim; Himalayas to Formosa 1493

Cisticolas, also called Fantail Warblers, fly lark-like over grain fields, calling on the wing.

Golden-headed Cisticola, *Cisticola exilis.*
244 m. (800') 11 cm. (4½") R.

Scarce; usually in scattered groups in tall grass in fields. Distinct golden head in summer (this plumage not recorded in Nepal). In winter outer tail feathers similar to Zitting Cisticola but only buff tipped (not white) and underparts darker. Nests in plains and low foothills east of Nepal. Found once in winter at edge of field in the western *tarai* (RLF). Should occur most frequently in E. Nepal; status here unclear. 🌓 Nepal; India to Australia 1497

Zitting Cisticola (Streaked Fantail Warbler), *Cisticola juncidis.*
274-1830 m. (900-6,000') 10 cm. (4") R.

Fairly common; over damp rice fields in summer. Easily told from Golden-headed Cisticola in summer by dark (not golden) head. Both species very similar in winter. White tips to outer tail feathers (not buff) and paler underneath distinguish *C. juncidis*. Pale tips to outer tail feathers do not show well in illustration. Single or in pairs, perching on clods of earth between rice paddies or on telephone wires. Occasionally flares out tail. Flutters into the air like a finch lark with roller-coaster flight and calls at the high point of each undulation. Song a high, metallic *zeek* repeated at intervals. ✻ KV: over cultivated fields from March to October. 🌓 Nepal; Europe, Africa, Asia, Australia 1498

Ashy Prinia, *Prinia socialis.*
76-305 m. (250-1,000') 13 cm. (5") R.

Fairly common; in tall reeds or bushes at edges of forest and cultivations. Look for pri with uniform dark, slaty-gray above shifting to brownish on rump and tail. Underpa strongly ochraceous, lightest on chin and cheeks. In winter, upperparts of western ta birds change from slate-gray to brownish; tail lengthens. Solitary or in pairs, on or ne ground, staying close to cover. Song a sprightly *jimmy-jimmy-jimmy* (AR). ● Nep the Indian Subcontinent to W. Burma, Sri Lanka 15

Hodgson's Prinia (Franklin's Wren Warbler), *Prinia hodgsonii.*
152-1525 m. (500-5,000') 13 cm. (5") R.

Common; among thorn bushes in open, sunny places and swamp grass. Ashy above exce for brown rump. The only prinia that is white below with gray breast band; flanks gray and t white-tipped. Gray pectoral band indistinct in many individuals, especially in winter. sociable bird, gathering in large flocks from 20-30 in winter. Moves jerkily through lo vegetation in scattered parties. Momentarily mounts a tall grass stalk to sing or to s better. ● Kashmir, Garhwal, Nepal, Sikkim; Himalayas to S.E. Asia 15

Gray-capped Prinia (Hodgson's Wren Warbler), *Prinia cinereocapilla.*
152-1067 m. (500-3,500') 13 cm. (5") R.

Fairly common; at edges of open, sunny forest glades. Bright fulvous above with ashy he distinctly different from fulvous back. Buff eyebrow and black eye line; pale fulvous belo In small flocks often with other long-tailed warblers. Keeps near ground; partial to *Zizyph* bushes and tall grass. Parties move about in dimly lit shrubbery on forest floor, emergi on tall stalks to view intruders. Song a squeezed out *cheeeeeeeesum-zip-zip-zip*: also rapid *tzit* repeated 10-15 times. ● Nepal, Sikkim; India 15

Rufescent Prinia (Beavan's Wren Warbler), *Prinia rufescens.*
Low altitudes 10 cm. (4") R?

No confirmed sightings since Hodgson's days (1846). Previously included in curre Nepal list through misidentification. May occur in the eastern *tarai*. Look for a brownis prinia with distinctly rufous rump, tail and wings and a gray cap (summer). Summe plumage resembles Gray-capped Prinia but latter has buffy lores and eyebrow (vs whi lores and no eyebrow). Brown winter plumage retains rufous-washed rump, tail an wings thus distinguishing from other brown prinias. Should occur in patches of grass c bushes near forest; usually single or pairs. In S.E. Asia sings conspicuously, in spring, fron high grass perch. ● Nepal; Nepal to S.W. China and S.E. Asia 150

Jungle Prinia, *Prinia sylvatica.*
152-244 m. (500-800') 15 cm. (6") R.

Occasional; in tall grass and bushes in stony, uncultivated areas. Dull earthy-brown abov and buff below. Very similar to Plain Prinia; look for buffy eyebrow while lores appea dark buffy or brownish (*vs* Plain Prinia's nearly white lores and thin eyebrow). Sma parties up to five birds frequent tangled vegetation. Appears for a moment, then disappear to forage close to the ground among ginger, bamboo and other plants. Most common i the W. *tarai*. Song a repeated *pit-pritty* (Ali). ● Garhwal, Nepal; S. Asia 151

Plain Prinia, *Prinia subflava.*
152-305 m. (500-1,000') 15 cm. (6") R.

Occasional; in reed beds at edges of fields. Uniformly light brown above; the wings an tail may have a ruddy tinge. Face and underparts creamy and tail tipped white (seen from i front). Very like Jungle Prinia but appears "thinner" and with whitish "fore-face" (i.e nearly entire loral region white or pale buff and this color extends backwards into a thi: but noticeable eyebrow). In small groups among clumps of dry grass at edge of *sal* forest and cultivated fields. Noisy but fairly secretive. In flight, snaps wings as do other prinias Voice a *weet--weet--weet* (Baker). ● Nepal, Sikkim; Africa, Asia 1510, 151,

Yellow-bellied Prinia, *Prinia flaviventris.*
120-274 m. (400-900') 14 cm. (5¼") R.

Occasional; among clumps of elephant grass in sandy river courses. Long tail combined with bright yellow abdomen diagnostic. White breast and throat also easily seen. Single or in small parties. A feeble top-heavy flight accentuated by the long, floppy tail. Occasionally pops up out of a sea of grass, bracing itself on a curved stem to look around. Builds grass nest near ground in April (Karnali). Has a gallant little song; also a fast, raspy buzz *reeeeeeeeee* and a *tzetze-tze*. 🌢 Nepal; Pakistan to Sumatra
1525

Fulvous-streaked Prinia, *Prinia gracilis.*
152-1067 m. (500-3,500') 13 cm. (5") R.

Occasional; in grass along sandy stream beds and rice fields. The only pale prinia streaked above. In small parties, fluttering through tall grass and sugarcane fields. When perched may cock tail so that tip is above head level. Most frequent in E. Nepal *tarai* but also numerous, along Karnali River in grass bordering acacia trees. Call a *kit-kit-kit* (AR). 🌢 Nepal; Egypt to India
1508, 1590

Brown Hill Prinia, *Prinia criniger.*
274-2745 m. (900-9,000') 18 cm. (7") R.

Common; in grass and wayside bushes on steep, rocky hillsides. Streaked brown above and often with black streaks on breast (young lack streaks on breast); a very long tail. Quite tame, usually solitary. Perches on tall grass stalk, the top of a bush or low branches of small tree. Throws back head and holds tail at a low angle when singing. Voice sounds like a cork being turned in a bottle, a repeated *tzirt-tz-it-tzit*. ✻ KV: above Balaju, on Trisuli road and slopes S. of Chapagaon. 🌢 Kashmir, Garhwal, Nepal, Sikkim; Pakistan to Formosa 1527

Black-throated Hill Prinia, *Prinia atrogularis.*
1525-2440 m. (5,000-8,000) 16 cm. (6¼") R.

Occasional; on fern-covered hillsides and in forest clearings. Gray-brown with *black* upper breast, chin and throat. Less black on winter birds. Young resemble Brown Hill Prinia except for a faint indication of black on breast and a rather distinct, pale eyebrow. Solitary or in pairs; somewhat shy. Rather strong flight for a warbler. Recorded as far west as the Mewa Khola, Taplejung District. Song a raspy *tze*, two a second up to thirty or more times.
🌢 Nepal, Sikkim; Nepal to Sumatra
1529

Orphean Warbler, *Sylvia hortensis.*
152-274 m. (500-900') 15 cm. (6") M (?)

Scarce; in bushes and trees edging clearings in the *tarai* and *bhabar*. A large, distinctive warbler with top half of head black, contrasting with white throat (male). Remaining upperparts dark gray, underparts whitish. Female similar to male but has top half of head gray, decidedly darkest on cheeks. Female resembles female Lesser Whitethroat, *Sylvia curruca* (see p. 237) but much larger, chunkier and the bill strikingly longer and heavier. Primarily arboreal; movements rather sluggish and deliberate for a warbler. Single. A possible sight record by Richard C. Gregory-Smith at the edge of the Dharan Camp (E. Nepal) on 13 June 1975. Confirmed for Nepal by RLF when a male was observed for several minutes in low trees of the Shuklaphanta Wildlife Reserve (W. *tarai*). Probably occurs as an irregular winter visitor or passage migrant, especially in the western *tarai*. Alarm call a hard, rattling *trrr* (AR). 🌢 Kashmir, Nepal; S. Europe, Africa to India
1565

Large Grass Warbler, *Graminicola bengalensis.*
274 m. (900') 18 cm. (7") R.
Scarce; in tall grass bordering water. Dark above with a rufous rump. The undertail pattern an important field mark and quickly separates this species from other grass-haunting babblers or warblers. In small parties, keeping well under cover; feeds between roots and clumps of grass. Netted in Rapti Dun. Contact note a *mew* like an American Catbird. Said to be noisy in monsoon breeding season, singing from tops of reeds (Baker). ♣ Nepal; Nepal to Hainan Island 1534

Tailor Bird, *Orthotomus sutorius.*
120-1830 m. (400-6,000') 13 cm. (5") R.
Common; in city gardens, hedgerows and temple groves. A pale greenish bird with pale rusty forehead; whitish below. Long wren-like tail often cocked. In pairs or small scattered parties, constantly on the move. Nests stitched with spiderwebs into large leaves such as canna lilies. Two or three broods a year. Near the ground and easy prey for predators. Also works high up into figs and other trees. Call a loud, rapid *tik* about four per second up to 700 times. Also a repeated double note. (Golden-headed Tailor Bird, *O. cucullatus*, in Sikkim, see p. 337.) ♣ Garhwal, Nepal, Sikkim; Pakistan to Java 1536

Streaked Grasshopper Warbler, *Locustella lanceolata.*
213 m. (700') 13 cm. (5") W.
Scarce; a winter visitor found in February, in tall grass of Morang District (Bailey, 1938) and thickets near the Babai River of Bardia District (RLF, April 1972). An olive-brown warbler, heavily streaked above and finely streaked on throat and breast which are lightly washed with yellow in young birds (illustrated). Tail tipped pale brown (not white). Usually solitary in middle of dense thorn bushes close to ground; tail often cocked. When disturbed it shyly moves out of one bush and flies low over the ground to the next thicket. Contact note *chik*. (Grasshopper Warbler, *Locustella naevia*, see Sikkim list, p. 337.) ♣ Nepal; Europe, Asia 1544

Pallas's Grasshopper Warbler, *Locustella certhiola.*
120 m. (400') 13 cm. (5") W.
Scarce; a winter visitor found by Bailey near the Kosi River, eastern *tarai* in February 1937. This species told from Streaked Grasshopper Warbler by lack of streaking on underparts, rufous rump and also by *white* tips to tail feathers. Note the long undertail coverts which characterize grasshopper warblers. Said to be shy (Baker). More information on Nepal status needed. ♣ Nepal; Asia 1543

Striated Marsh Warbler, *Megalurus palustris.*
120-305 m. (400-1,000') 25 cm. (10") R.
Occasional; in grass along river courses of the *tarai* and *duns*. A very large warbler resembling some babblers but note the heavily streaked, bright fulvous upperparts and the distinct pale eyebrow. Solitary or in pairs near water under heavy cover. Partial to tamarisk shrubs; also found in scrub near cultivation. Perches on reeds; flicks wings and tail. In spring flies into air something like a lark, but after an ascent of 30 or more feet, quickly dives back to reeds. Song is a bright, strong *pit-pit-pity--peeu* with variations, most often heard at dawn. ♣ Nepal; India to Philippines 1548

Thick-billed Warbler, *Phragamaticola aedon*.
152-1342 m.   (500-4,400')   19 cm.   (7½")   W.

Occasional; in swamp grass and willows along wooded streams. A large warbler that looks much like a small babbler. Brown with no distinguishing marks. Pale rusty or fulvous wash over the body is perhaps the best field character. Bill shorter than Great Reed Warbler's but useful as a clue only for the experienced observer. Usually solitary, fairly close to the ground. Continually flicks tail and wings. Sometimes associated with the Dusky Leaf Warbler. Alarm call a loud *tschok* (Baker) but usually silent in winter. ❊ KV: along the Kalimati Stream and Vishnumati River in winter. ✦ Nepal, Sikkim; Asia   1549

Oriental Reed Warbler, *Acrocephalus orientalis*.
91 m.   (300')   20 cm.   (8")   W.

Scarce; in wet rice fields. Very similar to Clamorous Reed Warbler but slightly darker above with flanks warm buff (vs. pale buff) and faint dark-brown streaks (vs. no streaks) on lower throat and upper breast (often hard to see but distinctive if noted). Collected near Biratnagar, E. *tarai* on 9 Mar. (RLF). Probably a regular winter visitor in reeds and standing rice in southeastern Nepal. Alarm call a loud *chuck*. ✦ Nepal; eastern India, China, S. E. Asia   1554

Blyth's Reed Warbler, *Acrocephalus dumetorum*.
274-2745 m.   (900-9,000')   14 cm.   (5½")   M.

Fairly common; in hedges and gardens during migration. A small nondescript edition of the Great Reed Warbler but with only a *faint* eyebrow and dusky sides and breast. Slightly chunkier than paddyfield warblers, and slightly darker underneath but best distinguished by virtual lack of eyebrow (vs. fairly distinct eyebrows in the Paddyfields). Difficult to separate in field. Solitary and shy. Call a repeated *tik*. ❊ KV: a few along the Bagmati and Vishnumati Rivers in willows. ✦ Kashmir, Garhwal, Nepal; Europe, Asia   1556

Paddyfield Warbler, *Acrocephalus agricola*.
152 m.   (500')   13 cm.   (5")   W.

Occasional; in clumps of bamboo or reed beds bordering fields. Another nondescript, rufous-brown species with buff eyebrow and pale throat. Very similar and most difficult to distinguish in the field from the Blunt-winged Paddyfield Warbler. The Paddyfield, however, is somewhat browner above, especially noticeable on top of head, nape and upper back. Solitary, more often in open areas than other reed warblers. Not shy. Partial to clumps of bamboo. Alarm note *chik-chik*. ✦ Kashmir, Nepal; Asia   1558

Blunt-winged Paddyfield Warbler, *Acrocephalus concinens*.
213-1220 m.   (700-4,000')   13 cm.   (5")   W., M.

Occasional; among willows along river banks and in marsh reeds, tall grass and small shrubs. Very similar to Paddyfield Warbler but upperparts noticeably paler, especially on head and nape. In hand, 1st primary (ascending) much larger than 1st primary of Paddyfield (see wing diagrams). Resembles some leaf warblers but does not flick wings. ❊ KV: along the Vishnumati River in March. November. ✦ Kashmir, Nepal; Asia   1559 (?)

Lesser Whitethroat, *Sylvia curruca*.
854-1525 m.   (2,800-5,000')   13 cm.   (5")   W.

Scarce; probably only a migrant through Nepal. Paynter found it in Pokhara in October and H.S. Nepali in Kathmandu Valley in September. A distinctive warbler; dark gray above and white below with very dark cheeks. ❊ KV: one bird in scrub jungle in December (RLF).
✦ Kashmir, Nepal; Europe, Africa, Asia   1567

Booted Tree Warbler, *Hippolais caligata*.
No records since Hodgson. Similar to Paddyfield Warbler but paler and end of tail square, not rounded. Partial to acacia groves.
✦ Kashmir, Nepal, Sikkim; Africa, Asia   1562

Clamorous Reed Warbler (Great Reed Warbler), *Acrocephallus stentoreus*.
152-1830 m.   (500-6,000')   20 cm.   (8")   W.

Occasional; in reedy stream beds, marsh grass and among ferns bordering ricefields. Very similar to Oriental Reed Warbler but paler on back, lacking faint streaks on lower throat and upper breast. Also similar to Thick-billed Warbler but bill noticeably longer. Associates with buntings and leaf warblers, eating vegetation, insects, slugs. Usually stays out of sight near ground or water level. Song a loud, harsh *chuk-chuk-chew-you-re-chuk-chuk* (Waller). Also a loud alarm call and a repeated *chek*. ❊ KV: in hedges around Rani Bari in spring and fall. ✦ Kashmir, Nepal; Egypt to China   1550

Leaf Warblers (Willow Warblers) are small greenish-brown birds that are gregarious and much on the move. They flick wings restlessly and change positions frequently. They nest in the highest parts of their ranges. At first, difficult to separate species in field. One should look for head pattern, wingbars and tail color. Identification is a process of elimination.

Tytler's Leaf Warbler, *Phylloscopus tytleri.*
2135 m.   (7,000')   13 cm.   (5")   W.

Scarce; in oak-rhododendron forests. *No wingbar.* Olive brown above, grayish below; pale yellow eyebrow. Common in N.W. Himalayas but in Nepal only known from Dandeldhura District above Rupal. Noted in mixed flocks of warblers, nuthatches and tits in April. Nests near tree line 3507 m. (11,500') (Ali). Song *let's--kiss--him* (Osmaston). ♠ Kashmir, Garhwal, Nepal; S. Asia   1578

Brown Leaf Warbler (Chiffchaff), *Phylloscopus collybita.*
152-1372 m.   (500-4,500')   10 cm.   (4")   W.

Fairly common; among streamside willows, hedges and light forest on southern slopes of hills. *No wingbar.* A brown leaf warbler with a pale buff eyebrow and slightly *yellow at bend of wing.* Paler and with a shorter tail than Dusky Leaf Warbler which is often in the same habitat. Single, in vegetation with mixed hunting parties of other warblers and tits. Sometimes attracted to flowering rhododendrons in spring; feeds on insects. Quite agile as it moves through foliage. Call a sharp *tzit.* ❅ KV: among willows near streams in winter. ♠ Kashmir, Garhwal, Nepal, Sikkim; Europe, Africa, Asia   1575

Tickell's Leaf Warbler, *Phylloscopus affinis.*
152-4880 m.   (500-16,000')   11 cm.   (4½")   R.

Fairly common; in acacia trees of the *tarai* in winter and among willows and high altitude scrub above the tree line in summer. *No wingbar.* Although intensity of yellow varies, the fairly clear yellow underparts a good field mark. Also note the broad, yellow eyebrow. Eastern race, *P. a. subaffinis*, is paler and slightly larger. Single or in pairs usually near ground. Partial to *Caragana* bushes 3355 m. (11,000') upward. Very numerous in N. Dolpo District in summer. Scolds and chases shrikes near nest. Spends much time singing from a bush top. Song a loud chattering *chip----di-di-di-di, chip----zik-zik-zik* and *chip----twee-twee-twee-twee* repeated five or six times. Also a *tzip* in winter. ❅ KV: on passage, April, November; a few remain all winter. ♠ Kashmir, Garhwal, Nepal, Sikkim; Himalayas, Tibet, Yunnan
1579, 1580

Olivaceous Leaf Warbler, *Phylloscopus griseolus.*
152 m.   (500')   11 cm.   (4½")   W.

Occasional; among bushes and low branches of trees in thin forest of the *tarai.* Common in Bardia District in April. *No wingbar.* A darkish bird with a prominent yellow eyebrow. Similar to Smoky Leaf Warbler but not as dark and with buffy-yellow underparts (not greenish). Dusky Leaf Warbler has no yellow. Solitary or in small, scattered flocks, thoroughly examining leaves and branches before moving on. Partial to acacia trees and often with other leaf warblers. Call a *pick* (AR). ♠ Kashmir, Nepal; Asia   1581

Smoky Leaf Warbler, *Phylloscopus fuliginventer.*
152-4575 m.   (500-15,000')   11 cm.   (4½")   W., S. (?)

Scarce; along water's edge in tall grass of lowlands. *No wingbar.* The darkest Nepal leaf warbler, sooty-brown above, greenish below with center of breast yellowish. Could be confused with Olivaceous Leaf Warbler but is darker. Also note dull green overall (not bright yellow). Common in Bengal in winter. Noted in W. *tarai* in winter (RLF). May occur in N. Nepal in summer at 3660-4575 m. (12,000-15,000'). Clambers around rocks. Call a repeated *tsli* and a drawn-out *t--s--u--s--i* (Desfayes). ♠ Nepal, Sikkim; Nepal to Bhutan, Tibet   1582

Dusky Leaf Warbler, *Phylloscopus fuscatus.*
120-1372 m.   (400-4,500')   11 cm.   (4½")   W.

Occasional; in cultivated fields along stream banks and wooded groves. *No wingbar.* A brown leaf warbler, darkish above with prominent buffy eyebrow. Very similar to Brown Leaf Warbler but overall darker and a comparatively longer tail. Also resembles Blyth's Reed Warbler (see p. 236) but smaller, darker and shorter tail. Solitary or in small, scattered groups. Winters in reeds of the *tarai* with buntings, wagtails and Bluethroats. Feeds close to the ground but occasionally fairly high in willows. Alarm call a *turk;* song a rapid *chichichichichitzzz.* ❅ KV: winters along streams in low vegetation and willows. ♠ Nepal, Sikkim; Asia   1584, 1586

Gray-faced Leaf Warbler, *Phylloscopus maculipennis.*
1525-3202 m. (5,000-10,500') 10 cm. (4") R.

Occasional; in forest glades often near water. The only leaf warbler with gray face and breast. One and a half wingbars; yellow below, yellow rump and white in tail. In middle and tops of trees often in company with other small birds. Very restless; fluttering shows white in tail. Usually above 2440 m. (8,000') in summer. Calls a great deal, a high-pitched *tzip.* The usual song *ti-ti--whee-tew;* also *whee-teew--whee-teew.* ❀ KV: winter and spring at Godaveri and Sheopuri ridge. ♠ Kashmir, Garhwal, Nepal, Sikkim; Himalayas to Annam
1598, 1599

Dull Green Leaf Warbler, *Phylloscopus trochiloides (nitidus).*
274-4270 m. (900-14,000') 11 cm. (4½") R.

Fairly common; in undergrowth as well as tall forest trees. Very similar to Large-billed Leaf Warbler, also showing one short wingbar. Habitat differences and call distinct and diagnostic. Only with practice does size and weaker bill become evident. Green of western race *(P. t. nitidus)* brighter than common form. Single or in scattered, mixed parties. Rather tame and can be observed for long periods near the tree line in summer. Among Blue Pines and other conifers in Dolpo and Khumbu. Song a loud, double note, the second often higher-pitched, *which-chi, plee-tzu, ziit-wee* and *zeet-tu.* Also a *tik.* ❀ KV: a spring and fall migrant. ♠ Kashmir, Garhwal, Nepal, Sikkim; Europe, Asia
1602, 1604, 1605

Large-billed Leaf Warbler, *Phylloscopus magnirostris.*
274-3507 m. (900-11,500') 13 cm. (5") R.

Occasional; in thick vegetation along mountain streams. Dark olive-green above, 1½ wingbars, pale, broad eyebrow, grayish-yellow below. Often shows only one short wingbar. Very similar to Dull Green Leaf Warbler but with practice the larger size and heavier bill are helpful pointers. Distinct habitat differences in summer also useful identification aid. Solitary and almost always near running water. Sometimes clings to riverside cliffs and often in tangled thickets. Moves slower than most other leaf warblers, staying for some time on one perch. A loud song heard above gurgling water, five syllables in three descending notes *tri--ti-ti---ri-ri;* also a double *tsip-tsee.* The song is often the first indication of the bird's presence. ❀ KV: in surrounding hills in April. ♠ Kashmir, Garhwal, Nepal, Sikkim; Asia
1601

Plain Leaf Warbler, *Phylloscopus inornatus.*
274-3965 m. (900-13,000') 10 cm. (4") R.

Common; in gardens, groves, bushes in winter; nests in pine forests in summer. One of the smallest leaf warblers. Somewhat pale above with 1½ white wingbars and pale eyebrow. Rather nondescript with few identifying marks. Can be told from other leaf warblers by process of elimination, i.e., no yellow rump, no coronal bands, no white in tail. Among busy, mixed hunting parties. Sings from top of Blue Pines around Ringmo Lake at 3660 m. (12,000'). Call in winter a loud, slow *chi--leeep.* Song in summer a high-pitched, weak *zilip-zilip* often with an added descending buzz *zeeeeeeeeuuuuuuu.* ❀ KV: in winter among shrubs and trees. ♠ Kashmir, Garhwal, Nepal, Sikkim; Europe, Asia
1590, 1592

Orange-barred Leaf Warbler, *Phylloscopus pulcher*.
915-3965 m. (3,000-13,000') 10 cm. (4") R.

Common; in oak-rhododendron forests. Two orangy wingbars (first may be hard to see but second prominent); orange tinge noted in good light, otherwise appears yellowish. Also check white in tail (best seen from beneath when tail is flared) and pale rump. Flits busily among trees, remaining until late October as high as 3965 m. (13,000') in Langtang. Often with other species in mixed hunting parties in upper branches of trees. Around flowering rhododendrons, forehead in spring may turn pale from accumulated pollen. Song a squeezed-out *tzzzzzzzzzzzzt* and *tzi*. ❊ KV: winters in oak forests; a few nest here.
🌢 Kashmir, Garhwal, Nepal, Sikkim; Himalayas to Szechuan 1587, 1589

Yellow-rumped Leaf Warbler, *Phylloscopus proregulus*.
274-3812 m. (900-12,500') 9 cm. (3½") R.

Common; among barberry bushes and shrubs as well as lofty trees. A small-sized leaf warbler with distinct wingbars. Look for a bright yellow rump and yellow eyebrow. An excellent identification clue — hovers at end of branches. Partial to alders; several work in a tree together. Nests in conifer forests. Call a *tsip-tsip;* the second syllable two notes higher than the first. ❊ KV: among oaks and mixed forest trees. (Brook's Leaf Warbler, *P. subviridis*, in Kashmir, see p. 335.) 🌢 Kashmir, Garhwal, Nepal, Sikkim; Asia 1594, 1595

Crowned Leaf Warbler, *Phylloscopus reguloides*.
274-3507 m. (900-11,500') 11 cm. (4¼") R.

Common; in upper half of tall trees. Green above with diffused, pale yellow line through crown, edged with darker lines. Prominent yellow eyebrow and wingbars. Pale below, sometimes with an uneven yellowish wash. Very similar to Large Crowned Leaf Warbler but smaller and bill noticeably weaker. Pairs or small parties with other birds. Partial to maples and flowering rhododendrons. A few nest on Sheopuri above 2440 m. (8,000'). Song a bright, varied warble of three or four notes per phrase, preceded by a soft *zit: zit-----wherchee-tee, whee-chee-te-wheet,* a repeated *chee-wee-tee* and a single *chi.* ❊ KV: winters in Rani Bari, Gorkarna; summers on Sheopuri. 🌢 Kashmir, Garhwal, Nepal, Sikkim; Kashmir to S.E. Asia 1609

Large Crowned Leaf Warbler, *Phylloscopus occipitalis*.
1525-1982 m. (5,000-6,500') 13 cm. (5") R.

Fairly common; in uppermost sections of oaks and pines in W. Nepal. A large, somewhat pale leaf warbler; olive-green above and yellowish-white below. Note the pale wingbar and eyebrow, and dark lines over crown. Very much like Crowned Leaf Warbler but larger and head markings comparatively less distinct. Actively flits about after insects like a flycatcher. In small, scattered parties with other warblers, tits and nuthatches. May also search carefully through leaves and branches like a tit. Contact note a repeated *cheep-wip.* Song said to be a repeated, squeaky *chi-chi-chi-chwei-chwei-chwei-chwei* (Ali). 🌢 Kashmir, Garhwal, Nepal; Asia 1606

Yellow-throated Leaf Warbler (Small Crowned), *Phylloscopus cantator*.
305 m. (1,000') 10 cm. (4") R. (?)

Scarce; among trees of eastern *tarai* in winter; up to 2441 (8,000') in Sikkim in summer (Ali). The only leaf warbler with a bright yellow throat and white lower breast. Also note crown pattern and wingbars. Very active; jerky wing movements, spreads tail and flicks it upward when calling. In mixed hunting parties among low branches and shrubs. Rather shy, keeping well under cover. Call a loud, incessant *pio--pio* (AR). 🌢 Nepal, Sikkim; Nepal to Hainan Island 1612

Seicercus and Abroscopus Warblers, often called Flycatcher Warblers, are somewhat lethargic when compared with the restless leaf warblers. Many are brightly colored.

Allied Warbler, *Seicercus affinis*. 10 cm. (4"). No data since 1854. Green above, yellow below with black and gray streaked crown and white eye-ring (Gray-cheeked Warbler has all gray crown). Possibly survives in eastern Nepal in evergreen *tarai* forests in winter. ♣ Nepal, Sikkim; Nepal to Annam 1613

Yellow-eyed Warbler (Black-browed Warbler), *Seicercus burkii*.
152-3660 m. (500-12,000') 11 cm. (4½") R.
Fairly common; in low parts of trees and bushes of open or dense forests. Dark olive-green above, yellow below with *bright yellow eye-ring*. Grayish bands on head. Usually in pairs; actively moves fairly close to the ground. Confiding but hard to see in their dimly-lit haunts. Much altitudinal movement, nesting among high altitude rhododendrons. In winter, a repeated *nrip* at several-second intervals. A cheery, oft-repeated warble in spring. ❊ KV: Rani Bari, Godaveri and surrounding hills in cold weather. ♣ Kashmir, Garhwal, Nepal, Sikkim; Pakistan to S.E. Asia 1615

Gray-headed Warbler, *Seicercus xanthoschistos*.
244-2592 m. (800-8,500') 10 cm. (4") R.
Common; flitting through thickets and forest trees. Underparts entirely bright yellow, the most conspicuous field character. Look for gray head with white eyebrow (lacks white eye-ring of Gray-cheeked and Allied Warblers). Should not be confused with Gray-headed Flycatcher which has gray throat and breast as well as semi-crest. Shows white in tail as it flits among trees. Two or three in company with leaf warblers, White-eyes and tits. Restlessly examines leaves and twigs. Hovers as well as flies out after insects. Not very shy. Song a cheery warble *tsiri-siri-trip-ottzee-pseet-tzerra*. ❊ KV: among trees surrounding the Valley.
♣ Kashmir, Garhwal, Nepal, Sikkim; Pakistan to Burma 1616, 1617

Gray-cheeked Warbler, *Seicercus poliogenys*.
2440 m. (8,000') 11 cm. (4½") R.
Scarce; among thick matted vines and bamboo forests. Similar to Gray-headed Warbler but with *gray cheeks and chin* (not yellow) and a conspicuous *white eye-ring*. Hangs on vines and turns, tit-like, upside-down when feeding. Less active than leaf warblers. Usually in mixed hunting parties. Occasional in E. Nepal. ❊ KV: once seen near road above Godaveri School. ♣ Nepal, Sikkim; Nepal to S.E. Asia 1620

Chestnut-crowned Warbler (Chestnut-headed), *Seicercus castaniceps*.
274-2440 m. (900-8,000') 10 cm. (4") R.
Occasional; in upper parts of tall oaks. Found around flowering rhododendron in spring. A sprightly bird, the bright chestnut crown and white eye-ring show well in most lights. Solitary or in pairs among mixed hunting parties of leaf warblers and tits. Flicks wings like a leaf warbler. Quite active and often difficult to locate. Known from as far west as Annapurna Himal. Works through tops of small trees in mixed forest. Call a *chi-chi* and a buzzing alarm call *z-z-z-z-z*. ❊ KV: in spring in surrounding forests at about 2287 m. (7,500'). ♣ Nepal, Sikkim; Nepal to Sumatra 1621

Yellow-bellied Warbler, *Abroscopus superciliaris.*
244-1525 m. (800-5,000') 10 cm. (4") R.

Occasional; at edges of forest, in wooded ravines and groves of bamboo. No other Nepal warbler is bright yellow below with a conspicuous *white* throat and upper breast. Solitary or in pairs in mixed hunting parties. Often near little forest streams usually near bamboos. Flies after insects from low branches. Most common about 610 m. (2,000'). A bright song *chew-do-due--tee-do-dee.* While feeding, a high squeaky *ptee-ptee-ptee-plew.* ◀ Nepal, Sikkim; Nepal to S.E. Asia   1622

Black-faced Warbler, *Abroscopus schisticeps.*
1525-2440 m. (5,000-8,000') 10 cm. (4") R.

Occasional; in mixed temperate and oak forests. A small gray and yellow bird with black face mask. Differs from Yellow-bellied Fantail Flycatcher in behavior as well as shorter tail (with no white) and yellow (not white) abdomen. In wet regions where trees are moss-covered, parties of 10-15 move quickly through trees at medium height, often with other species. It occasionally hunts through large bushes. Inquisitive, approaching within a few feet. Occurs as far west as Annapurna Himal. Alarm call a rapid, high-pitched *tz-tz-tz-tz-tz-tz.* ✲ KV: about 2135 m. (7,000') on Phulchowki, Sheopuri. ◀ Nepal, Sikkim; Nepal to Tonkin   1624

Goldcrest, *Regulus regulus.*
2440-3965 m. (8,000-13,000') 10 cm. (4") R.

Occasional; among conifers. Greenish-gray with diagnostic head pattern. Eye-ring and white wingbars very conspicuous in the field. In small parties constantly on the move. Sometimes hovers and hangs upside-down. Stance in illustration too erect; should be more crouched. Occasionally with other species but most often in homogeneous flocks. Attracted to flowering rhododendrons in spring. Feeds among pines in Jumla and fir in Khumbu. Song a *ti-ti-ti----swee---tee-tee* with variations. Also a frequent high-pitched *tzit-tzit.* ◀ Kashmir, Garhwal, Nepal, Sikkim; Europe, Asia   1629, 1630

White-throated Warbler, *Abroscopus albogularis.*
120-1220 m. (400-4,000') 10 cm. (4") R.

Scarce; in scrub jungle, bamboo clumps and thin forests of the eastern *tarai* and low foothills. Brown above with rufous-brown crown; chestnut eyebrow and cheeks (lacks white eye-ring of Chestnut-crowned Warbler, see p. 244). Below, black and white throat, pale abdomen. Like a Goldcrest, it moves in small parties, hovering at the tips of twigs while twittering constantly (Stanford). Usually feeds among low branches and bushes. So far, only recorded from the eastern *tarai.* ◀ Nepal, Sikkim; Nepal to S. China   1626

Broad-billed Warbler, *Abroscopus hodgsoni.*
No recent data. An active and colorful forest bird. Look for chestnut head and crown, *gray throat and breast* and bright yellow abdomen (the White-throated Warbler has a white throat with black spots and a pale yellow breast). May still be found in undergrowth and bamboo forests of E. Nepal. ◀ Nepal, Sikkim; Nepal to Tonkin   1627

Stoliczka's Tit Warbler, *Leptopoecile sophiae.*
2745-4575 m. (9,000-15,000') 10 cm. (4") R.

Occasional; among *Caragana* shrubs in the semi-deserts of Dolpo, Mustang and Manang Districts. Unmistakable. Rufous head in male and lilac lower back and rump; female and young, paler. In pairs or small parties; climbs to top of bush for better view. Homogeneous flocks among cypress and juniper bushes near Jomosom in winter. Rather shy in summer; nests among *Caragana* above 3965 m. (13,000'). Flight pattern swift, aided by heavy winds which blow across its high altitude haunts. Call a high-pitched *zip.* ◀ Nepal, Sikkim; C. Asia   1634

THRUSHES, CHATS and ALLIES (Turdidae) include shortwings, chats, bush robins, redstarts, Grandala, forktails, cochoas, rock thrushes, whistling thrushes, ground thrushes, robins, mountain thrushes, blackbirds and thrushes. These vary from small to moderate-sized birds; most have strong legs and wings. Thrushes are among the best singers of the Himalayas.

Gould's Shortwing, *Brachypteryx stellata*.
1982-3812 m. (6,500-12,500') 13 cm. (5") R.

Scarce; among fir and rhododendrons near damp ravines and running water; also on rocky hillsides. Maroon above and dark gray below with white, triangular spots on abdomen; sexes alike. Solitary or in loose pairs, hopping over mossy logs, feeding in low bushes or on the ground. Exceptionally strong legs and short wings. Shy and hard to see. Summer, among juniper and rhododendron groves about 3660 m. (12,000'). Song a thin, lisping *zi-zi-zi-zi-zi*, sung near the tops of junipers. ◆ Garhwal, Nepal, Sikkim; Himalayas to Tonkin   1635

White-browed Shortwing, *Brachypteryx montana*.
244-3660 m. (800-12,000') 14 cm. (5½") R.

Fairly common; in densely wooded oak-rhododendron forests near streams. White eyebrow of dark male seen when bird is excited. Told from dark Lesser Shortwing by deep ashy abdomen (not pale ashy). Female separated from female Lesser Shortwing by rusty face and ashy-brown underparts (not tan). Young male like female but has white eyebrow. Single or in pairs. Flicks wings when it calls. Partial to bamboos in summer. Alarm note a quick *fek*. Song a strong, high-pitched warble lasting 3-4 seconds; general theme repeated but notes constantly varied. ◆ Nepal, Sikkim; Nepal to Philippines   1640

Lesser Shortwing, *Brachypteryx leucophrys*.
120-1982 m. (400-6,500') 11 cm. (4½") R.

Scarce; in cutover scrub jungle. Older(?) males are dark blueish-gray above; pale ashy below with gray breast and flanks (this phase not shown as yet not seen in Nepal). Most(?) males in Nepal resemble female plumage, a rusty-brown above and pale tan below (not ashy-brown of White-browed Shortwing). Crepuscular; hops along forest trails at dusk, also under ferns and tangled vegetation. Solitary and shy. Wintering records unsatisfactory; may descend to 120 m. (400') in the *tarai*. Contact note a *seep* (Ali) and alarm call a *chirp* followed by *tak-tak-tak* (Smythies). (Rusty-bellied Shortwing, *B. hyperythra*, rare in Sikkim, see p. 337.) ◆ Nepal, Sikkim; Himalayas to S.E. Asia   1639

Himalayan Rubythroat, *Erithacus pectoralis*.
274-5185 m. (900-17,000') 15 cm. (6") R.

Occasional; in heavy foliage and swamp grass of the lowlands; nests among *Caragana* bushes above the tree line. Male blackish and *gray* with a deep crimson throat patch and broad white eyebrow (Tibetan race has, in addition, a broad white cheek stripe). Female is a darker gray-brown than the Eurasian Rubythroat female, with a whitish throat and tips to tail. Two subspecies and a Eurasian Rubythroat caught in the same mist net in Rapti Dun in November. In Dolpo, most common on northern slopes. Cocks tail and droops wings as it hops on ground. Males sing from rocks or bush tops at about 4270 m. (14,000') in summer. Song a pleasing warble of 4 or 5 phrases interspersed with chips, squeaks and a rattle (one sequence lasted 17 seconds). Alarm a quick, loud *ke*. ❉ KV: a few here in winter (Nagarjung). ◆ Kashmir, Garhwal, Nepal, Sikkim; Asia   1647, 1648, 1649

Eurasian Rubythroat, *Erithacus calliope*.
274-1372 m. (900-4,500') 15 cm. (6") W.

Fairly common; wintering in wet ravines of the foothills and *tarai*. Male brown above (male Himalayan Rubythroat gray) with a large ruby patch on chin and throat. Female has white throat and uniform tail (not tipped white as in female Himalayan Rubythroat). Hops on ground with tail cocked. A strong flier but usually keeps well hidden in tall grass and in hedgerows. Will mount branches of small trees at edges of damp *tarai* waste land. Nests in Siberia. Alarm a metallic *chep-chep*. ❉ KV: at edges of fields in bushes on migration, March-April. ◆ Nepal, Sikkim; Europe, Asia   1643

Bluethroat, *Erithacus svecicus*.
120-1372 m. (400-4,500') 15 cm. (6") W.

Fairly common; in damp, shady ravines. Intensity and extent of blue of throat varies considerably from male to male. The rufous tail very noticeable as bird dives into bushy cover. Female lacks blue throat; is distinguished from female rubythroats by rufous on tail. English Robin-like, it often hops on wet soil with tail cocked. Strong, short flight, soon disappearing into next tussock of grass. Rather secretive. Call a *vek*. ❉ KV: in hedges and gardens during spring and fall migration; a few remain all winter. ◆ Kashmir, Garhwal, Nepal, Sikkim; Europe, Africa, Asia, N. America   1644

Blue Chat, *Erithacus brunneus*.
274-3446 m. (900-11,300') 15 cm. (6") S.

Fairly common; on ground or in low trees near water. Male dark steel-blue above and chestnut below. A white eyebrow extends to the nape. Told from the male White-browed Bush Robin by bright chestnut below (not orange-rufous) and a narrow (not wide) eyebrow. Female pale chestnut below (not yellowish-brown like female White-browed Bush Robin). Single or in pairs, somewhat shy. Above 2135 m. (7,000') in summer and most common in damp forests from 2440-3050 m. (8,000-10,000'). Often sings from a low branch with chestnut breast puffed out. Song a penetrating, rapid *tee-tee-three-four-----amoebic*, of a second's duration, then repeated without much variation. ❊ KV: nests on north face of Sheopuri; calls in April. ❦ Kashmir, Garhwal, Nepal, Sikkim: Asia   1650

White-browed Bush Robin, *Erithacus indicus*.
2135-3965 m. (7,000-13,000') 15 cm. (6") R.

Occasional; at edges of juniper and rhododendron forests. Male slaty-blue, slightly paler than the Blue Chat. Look for *black sides of head* and neck; orange-rufous below; broad white eyebrow to nape. Female yellowish-brown (not pale chestnut) with a short, narrow eyebrow. This species and the similar Blue Chat are usually separated altitudinally, the robin rarely below 3050 m. (10,000') in summer. Partial to dense undergrowth such as bamboo; usually near water. Little altitudinal movement, 3507 m. (11,500') in December. Alarm call a repeated *trrrrr*. Song a bubbling, double phrase combined to produce an unusual echo effect *shri-de-de-dew-----de-de-dew*. ❦ Garhwal, Nepal, Sikkim; Himalayas to Formosa   1659

Orange-flanked Bush Robin, *Erithacus cyanurus*.
1372-4117 m. (4,500-13,500') 15 cm. (6") R.

Fairly common; in low bushes of forest and among open glades. Unmistakable. Male blue above and ashy and white below. Orange flanks clearly seen in cold weather with feathers puffed out but at other times, orange mostly hidden under closed wings. Female (and young males) brown with orange flanks and a *blue tail*. Single or in loose pairs; in summer at bases of tall conifers and rhododendrons at upper altitude limit. Sits fairly upright, spreads tail and twitches it upward at 3-4-second intervals. Flies to ground and also clings to tree trunks for insects. Song a lazy, three-syllable *dwee-dew-dew*, or *dweww-dew-dwee-dee* at about two phrases per minute, a fast *klik* and an alarm, *drrrrrr*. ❊ KV: along forest paths on surrounding hills. ❦ Kashmir, Garhwal, Nepal, Sikkim; Lapland to S.E. Asia   1654, 1655

Golden Bush Robin, *Erithacus chrysaeus*.
1372-4270 m. (4,500-14,000') 14 cm. (5½") R.

Occasional; in cutover scrub in winter; above 3660 m. (12,000') in summer. Male distinctive bright gold and black; female yellow and olive-brown. Young speckled brown, with yellow tail. Single or in small, loose parties. Shy in winter, bold in summer. Forages on ground and in low bushes. More often heard than seen. In winter an observer rarely has more than a fleeting glimpse of something yellow disappearing into a bush ahead. Song a high, wispy *tze-du-tee-tse* with variations, ending in a lower *chur-r-r-r*. Alarm a loud, repeated *drrrrr*. ❊ KV: in dense shrubbery at Godaveri, Kakani, Chandragiri, in winter. ❦ Kashmir, Garhwal, Nepal, Sikkim; Kashmir to Tonkin   1658

Rufous-bellied Bush Robin, *Erithacus hyperythrus*.
2135-3355 m. (7,000-11,000') 15 cm. (6") R.

Scarce; in dense mixed forests near water. Male the only chat or flycatcher with underparts *entirely* deep orange-chestnut and no white eyebrow. Female is brown above and orange-brown below with a blue rump and tail (also separated from female Orange-flanked Bush Robin by lack of orange flanks). Usually solitary, on low branches; frequently flicks its tail and wings. Rather sluggish in its movements. Young just able to fly on 3 June at 3202 m. (10,500') in Helumbu. Known from Kosi-Gandaki watershed ridge eastward. Song a lisping warble *zeew---zee---zwee---zwee (zwe)*; and an alarm *duk-duk-duk-squeak*. ❦ Nepal, Sikkim; Nepal to W. China   1660

Shama, *Copsychus malabaricus*.
120-305 m. (400-1,000') 28 cm. (11") R.
Fairly common; both in thin and dense lowland forests. Male glossy black, chestnut breast and *white rump*; the very long tail conspicuous in flight. In the female, brown replaces black of male. Usually solitary or in pairs, working in low trees or flitting to the ground for insects. Rather shy, moving behind sheltering leaves. A bird of Indian poets. "Shama" is a favorite girl's name. One of the most beautiful of songs, sustained for many seconds, often heard in the still jungle air at dusk. Alarm *chur-chi-chur-r-r; chir-chur.* ♣ Nepal, Sikkim; India to S.E. Asia
1667

Grandala, *Grandala coelicolor*.
3355-5032 m. (11,000-16,500') 23 cm. (9") R.
Fairly common; on steep rocky slopes well above tree line. Male unmistakable. A deep glistening blue with black wings and tail. Female streaked brown with white wing patch. In flight the light middle part of wing stands out. In summer loose flocks up to 50 or more birds "flow" over the ground when feeding. Advance birds arrive on grassy knoll, hop about and continue on as other birds assemble. Males often separate into large flocks in winter when the brilliant blue of 300 birds against snow is unforgettable. Will dig with bill in soft, shallow snow, burying entire head, with wings flicking out to side. Perches on rocks like a thrush, then cranes neck and assumes an erect stance (shown in illustration). Descends temporarily in winter to trees. Flight behavior somewhat swallow-like, circling slowly for long periods catching insects on the wing. Song a subdued, oft-repeated *galeb--che--chew--de--dew* with variations. Flight call *tew-wee.* ♣ Kashmir, Garhwal, Nepal, Sikkim; Himalayas to Sikiang
1683

White-tailed Blue Robin, *Cinclidium leucurum*.
1525-2745 m. (5,000-9,000') 18 cm. (7") R.
Occasional; under heavy foliage in watered ravines. Male appears black with white in the tail (the white conspicuous as bird fans tail). The blue eyebrow and shoulder patch only seen in good light. Female brown with white in tail. Single, or in pairs near ground in darkest and densest forests. Partial to bamboos and moss-encrusted undergrowth. When perching, slowly depresses, then spreads tail. Song a twinkling, silvery *do-de-de----dl* with variations, usually the first indication of the bird's presence. ❋ KV: heard in spring, Phulchowki, Sheopuri, 2135-2440 m. (7,000-8,000'). ♣ Nepal, Sikkim; Nepal to S.E. Asia
1681

Blue-fronted Long-tailed Robin, *Cinclidium frontale*. 19 cm. (7½"). No data since 1854. Dark with pale blue forehead. Very similar to White-tailed Blue Robin but with no white in tail. May survive in dense forests of eastern Nepal. ♣ Nepal, Sikkim; Nepal to Laos
1682

Robin Dayal (Magpie Robin), *Copsychus saularis*.
120-1830 m. (400-6,000') 19 cm. (7½") R.
Common; the garden singer in city, village and grove. Male black and white with black bib. Female gray and white with gray bib. Young mottled brownish-gray with brown bib. Told from Pied Wagtail by color pattern, stouter build and shorter tail. Tail usually cocked. Wings dropped and flicked as bird calls. Hops on lawns; strong flight. Tame. Nests in holes in brick walls and trees. Song a strong, varied melody for many seconds. Alarm, a repeated *ssheeeee* and contact note *chir---eet.* ❋ KV: on roof tops; the first singer on a spring morning, beginning at 4:30 A.M. or earlier. ♣ Garhwal, Nepal, Sikkim; Pakistan to Philippines
1661

Eversmann's Redstart, *Phoenicurus erythronotus.*
2287-3050 m. (7,500-10,000')   19 cm.   (7½")   W.
Occasional; in hedgerows bordering fields. Male gray head, chestnut throat and breast tinged with gray. Distinctive white wing and shoulder patches. Female brown with pale, indistinct eye-ring, white wing patch. Single or in widely scattered pairs on stone walls and in shrubs. Violently flicks tail as it leans forward to call. Fairly common around Rara Lake in February; also Jumla and Jomosom. Alarm a loud, nasal, rasping *chaaaaaaaan.*
🌶 Kashmir, Garhwal, Nepal; C. Asia   1669

Blue-headed Redstart, *Phoenicurus caeruleocephalus.*
1372-3660 m. (4,500-12,000')   15 cm.   (6")   R.
Fairly common; in open scrub and cutover forests. Male a small gray and white "robin-like" bird with blue-gray crown and nape (pale blue in summer). Female is brown with pale eye-ring and diagnostic reddish-brown rump. Single or in small, scattered parties on tops of bushes. Not very shy. Moves tail from side to side. Flight slightly undulating. Very common on open hills at 2745 m. (9,000') on Jumla-Rara trail in January. In winter, separate flocks of males and females noted. Alarm call a rapidly repeated *tik* like the sound of a finger running down a small comb. ❈ KV: winters on Sheopuri and Nagarjung. 🌶 Kashmir, Garhwal, Nepal, Sikkim; C. Asia   1670

Black Redstart, *Phoenicurus ochruros.*
1525-4575 m. (5,000-15,000')   15 cm.   (6")   R., M.
Common; in grassy meadows and around villages above the tree line. Male grayish back, brown abdomen, chestnut tail. Very dark males rarely seen in Nepal. Female brown with pale eye-ring and a two-toned chestnut and brown tail. Easily confused with the female Hodgson's Redstart which is gray-brown (not brown). The similar Blue-fronted Redstart female has a *black* tipped tail. "Shivers" tail more than other redstarts. Males often breed in "female" plumage. Solitary or in loose pairs; partial to open country around villages and *Caragana* scrub. Often nests in *chortans* and *mani* walls. Common in Dolpo; remains in Langtang Valley until October. Song a ringing *zrrrrrreeeee;* alarm a *tzip,* also a *tuk-tuk.*
❈ KV: on open, stony ground during migration. 🌶 Kashmir, Garhwal, Nepal, Sikkim; Europe, Africa, Asia   1672

Hodgson's Redstart, *Phoenicurus hodgsoni.*
762-2806 m. (2,500-9,200')   15 cm.   (6")   W.
Occasional; in open grassy areas interspersed with bushes. Male gray above with black face, white forehead. Also note white wing patch and rufous abdomen, very reminiscent of the European Redstart (*P. phoenicurus*). Female *brownish-gray* (not brown of female Black Redstart) with a pale rufous and black tail (but not tipped black as female Blue-fronted Redstart). Single or in scattered pairs; perches on tops of shrubs or hops on ground. Fans tail while resting but not much "shivering." Migrating birds in Jomosom, 2745 m. (9,000') in mid-March. ❈ KV: at Godaveri, Chobar Gorge, Anandaban, mostly in female plumage. (Daurian Redstart, *P. auroreus,* occurs in Sikkim, see p. 337.) 🌶 Nepal, Sikkim; C. Asia   1674

Blue-fronted Redstart, *Phoenicurus frontalis.*
762-4880 m. (2,500-16,000')   16 cm.   (6½")   R., M.
Fairly common; on low tree branches, walls around fields or in open groves. Male dark blue head with light blue forehead and eyebrow, orange-chestnut below. Look for chestnut *tail tipped black.* Female light brown with diagnostic chestnut *tail tipped black.* Usually solitary and not very shy. Flicks tail but does not "shiver" it as Black Redstart. Feeds in undergrowth. Nests above 3660 m. (12,000') in Dolpo. Sings from boulders on barren slopes above tree line (Dolpo). Remains in Langtang Valley into late October where it is largely confined to birch-rhododendron groves (Black Redstart in nearby *open* country). Alarm a quick *tze-tze.* ❈ KV: winter, in open glades. 🌶 Kashmir, Garhwal, Nepal, Sikkim; C. Asia to Tonkin   1675

Guldenstadt's Redstart, *Phoenicurus erythrogaster.*
2745-5642 m. (9,000-18,500') 19 cm. (7½") W.
Fairly scarce; on glacier moraine rocks. Male chestnut with black head and grayish-white cap. Distinguished from similar White-capped River Chat by the white patch on black wings, very conspicuous in flight. Female pale brown with rufous rump and tail. Single or in scattered pairs in glacial valleys. As high as 5490 m. (18,000') in Khumbu (Diesselhorst). Fairly common on glacial moraine boulders as well as in rhododendron-ephedra scrub (upper Langtang Valley). Scarce around Jomosom. Active; eats orange *Ephedra* berries. Moves tail and wings less violently than the Black Redstart. Call *drrrrr* when two males chase each other; contact note a weak *lik*. ♦ Kashmir, Garhwal, Nepal, Sikkim; C. Asia 1678

White-capped River Chat (White-capped Redstart), *Chaimarrornis leucocephalus.*
244-4880 m. (800-16,000') 19 cm. (7½") R.
Common; on rushing streams and fast flowing rivers. Crown and nape white, remainder black and maroon. Resembles male Guldenstadt's Redstart but latter has white in wing and tail not tipped black. Solitary or in pairs; skims from rock to rock, fanning and pumping tail while resting. In summer, may stray over high altitude meadows some distance from water. In winter often associates with Plumbeous Redstart; sometimes on grassy stretches. Song a ringing *s-r-e-e-e-e* sung from a boulder in water. ✵ KV: conspicuous at edge of streams, pools and on grassy banks. ♦ Kashmir, Garhwal, Nepal, Sikkim; Turkestan to Tonkin 1716

White-throated Redstart, *Phoenicurus schisticeps.*
2592-4422 m. (8,500-14,500') 15 cm. (6") R., W.
Occasional; on steep, rocky slopes among shrubs. Male is chestnut, black and blue with *white throat patch.* White wing patch very conspicuous in flight. Female is brown with diagnostic white throat patch (sometimes hard to see) and white wing patch. Single or widely scattered parties in open country. Perches on rocks or shrubs, flicks wings and tail. Fairly shy; flight is swift and distant. Seen as far west as the Jumla-Rara trail. Moves down to Khumjung in Khumbu the first week in November. On Gosainkund ridge at 3965 m. (13,000') in January. ♦ Nepal, Sikkim; Himalayas to China 1676

White-bellied Redstart (Hodgson's Shortwing), *Hodgsonius phoenicuroides.*
213-4270 m. (700-14,000') 19 cm. (7½") R.
Occasional; in brush country of the *tarai* in winter; at or above the tree line in summer. Male slaty-blue with white abdomen and a long tail marked at base with orange. Female olive-brown with whitish abdomen and a long tail. Similar brownish warblers have shorter tails and lack white on abdomen. In summer, fairly common in limited habitat range of thorny undergrowth under cypress and juniper shrubs in the Trans-Himalayan zone. Rather shy, it hops on ground and cocks tail like a Robin Dayal. Boldly scolds animals near nest. In winter is confined to thick vegetation at low altitudes. Calls a soft *chee-chee-you-wee*, a lazy *jew-jew-wea-jew-eee* and a sharp alarm *trik*. ✵ KV: western rim of Valley in spring and autumn. ♦ Kashmir, Garhwal, Nepal, Sikkim; Himalayas to Laos 1680

Plumbeous Redstart, *Rhyacornis fuliginosus.*
762-4117 m. (2,500-13,500') 14 cm. (5½") R.
Common; on flat rocks and boulders in running water. Male slaty-blue with broad rufous-maroon tail. Female blueish-gray with white. Tail is constantly moved up and down and flared widely so that white is very conspicuous. Tame and easily watched. Single or in scattered twos or threes always associated with water. Actively hunts insects at dusk; feeds on fruit and insects from bushes at the water's edge. Song a ringing *seeeeeeeeeeeeee*. ✵ KV: Chobar, Sundarijal, Godaveri streams in winter. ♦ Kashmir, Garhwal, Nepal, Sikkim; Pakistan to Formosa 1679

Little Forktail, *Enicurus scouleri.*
366-4239 m. (1,200-13,900') 13 cm. (5") R.
Occasional; moving among rocks of rushing streams or along river banks. Small black and white bird with a fairly short, slightly forked tail. Young, brown and white. Easily told from Pied Wagtail by short tail and small size. Usually solitary, actively catching insects among rocks in flowing water. Flares tail like redstarts. Nest found as low as 2379 m. (7,800') in a rock niche near a waterfall in May. ✤ KV: scarce, along streams in spring. ◖ Kashmir, Garhwal, Nepal, Sikkim; Himalayas to Formosa 1684

Black-backed Forktail, *Enicurus immaculatus.*
152-1372 m. (500-4,500') 22 cm. (8½") R.
Fairly common; on streams of foothills. Black and white with *plain black back*. Resembles Little Forktail but a much larger bird and much longer tail. Told from Pied Wagtail by heavier build and forked tail. Solitary or in pairs along comparatively open streams and lakes such as Phewa Tal, Pokhara. Nests at elevation lower than other forktails. Call a double *curt-seeeee* the last note higher than the first. ◖ Garhwal, Nepal, Sikkim: Himalayas to Thailand 1685

Slaty-backed Forktail, *Enicurus schistaceus.*
915-1677 m. (3,000-5,500') 24 cm. (9½") R.
Occasional; along large streams and lakes. Similar to Black-backed Forktail but with a *gray back*. Told from gray-backed Pied Wagtail by heavier build and forked tail. Hugs margins of lakes or streams, staying under overhanging vegetation. Skims from stone to stone in undulating flight like a wagtail. Single and in pairs. Call a mellow *cheet.* ✤ KV: Sundarijal Reservoir; lower Godaveri. ◖ Nepal, Sikkim; Kumaon to S. China 1686

Spotted Forktail, *Enicurus maculatus.*
290-2745 m. (950-9,000') 27 cm. (10½") R.
Fairly common; on forest streams of the mid-Himalayas. This strikingly handsome black and white species has *white spots* on its black collar and back, a long, deeply forked black and white tail and white legs. Young, upper half dark chocolate. One or two along small streams under tangled thickets. Fairly shy. When disturbed, flies into shrubbery and then circles back down the stream bed. When perched on a spray-soaked boulder, moves its whole body this way and that, slowly lifting tail up and down. Call a penetrating *jeet-jeet-jeeeeeeeet-jit-jit* like that of a Whistling Thrush. Also a hissing *chee-chee-chit.* ✤ KV: Godaveri streams; Royal Botanic Gardens. (Black-breasted Forktail, *E. leschenaulti,* in Sikkim, see p. 337.) ◖ Kashmir, Garhwal, Nepal, Sikkim; Himalayas to Yunnan 1688, 1689

Collared Bush Chat (Stone Chat), *Saxicola torquata*.
274-4880 m. (900-16,000') 13 cm. (5") R.
Common; on tops of bushes along fields. Male dark brown and fulvous above with white shoulder patch and white sides of neck. The white on underparts variable depending on the race. Female is brown-fulvous with pale underparts. White of the wing especially noticeable in flight. Usually in pairs. Periodically twitches tail. The very rufous-breasted *S. t. przevalskii* breeds from 2745 m. (9,000') upward in *Caragana* desert country of Trans-Himalayan Nepal; nest with 4 eggs 20 June, 4575 m. (15,000'), Dolpo. The pale *S. t. indica* breeds up to 2897 m. (9,500'). Song a short melody; alarm a repeated *tzup* or *tik*. ❈ KV: in winter throughout Valley on bushes, fences, wires. ♠ Kashmir, Garhwal, Nepal, Sikkim; Europe, Africa, Asia 1695, 1696, 1697

White-tailed Bush Chat, *Saxicola leucura*.
274-1830 m. (900-6,000') 13 cm. (5") R.
Occasional; in high elephant grass bordering rivers in Rapti Dun. Male very similar to male Collared Bush Chat but with rufous patch on breast very small. *White* at base of tail easily seen on close inspection. Female very similar to female Collared Bush Chat but slightly paler. Both species occur in same habitat and females difficult to differentiate without considerable practice. Solitary or in pairs; perches on grass stalks in river beds. Also noted in bushes on dry open slopes of midland Nepal. Seasonal movements not well understood. ❈ KV: a pair below Tokha Sanitarium in April; Taudha Lake in May. ♠ Nepal; Pakistan to Burma 1699

Dark-gray Bush Chat, *Saxicola ferrea*.
274-3355 m. (900-11,000') 15 cm. (6") R.
Fairly common; in secondary forests and open glades. Male gray with black face mask and white eyebrow. Female brown, dark brown face mask, white throat; outer tail feathers rufous. In ones or twos on top of shrubs, on large boulders or on low branches of trees. Not very shy; flicks tail when perched. Rarely found above 2135 m. (7,000') in winter. Call *zeeeeee-chunk*. Alarm *breeeez*, and *tserp-tserp*. ❈ KV: Nagarjung; nests on top of Sheopuri in spring. ♠ Kashmir, Garhwal, Nepal, Sikkim; Pakistan to S. China 1705

Pied Bush Chat, *Saxicola caprata*.
244-2440 m. (800-8,000') 13 cm. (5") R.
Common; in open country, fields and gardens. Male looks mostly black when perched, but shows much white on tail coverts, abdomen and wing patch in flight. Female is fairly uniformly brown but slight streaking noticeable at close range. Single or in pairs, boldly hawking insects in air or from ground. May sit on one perch a long time, flicking wings and tail. Nests on ground; cuckoos parasitize it. Song a soft *preep-pretty-seeeeer; pree-pretty lessup-chur-rip*. Contact notes a short *phir; pritche-chew*. Begins to sing in February. ❈ KV: on bushes, wires in urban and rural areas. ♠ Kashmir, Garhwal, Nepal, Sikkim; Asia to New Guinea 1700

Indian Robin, *Saxicoloides fulicata*.
120-274 m. (400-900') 16 cm. (6½") R.
Occasional; in gardens and fields bordering villages; in scrub forest. Male glossy black and chestnut. Note white shoulder patch. Female dark brown, paler below. Single or in loose pairs hopping on the ground or perched on a rock. *Tail constantly cocked* and held at an acute angle in breeding season. "Shivers" wings and flips tail. Nests in holes in walls of houses or under bridges. Common in cutover scrub north of Nepalganj, Banki District. Call a rapid *chee-chee-chew-whee-chew*. ♠ Nepal; S. Asia 1717, 1718

Blue-headed Rock Thrush, *Monticola cinclorhynchus*.
274-2135 m. (900-7,000') 18 cm. (7") S.

Fairly common; in pine forests and open, rocky slopes with stunted trees. Male outstanding cobalt-blue and orange; white wing patch conspicuous in flight. Female is olive-brown and profusely speckled. Single or in pairs usually above 1525 m. (5,000') in summer. Not very shy; moderate flight. Male sings from pines and stunted oaks; female often lower in shrubs. Song a clear, repeated *riti-prilee-prileer*, also *seer-twik-twik*. ❅ KV: open hillsides in summer. ♣ Kashmir, Garhwal, Nepal, Sikkim; Afghanistan to Burma   1723

Chestnut-bellied Rock Thrush, *Monticola rufiventris*.
1372-3355 m. (4,500-11,000') 23 cm. (9") R.

Fairly common; rather high up in tall forest trees. Male dark blue and maroon. Female barred brown and fulvous; look for a conspicuous tan patch on neck just below ear. Single or in pairs. Flight strong. Leans forward and jerks tail when perched. A forest bird not found on rocks. Often remains between 2135-2440 m. (7,000-8,000') in winter. Spring courting flight consists of sailing out over mountain slope in a wide horizontal arc, tail wide-spread, then gliding back to original perch. Song an ascending *jero--terry--three; phir-tar-ree* and a wistful *kari-mee-surgee*. Alarm note a loud, rasping *czaaaaaa*. ❅ KV: pine and oak forests of Phulchowki, Nagarjung, Sheopuri. ♣ Garhwal, Nepal, Sikkim; Pakistan to S.E. Asia 1724

Blue Rock Thrush, *Monticola solitarius*.
120-3355 m. (400-11,000') 23 cm. (9") R.

Occasional; in open country or rocky stream beds. Male gray-blue, brightest around the head. Female gray-brown, lightly barred. Single or in pairs. Nests in summer in the Trans-Himalayas from 2592 m. (8,500') above Tukuche to about 4880 m. (16,000') in Dolpo. Male sings for long periods from large rocks or high on steep cliffs and stunted cypress shrubs. Hops among boulders and grass clumps for insects. Descends in winter to lowlands; found along rivers or sometimes in crumbling buildings. Song a short, pleasant warble, frequently repeated. Contact note a *pok*. (Eurasian Rock Thrush, *M. saxatilis*, rare in Kashmir, see p. 335.) ♣ Kashmir, Garhwal, Nepal, Sikkim; Europe, Africa, Asia   1726

Purple Cochoa, *Cochoa purpurea*.
915-2287 m. (3,000-7,500') 25 cm. (10") R. (?)

Scarce; among tall trees in mixed forests of eastern Nepal. Male, chunky, pale purplish-brown thrush with purplish-gray forehead, nape and pale wing patch. In female, a reddish-brown hue replaces the purple. Solitary or up to three in a flock, well hidden in leafy forest trees. Most often seen in spring when singing from the top of a tall oak or chestnut. Descends to ground for insects. Rather lethargic movements; slow flight. Moves up into oak-chestnut forests in Ilam District in May. Song a broad flute-like *peeeeee*; also *peeee-you-peeee*, like the music of a shepherd's bamboo flute (the pitch drops one note in the middle of the phrase). ♣ Nepal, Sikkim; Himalayas to S.E. Asia   1690

Green Cochoa, *Cochoa viridis*. 28 cm. (11").
No data since 1846. A plump, green thrush with pale blue on head; wing, white, black and rufous. May occur in dense forests below 1830 m. (6,000'). ♣ Nepal, Sikkim; Himalayas to Fukien   1691

Isabelline Wheatear, *Oenanthe isabellina.*
1372 m.   (4,500')   16 cm.   (6¼")   M.

Scarce; found twice in potato fields along the Manora in KV in April (RLF). Buffy; white rump and white and black tail. Possibly a vagrant. Migratory route in Nepal unknown.
🌜 Nepal; Europe, Asia   1706

Desert Wheatear, *Oenanthe deserti.*
2592-4880 m.   (8,500-16,000')   15 cm.   (6")   R.

Scarce; in desert biotope. Male has black throat; note that basal half of tail is entirely white. Female a pale sandy buff. First sight record for Nepal, April 1972 by Jarman and Howard on sandy banks near Tukuche 2592 m. (8,500'). Collected by J. Martens in Dolpo, June 1973. Perches on ground as well as on bushes. Song a mournful *teee-ti-ti-ti* (Ali). (Pied Wheatear, *O. picata* and Pleschanka's Wheatear, *O. pleschanka*, winter stragglers in Kashmir, see p. 335.)   🌜 Kashmir, Garhwal, Nepal; Africa, Asia   1709

Pied Ground Thrush, *Zoothera wardii.*
1525-3050 m.   (5,000-10,000')   22 cm.   (8½")   S.

Occasional; along streams under dense vegetation. Male black and white with broad white eyebrow. Female olive-brown, also with a white eyebrow. Solitary or in loose pairs along streams; on steep, open hillsides during migration. Nests usually above 2440 m. (8,000'). Males engage in combat, tumbling to the ground (May). Secretive, although in spring male sings for a short period from tree top as dawn breaks. Song a short, mellow warble *ple-dee*, phrases sometimes ending in a *zik*. Song reminds one of a bulbul's notes. Alarm a spitting *ptz-ptz-ptz-ptz.*   🌜 Garhwal, Nepal, Sikkim; S. Asia   1731

Orange-headed Ground Thrush, *Zoothera citrina.*
120-1830 m.   (400-6,000')   23 cm.   (9")   R.

Fairly common; both in light and heavy forests. Male orange and ashy-blue back with white shoulder patch. Female, brown replaces ashy-blue. Often solitary, low in bushes or on ground. Rather shy; partial to watered ravines. On ground it scatters dry leaves about with vigor. Often kept as a caged bird. Song a beautiful, varied series of spaced phrases a second or more long: *wheeper-pree-preeteelee; wheeoo-peerper-wheechee-leet-wheechee-leet; pir-whoo-peer-rate-rate.* ❉ KV: summer in oak forests of Phulchowki and surrounding hills.
🌜 Kashmir, Garhwal, Nepal, Sikkim; Pakistan to S.E. Asia   1733

Plain-backed Mountain Thrush, *Zoothera mollissima*.
1525-3965 m. (5,000-13,000') 25 cm. (10") R.

Fairly common; in fir forests and alpine meadows near water. Brownish above and fulvous below with crescent spots. Very similar to Long-tailed Mountain Thrush but *lacks wingbar* and has darker back and shorter tail. Single or in small family groups on open hillsides or in underbrush near tree line in summer; in midland forests in winter. Young seen in July-August at 3965 m. (13,000'). Sings from tree tops or rocks in light rain and at dawn and dusk. Silent in winter and easily overlooked. Song chirps, trills and squeaks of 3-4-second durations at 5-10-second intervals, often beginning with a *plee-too*, a *plee-chu* or a *ti-ti-ti* and usually ending with a descending *chup-ple-oop*. ❀ KV: winter, Godaveri and up Phulchowki road. ♪ Kashmir, Garhwal, Nepal, Sikkim; Pakistan to Tonkin   1739

Long-tailed Mountain Thrush, *Zoothera dixoni*.
1525-3965 m. (5,000-13,000') 27 cm. (10½") R.

Occasional; in underbrush of birch and fir forests in summer; mid-Himalayas in winter. Similar to Plain-backed Mountain Thrush but has a longer tail, *two narrow fulvous wingbars* and back is a shade paler. Single or in pairs often on the ground. Nests in forest at slightly lower elevations than the Plain-backed species. Nest with 3 eggs in May at 3507 m. (11,500'). Young flying 2 August at 3507 m. in juniper forest. Song unrecorded. ❀ KV: sparingly on surrounding hills in winter. ♪ Garhwal, Nepal, Sikkim; Himalayas to S.E. Asia   1740

Speckled Mountain Thrush (Small-billed Mountain Thrush), *Zoothera dauma*.
120-3538 m. (400-11,600') 27 cm. (10½") R.

Fairly common; in forests and thick undergrowth, often near water. The only mountain thrush speckled both above and below. A broad, pale wingbar and a dark under wingbar conspicuous in flight. Solitary and rather shy. Active on ground; flies up swiftly into middle of tree. Nests in May and June from 2318 m. (7,600') to tree line (nest with 4 eggs, 1 June). Has a slow song for a *Zoothera;* frequently sings *before dawn* and often warbles from tree tops in light rain. Song of short phrases, usually repeated twice or more before going on to next: *pur-loo-tree-lay; dur-lee-dur-lee; drr-drr-chew-you-we-eeee*. ❀ KV: nests on Sheopuri; winters on Valley floor. ♪ Kashmir, Garhwal, Nepal, Sikkim; Europe, Asia, Australia   1741

Large Long-billed Thrush, *Zoothera monticola*.
244-3111 m. (800-10,200') 28 cm. (11") R.

Occasional; on damp forest floor. Large, curved bill distinguishes this thrush from all species except the Lesser Long-billed Thrush which is slightly smaller and olive-brown (not brown). Usually solitary and shy, flying close to the ground. Active at dawn and dusk. Probes with bill in wet soil. Nest found in May at 2287 m. (7,500'). Song, resembling one rendition of the Gray-winged Blackbird's, a loud, slow, plaintive whistle of two or three notes *te-e-uw* (middle "e" higher); *tew-tew-tew*. Alarm note a loud *zaaaaaaaa*. ❀ KV: scarce, passing through Thankot area in April. ♪ Garhwal, Nepal, Sikkim; Himalayas to Tonkin   1745

Lesser Long-billed Thrush, *Zoothera marginata*.
274-2440 m. (900-8,000') 25 cm. (10") R.

Scarce; on forest floor near streams. A small edition of the Large Long-billed Thrush but back olive-brown (not dark brown) and markings of underparts olive-brown (not brownish-black). Another solitary species haunting dense undergrowth. Quite shy and flies into a tree when disturbed. Active at dusk. Nests at a lower elevation than the larger bird but may associate with it in winter. Song not heard. ♪ Nepal, Sikkim; Nepal to S.E. Asia   1746

White-collared Blackbird, *Turdus albocinctus*.
1525-3446 m. (5,000-11,300') 28 cm. (11") R.

Fairly common; in upper parts of tall trees. Male black with broad white neck band; female brown with dirty white collar. Solitary or in loose pairs in summer; small flocks in winter. Restricted to forests; prefers large oaks. Somewhat shy, staying rather high in tree when disturbed. Fond of fruit such as *Hedera nipalensis*. Sings a "sad," broken song at twilight when other birds are silent. Each phrase is repeated three, or more often four, times with about a ten-second interval. ❀ KV: on Sheopuri, Phulchowki, above 2135 m. (7,000').
❁ Garhwal, Nepal, Sikkim; Himalayas to Burma   1749

Gray-winged Blackbird, *Turdus boulboul*.
120-2745 m. (400-9,000') 29 cm. (11¼") R.

Common; among tall forest trees. Male black with pale gray wingbar and orange bill. Female olive-brown with bright orange bill (varying to bright yellow); pale wingbar distinguishes it from the female Eurasian Blackbird. Somewhat shy; flies into the middle of a tree, then hops upward staying close to trunk. In the *tarai* in winter; sometimes eats decayed matter. Nests in moss-covered tree crotch or tree stump near ground. Sings during the day but is at its best in the gathering dusk. The song is a fine, sustained melody of many notes. Dr. Salim Ali's favorite Himalayan songster. Phrases *chir-bles-we-bullie-dee; we-put-kur-we-put-kur; who-bori-cha-let-cha-he*. Contact note *churi*. ❀ KV: nests in oaks on Sheopuri at about 2440 m. (8,000'). ❁ Kashmir, Garhwal, Nepal, Sikkim; Pakistan to Tonkin   1750

Eurasian Blackbird, *Turdus merula*.
244-4270 m. (800-14,000') 28 cm. (11") R. (?)

Scarce; three sight records: on Gosainkund trail in June at 4270 m. (14,000'), (Desfayes); above Gatlang (Ganesh Himal) in May and in *tarai* in January (RLF). Male all black except brown primaries and yellow bill. Female very similar to female Gray-winged Blackbird but lacks wingbar; bill greenish-yellow (not orange or bright yellow). ❁ Kashmir, Garhwal, Nepal, Sikkim; Europe, Africa, Asia   1752

Whistling Thrush, *Myiophoneus caeruleus*.
213-4575 m. (700-15,000') 30 cm. (12") R.

Common; near rushing water in wooded ravines. Blue-black (usually looks black) with bright yellow lower mandible. Some feathers flecked to give a slightly spotted appearance but seen only when light is reflected at just the right angle. Larger and stronger-legged than the Eurasian Blackbird. Single or in pairs. After landing on branch or rock, slowly depresses and flares tail. Often chases another through trees. A powerful and delightful song of sustained, silvery notes heard at dawn or on dim, rainy days. Song penetrates above the sound of waterfalls. Also a hissing *k-a-a-a* and a loud *cheet-chi-cheet* like that of the Spotted Forktail. ❀ KV: along forest motor roads and wooded streams. ❁ Kashmir, Garhwal, Nepal, Sikkim; Turkestan to Java   1729

Tickell's Thrush, *Turdus unicolor.*
1525-2745 m. (5,000-9,000') 25 cm. (10") S.

Fairly common; in oak and scrub forests and grassy hillsides. Male pale gray and white, sometimes lightly spotted on throat. Female olive-brown with brown marks on pale throat and upper breast. Female very similar to Black-throated Thrush in non-breeding plumage but is smaller and has a light rufous wash on flanks. Also very like the Dark Thrush (rare in Nepal) but lacks rufous wash on breast. Single or in small parties; more of a noontime singer than other Himalayan thrushes. Fairly shy and quickly takes to cover. Nests in crotches of smallish trees at about 2440 m. (8,000'). Song a relaxed warble, *dew-dew* and variations, each short phrase ending in a characteristic high squeak. ✲ KV: nests on southern slopes of Sheopuri.
♠ Kashmir, Garhwal, Nepal, Sikkim; S. Asia   1748

Gray-headed Thrush, *Turdus rubrocanus.*
915-2745 m. (3,000-9,000') 28 cm. (11") M., W.

Scarce; in tree tops or feeding on ground. Male, gray head, neck and throat contrasts sharply with chestnut body. Female similar but duller. Single, pairs or small parties. Flies with a strong thrush wingbeat. Associates with other thrushes in fruiting trees such as wild pears. Not known to nest in Nepal but may do so in the extreme N.W. Song a fine warble sung from tops of tall conifers at dusk. ✲ KV: winter, Godaveri; oak forest on Chandragiri. ♠ Kashmir, Garhwal, Nepal, Sikkim(?); Pakistan to S. China   1758, 1759

Black/Red-throated Thrush, *Turdus ruficollis.*
120-3660 m. (400-12,000') 25 cm. (10") W.

Fairly common; from dense forest to grassy slopes with scattered trees. Two very distinct subspecies (considered full species by some). Black-throated race fairly common in midland Nepal. Most birds are gray above, pale below with streaks on sides of throat and upper breast. Resembles female Tickell's Thrush but is larger and lacks rufous wash on flanks. Individuals with solid black throats fairly unusual. *T. r. ruficollis*, the red-throated form with upper breast and tail reddish, is common only north of the main Himalayas (Jomosom). When perching, tilts tail up and flicks wings. Hops in fields and along river banks but also spends much time in trees. In loose flocks of 5-50 in winter; often feeds in fruiting trees. Contact note a short *puk*, *peer-up;* alarm a *pee-wit*, *chip-chi-chip.* ✲ KV: a common forest and field bird in winter. (Dusky Thrush, *Turdus naumanni,* see Sikkim list, p. 337.) ♠ Kashmir, Garhwal, Nepal, Sikkim; Europe, Asia   1763, 1764

Mistle Thrush, *Turdus viscivorus.*
1525-3660 m. (5,000-12,000') 29 cm. (11¼") R.

Fairly common; in pine and oak forests of W. Nepal. Pale brownish-gray with large, dark spots below (larger and paler bird than spotted mountain thrushes; *spots are round,* not crescent-shaped). Inhabits wild ridges such as Khali Lagna, Jumla District. Single or pairs seen as high as 3660 m. (12,000') in January. Fairly common around Rara Lake and noted as far east as Dhorpatan, Baglung District. Song a dissected melody heard in spring. A harsh nasal contact and alarm note, *chaaa.* ♠ Kashmir, Garhwal, Nepal; Europe, Africa, Asia   1768

Dark Thrush, *Turdus obscurus.*
2135 m. (7,000') 20 cm. (8") M.

Scarce; appears to be a straggler in Nepal. Reported from the Singalila Ridge by Stevens (1925). Recently netted by Ted Cronin in Arun River area (1973). Male olive-brown above with distinct white eyebrow. Also note pale underparts with streaked gray neck and rufous on flanks and breast. Female similar but lacks gray neck. (Striking Kessler's Thrush, *T. kessleri*, rare in winter in Sikkim, see p. 337.) ♠ Nepal, Sikkim; C. and E. Asia   1762

WREN (Troglodytidae). The Wren is a tiny, brown bird with strong legs and a cocked tail. An American family with only one species in Eurasia.

Wren (Winter Wren), *Troglodytes troglodytes*.
2440-4575 m. (8,000-15,000') 9 cm. (3½") R.

Fairly common; popping out of stone walls and from between rocks above the tree line. Dark rufous-brown, paler below with heavy barring except chin and upper breast. A perky, inquisitive little bird which bobs up and down through bushes and among rocks. Found among *Cotoneaster* and *Ephedra* bushes in Mugu, Langtang and Khumbu. Has a short song and a loud alarm note *tzip*. ❋ KV: among stone ruins on top of Sheopuri in winter. ◖ Kashmir, Garhwal, Nepal, Sikkim; Holarctic 1771

DIPPERS (Cinclidae) are plump birds with short, strong bills, stubby tails, stout, long legs and dense feathers adapted to keeping the bird dry under water. Sexes alike.

White-breasted Dipper, *Cinclus cinclus*.
3873-4575 m. (12,700-15,000') 18 cm. (7") R.

Fairly common; on rushing streams and rivers of Trans-Himalayan Nepal (Dolpo and Mustang). Dull brown to gray with a distinctive white chin, throat and upper breast. Young (seen from mid-June onward) a "fuzzy" gray, dark-tipped feathers and paler throat. Single on rocks in mid-stream or along edge in shallow pools but sometimes bobs around like a cork in deeper water. When standing, continually does "deep-knee-bends;" flicks wings and tail. Nest in Dolpo behind a waterfall reached by diving into pool and swimming under the falls. Both parents feed young. Call a *zeet*. ◖ Kashmir, Nepal, Sikkim; Europe, Africa, Asia 1773

Brown Dipper, *Cinclus pallasii*.
457-4575 m. (1,500-15,000') 18 cm. (7") R.

Fairly common; skimming over the surface of rushing water. Similar in shape to White-breasted Dipper but adults wholly chocolate-brown, pale edges to upperwing coverts. Young gray. Solitary or in scattered family parties in spring. Bobs up and down on spray-soaked rocks; short, direct flight with rapid wingbeat. Much in the open; somewhat shy. Nests at fairly low altitudes in January-February, then moves uphill [found with White-breasted species in Dolpo in summer 4270 m. (14,000')]. A loud, bubbling song sung from ice-encrusted boulders (Jumla) in February. Alarm a loud, repeated *jeeeet*. ❋ KV: sometimes nests in stone wall at Sundarijal Tal (January). ◖ Kashmir, Garhwal, Nepal, Sikkim; Transcaspia to Japan 1775

ACCENTORS (Prunellidae) superficially resemble sparrows but have tapering, sharp-pointed bills, pointed wings and fairly long, square tails. Most are heavily streaked above and lightly marked below. Sexes alike. Pairs (summer) or small parties found on open slopes or in light forest during winter. Behavior is reminiscent of both chats and finches.

Altai Accentor, *Prunella himalayana*.
2135-4270 m. (7,000-14,000') 15 cm. (6") W.

Fairly common; wintering on grassy slopes from snow line downwards. Similar to Alpine Accentor but head and rump grayer and white throat flecked (not closely barred) with black. Not yet recorded from Nepal in summer. Collects in vast flocks in winter to feed on grassy slopes from Darchula hills to Sandakphu (Sikkim border). Associates at times with Hodgson's Mountain Finch. Hops about with body parallel to ground and at times lifts head to look around. When alarmed, flies up with others in a compact group to circle and turn together. After disturbance, may land on a bare branch rather than on the ground. Noted as late as mid-May [Gosainkund, 4270 m. (14,000')]. Voice a double *tee-tee*. ◖ Kashmir, Garhwal, Nepal, Sikkim; C. Asia 1780

Alpine Accentor, *Prunella collaris*.
2440-5490 m. (8,000-18,000') 15 cm. (6") R.

Occasional; well above the tree line for most of the year. Brown with grayish-brown head and breast. Distinctive throat is white, *narrowly barred with black*. Also look for rufous flanks which are puffed out in cold weather. Solitary or in pairs and virtually never in flocks. Rarely below 4575 m. (15,000') in summer; noted as low as 2440 m. (8,000') in winter at Jumla. Prefers grassy slopes. Hops about on ground searching for seeds and insects among clumps of grass and under stones. Very tame in Thangboche Monastery complex (Khumbu). Song six notes slurring upward to a final *tee-dee*. Alarm a high-pitched *tsip*. ◖ Kashmir, Garhwal, Nepal, Sikkim; Europe, Africa, Asia 1779

Robin Accentor, *Prunella rubeculoides.*
2745-4880 m. (9,000-16,000') 16 cm. (6½") R.
Common; in Trans-Himalayan Nepal; fairly common in Khumbu above 3812 m. (12,500'). Uniform gray head and throat contrasts with rufous breast. Distinguished from Rufous-breasted Accentor by *gray throat* (not white) and lacks eyebrow. Single or in pairs among *Caragana* bushes; easily approached. Hops among grassy spots. Several birds chase each other in spring; courtship display includes much quivering. Descends as low as Jomosom, 2745 m. (9,000') in winter; nests above 3965 m. (13,000') in Khumbu (Diesselhorst) and the Trans-Himalayas. Song two high-pitched phrases *tzwe--e--you, tzwe--e--you* with variations. Alarm a ringing *pi-pi-pi-pi-pi* sounded from tops of bushes. ♠ Kashmir, Garhwal, Nepal, Sikkim; Himalayas to Shensi 1781

Rufous-breasted Accentor, *Prunella strophiata.*
1982-4880 m. (6,500-16,000') 15 cm. (6") R.
Fairly common; in cutover scrub and open country above the tree line. Heavily streaked with diagnostic *broad rufous breast band* and *rufous eyebrow*. In pairs or small parties in fields near villages or old cattle sheds. Rests atop small bushes; often associates with other bush birds such as White-browed Tit Babblers. Common in hedges around Jumla 2440 m. (8,000') in winter. In summer, commonest just above the tree line where nests are placed in barberry and juniper bushes. Song a rapid staccato *te-te-te-te-te;* also a *chr-r-r-r.* ❀ KV: southern slopes of Sheopuri in winter. ♠ Kashmir, Garhwal, Nepal, Sikkim; Afghanistan to Shensi
1782, 1783

Black-throated Accentor, *Prunella atrogularis.*
2440-3050 m. (8,000-10,000') 15 cm. (6") W.
Fairly common; in fields and hedges of far N.W. Nepal. Brown with a black face mask and *black throat*. In small flocks feeding under bushes at edges of fields. When disturbed, first seeks shelter in bushes but if pressed will fly strongly away. Usually hugs vicinity of bushes and stone walls. Noted only in winter with rose finches, buntings and other accentors around Jumla, Mugu, Humla. ♠ Kashmir, Garhwal, Nepal; C. Asia 1786

Brown Accentor, *Prunella fulvescens.*
2745-4880 m. (9,000-16,000') 15 cm. (6") R.
Common; in desert biotope of the Trans-Himalayas. A pale, brownish-gray species with conspicuous dark brown mask. Like the Black-throated Accentor but with uniformly pale (not black) throat. Pairs or small parties, in stony wastes of the Dolpo desert country; sometimes with Tibetan Snow Finches. Feeds mostly on the ground. Chase each other over ground or through *Caragana* clumps. Sings lustily from a bush top. Nest building in June at 4270 m. (14,000'). Down as low as Jumla 2440 m. (8,000') in winter. Song variable, somewhat like a warbler's, a soft *tuk* followed by a 4-5-syllable phrase *tuk---tileep-tilee--tileep-tileep;* also *tuk---seep-seep-see-seep* and *tuk----teew-teew.* ♠ Kashmir, Nepal; C. Asia 1785

Maroon-backed Accentor, *Prunella immaculata.*
1830-2440 m. (6,000-8,000') 16 cm. (6½") W.
Occasional; in forests or at edges of fields. Gray with a *maroon lower back* and *upper wing coverts*. Pale yellow eye seen at close range. In small, close parties, pecking at wild pears from leafless trees or hopping on ground for seeds. Somewhat shy, flying quickly from ground into trees. Noted so far only in winter but may nest in Nepal above 4575 m. (15,000') as in Sikkim (Ali). Has a double note. ❀ KV: in grassy glades on Sheopuri at about 2287 m. (7,500') in winter. ♠ Nepal, Sikkim; Nepal to Szechuan 1788

TITMICE (Paridae) are mostly small, energetic birds, working in flocks through trees and bushes, often with nuthatches and warblers. Many species are crested. They are acrobatic and may hang upside-down while searching for insects or berries; can be watched at close range. Sexes similar.

Sultan Tit, *Melanochlora sultanea*.
274-1372 m. (900-4,500') 22 cm. (8½") R.

Scarce; in both heavy and thin stands of trees in low foothills. The *only large tit*, the size of a bulbul. Unmistakable; a flaring yellow crest and yellow abdomen, otherwise shiny black. In female, black is replaced by dark brown. Single or in pairs in tall trees, along streams, roads and fields. Largely restricted to the Churias (outermost Himalayas). In action, much like other tits, acrobatically creeping around and under branches or hovering in front of twigs. Song a loud, mellow *pee-del-pee-del*, the pitch falling on the "del." Alarm a buzzing *durrrrrrr*. ♦ Nepal, Sikkim; Nepal to Sumatra   1789

Gray Tit, *Parus major*.
120-2440 m. (400-8,000') 14 cm. (5½") R.

Common; in acacia groves and scrub land. Blue-gray and black with white cheek patch and wingbar. Moves through the middle or lower levels of trees. Balances upside-down on a twig while prying into curled leaves; probes into flowers. Nests rather early in spring in walls or holes of trees. Uncommon above 1525 m. (5,000'). Song a bright *bree-bree-chi; wheat-wheat-ear; tee-tee---tee-ter-tee-ter*. ✤ KV: in temple groves and light pine forest above Balaju. ♦ Kashmir, Garhwal, Nepal, Sikkim(?); Europe, Africa, Asia   1793

Green-backed Tit, *Parus monticolus*.
1372-3660 m. (4,500-12,000') 13 cm. (5") R.

Common; in oak-rhododendron forests. Black head, no crest and *white cheeks*. Bright yellow below with black bib and mid-line. Green back not conspicuous. In small parties or mixed groups in the middle or low parts of trees; also in bushes. May descend to the ground after insects or cling to bole of tree while searching for food. Rarely above 2745 m. (9,000') in winter. A cheery, fearless species, often calling with a bright, drawn-out *teeeee-churrrrr, teeeee-churrrrr*, a *pic-tee* and a *pz-pz-pz-peer*. ✤ KV: in oak forest around the Valley. ♦ Kashmir, Garhwal, Nepal, Sikkim; Pakistan to Formosa   1799

Yellow-cheeked Tit, *Parus xanthogenys*.
305-2287 m. (1,000-7,500') 14 cm. (5½") R.

Common; in groves, thin forest and at the edge of heavy forest. Black crest, yellow cheeks; yellow below with wide, black median stripe. Told from very similar Black-spotted Yellow Tit by *black forehead* (not yellow) and *yellow*-tipped wing coverts (not white). In pairs or small parties usually by themselves; sometimes with other tits. When agitated, raises crest, flicks wings and tail. Song a bright *miss-us-spitti-baar;* also *sz-sz-sz-tsirp* and an alarm call, *tst-reet*. ✤ KV: frequent in Chapagaon, Gokarna, Gaucher, Godaveri forests. ♦ Kashmir, Garhwal, Nepal, Sikkim(?); S. Asia   1809

Black-spotted Yellow Tit, *Parus spilonotus*.
1982-2440 m. (6,500-8,000') 14 cm. (5½") R.

Occasional; in oak forests of Ilam District, E. Nepal. Very similar to Yellow-cheeked Tit but *forehead* is *yellow* (not black); back is streaked with black. Moves through low trees in small parties; flies short distances from one tree to the next in follow-the-leader fashion. Also spends time towards tops of tall trees. Acrobatic behavior. A subdued contact note when feeding. Song is a bright *pe-tee-tee-tee*, often following phrase similar to that of Yellow-Cheeked Tit. ♦ Nepal, Sikkim; Nepal to Thailand   1812

Coal Tit, *Parus ater*.
2287-3965 m. (7,500-13,000') 11 cm. (4½") R.

Fairly common; among oak, fir, juniper and hemlock forests. Nepal's tiniest black tit with a thin black crest sporting three or four elongated feathers. Note white spots on wings and *pale buffy-fawn belly*. Often in large homogeneous flocks, even in spring; associates with other small birds. At times rather high in trees, jerking, jumping and fluttering about. Conversely, will work among fallen logs on forest floor. Swarms around owls. Considerable altitudinal movement in cold weather, descending to 2287 m. (7,500') in winter but rarely below 2897 m. (9,500') in summer. Song a fairly low-pitched, slow *wee-tsee---wee-tsee---wee-tsee.* Contact note a *psip*. Hybridizes with the Spot-winged Black Tit in the Dhaulagiri area (Martens). Look for hybrids around Dhorpatan and S. Dolpo. ✣ KV: the only black tit here in winter, top of Sheopuri. ✦ Nepal, Sikkim; Europe, Africa, Asia 1803

Spot-winged Black Tit (Crested Black Tit), *Parus melanolophus*.
2135-3812 m. (7,000-12,500') 11 cm. (4½") R.

Common; on northern slopes among oaks and conifers of N.W. Nepal. Numerous in forests of S. Dolpo. A "typical" black tit with black crest and breast, uniform dark gray belly and a double row of pale spots on wing forming "bars." Small parties in spring; large flocks up to 40 in winter. Often with creepers, warblers and tits. Constantly flipping about in the upper half of trees. Song a weak *peak-you* repeated about four times followed by a *pau-see*. Alarm a high squeak. J. Martens discovered this species interbreeding with Coal Tit, *P. ater aemodius*, in Dhaulagiri area (1973). ✦ Kashmir, Garhwal, Nepal; Afghanistan to Nepal 1802

Simla Black Tit, *Parus rufonuchalis*.
2867-3965 m. (9,400-13,000') 13 cm. (5") R.

Fairly common; in conifers, oaks and rhododendrons. The largest and darkest of the black tits with black crest and head. Black extends onto abdomen. Underparts usually show no rufous. No white spots on wings. Very similar to Sikkim Black Tit but larger, black descends farther on breast and E-W ranges never overlap. In pairs or small parties at tops of firs and Blue Pines or other trees. Not as active as other black tits but associates with them as well as with nuthatches and warblers. Song a somewhat thrush-like *leu-ti-tee-de* and a *sue--whee*. Taped song of Sikkim Black Tit (see next species) elicited no response from this tit (J. Martens). ✦ Kashmir, Garhwal, Nepal; Afghanistan to Nepal 1804

Rufous-breasted Black Tit, *Parus rubidiventris*.
2257-4575 m. (7,400-15,000') 11 cm. (4½") R.

Common; in oak-rhododendron forests and scrub rhododendrons above tree line. *No wing spots*. The western race, *P. r. rubidiventris* has all lower breast and belly rufous; the rufous is replaced by gray in the eastern race, *P. r. beavani* (Sikkim Black Tit). Usually well above 3050 m. (10,000') with little altitudinal change. One specimen (a stray?) at base of a talus fan near Trupak Glacier, Langtang at 4574 m. (15,000'). In flocks with other species working on mountain ash berries and fir cones. Descends to pools at evening to drink. Song a *tzuk-ti-ti-ti-ti-ti* (the "ti"s a rapid, lilting whistle). Alarm a *churrrr*. J. Martens, by taping calls of the two races, found they were very similar and elicited immediate responses. ✦ Garhwal, Nepal, Sikkim; Garhwal to China (Shensi) 1805/1804½

Crested Brown Tit, *Parus dichrous*.
2745-3812 m. (9,000-12,500') 13 cm. (5") R.

Fairly common; in leafy canopies of oak-conifer-rhododendron forests. A gray bird (not brown). Besides a prominent crest, the pale fulvous band on sides of neck the most conspicuous feature (looks somewhat like the Stripe-throated Yuhina, see p. 208, but has the pale collar and lacks throat markings and color on wings). Pairs or small parties; rather shy, unobtrusive and silent except when alarmed. Usually a few in a mixed hunting party low in trees and in bushes. Alarm a rapid, moderately-pitched *cheea, cheea*, a *ti-ti-ti-ti-ti;* song a *whee-whee-tz-tz-tz*. ✦ Kashmir, Garhwal, Nepal, Sikkim; Himalayas to Kansu 1808

Fire-capped Tit, *Cephalopyrus flammiceps.*
2745 m. (9,000') 9 cm. (3½") R.

Scarce; recent sight record in maple forest near Chedang Kund, 2745 m. (9,000') on slopes of Ganesh Himal in April (RLF and members of Sierra Club Natural History Trek, 1971). A small warbler-like species. Male with flaming orange head and throat; female has greenish-gray head, a yellowish breast, gray throat. Status in Nepal unclear. Strong flight like a Goldfinch. Works towards tops of trees. Song is soft and bubbling. ♠ Kashmir, Garhwal, Nepal, Sikkim; Afghanistan to Yunnan   1816

Red-headed Tit, *Aegithalos concinnus.*
1067-2592 m. (3,500-8,500') 11 cm. (4½") R.

Common; in mixed forests and bamboo groves. Look for conspicuous chestnut crown bordered with white; also a broad black eye bar and a black bib on pale throat. At close range, pale cream eye conspicuous. A tiny species with a long tail. In small parties buzzing about in trees or low shrubs. Very active; a weak flight. Roosts apart from other species but feeds with them. Nests early; a round ball of moss lined with feathers; entrance through hole at the side. Song a very high, thin *tur-r-r-tait-yeat-yeat-yeat*. Alarm a rapidly repeated *tzit*. ❋ KV: frequents forests of surrounding hills. ♠ Kashmir, Garhwal, Nepal, Sikkim; Pakistan to Formosa   1818, 1819

Yellow-browed Tit, *Parus modestus.*
1830-3660 m. (6,000-12,000') 10 cm. (4") R.

Fairly common; in tops of oak trees. Looks like a tiny leaf warbler but slightly elevated semi-crest distinguishes it from all warblers. The yellow brow usually invisible except at close range when the bird is alarmed. In pairs or small hunting parties, often in company with other species. Constantly flicking wings and frequently hanging upside-down. Call a high *tee* repeated about three times in two seconds; alarm note is a high, almost inaudible *tzee-tzee*, rapidly repeated. ❋ KV: in surrounding forests 2135-2440 m. (7,000-8,000'). The first known nest of this species discovered on a bird walk on Phulchowki at 2440 m. (8,000') by the D. E. Boster family (1969). Nest made of hair in hole of rhododendron trunk, three feet above the ground. Young about two weeks old on 3rd of May. Both parents fed insect larvae to young; extremely bold when doing so. ♠ Kashmir, Garhwal, Nepal, Sikkim; Himalayas to Fukien   1814

White-throated Tit, *Aegithalos niveogularis.*
3050-3965 m. (10,000-13,000') 11 cm. (4½") R.

Occasional; in N.W. Nepal as far east as Ringmo Lake, Dolpo District; in scrub and bushes in birch and pine forests. Pale grayish-brown. Look for large pale bib, black eyebrow and black encompassing much of the face. A pale buff stripe from bill to crown is also conspicuous. In small parties, even in spring; usually fairly close to the ground. Active, but lingers longer in an area than most other tits. Often with leaf warblers. Call a high, rapid, repeated *tze-tze-tze* like the Red-headed Tit. (White-cheeked Tit. *A. leucogenys*, in Kashmir, see p. 335.) ♠ Kashmir, Garhwal, Nepal; Chitral to Nepal   1822

Rufous-fronted Tit, *Aegithalos iouschistos.*
2592-3355 m. (8,500-11,000') 11 cm. (4½") R.

Occasional; in oak, rhododendron, chestnut and hemlock forests. Another crestless, long-tailed mite. Has black crown, wide fulvous band over top of head from bill to nape and pale throat patch. Resembles somewhat the White-throated Tit but more rufous below, darker above and much less white on throat. Usually in small homogeneous parties but sometimes with warblers, nuthatches and other tits. In low parts of tall trees and bushes. A confiding bird but a bit shier than other tits. Very little seasonal movement. First known nest of this species discovered in an oak at 2745 m. (9,000') in Ilam District in May 1970 (Lee Miller and RLF). Nest is a ball lined with feathers and studded outside with lichens; the entrance hole at side. Both parents feed young. Alarm call a shrill *zeet* and a *trr-trr-trr;* contact note *tik-tik*. ♠ C. Nepal (Dhaulagiri) eastward, Sikkim; Himalayas   1823

NUTHATCHES (Sittidae) are chunky little birds with long, well-developed bills, small, short legs, short tails, and pointed wings. A strong undulating flight. Sexes similar in most cases. Among the few Himalayan birds that work head first down tree trunks. Differences in altitude and habitat help to distinguish species.

Eurasian Nuthatch (European Nuthatch), *Sitta europaea*.
3050-3507 m. *(10,000-11,500')* 13 cm. (5") R.

Fairly common; in oak-spruce-pine forests of N.W. Nepal (Dolpo, Jumla, Mugu, Humla). Blue-gray above and fulvous to rufous below. A black line through eye extends to nape. Silver-gray ear patch noticeable. Very similar to Chestnut-bellied Nuthatch but range never overlaps. Also note that the female Chestnut-bellied Nuthatch has cinnamon-brown underparts (not rufous) while the White-tailed Nuthatch is *pale* fulvous below. Moves in pairs up and down tree trunks and along large branches; probes and hammers on both conifers and oaks. Near Rara Lake in the same area as the White-cheeked Nuthatch but not seen with them. Alarm a loud, repeated, rasping *kaaaaa*. ♣ Kashmir, Garhwal, Nepal; Europe, Africa, Asia 1824

Chestnut-bellied Nuthatch, *Sitta castanea*.
152-1830 m. (500-6,000') 14 cm. (5½") R.

Common; in upper half of forest trees. Blue-gray above; below, male maroon and female cinnamon-brown, palest on chin and throat. Some white in tail. Separated from similar Eurasian Nuthatch, which is rufous below, by habitat and altitude. Usually in pairs, often with other birds which they seem to pilot on to the next tree. Quite noisy. Song a faint "police whistle" trill *veveveveve;* also a rapid *tir-tir-tir-tir-tir*. Alarm a loud *bzirp*. ❊ KV: in forest groves of the Valley floor. ♣ Garhwal, Nepal, Sikkim; Himalayas to S.E. Asia
1827, 1828, 1830

White-cheeked Nuthatch, *Sitta leucopsis*.
2745-3812 m. *(9,000-12,500')* 13 cm. (5") R.

Fairly common; among conifers of N.W. Nepal and as far east as Suli Gad River, Dolpo District. Blue-gray with a distinctive black crown and nape contrasting with *white face and throat*. In pairs, often in mixed hunting parties. Works energetically on branches towards the tops of trees where it may pause to call loudly. Voice a hard, nasal *chaaaaa* repeated at intervals. When excited, continues to call long after visible danger has passed. ♣ Kashmir, Garhwal, Nepal; Afghanistan to Kansu 1832

Velvet-fronted Nuthatch, *Sitta frontalis*.
152-2013 m. (500-6,600') 13 cm. (5") R.

Fairly common; especially in *sal* forests of the *tarai*. Bright blue above, pinkish-gray below with *bright coral-red bill*, the most conspicuous feature. Female is illustrated here; male similar but also has black line from eye to nape. In pairs or small parties with other nuthatches, tits, minivets and drongos. Very agile, working through middle of trees and along large branches. Easily seen; noisy. Voice *did-did-cadcaddidididideee; chip-chip-chee-chee-chee;* a faint *tilk* and a *chip*. ❊ KV: in groves on the Valley floor. ♣ Nepal, Sikkim; India to Philippines 1838

White-tailed Nuthatch, *Sitta himalayensis*.
915-3141 m. (3,000-10,300') 13 cm. (5") R.

Common; in oak-rhododendrons at 1525-2135 m. (5,000-7,000') and maple-hemlock forests at 2745-3050 m. (9,000-10,000'). Blue-gray and fulvous with black band from bill through eye to nape. White in center and at base of tail hard to see except from above. In pairs or small parties, usually with other species. Frequently in upper half of tree. Calls loudly from dead branches or while heading down tree trunk with head raised to a horizontal position. Not often below 1830 m. (6,000'). Voice a loud, rapid *ti-ti-ti-ti-ti* and a gentle *preeee* at two-second intervals. Contact note *ti-tik*. ❊ KV: in oak forests surrounding Valley. (Beautiful Nuthatch, *S. formosa*, rare resident, Sikkim, see p. 337.) ♣ Garhwal, Nepal, Sikkim; Kulu to Tonkin 1834

Wall Creeper (Sittidae; sub-family Tichodromadinae). The Wall Creeper, although classified with nuthatches, does not greatly resemble them either in behavior or superficial anatomy. The long bill is slender and decurved. It constantly flicks wings; flight, a moth-like flutter, exposes crimson on wings. It hitches up vertical surfaces like a creeper.

Wall Creeper, *Tichodroma muraria*.
549-4575 m. (1,800-15,000') 18 cm. (7") W., R. (?)
Occasional; on cliffs, boulders in rivers and high clay banks. Pale gray with crimson wing pattern and white spots, most conspicuous in flight. Throat pale in winter (illustrated); black in summer. Solitary, active and fairly bold. Erratic, jerky flight. Seen in June in Dolpo and Khumbu and may nest in Trans-Himalayan Nepal. Song (in Europe) a rising *zee-zee-zee-tui* (Bruun). ◐ Kashmir, Garhwal, Nepal, Sikkim; Europe, Africa, Asia 1839

TREE CREEPERS (Certhiidae) are small, mottled brown birds with long, stiff tails and long, decurved bills. They hitch their way up tree trunks in the manner of woodpeckers, using their tails for support. Sexes alike. They probe crevices of bark for insects but do not hammer trees as do nuthatches and woodpeckers.

Northern Tree Creeper (Brown Creeper), *Certhia familiaris*.
2287-3965 m. (7,500-13,000') 15 cm. (6") R.
Occasional; in conifer, birch and rhododendron forests. Below, *white from chin to abdomen* with fulvous flanks and an unbarred tail. Solitary or in small parties, often with other species. Partial to hemlock and fir trees. Usually is busy on lower half of main trunk; when about half way up the tree, it flips off and flutters to base of next tree. Voice a high-pitched, rising then descending *tzee---tzee--tze-tzizitze*. Also a quick *tzit*. ◐ Kashmir, Garhwal, Nepal, Sikkim; Europe, Asia, N. America 1843

Himalayan Tree Creeper, *Certhia himalayana*.
305-2745 m. (1,000-9,000') 15 cm. (6") R.
Occasional; in oak forests, descending to low foothills in winter. Similar to Northern Tree Creeper but grayish-tan below (not white). Also look for diagnostic *cross bars on tail*. Single or in pairs often with other species. Feeds on boles of large trees from about five feet above the ground to the middle level. Sometimes pursues insects into the air like an uncoordinated flycatcher. Known in W. Nepal as far east as the Kali Gandaki Valley. Song in spring a loud, mellow *lu-lu-lu-lu* whistle; also a high-pitched squeak. ◐ Kashmir, Garhwal, Nepal; Turkestan to Nepal; again in Burma and S. China 1848

Nepal Tree Creeper, *Certhia nipalensis*.
1830-3660 m. (6,000-12,000') 15 cm. (6") R.
Fairly common; in wet oak and conifer forests. Differs from other tree creepers in having throat pale fulvous (not white or brown) and *deep fulvous* on sides of breast and flanks. Pale eyebrow curves strongly downward, then around cheek and is good field mark. Solitary or in loose pairs on low branches and tree trunks. Forages among epiphytes such as moss and ferns, along with other creepers, tits and nuthatches. Sometimes found in dwarf bamboo. Known as far west as Bajhang District, N.W. Nepal. Call a low squeak (Baker). ◐ Nepal, Sikkim; Nepal to Bhutan 1851

Sikkim Tree Creeper, *Certhia discolor*.
305-3050 m. (1,000-10,000') 15 cm. (6") R.
Fairly common; in oak and mixed forests. Throat brown (neither white as in Northern and Himalayan Tree Creepers nor pale fulvous as in Nepal Tree Creeper), grayish-brown below with a *bright rufous tail*. One or two in mixed hunting parties. The common tree creeper at moderate elevations. Seen in foothills in winter but also noted as high as 3050 m. (10,000') in December. Extends as far west as the Kali Gandaki River. Voice a loud, mellow trilling *tritititititit* for about two seconds, repeated at seven or eight-second intervals. Contact note a repeated *tzit*. ❄ KV: in oak forests with warblers and tits. ◐ Nepal, Sikkim; Nepal to S.E. Asia 1849

PIPITS and WAGTAILS (Motacillidae). Pipits are brown, heavily streaked above and less so below. Wings and legs are strong. Tails in some species are pumped up and down. Pipits resemble larks but are slenderer and tails longer. Sexes alike. In spring, males flutter weakly into the air with undulating flight. Field identifications often difficult, particularly with young birds. Pipits show pale lateral tail feathers in flight. Wagtails begin on p. 290.

Hodgson's Tree Pipit, *Anthus hodgsoni.*
274-3751 m.   (900-12,300')   15 cm.   (6")   R., W.

Common; in grassy meadows in summer and shaded glades in winter. Very heavily streaked above and below. Has greenish wash on back and a conspicuous buffy eyebrow in contrast to the much paler Eurasian Tree Pipit with almost no eyebrow. In summer usually above 2440 m. (8,000') around cattle sheds but nests as low as 2135 m. (7,000') in Ilam District. Small, scattered flocks feed on ground in winter. When disturbed, quickly flies into tree and pumps tail. Song a bubbling *chirr-eep-zip-zip-zip* given on the wing or from a top of a dead tree. Also a faint *tzip* when flying off ground. ✹ KV: October-April on Valley floor; May, nests on rim of Sheopuri. ✺ Garhwal, Nepal, Sikkim ; Asia   1852, 1853

Upland Pipit, *Anthus sylvanus.*
1372-2745 m.   (4,500-9,000')   18 cm.   (7")   R.

Fairly common; on steep rocky and grassy stretches. A fulvous-gray bird with thin, dark brown streaks, least apparent on lower abdomen. Has a rather short and sharp-pointed tail for a pipit. Solitary, mounts rocks or raised clods of earth; rarely associates with other birds. Usually on south faces of hills in rocky areas. Not shy, but blends into background, so hard to see. In spring, flutters into air, circles while singing, then glides to another suitable rock. Song a slow, raspy *feer-cheeee* or *purrrr-tseeee* repeated seven or eight times; sounds like a squeaky gate. ✹ KV: on grassy, southern slopes of Valley. ✺ Kashmir, Garhwal, Nepal, Sikkim ; Afghanistan to Yunnan   1873

Paddyfield Pipit (Richard's Pipit), *Anthus novaeseelandiae.*
152-1830 m.   (500-6,000')   15 cm.   (6")   R., W.

Common; at edges and banks of terraced fields and open meadows. Pale fulvous and tan with *faint marks on breast*. Legs pale (pinkish). White outer tail feathers conspicuous in flight. Spends much time running over the ground looking for food. Flight strong and undulating. In spring, shoots up into air as it sings a weak, little song, then "parachutes" down again; also from a mound a ringing *dee-dee-dee-dee-dee-dee*, with neck outstretched. Nests in a sheltered spot on the ground. Flies up with a *tseep*. A very much larger and more richly colored race, Richard's Pipit, *A. n. richardi*, which some scientists now consider a full species, is an occasional winter visitor. Similar to Blyth's Pipit but is usually slightly paler and without noticeable fulvous wash. Hind claw is much longer than hind toe (but this can be seen best in a museum !). ✹ KV: *A. n. rufulus* is the common pipit here. (Meadow Pipit, *Anthus pratensis*, see Kashmir list, p. 335.) ✺ Nepal, Sikkim ; Europe, Africa, Asia, Australia   1857, 1859

Blyth's Pipit, *Anthus godlewskii.*
1342-3873 m.   (4,400-12,700')   18 cm.   (7")   W., M.

Occasional; in grassy meadows. A large, pale pipit. Note pale fulvous throat and abdomen with a darker wash on breast and flanks. Very similar to *A. n. richardi* but overall slightly richer fulvous. Hind claw about same length as hind toe. An autumn migrant in small flocks on open ground. Rises with a single harsh note. ✹ KV: in fallow fields east of airport in November. ✺ Nepal, Sikkim ; C. Asia to Sri Lanka   1863

Red-throated Pipit, *Anthus cervinus*.
5185 m. (17,000') 14 cm. (5½") W.

Scarce; an uncommon visitor found on steep, rocky slopes of Dhaulagiri above Tukuche in December (Carl Taylor). A brick-pink wash on throat (not the purplish-pink of Rose-breasted Pipit). Rump heavily streaked. Found in open country above tree line. Nepal status uncertain. ♦ Nepal; Europe, Africa, Asia, N. America
1864

Rose-breasted Pipit (Hodgson's Pipit), *Anthus roseatus*.
762-4880 m. (2,500-16,000') 16 cm. (6¼") R, M.

Fairly common; on wet, grassy stream banks in winter and on migration; above the tree line in summer. A dark, heavily streaked pipit. A faint lilac-rose throat, breast and upper abdomen, most distinct in spring. No lilac-rose on many young and winter birds. Young very heavily streaked above and differentiated from Hodgson's Tree Pipit by lack of buffy eyebrow. Creeps along edges of streams holding body almost parallel to the ground, giving a hunched-over appearance. In summer one of the most conspicuous birds above the tree line. Works among rocks, grass clumps and bushes. Undulating flight. Song a brief melody often sung on the wing, also a short *tsip*. ❖ KV: Bagmati River above Chobar in March. ♦ Kashmir, Garhwal, Nepal, Sikkim; C. Asia
1865

Brown Rock Pipit, *Anthus similis*.
244-1982 m. (800-6,500') 23 cm. (9") R.

Scarce; on dry, rocky slopes of the low foothills. A heavy grayish-brown pipit with pronounced eyebrow (lacking in illustration). Sandy-brown below with a few dark markings on breast; *no* white outer tail feathers. Solitary, in bushes and in cultivated fields. Known only from far western Nepal. A courting flight and song in spring. Also a *tzip*. ♦ Kashmir, Garhwal, Nepal; Africa, Asia
1867

Water Pipit, *Anthus spinoletta*.
152-2135 m. (500-7,000') 16 cm. (6¼") W.

Scarce; in open cultivated fields in vicinity of streams. Resembles the Paddyfield Pipit but plumage is somewhat variable. Note blackish legs and pinkish wash on throat and breast in spring; breast and flanks not heavily streaked as in Rose-breasted Pipit. Numbers in western Pokhara Valley in winter in cutover rice fields with other pipits and larks. Flies up with a *tsi*.
♦ Kashmir, Nepal, Sikkim; Europe, Africa, Asia, C. and N. America
1872

Eurasian Tree Pipit (Tree Pipit), *Anthus trivialis*.
274-2135 m. (900-7,000') 15 cm. (6") W.

Scarce; only a few records for Nepal. Paler and browner (not olive-green) than Hodgson's Tree Pipit. Feeds in fields as well as on ground in forest groves. When disturbed, flies into tree in typical tree pipit fashion and pumps its tail. Behavior and pale color good identification aids. Leaves ground with a *tseep* (AR). ♦ Kashmir, Garhwal, Nepal, Sikkim; Europe, Africa, Asia
1854

Wagtails are similar to pipits in body shape but tails are longer and are constantly pumped up and down. Often near water or in open fields. Most Nepal species are migratory, arriving in September and leaving in April-May. Sexes alike.

Yellow Wagtail, *Motacilla flava*.
152-1525 m. (500-5,000') 18 cm. (7") W.

Occasional; in freshly plowed fields of the *tarai* and also in shallow water and marshlands. Three distinct races; the most common form has a gray head (illustrated); others gray-blue and black. Note mottled gray and yellow breast and yellow abdomen. Distinguished from the similar Gray Wagtail by the *olive-green* (not gray) back and a somewhat shorter tail. Small flocks feed at edges of pools and chase after insects disturbed by cattle. Roosts in colonies in grass and reeds. Upon flying, gives a *sveeeee---sit*. ✣ KV: fields along Manora in November; March-April. ⚜ Kashmir, Garhwal, Nepal; Europe, Africa, Asia, N. America 1875, 1876, 1878

Gray Wagtail, *Motacilla caspica*.
152-3965 m. (500-13,000') 20 cm. (8") R., W.

Occasional; along wooded margins of streams; at edges of mountain roads on migration. Very similar to Yellow Wagtail but *back gray* (not greenish) and has a longer tail. A white throat turns black in spring (illustration shows partial change). Noted between Dhorpatan and Tarakot in June and nesting near Marpha, Mustang District in early July. Moves down through mist and rain in late August and September, one of the earliest "winter" arrivals in the lowlands. A spring song *blu-blu-blu-chi-chi-tzureeeessoo*. Also a bright *see-seep* on the wing. ✣ KV: along small streams, usually near bridge at Godaveri Village. ⚜ Kashmir, Garhwal, Nepal, Sikkim; Europe, Africa, Asia, New Guinea 1884

Yellow-headed Wagtail, *Motacilla citreola*.
120-3965 m. (400-13,000') 18 cm. (7") W.

Occasional; along stream beds and wet fields. Unmistakable in summer. In winter some yellow on head of most birds (no other wagtails here have yellow on head). Usually winter south of Nepal but a few stay to wander about shallow, flooded fields of the *tarai*. Darts here and there capturing insects. Undulating flight. Has a quick *cheep*. ✣ KV: along the Manora and Bagmati Rivers in winter and spring. ⚜ Kashmir, Garhwal, Nepal; C. Asia to India 1881, 1883

Pied Wagtail (White Wagtail), *Motacilla alba*.
120-4514 m. (400-14,800') 19 cm. (7½") M., W.

Common; moves along river courses on migration. An extremely varied wagtail with many combinations of black white and gray depending on which of the six subspecies viewed. *M.a. alboides*, a nesting bird in Trans-Himalayan Nepal, is similar to resident Large Pied Wagtail but has white eyebrows meeting on white forehead (not black forehead). Subspecies intermingle in winter: *M.a. alboides, dukhunensis* and *leucopsis* are common, with *ocularis* and *personata* occasional; *baicalensis*, scarce. Young are brownish-gray and white. Migrate in large, loose flocks, crossing the Himalayas on a broad front. Actively running here and there on sandy islands in rivers. A bright, warbling song in spring and a familiar *see-seep* contact note. Movements of races not clearly known. ✣ KV: here in winter; abundant in spring. ⚜ Kashmir, Garhwal, Nepal, Sikkim; Europe, Africa, Asia, N. America 1885, 1886, 1887, 1888, 1889, 1890

Large Pied Wagtail, *Motacilla maderaspatensis*.
120-1586 m. (400-5,200') 24 cm. (9½") R.

Fairly common; along sandy and rocky banks of large rivers in the *tarai* and foothills. Nepal's largest wagtail. Black and white with extensive white eyebrow on black head. Differs from Pied Wagtail *(M.a. alboides)* in having a *black* (not white) forehead. Single or in pairs, constantly pumping tail as it feeds. Much chasing of female in spring courtship. Sings atop rocks, often near water's edge. Song begins with a *tsip-tsip-tsip-zeer* and ends in *pheer-cheer-zweet-zweet* lasting three to six seconds. ✣ KV: along rivers in spring; above Chobar Gorge. (Forest Wagtail, *M. indica*, in Kashmir [once] and Sikkim, see p. 335.) ⚜ Kashmir, Garhwal, Nepal, Sikkim; S. Asia 1891

FLOWERPECKERS (Dicaeidae) are tiny, nectar-sipping birds often feeding in clusters of flowering mistletoe. Bills are short and usually sharp; tails are short. Sexes alike in several species. They have frequent, high-pitched notes.

Yellow-bellied Flowerpecker, *Dicaeum melanozanthum.*
1220-2440 m. (4,000-8,000') 13 cm. (5") R.

Occasional; in flowering and fruiting trees. A "large" black and yellow species with middle of throat and breast white. Female is grayish-brown and pale yellow-olive with a distinct white line down throat and breast. In pairs or small parties. Actions quite finch-like and less "nervous" than small flowerpeckers. Usually in bushy country at edge of forest. Nesting data unrecorded. Male pursuing female in April at 2440 m. (8,000') in upper Trisuli Valley. Alarm call an agitated *zit-zit-zit-zit*. ❊ KV: winter Nagarjung, Rani Bari and above Tokha. ♠ Nepal, Sikkim; Nepal to Tonkin 1896

Yellow-vented Flowerpecker, *Dicaeum chrysorrheum.*
244 m. (800') 9 cm. (3½") R.

Scarce; recently noted in mistletoe on acacias along the Tamur River, E. Nepal. Yellow-orange vent most conspicuous feature; also note bold streaking. Single birds working in mistletoe clumps sometimes with Plain-colored Flowerpeckers. Flight is strong and birds appear to travel considerable distances between feeding trees. Call, sometimes given when hunting, a *zeet*. ♠ Nepal, Sikkim; Nepal to S.E. Asia 1895

Thick-billed Flowerpecker, *Dicaeum agile.*
152-1982 m. (500-6,500') 10 cm. (4") R., S.

Fairly common; in temple groves and forests. Pale greenish-brown above; below, yellowish-white with *indistinct brown streaking*. Swollen bill noted at close range. Moves in loose parties; may hang upside-down when eating wild fruit. Much chattering; flies quickly from one tree to the next. Usually below 915 m. (3,000') in winter. Attracted by flowering shrubs, vines and trees. Call a *chik-chik-chik-chik* (Ali). ❊ KV: in summer in Gokarna, Rani Bari and Valley floor groves. ♠ Garhwal, Nepal, Sikkim; India to Philippines 1892

Tickell's Flowerpecker, *Dicaeum erythrorhynchos.*
152-305 m. (500-1,000') 9 cm. (3½") R.

Fairly common; in mango groves and at edges of cultivation. Uniformly ashy-olive with brown wings and tail. A *pale, curved bill* the most conspicuous field mark (not dark as in the Plain-colored Flowerpecker). Pairs in spring and up to ten or more together in winter. Usually high in forest trees and difficult to see. Frequents clumps of mistletoe. Active and noisy. Call a high-pitched *pit* repeated at intervals. ♠ Garhwal, Nepal, Sikkim; S. Asia 1899

Plain-colored Flowerpecker, *Dicaeum concolor.*
305-1525 m. (1,000-5,000') 8 cm. (3") R.

Fairly common; around vines with fruit or flowers, also shrubs and trees. Dark gray with *dark bill*. One of Nepal's tiniest birds. Very active and constantly on the move, eating insects and sipping nectar. In pairs or small parties, often in tops of rather tall trees. Call *tik-tik-tik* (Baker). ❊ KV: mostly in summer in groves of Valley floor. ♠ Nepal, Sikkim; India to Formosa 1901

Scarlet-backed Flowerpecker, *Dicaeum cruentatum.*
152-2135 m. (500-7,000') 9 cm. (3½") R.(?)

Scarce; one sight record from Ilam District 2135 m. (7,000'). Male unmistakable with deep red on back. Female brown and sooty-gray with red on rump. Should be found in S.E. Nepal. Additional data needed on status in Nepal. ♠ Nepal, Sikkim; Nepal to S.E. Asia 1904

Fire-breasted Flowerpecker, *Dicaeum ignipectus.*
915-2440 m. (3,000-8,000') 9 cm. (3½") R.

Common; in subtropical and oak forests of midland Nepal. Male, crimson breast patch diagnostic. Male looks black above except in good light when iridescence shines. Female may be confused with other flowerpeckers but is the only one with *dark back* and *buffy* underparts. Note bill is not swollen, pale or strongly decurved. Actively buzzes from one place to another. When disturbed, scolds loudly from a vantage point and shifts body this way and that without changing foot position. Alarm a high-pitched, repeated *tsik*, about two per second. ❊ KV: Valley floor in winter; oak-rhododendron forests in summer. ♠ Kashmir, Garhwal, Nepal, Sikkim; India to Formosa 1905

SUNBIRDS (Nectariniidae). Male sunbirds are brilliantly-colored with long, slender, decurved bills and most have pointed tails. Females have short tails and are drab-colored. They are active among flowers and occupy a niche similar to that of hummingbirds of the Americas.

Fire-tailed Sunbird, *Aethopyga ignicauda.*
610-3965 m. (2,000-13,000') 20 cm. (8") R.
Fairly common; in mixed foothill forests in winter to high altitude rhododendrons in summer. Male unmistakable in breeding dress with a magnificent, long, red tail. Male in eclipse plumage, drab olive-gray except for short red tail and yellow rump. Female a drab olive-gray with yellow wash on abdomen and *rufous tinge* to *wings and tail.* Much singing in summer. Female dashes back and forth with nesting material; male dances on nearby branches rarely assisting female. Shoots out above rhododendron grove for insects. In winter small flocks gather in flowering *Leucoseptrum* trees. ❊ KV: Godaveri and Sundarijal often with other sunbirds. ❦ Garhwal, Nepal, Sikkim; India to Sikiang 1930

Mrs. Gould's Sunbird, *Aethopyga gouldiae.*
2531-3355 m. (8,300-11,000') 15 cm. (6") R.
Scarce; in undergrowth and low parts of trees in damp ravines. The only sunbird in Nepal with lemon-yellow breast and *red back extending to upper rump.* Female sunbirds hard to distinguish in field. Female is olive-gray with *dull yellow rump* and yellowish on abdomen. Note comparatively short bill. Rather shy and constantly on the move. In winter, usually on north-facing slope in moderate-height shrubbery. Usually found near flowering rhododendron trees and mistletoe in spring. Descends around mid-day to drink at pools. Call a quick, repeated *tzip;* alarm a *tshi-stshi-ti-ti-ti;* a lisping *squeeeeee* rising in middle. ❊ KV: on Phulchowki. ❦ Garhwal, Nepal, Sikkim; India to S.E. Asia 1919

Nepal Sunbird, *Aethopyga nipalensis.*
305-3355 m. (1,000-11,000') 14 cm. (5½") R.
Common; a bird of the oak-rhododendron forests. Male dark iridescent green head and bright yellow breast somewhat streaked with red. Easily confused with Mrs. Gould's Sunbird but *lower back is dark green* (not red) and tail iridescent green (not purple). Female similar to Mrs. Gould's female but undertail coverts yellow (not yellowish-gray) and tail feathers tipped pale buff. Solitary or in scattered groups. Rarely below 1830 m. (6,000') in summer or above 2745 m. (9,000') in winter. Calls a *twit-zig-zig-zig,* a repeated *bee—tzree* and a *tzweeeet.* Contact note *reet.* ❊ KV: along Godaveri-Phulchowki road; Sheopuri in flowering pear trees. ❦ Garhwal, Nepal, Sikkim; Himalayas to Malaya 1922, 1923

Black-breasted Sunbird, *Aethopyga saturata.*
305-1830 m. (1,000-6,000') 15 cm. (6") R.
Occasional; in thin forests of the lowlands. Male is the only dark sunbird with a long tail (Purple Sunbird male has short tail). Female gray-green (grayer than other similar female sunbirds), faint yellow rump with under tail feathers tipped whitish. Responds to squeaks and whistles. In ones and twos along roadsides and forest trails. Partial to hot river valleys. Most often in E. Nepal. Song a lively twitter. ❊ KV: in *Leucoseptrum* trees at Godaveri in spring. ❦ Garhwal, Nepal, Sikkim; Himalayas to Malaya 1925

Scarlet-breasted Sunbird (Yellow-backed Sunbird), *Aethopyga siparaja.*
244-1677 m. (800-5,500') 14 cm. (5½") R.
Fairly common; among shrubs along hot roads and river beds in fairly open country. Male the only Nepal sunbird with brilliant red and green underparts. Yellow of lower rump largely obscured by longer upper rump feathers. Female dull green below. A busy creature, single or in pairs. Often hovers and returns to same branch after examining flowers, piercing their bases for nectar or searching through leaves for insects. Partial to *Woodfordia* flowers of the warm lowlands. Usually found below 915 m. (3,000'). Call a sharp trill (Baker). ❊ KV: scarce; in low trees in places like Gokarna Forest. ❦ Garhwal, Nepal, Sikkim; India to Philippines 1927

Rubycheek, *Anthreptes singalensis.*
120-457 m. (400-1,500') 11 cm. (4½") R.

Scarce; in forests of foothills and the *tarai* of E. Nepal. Male glossy green above and ferruginous from chin to abdomen. Female has diagnostic rufous wash from chin to abdomen. Bill long and nearly straight. Solitary or in pairs, continually flitting about on low branches or bushes near sunny glades. Around villages as well as in forests. In mixed flocks. Actions reminiscent of a tit. Call a constant twitter, *tear-tear*. ● Nepal, Sikkim; Nepal to S.E. Asia   1906

Purple Sunbird, *Nectarinia asiatica.*
152-1830 m. (500-6,000') 10 cm. (4") R.

Common; in flowering shrubs and trees around houses and in open country. Male is shiny, iridescent blue-black with yellow patch on side of breast under wing. Assumes female-colored plumage from summer to late winter but retains a dark median line down throat and breast. Female, the only female sunbird with clear, pale yellow below. Single or in pairs in lowlands and up into hot river valleys in February; moves uphill after nesting. Probes cannas, banana flowers and is fond of spiders. Quite noisy and constantly on the move. Song a bright warble *swi-swi-swi-a-col-a-oli*. Contact note a repeated *sweet*. ✣ KV: a few in winter; common from June to November, often in Bottlebrush trees. ● Garhwal, Nepal; Muscat to S.E. Asia   1917

Spiderhunters (in the Sunbird Family) are bulkier than sunbirds and have heavier, longer, decurved bills. They lack iridescence. Sexes alike. In Nepal they are found mainly below 457 m. (1,500') altitude.

Little Spiderhunter, *Arachnothera longirostris.*
120-305 m. (400-1,000') 14 cm. (5½") R.

Scarce; along watered ravines and streams in the vicinity of wild bananas. Olive-green above with gray throat and breast and yellow abdomen. Dark, heavy, decurved bill conspicuous. Single or in small parties among bamboos, banana plants and low parts of forest trees. Inquisitive, responding to squeaking noises. Constantly on the move, flitting among tangles of vines and bushes. Pecks at flowers. So far only recorded from the *tarai* in Jhapa District near the Mechi River and the Churia foothills on the Sunischari-Ilam Road. Call a rapidly repeated, metallic *cheet*. ● Nepal; India to S.E. Asia   1931

Streaked Spiderhunter, *Arachnothera magna.*
152-457 m. (500-1,500') 18 cm. (7") R.

Fairly common; in tangled thickets and *sal* forests. A boldly streaked yellowish-green bird with a great, decurved bill and *bright orange legs*. Single or in scattered pairs. Sits upright on branch, constantly moving head this way and that. Restless, flying from one tree top to another with a strong, undulating flight. Two birds, possibly stragglers, recently netted by T. Cronin at nearly 2135 m. (7,000') in the Arun Valley. Very vocal; one of the characteristic sounds of the *tarai* and foothills. Call a loud, metallic *chi-chi-chi*, repeated at intervals. ● Nepal, Sikkim; India to Malaya   1932

WHITE-EYE (Zosteropidae). The single species in Nepal is a small warbler-like bird, predominantly greenish-yellow with a wide, white ring around the eye. It is active and gregarious; sexes alike.

White-eye, *Zosterops palpebrosa.*
120-2440 m. (400-8,000') 11 cm. (4½") R.

Common; in tall trees as well as undergrowth in mixed forests. A bright yellow throat and breast usually first field mark noted; then look for white eye-ring and greenish head (Gray-cheeked Warbler has an eye-ring but head is gray not greenish). Ten to twenty in a flock; buzzes along in follow-the-leader fashion. Often with warblers and tits. In pairs in spring. Resembles warblers but does not flick wings and tail. May hang upside-down while searching for insects. Confiding; may build nest in garden near house. Call a small snatch of song in spring; a plaintive *tear-tear-tear* contact note when foraging. ✣ KV: common in thin forests and temple groves. ● Kashmir, Garhwal, Nepal. Sikkim; Pakistan to Philippines   1933

SPARROWS and WEAVER BIRDS (Ploceidae). Ploceids (including the English Sparrow and similar species) are rather small, plump birds with thick, pointed bills, rounded wings and well-developed legs. Most are gregarious and several species live close to human habitations. Sexes usually dissimilar.

House Sparrow (English Sparrow), *Passer domesticus.*
120-2135 m. (400-7,000') 13 cm. (5") R.

Abundant; on city streets, under eaves of houses and in adjoining fields or gardens. Male is streaked brownish with a gray crown, bright white cheek, prominent black bib and white wingbar. Female earthy-brown, streaked on back. Male similar to Tree Sparrow but has gray crown (not rufous) and cheek lacks black patch. In loose flocks scattered throughout cities and towns. In warm weather, much courting activity including dancing, quivering and battling. In cold weather, gather at dusk in large chirping parties in leafy trees. Call a variety of twitters, chirps and squeaks. ❊ KV: streets of cities and towns; very few in rural areas.
🍃 Kashmir, Garhwal, Nepal, Sikkim; Europe, Africa, Asia, introduced elsewhere   1938, 1939

Tree Sparrow, *Passer montanus.*
610-4270 m. (2,000-14,000') 13 cm. (5") R.

Abundant; in suburbs and fields at edge of towns and villages. Resembles male House Sparrow but has *chestnut head* and neck (not gray); a conspicuous black dot on white ear patch. Sexes alike. Parties forage busily on grass lawns, in gardens and fields for seeds and scraps of food. Nests under eaves and in holes in brick walls alongside House Sparrow, the ecological differences not yet entirely clear. In northern Nepal, flocks up to 100 feed in fallow fields. When alarmed, the whole flock swarms into a protective hedge and then gradually returns to the field. Birds in Jumla town are blackened with soot in winter. Calls similar to those of House Sparrow though apparently a little less shrill. Introduced around St. Louis, Missouri, U.S.A. ❊ KV: the common sparrow of suburbs and fields. 🍃 Nepal, Sikkim; Europe, Asia   1942, 1943

Cinnamon Sparrow, *Passer rutilans.*
762-4270 m. (2,500-14,000') 14 cm. (5½") R.

Fairly common; in northern Nepal, at edges of fields and forest and perching on village houses. Male bright cinnamon above with white wingbar, pale yellowish on upper abdomen. Female is grayish-brown with dark streaks on back. Look for broad fulvous eyebrow and a distinct white wingbar. In small parties clustered around nesting sites which are holes high in trees, walls of houses or cliffs. Rather shy but rests on exposed branches. A common bird in northern Dolpo in summer, feeding in fields and nesting under eaves. Appears to descend in cold months, common around Tukuche, 2592 m. (8,500'), in winter. Song a throaty, repeated *chul-lup.* 🍃 Kashmir, Garhwal, Nepal, Sikkim; Himalayas to Formosa   1946

Yellow-throated Sparrow, *Petronia xanthocollis.*
120-1525 m. (400-5,000') 15 cm. (6") R.

Occasional; in thin, open forests and scrub jungle of the lowlands. Male brown and gray with *chestnut shoulder patch* and white wingbar. The yellow throat patch may be missed in poor light. Female pale brown and lacks yellow throat. Usually in pairs in spring and summer, in thin forest far from civilization. Rarely over 915 m. (3,000') elevation. Large flocks may collect in winter. A sparrow chirping well within a forest is likely to be this species. A flock in W. Nepal swooped down to feed in a short grassy glade much like mountain finches would. Chirps for long periods, a repeated mellow *chul-leep.* 🍃 Garhwal, Nepal; Iraq to India   1949

Tibetan Snow Finch, *Montifringilla adamsi.*
3660-5185 m. (12,000-17,000') 18 cm. (7") R.

Common; in desert steppes of the Nepal Trans-Himalayas (Dolpo, Mustang). Gray-brown with indistinct black throat. White tail feathers and wing patch very noticeable in flight. Female slightly duller than male. In ones or twos in summer; runs on ground or awkwardly jumps into air after insects. Searches under rocks and near cultivations. Occupies the most barren and rocky country. Tame, perches on walls of houses and on prayer flag poles. Feeds with Brandt's Mountain Finch. Parents cram bills with insects and feed young in holes of banks or *mani* walls. Strong fliers, gliding more than most finches. Calls on wing, *chew-cheep;* alarm a nasal *chaap-chaap;* in spring a very coarse, buzzy *cheep (ti) twee,* the "ti" sometimes omitted. (Mandelli's Snow Finch, *M. taczanowskii,* Red-necked Snow Finch, *M. ruficollis,* Blanford's Snow Finch, *M. blanfordi,* see p. 323. Mongolian Snow Finch, *M. davidiana,* in N. Sikkim, see p. 337.) 🍃 Kashmir, Nepal, Sikkim; Himalayas and C. Asia   1952

Two finches (Family, Fringillidae) are placed on this page; weaver finches then continue. For Fringillidae description see page 304.

Brambling, *Fringilla montifringilla*.
2440-3050 m. (8,000-10,000') 16 cm. (6½") W.
Occasional; in bushes bordering fields and in conifer forests. Male pale brown with broad, orangy breast band; white abdomen and rump, two white wingbars. Female, duller than male but with pale orangy breast band conspicuous from a distance. Sometimes solitary or in pairs but usually in flocks of 4-15. Shy, sits on tops of bushes when disturbed. Feeds on ground at edge of forest. Strong flight. In N.W. Nepal in winter around Rara Lake and Jumla town. Call note not recorded in Nepal; said to be *tjeak-tjeak* in Europe (Brunn). ♣ Kashmir, Garhwal, Nepal; Europe, Africa, Asia   1980

Chaffinch, *Fringilla coelebs*.
2440-3050 m. (8,000-10,000') 18 cm. (7") W.
Occasional; in conifers or bushes near fields. Male olive-gray and orangy-chestnut with broad, dark line from bill to sides of neck, a white shoulder patch and fulvous wingbar. Female drab brown with white shoulder patch and pale fulvous wingbar. Single or in parties up to fifteen birds; feeds on fallow ground near hedges. Wingbeat noticeably heavy as compared to mountain finch's. A strong flight. Sits at very top of tall conifers in winter sun. Found in Jumla and Mugu Districts. Recently seen as far east as the Kali Gandaki Valley (Madge, *et al*, 1973). Call a two-note whistle that carries far through the stillness of the coniferous forests of N.W. Nepal; also a nasal *cheek*. ♣ Nepal; Europe, Africa, Asia   1979

Baya Weaver, *Ploceus philippinus*.
120-1372 m. (400-4,500') 15 cm. (6") R.
Common; in open country with scattered bushes and tall trees; near water in the foothills and lowlands. Male streaked brown above, bright yellow cap and upper breast in summer, buff below. Male in winter like female with little or no yellow. Distinguished from female House Sparrow by larger bill and heavier streaks on back; from Black-throated Weaver by lack of any black feathers on throat or upper breast. Lives in colonies; very noisy. Long, retort-like nests built by males. Males may begin several but only finish those chosen by females. Some birds steal grass from other nests being built nearby. Much calling and quivering. Call quite varied with a *jejejejejej;psh-pssh-peep;* a prolonged *pep-pur-chhhhhhheeeeeeeeeeeee;* a short *chik*. ✤ KV: nests mostly in August and September in many parts of Valley. ♣ Nepal; Pakistan to S.E. Asia   1957, 1959

Black-throated Weaver, *Ploceus benghalensis*.
120-244 m. (400-800') 14 cm. (5½") R.
Occasional; in marshes of the *tarai*. Brown back heavily streaked with black. Like Baya Weaver in winter but always has a few black throat or upper breast feathers visible. Large flocks (60-70) in winter; eats seeds from grass stalks and raids ripening grain fields. Roosts and nests in colonies. Voice a series of squeaks and chirps, somewhat quieter than the Baya.
♣ Nepal; S. Asia   1961

Red Munia, *Estrilda amandava.*
120-305 m. (400-1,000') 11 cm. (4½") R.

Occasional; in small parties in tall grass of the *duns* and *tarai*. Male a tiny red bird boldly spotted with white, the red darkening towards the tail. Female and non-breeding male, brown with red bill, crimson rump and numerous white spots. Feeds on grass seeds both high on grass stalks or on ground. Often associated with weavers and buntings. When flushed, flock buzzes off together in fairly close formation to land on a fence or in tall grass. Bird dealers crowd numbers together in small cages. Call a high, repeated *tsi*. 🦢 Nepal; Pakistan to Lesser Sunda Islands 1964

White-throated Munia, *Lonchura malabarica.*
120-305 m. (400-1,000') 11 cm. (4½") R.

Occasional; in dry, open country. Brown with white rump and black tail; buffy-white below. Also has white ear patch. Sexes alike. In small flocks, busily feeding on the ground or around cactus and agave hedges near villages. A flock occupied old weaver nests in a Palmyra Palm near Biratnagar airport in November. Call a feeble chirping. 🦢 Nepal; Africa, Asia 1966

Sharp-tailed Munia, *Lonchura striata.*
305-1372 m. (1,000-4,500') 13 cm. (5") R.

Fairly common; among bamboo and tangled thickets of the lowlands. Dark chocolate-brown with a pointed, dark tail. Fine fulvous streaks on neck and back, with fine stippling on gray abdomen. In small flocks and rather shy. Partial to leafy trees and shrubs where they are not easily seen. Constructs nests in forest from long strips of grass. Strong buzzing flight for short distances. Eats seeds and berries. Call a metallic, high-pitched, repeated *cheep*. ❊ KV: occasionally a small party in Rani Bari. 🦢 Garhwal, Nepal, Sikkim; India to Sumatra 1967

Spotted Munia, *Lonchura punctulata.*
244-1525 m. (800-5,000') 13 cm. (5") R.

Common; in gardens and bushes in towns, cities and near fields. Breeding male chocolate and light brown above; gray below with conspicuous brown crescent edges to feathers. Female and young male plain rufous-brown, heads darker. Feeds in small, scattered groups on ground. Roosts in a compact row on a branch. Flies in close formation. Confiding, may nest in vines on verandas. Call a distinct, plaintive *peer—peer*. ❊ KV: in hedges, gardens, fields around houses. 🦢 Garhwal, Nepal, Sikkim; India to Philippines 1974

Black-headed Munia, *Lonchura malacca.*
120-1372 m. (400-4,500') 11 cm. (4½") R.

Occasional; in small flocks in ripening grain fields of the lowlands. Black head and upper breast contrasts with white lower breast and abdomen; chestnut back and tail. Small, scattered parties work through rice fields of western Rapti Valley in winter. Wanders upwards in summer. A flock in Jhapa town contained about 150 birds along with 50 Spotted Munias, feeding on threshing floor in open courtyard. A low, fast flight. Call a high, metallic chitter. ❊ KV: a few here in summer at edge of fields on Manora. 🦢 Garhwal, Nepal; India to Australia
1976, 1977

FINCHES and ALLIES (Fringillidae). Finches are rather gregarious, small birds with heavy beaks but generally not as thick as those of weaver finches. Legs are strong and tails usually notched. Males are often more colorful than females.

Allied Grosbeak, *Mycerobas affinis*.
2440-3660 m. (8,000-12,000') 24 cm. (9½") R.

Fairly common; in mixed broad-leafed and conifer forests. Males black and bronzy-yellow above with *no* white wing patch; yellow below. Female and immature birds, gray head and olive-green body. In small parties among forest trees; fond of maple *(Acer)*, eating seeds and nipping off tips of fresh twigs. Perches in one place, reaching out with thick bill to grasp food. Also feeds on ground. Flies in a compact flock. Call a clear *dip-di-chichpapdee; dip-dip di-di-de-do.* (Black-and-Yellow Grosbeak, *M. icterioides*, resident in Kashmir, see p. 335.)
🍂 Kashmir, Garhwal, Nepal, Sikkim; Pakistan to Burma and Kansu   1983

Spot-winged Grosbeak, *Mycerobas melanozanthos*.
1220-3355 m. (4,000-11,000') 23 cm. (9") R.

Occasional; in fir-hemlock-maple forests. Male black with lemon-yellow breast and abdomen. Large, oval, yellow spots on secondaries and a very obvious white wing patch in flight. Female profusely spotted. In close flocks in winter; pairs in spring. Feeds in fruiting trees. May take shelter in empty cattle sheds. A heavy flight. Sits quietly and is easily overlooked. Voice a harsh *krrr* and song is a loud, mellow *tew-tew--teeeu.* ❊ KV: Rani Bari; Balaju in winter after cold snap. 🍂 Kashmir, Garhwal, Nepal, Sikkim; Himalayas to Yunnan   1986

White-winged Grosbeak, *Mycerobas carnipes*.
2135-4270 m. (7,000-14,000') 24 cm. (9½") R.

Common; in juniper forests and alpine scrub, often near old cattle sheds. Male diagnostic black with olive-green abdomen and flanks; white wing patch conspicuous in flight. Gray replaces black in females and young males. Black birds much less common than gray. In scattered flocks in winter, usually above 3050 m. (10,000') where they feed on juniper berries. Flies about between bushes and is quite easy to observe. Pairs in summer; build nests in August (Helumbu) using strips of juniper bark. Fairly confiding; easily watched. Call a rather harsh *add-a-dit; un-di-di-di-dit.* ❊ KV: occasional; eating *Randia tetrasperma* and dogwood berries on Sheopuri above Tokha Sanitarium. 🍂 Kashmir, Garhwal, Nepal, Sikkim; Transcaspia to Szechuan   1985

Himalayan Goldfinch (Green Finch), *Carduelis spinoides*.
274-3965 m. (900-13,000') 13 cm. (5") R.

Common; in trees above cultivated fields. Male in breeding plumage is a brilliant yellow, green and black. Females and non-breeding males are dull green and yellow, streaked below. Small to large flocks over 100 birds. Resembles the American Goldfinch in both habits and color pattern. Strong, undulating flight. A seed-eater partial to *Cannabis*. Calls a high-pitched twitter, *ti-test—ti-teet; tsit-tsit-tsit-ur-tsiit-ur;* and a nasal *tweeeeeeee.* ❊ KV: in city gardens; alders along Bhaktapur-Banepa road. 🍂 Kashmir, Garhwal, Nepal, Sikkim; Pakistan to Tonkin   1990

Eurasian Goldfinch, *Carduelis carduelis*.
152-3660 m. (500-12,000') 14 cm. (5½") R.

Scarce; in tops of bushes and leafless trees in winter. In flight appears black and white with wings flashing yellow. Face looks as if dipped in a bottle of red ink, bill first! Black and yellow shoulder patch and primaries are unmistakable. Female paler. In small parties and up to 100 in winter. Feeds on ground in fallow fields and in trees with seeds. Constant conversation and shifting of positions. Swift flight. In hedgerows near farmers working in fields [July, Tukuche, 2592 m. (8,500')]; also in Nepalgunj, 152 m. (500'), in January (H.S. Nepali). Known as far east as Helumbu. Song from an exposed perch *chew-e-e-e;* contact note a *pu-pic-pic.* 🍂 Kashmir, Garhwal, Nepal; Europe, Africa, Asia   1989

Tibetan Siskin, *Carduelis thibetana.*
 1525-3355 m. (5,000-11,000') 13 cm. (5") W.
Scarce; in alders *(Alnus nepalensis).* Greenish-brown with bright yellow on face, eyebrow and throat; dull yellow on cheeks, neck and breast. Female paler than male and streaked with brown except on throat and breast. In large flocks of 50-75 birds eating seeds high in alder trees. Sits concealed, only occasionally changing position or clinging to underside of a twig. Located by their constant, faint, high-pitched twittering. Noted northwest of Pokhara (E. Forster). ✻ KV: Royal Botanic Gardens area, Godaveri in January. ♠ Nepal, Sikkim; Nepal to Yunnan
1993

Tibetan Twite, *Acanthis flavirostris.*
 3965-4575 m. (13,000-15,000') 15 cm. (6") R.
Fairly common; in desert biotope of north Nepal (Dolpo, Mustang). Pale, nondescript, brown bird, finely streaked. When alighting, pale edges of the flared tail feathers noticeable. Faint pink on rump hard to see. Single or in small parties busily feeding on grassy or stony flats in northern Nepal. Avoids bushes; is found in the bleakest regions. Quite tame, flying but a short distance when disturbed. Seen also at edges of villages, sometimes in company with mountain finches and larks. Flight call a rapid *chew-chew* somewhat low-pitched for so small a bird.
♠ Kashmir, Nepal, Sikkim; Europe, Asia
1996

Linnet, *Acanthis cannabina.*
 2379-2409 m. (7,800-7,900') 14 cm. (5½") W.
Scarce; in hedges and open, grassy meadows in Jumla District in winter. Male has gray head, streaked on crown and warm brown back. Pale below with pink breast (pink shade quite variable). Wings pale-edged, noticeable in flight. Female similar but lacks pink on breast. In small flocks, feeding on open, grassy plains such as Jumla airstrip in February. After being disturbed, flock flies around and finally when one bird settles on a bush, a second is drawn to the spot and gently alights. Call a high twitter. ♠ Nepal; Europe, Africa, Asia
1994

Gold-fronted Finch, *Serinus pusillus.*
 2135-4575 m. (7,000-15,000') 13 cm. (5") R.
Fairly common; in desert biotope of N. Nepal in summer and in hedges and low trees in winter. Distinctive dark head with *orangy-gold half crown;* body heavily streaked. In small and large flocks. May feed on ground near cattle sheds but also nibbles fresh tips of stream-side bushes *(Hippophae).* Somewhat shy but frequents edges of villages, perching on *chortans.* Moves downward in winter (Rara Lake). Known as far east as the Kali Gandaki Valley. Spring song a buzzing warble somewhat like that of a Himalayan Goldfinch. Alarm a high, rapid *tititititit,* rising in pitch. ♠ Kashmir, Garhwal, Nepal; Caucasus to Nepal 1998

Red-browed Finch, *Callacanthis burtoni.*
 2287-3355 m. (7,500-11,000') 18 cm. (7") W.
Scarce; in oak and hemlock forests in winter; rhododendron-fir forests in spring. Male has conspicuous red "spectacles" and eyebrow. Female has yellow "spectacles." Note white spots on wing. Confiding, works on ground or in low bushes. Seen pecking deep into flowers and eating bark of *Rhododendron barbatum* on slopes of Ganesh Himal, 3355 m. (11,000'). In flocks of 4 to 15 or more. Very tame. Contact note a light *chip.* ✻ KV: a flock seen on Christmas bird count, January 1972 at top of Phulchowki. ♠ Kashmir, Garhwal, Nepal, Sikkim; Himalayas
1997

Hodgson's Mountain Finch, *Leucosticte nemoricola*.
2135-5185 m. (7,000-17,000') 18 cm. (7") R.

Common; in open meadows and rocky slopes below the snow line. Nondescript brown, streaked above, indistinct eyebrow and wingbar. Face has a *light* rufous wash. Large flocks collect in both summer and winter, swooping about over grassy slopes near abandoned yak shelters. Perhaps the most conspicuous bird above 4575 m. (15,000'). Very sociable, chasing each other over melting snow. Marked altitudinal shift in winter. May sun in top of leafless tree as low as 2135 m. (7,000'). Flight call *pretty-boy*. ♠ Kashmir, Garhwal, Nepal, Sikkim; Afghanistan to Kansu 2000

Brandt's Mountain Finch, *Leucosticte brandti*.
4117-5185 m. (13,500-17,000') 18 cm. (7") R.

Fairly common; at edges of snow fields and in desert biotope of N. Nepal. Grayish-brown with a *dark face*. Pink rump difficult to see but white in tail shows in flight. Small to large flocks in open country of rocky slopes and short grassy meadows. Occasionally alights on *Caragana* bushes and hops about in barley fields. Rests on boulders and rock walls; very tame. Strong flight. Very little altitudinal movement apparent. Flight call *twee-ti-ti* and *peek-peek*. ♠ Kashmir, Nepal, Sikkim; C. Asia 2003

Common Rose Finch, *Carpodacus erythrinus*.
244-3934 m. (800-12,900') 15 cm. (6") W., R.

Fairly common; in bushes near fields or in high altitude scrub. A variable species with three races in Nepal. Male of breeding race, *roseatus*, has glistening crimson head and throat. Male of other common race, *erythrinus*, has only light wash of pink on head and neck. Female is pale with darker streaks. Most birds winter in lowland Nepal or India and return north to their breeding grounds early in June. Active among *Caragana* bushes in Dolpo where pink males and birds in female plumage sing for long periods. Nests in August. Song a bright, whistling *tu-whee-chu; pe-te-te-whee-chew*. ❈ KV: in wayside bushes in December and again in April-May. ♠ Kashmir, Garhwal, Nepal, Sikkim; Europe, Asia 2011, 2012, 2013

Nepal Rose Finch, *Carpodacus nipalensis*.
1372-4270 m. (4,500-14,000') 16 cm. (6½") R.

Occasional; in mixed temperate forests to above the tree line in high altitude scrub. Male is dark with crimson forehead, fore-crown and eyebrow; the back part of crown and nape dark red. Very similar to Blanford's Rose Finch which has a uniform light crimson crown, nape and throat. Female is dark rufous-brown above, grayish-brown below and completely unstreaked (female Blanford's Rose Finch is lighter with crimson and brown on the rump and tail). Small flocks in winter; large flocks among rhododendrons in spring. Fairly shy, keeping to shaded ravines on northern slopes. Above tree line in summer, nesting on cliffs and steep, grassy slopes. Song a monotonous chipping. Alarm *cha-a-rrr*. ❈ KV: in undergrowth on rim of Valley in winter. ♠ Kashmir, Garhwal, Nepal, Sikkim; Himalayas to Tonkin 2015

Blanford's Rose Finch, *Carpodacus rubescens*.
2440-3050 m. (8,000-10,000') 15 cm. (6") R.

Scarce; in open glades among fir and birch forests. Similar to Nepal Rose Finch but male has light red hind-crown and nape (not dark). Female, has wings, rump and tail edged with crimson (not brown). The crimson seen in good light at close range. In the Sunkosi watershed at 2440 m. (8,000') (Polunin). Seasonal movements not fully known. Call a persistent clacking note (Ludlow). ♠ Nepal, Sikkim; Nepal to Kansu 2016

Vinaceous Rose Finch, *Carpodacus vinaceus.*
915-2745 m. (3,000-9,000') 15 cm. (6") R.
Scarce; in wet bamboo and bushy areas near forest. Male dark with glistening pink eyebrow. Note spots on secondaries. Smaller and more uniformly marked than similar male Spot-winged Rose Finch. Female slightly darker than female Pink-browed Rose Finch and with narrower eyebrow; also habitat differences helpful in identification (Pink-browed usually in slightly drier country). Lacks spots of female Spot-winged Rose Finch. At times noted with both similar species. First identified in Nepal by Jochen Martens in the Upper Kali Gandaki area, 1972. Contact note is a loud, high-pitched *weeeep.* ♪ Nepal; China   2017a

Pink-browed Rose Finch, *Carpodacus rhodochrous.*
915-3965 m. (3,000-13,000') 15 cm. (6") R.
Occasional; in oak forests in winter; dwarf juniper and rhododendrons in summer. Male, very broad, distinctive, pink eyebrow contrasting with dark reddish head. Female is strongly streaked brown with a broad fulvous eyebrow; slightly paler than Vinaceous Rose Finch but hard to distinguish in field. Small flocks scattered among bushes or on ground at edge of forest glades. Fond of seeds of *Cyathula* plants. When disturbed flies into bushes rather than trees. Wintering flocks often of one sex. Call a loud *per-lee* and *chew-wee.* ✿ KV: in bushes on southern slopes of hills in winter. (Red-mantled Rose Finch, *C. rhodochlamys,* in Kashmir, see p. 335.) ♪ Kashmir, Garhwal, Nepal, Sikkim; Himalayas   2017

Spot-winged Rose Finch, *Carpodacus rhodopeplus.*
2135-3965 m. (7,000-13,000') 18 cm. (7") R.
Occasional; on grassy slopes above tree line in summer; in bushes and forests in winter. Male very dark above with glistening, broad, pink eyebrow. Resembles male Vinaceous Rose Finch but larger, darker and spots on wing form a bar. Female is streaked brown, distinguished from other female rose finches by *pale tips* to some secondaries. In pairs or small parties among tangled thickets in damp ravines in winter. Somewhat shy. Breeds in August in rhododendron scrub about 3965 m. (13,000'). ✿ KV: in damp ravines along Sheopuri ridge in winter. ♪ Garhwal, Nepal, Sikkim; Himalayas to Szechuan   2019

Beautiful Rose Finch, *Carpodacus pulcherrimus.*
2745-4575 m. (9,000-15,000') 15 cm. (6") R.
Common; flocks together in winter and hugs bushes bordering fields. Streaked male is grayish above, very pale pink below. It should not be confused with any other rose finch. Female nondescript gray-brown and heavily streaked. Told from other female rose finches by lack of prominent eyebrow and no fulvous wash. The common rose finch over much of northern Nepal, widely distributed at all times of year. In pairs and small parties in summer on stony hillsides above tree line. Fond of *Caragana* scrub. Call a harsh *chaaannn* as it flies; also a breeding song (Baker). ♪ Garhwal, Nepal, Sikkim; C. Asia   2023

Edward's Rose Finch (Large Rose Finch), *Carpodacus edwardsii.*
1067-2897 m. (3,500-9,500') 16 cm. (6½") R.
Scarce; under bushes where seeds are available. Male dark with crimson-brown head contrasting with pink cheeks and throat. Could be confused with Spot-winged Rose Finch but has *no* wing spots. Female resembles female Vinaceous Rose Finch but is more profusely streaked; also note lack of wing spotting which at once separates it from female Spot-winged. Single or in small parties. Usually shy; flips tail and wings when agitated. Quickly steals away from intruder. Winters at low elevations but apparently moves up into juniper-rhododendron stands to nest. Alarm call a rasping *che-wee.* ♪ Nepal, Sikkim; Nepal to Kansu   2025

Great Rose Finch, *Carpodacus rubicilla.*
3660-4880 m. (12,000-16,000') 20 cm. (8") R.

Occasional; on rocky hillsides with little or no shrubbery. A very *large, pale* rose finch, sandy above and pink below. The silvery centers to feathers on head and throat give a spotted appearance. Similar to Eastern Great Rose Finch but *paler* and *back* almost *uniform brown.* Female is very pale; white margins on outer tail feathers. Single or in pairs on open hillsides. Fairly tame; feeds on grass seeds at edges of villages. Perches on bushes to look around. Known from Dolpo (RLF) and Khumbu (Diesselhorst). Not seen below 3660 m. (12,000') in summer; probably little altitudinal movement. Song a loud, mournfully slow *weep;* also a series of low chuckles. ♣ Kashmir, Nepal, Sikkim; C. Asia   2027

Eastern Great Rose Finch, *Carpodacus rubicilloides.*
2440-4575 m. (8,000-15,000') 19 cm. (7½") R.

Occasional; frequenting ravines and thickets in winter; open, stony ground in summer. Male similar to Great Rose Finch but much darker and center of crown to back decidedly streaked. Female brown and streaked with darker brown. In small, scattered flocks around cultivations. Both of these large rose finches occur together in summer in Dolpo; ecological distinctions not yet clear. Descends as low as Jomosom in winter 2745 m. (9,000'). Somewhat shy; perches on tops of bushes when alarmed and flies sway on strong wings. Voice not recorded. ♣ Kashmir, Nepal, Sikkim; C. Asia   2028

White-browed Rose Finch, *Carpodacus thura.*
2440-3965 m. (8,000-13,000') 19 cm. (7½") R.

Common; in open glades and alpine meadows. Male has glistening pink eyebrow ending in white on nape but white not especially noticed at first glance. Female streaked brown with bright rufous throat and breast and a *golden rump.* A large, tame bird often on ground eating seeds and berries. Usually solitary or in small, scattered flocks. Partial to barberry bushes. Little altitudinal movement, remaining at 3660 m. (12,000') in December, eating juniper berries. Breeds among dwarf juniper and rhododendron bushes in August; the tenacious female on nest may be approached to within a foot before she flushes. Call a sharp, buzzy *deep-deep; deep-de-de-de-de.* ♣ Kashmir, Garhwal, Nepal, Sikkim; C. Asia.   2021

Red-breasted Rose Finch (Red-faced Rose Finch), *Carpodacus puniceus.*
2745-5490 m. (9,000-18,000') 20 cm. (8") R.

Occasional; on grassy, stony slopes above the tree line; on rocks in snow at 4575m. (15,000') in late December. May ascend to 5490 m. (18,000') in summer. In bad, winter weather down to Jomosom 2745 m. (9,000'). Resembles Great Rose Finch but has less swollen bill, less extensive red on head and a distinct dark band through eye. Female streaked brown with slight *greenish* tinge on rump. Solitary or pairs in summer and in groups of 8-10 birds in winter. At the highest elevations; in deep snow it works down into the cracks between large boulders and the snow, often spending long periods hunting and digging beneath one rock. Song a soft *twiddle-le-de* and a cat-like *m-a-a-a-u.* ♣ Kashmir, Garhwal, Nepal, Sikkim; C. Asia   2031

Juniper Finch (Red-fronted Finch), *Propyrrhula subhimachala.*
2592-3965 m. (8,500-13,000') 19 cm. (7½") R.

Occasional; rarely far from junipers. Red rump of male is conspicuous in flight. Orange replaces red in some birds (young males?). Rump of female greenish-yellow, easily seen in flight. In small parties among low trees and bushes. Rather sluggish. Males engage in fierce "song battles" at about 3660 m. (12,000') in August with female perched attentively nearby. Little altitudinal movement though sometimes descends to oak forests. Food of barberries, peeling outer layer to reach pulpy interior. Song a bright, varied warble; also a *ter-ter-tee.* ✻ KV: along wooded ridge just south of Phulchowki in November. ♣ Nepal, Sikkim; Himalayas to Sikiang   2033

Crossbill, *Loxia curvirostra.*
2592-3660 m. (8,500-12,000') 14 cm. (5½") R.
Occasional; in tops of hemlocks. Both sexes with sharp, crossed mandibles. Male is reddish above (brightest on rump) and mottled red and brown below, brightest on breast. In some birds red is replaced by orange. Female, rump and underparts with yellow wash. Crossed mandibles not easily detected. Birds often hard to see in tops of very tall trees; usually first located by their constant loud twittering. Flocks from 3-50 feed in hemlocks. Constantly on the go; may circle a tree several times before landing. In bad weather may seek shelter in unused yak sheds or under eaves of houses. Call a rapid, twittering *vic-vic-vic-vic-vic.* ♣ Garhwal, Nepal, Sikkim; Europe, Asia, N. and C. America 2032

Scarlet Finch, *Haematospiza sipahi.*
518-2440 m. (1,700-8,000') 18 cm. (7") R.
Occasional; in heavy forest ravines and edges of forest clearings. Male is brilliant scarlet with brown wings and tail. Female yellowish-olive green with bright orangy-yellow rump. Female color pattern resembles Himalayan Honeyguide's (see p. 138) but lacks yellow on head. Perches conspicuously on ends of branches or in tops of trees. Feeds close to the ground in raspberry bushes and on stinging nettle seeds. In pairs or small groups; in winter, birds in female plumage more numerous than adult males. Returns to same winter feeding grounds in successive years; seasonal movements not clear. At 1525 m. (5,000') in February and March, then at 2135 m. (7,000') in May. Call clear, oily notes *par-ree-reeeeeee,* a loud *pleeau,* a *chew-we-auh.* ❊ KV: February-April along forested stream above Godaveri School. ♣ Garhwal, Nepal, Sikkim, Himalayas to Tonkin 2034

Gold-crowned Black Finch, *Pyrrhoplectes epauletta.*
1525-3355 m. (5,000-11,000') 15 cm. (6") R.
Occasional; in oak-rhododendron forests. Male a striking black bird with shiny golden-orange hind-crown and upper nape. Also note long white margins to secondaries. Female rich brown. The light margins to secondaries distinguish her from other finches. Usually in small parties low in foliage, often descending to feed on ground. Also fond of tips of oak twigs. Keeps to interior of bushes. Frequently with other species. Nest not yet discovered; may breed in rhododendron thickets over 3050 m. (10,000'). Seen on Ganesh Himal at 3355 m. (11,000') the first week of May. Calls a musical *purl-lee;* also a single high squeak, *ple-e-e,* and a rapid high-pitched *pi-pi-pi-pi.* ❊ KV: some in oak forests except during summer. ♣ Garhwal, Nepal, Sikkim; Himalayas to Sikiang 2035

Brown Bullfinch, *Pyrrhula nipalensis.*
1830-3050 m. (6,000-10,000') 16 cm. (6½") R.
Fairly common; in oak forests. Male ashy-brown with contrasting white rump, black wings and tail. Female similar to male but innermost secondaries *tipped yellow,* not crimson. Pairs or small parties in tall trees and bushes consuming buds, blossoms and seeds. Rather tame. Fond of eating tips of oak twigs. Little altitudinal movement. Noted calling loudly in early June with nesting materials in bill at 2379 m. (7,800'). Song a repeated mellow *her-dee-a-duuee;* alarm call a mellow *per-lee.* ❊ KV: in oak forests; probably nesting. (Gray-headed Bullfinch, *P. erythaca,* winter in Sikkim, see p. 337). ♣ Garhwal, Nepal, Sikkim; Himalayas to Formosa 2036

Red-headed Bullfinch, *Pyrrhula erythrocephala.*
1830-3965 m. (6,000-13,000') 14 cm. (5½") R.
Fairly common; in low bushes in forest. Male has black face with head and nape orangy-brown; orange breast. The white rump is conspicuous in flight. Female is similar to male except that head, back and breast are yellowish-green. In small parties in mixed forests, usually above 3050 m. (10,000') in summer. Often near a stream. Somewhat lethargic, spending much time sitting in one position. Nibbles petals of rhododendron flowers. Nests at about 3812 m. (12,500'), building in low bushes to as high as 40 feet up in juniper trees. Call *terp-terp-tee.* ❊ KV: northern slopes of Sheopuri. (Orange Bullfinch, *P. aurantiaca,* in Kashmir, see p. 335.) ♣ Kashmir, Garhwal, Nepal, Sikkim; Himalayas 2039

BUNTINGS (Emberizidae) are smallish birds with strongly pointed, conical bills, strong wings and legs. They feed gregariously on the ground or in bushes. They resemble finches but have longer tails and less swollen bills. Sexes usually slightly dissimilar.

Pine Bunting, *Emberiza leucocephalos*.
2287-3050 m. (7,500-10,000') 18 cm. (7") W.
Fairly common; in hedges bordering fields in N.W. Nepal. Male distinctive with rich chestnut face; white on top of head bordered in black. Also note white ear patch. Males and females in winter plumage are gray and brown streaked with rufous. Look for chestnut rump and rufous wash on breast and flanks. In loose flocks up to 20 or more birds, perching on bare trees in the morning sun. Fairly shy, flying a considerable distance when disturbed. Sometimes associated with Rock Buntings. Most frequent in Humla, Mugu and Jumla Districts and sparingly as far east as Kathmandu. Flies up with a clear *tee*. ✤ KV: occasionally in winter (Balaju, Thimi). ♠ Kashmir, Garhwal, Nepal; Europe, Asia 2042

Black-headed Bunting, *Emberiza melanocephala*.
1372 m. (4,500') 18 cm. (7") W.
Scarce; found in Kathmandu Valley in January (H.S. Nepali). One bird associating with about 200 Yellow-breasted Buntings in hedges bordering fields. A yellow bunting with a black head becoming brown in winter, chestnut back and no white on tail. Female is streaked brown above; no streaks below; yellow vent. Also should straggle into S.W. Nepal in winter. ♠ Nepal; Europe and Asia 2043

Red-headed Bunting, *Emberiza bruniceps*.
183 m. (600') 16 cm. (6½") M.
Scarce; one male seen in tamarisk along the Narayani River, C. Nepal. Male has chestnut crown, sides of head and throat; bright yellow below. Female virtually identical to female Black-headed Bunting but slightly smaller. Recently discovered in Nepal (thus not illustrated) by RLF and Harvey Gilston. One bird seen on 15 April 1975 following three days of strong, continuous westerly winds. Possibly a wind-blown vagrant. ♠ Nepal; Iran to India 2044

Chestnut Bunting, *Emberiza rutila*.
1525 m. (5,000') 14 cm. (5½") W.
Scarce; in bushes near open fields. Male unmistakable chestnut and yellow. Female streaked above; chestnut rump separates it from other similar buntings. Possibly a vagrant in Nepal. ✤ KV: found once in January at Godaveri (RLF). ♠ Nepal, Sikkim; Asia 2045

Yellow-breasted Bunting, *Emberiza aureola*.
305-1372 m. (1,000-4,500') 16 cm. (6½") W.
Fairly common; during migration, along river courses; winters in bushes and *dal* fields of the *duns* and *tarai*. Male rich chocolate and yellow. Look for black face and white wing patch. Female is olive-brown above and pale yellow below with black streaks on flanks. Wingbar rufous. Loose parties up to 200 or more individuals; not very shy and are easily seen as they perch quietly on bushes or in trees. Roosts in colonies. Flight call a trilling *tzick*. ✤ KV: migrate along Manora, a few remain most of the winter. (Ortolan Bunting, *E. hortulana*, straggler in Kashmir, see p. 335.) ♠ Nepal, Sikkim; Europe, Asia 2046

Black-faced Bunting, *Emberiza spodocephala*.
120-305 m. (400-1,000') 16 cm. (6½") W., M.
Scarce; passing through Nepal on migration. An olive-green and bright yellow bird with white outer tail feathers seen in flight. Female lacks black face of male. In small flocks. Partial to stands of long grass, usually in dry river courses and also near swamps. ✤ KV: on Vishnumati in November (H.S. Nepali). ♠ Nepal; Asia 2047

White-capped Bunting, *Emberiza stewarti*.
213-1372 m. (700-4,500') 16 cm. (6¼") W.

Scarce; in small flocks in winter. Male has gray head (no black lines), brown back and *white breast streaked with rufous*. Female is a streaked, pale brown bird with a rufous rump. Winters in the lowlands. Feeds among low vegetation, particularly *Zizyphus* bushes and in fallow fields. Perches on leafless trees in winter sunshine. ♣ Kashmir, Garhwal, Nepal; Iran to Nepal
2048

Gray-headed Bunting, *Emberiza fucata*.
183-915 m. (600-3,000') 15 cm. (6") R.

Occasional; along reedy streams and lakes and in ditches between rice fields. Winter male is heavily streaked; look for bright rufous cheeks; gray head is not outstanding. The similar Little Bunting has rufous cheeks and a rufous crown (not gray). Female paler but retains rufous cheeks. Breeding male has much black on throat and breast. In small parties, haunting marshes, grassland and scrub jungle. When disturbed flies up at a steep angle but soon levels off to drop again into cover. Common in reedy habitat such as Begnas Tal, Pokhara, east to Jhapa District. Breeding birds recently discovered near Dhaulagiri (J. Martens, H.S. Nepali, 1973). (Reed Bunting, *E. schoeniclus*, see p. 323.) ♣ Kashmir, Garhwal, Nepal; Asia
2055, 2055a

Rock Bunting, *Emberiza cia*.
2135-4422 m. (7,000-14,500') 18 cm. (7") R.

Common; in grassy, open country. In male look for the gray head with two broad black stripes over crown and another behind eye. Also a dark gular stripe around to nape. White outer tail feathers noticeable when alighting. Female is pale and lightly streaked. In small parties usually above 2440 m. (8,000'). Fond of weed seeds around old cattle sheds. Strong flight, moving up into tree or onto rock promontory when disturbed. Not very shy. Little seasonal movement. Common around Tukuche, 2592 m. (8,500') both summer and winter; young being fed here in late June. Scarce in the desert region of northern Dolpo. Call a *zeet* when taking flight; song a light, lispy *tik-chep-tee-zu* with variations. ♣ Kashmir, Garhwal, Nepal, Sikkim(?); Europe, Africa, Asia
2051(?), 2052

Little Bunting, *Emberiza pusilla*.
244-3050 m. (800-10,000') 14 cm. (5½") W.

Fairly common; in grassy meadows in the vicinity of streams. A small bunting with a *rufous head*, two broad, dark lines through crown, rufous ear patch, a pale, streaked breast. In small, loose flocks in plowed fields and along hedges. Flight, strong and undulating. Perches on tops of bushes. Leaves Nepal in late April or early May. Silent in winter except for a light *tick* contact note. ❊ KV: on Valley floor and grassy slopes of surrounding hills ♣ Kashmir, Garhwal, Nepal, Sikkim; Europe, Asia
2056

Crested Bunting, *Melophus lathami*.
120-2440 m. (400-8,000') 15 cm. (6") R.

Fairly common; in cultivated fields and on open hillsides among rocks and bushes. Both sexes have a distinctive crest. Male is glossy black with rufous wings and tail which show best in flight. The female has rufous wings and tail, the black replaced with dark gray. Single or in pairs, feeding on seeds and grain. Quite bold; spends much time walking on ground. At other occasions seen perched on tops of bushes or small trees. Flight strong and undulating. Song a chirping *chut-chut-cheere-choo*. Also at intervals a metallic *plit*. ❊ KV: along footpaths around the edge of the Valley. ♣ Kashmir, Garhwal, Nepal, Sikkim; Pakistan to S. China
2060

Mandelli's Snow Finch, *Montifringilla taczanowskii.*
 4819 m. (15,800') 15.5 cm. (6¼") R (?)
Scarce; in open, stony, Tibetan plateau-like country of north Mustang Dist. A dull appearing snow finch resembling the Tibetan Snow Finch, *Montifringilla adamsi* (see p. 298) but with the throat white (not black) and without the extensive white in wing. Also note that lateral tail feathers tipped white (not dark brown). First found in Nepal by Hari S. Nepali in June 1977. Noted within 100 m. of two other snow finch species. In flight, hugs the ground closely, just skimming the surface (Nepali). ♠ Nepal, Sikkim; Tibet   1953

Red-necked Snow Finch, *Montifringilla ruficollis.*
 4819 m. (15,800') 14. cm. (5½") R (?)
Scarce; in open, stony Tibetan steppe-like country of north Mustang Dist. Very similar to Blanford's Snow Finch but has throat white (not black) and sides of neck bright rufous (not dull rufous). Also note black mustachial streaks. In flight, the white on shoulders shows well (Blanford's lacks white on shoulders). Both this species and Blanford's noted feeding together near openings of mouse-hare burrows (Nepali). ♠ Nepal, Sikkim; Tibet to Sinkiang 1954

Blanford's Snow Finch, *Montifringilla blanfordi.*
 4819 m. (15,800') 14 cm. (5½") R (?)
Scarce; in open, stony Tibetan plateau-like country of north Mustang Dist. Very similar to Red-necked Snow Finch but lacks the white on shoulders and has a dull black throat (not white) and a black mark at the forehead part. Note the *pale rufous* on neck but this should not be confused with the bright rufous of the Red-necked species. First found in Nepal by Hari S. Nepali in June 1977. Closely associated with other snow finches and mouse-hare burrows. Paired in summer. ♠ Nepal, Sikkim; Tibet   1955

Mongolian Desert Finch, *Rhodopechys mongolica.*
 3507 m. (11,500') 15 cm. (6") R (?)
Scarce; in open desert-like country of the Muktinath Valley (Mustang Dist.). A pale finch with a pink supercillium and a faintly pink rump. Amount of pink quite variable, least pronounced in female. Bill pale yellowish. Considerable white in wing distinguishes this species from other *Rhodopechys* finches. Gregarious. Feeds among stones and at bases of grass clumps. A flock of 16 birds noted (and 2 photographed) on 25 June 1976 (RLF). A flock of 34 on 09 Feb. 1982 near Jomsom (P. Pyle). Call note a distinct *weep weep*. ♠ Nepal; Caucasus south to Ladakh and east to Mongolia   2007

Streaked Weaver, *Ploceus manyar.*
 120 m. (400') 15 cm. (6") R.
Scarce; in reeds of eastern *tarai*. Wintering males and females told from other weavers by boldly streaked breast and flanks. Also look for yellow patch on side of neck. Breeding male has golden crown and dark face and throat. First noted in Nepal by Stephen Madge and party (Feb.1974) and confirmed by RLF and Harvey Gilston (one bird photographed). R. Gregory-Smith records the bird as "common" at the Barrage. ♠ Nepal; Pakistan to Bali   1962 (?)

Hodgson's Bush Chat, *Saxicola insignis.*
76-1372 m. (250-4,500') 16 cm. (6½") W.
Scarce; in reeds at the Kosi Barrage or at edge of fields in Kathmandu Valley. Very similar to Collared Bush Chat (see p. 261) but larger and male flashes much more white in flight. Look for *white throat* and white collar (this collar completely encircles hind neck and shows clearly in RLF photographs taken at the Barrage but apparently some males (partly immature?) lack collar; (more information needed). Female similar to imm. male (shown here) except *no white* on shoulders or wings (wings show two buffy bars). Solitary; perches on ground, grass stalks or small bushes. Somewhat shy. Rediscovered in Nepal at the Kosi Barrage on 11 April 1975 (RLF, H. Gilston); regular winter reports in subsequent years. ❀ KV: two imm. males collected along Manhora river in Oct. by H.S. Nepali.
◆ Nepal; C. Asia, winter S. Asia 1694

Jerdon's Bush Chat, *Saxicola jerdoni.*
76 m. (250') 15 cm. (6") S.
Scarce; in reeds near the Kosi Barrage (E. Nepal *tarai*). Male, all black above, all white below. Unmistakable. Female, brown above, pale buff below, lightening to white on the throat. Usually single; shy. Often flares tail. Feeds on ground; perches on reeds. Discovered in Nepal by Richard C. Gregory-Smith when he noted a male at the Kosi Barrage on 11 May 1975; another male seen on 19 June 1976 along with a spotted bird—possibly a juvenile of this species. Alarm call a *chirrr* (AR). ◆ Nepal; Nepal to Vietnam 1704

Brown Rock Chat, *Cercomela fusca.*
76-91 m. (250-300') 16 cm. (6½") R? W?
Scarce; in open country along the Indian border. A uniform ferruginous-brown bird with no distinguishing features. Differs from female Indian Robin, *Saxicoloides fulicata*, by lack of rusty undertail coverts. Usually solitary. Stands upright and often cocks tail; partial to stony areas. Collected in Nepal at the Kosi Barrage on 12 Mar. 1969 (RLF) and a possible sight record near Bhairhawa (RLF). ◆ Nepal; endemic to northern south Asia 1692

Little (Tibet) Owl, *Athene noctua.*
2745-4575 m. (9,000-15,000') 23 cm. (9") R.
Scarce; in desert biotope of Mustang and Dolpo Districts. A squat, yellow-eyed owl that blends into the rocky crags of its natural home. Only solitary birds noted. Discovered in Nepal for the first time by H. S. Nepali who collected a female from Phijor, Dolpo on 8 July 1978 and a male from Taku Do, Dolpo on 23 July 1978. Subsequently, has been noted several times in the Kagbeni region, Mustang District (F. Lambert and R. Grimmett on 15 Jan. 1979 and J. Wolstencroft on 3 April 1981). Call is a rather loud but plaintive *peew* (Nepali). ◆ Nepal, Sikkim; Europe and high central Asia 649

ADDITIONS

Tiger Bittern, *Gorsachius melanolophus.*
120 m. (400') 50 cm. (20") S.
Scarce; along streams in thick *bhabar* jungle. A heavy bittern; dark rufous above with back finely barred. Look for black nuchal crest. Pale buff throat streaked and pale buff underparts irregularly barred with dark brown. Solitary; shy. Single bird flushed from stream bank in dense jungle about 10 km. (6 mi.) S. of Dharan (E. Nepal) on 2 May and 30 May 1976 (Richard C. Gregory-Smith, 1976:4). Status and movements in Nepal uncertain. ♠ Nepal; Nepal to Sumatra 53

Bewick's Swan (Whistling Swan), *Cygnus columbianus.*
120 m. (400') 122 cm. (48") W.
Scarce; along Narayani River, edge of Royal Chitwan National Park. Plumage entirely white. Smaller than Whooper Swan, *Cygnus cygnus* (see p. 36) and with a comparatively smaller bill. Best diagnostic feature is yellow area at base of bill which in the Whooper is extensive and points sharply forward while, in the Bewick's, remains shortened and considerably rounded (i.e. truncated). One individual discovered on the Narayani by John Gooders on 23 Feb. 1978. Same bird (?) subsequently photographed by Michael Price as the latter sat filming Gharial crocodiles from a riverside blind. ♠ Nepal; North America, Europe, Asia 84

Large Whistling Teal (Fulvous Tree Duck), *Dendrocygna bicolor.*
76 m. (250') 50 cm. (20") Vagrant.
Scarce; in still water at the Kosi Barrage. Very similar to Lesser Whistling Teal, *D. javanica*, but has creamy white (not chestnut) upper tail coverts. Single bird discovered in Nepal on 12 Feb. 1979 by R. Grimmett. ♠ Nepal; S. Asia, Africa, N. and S. America 89

Baer's Pochard, *Aythya baeri.*
76 m. (250') 46 cm. (18") W.
Scarce; in large ponds at the Kosi Barrage. Very similar to White-eyed Pochard, *A. nyroca*, but head and neck glossed green (looks black in most lights) and distinctly darker than brown lower throat and breast (vs. uniform ferruginous). Also white (vs. no white) usually shows near the water line at a level below the shoulder (Ross and Wicks). Female difficult to distinguish in the field. First discovered in Nepal on 12 Feb. 1979 by R. Grimmett and F. Lambert. Up to 20 noted on 20 Feb. 1979. Regular and repeated sightings at the Barrage in subsequent years. ♠ Nepal; eastern S. Asia to N.E. Asia 110

Longtail Duck (Old Squaw), *Clangula hyemalis.*
76 m. (250') 30 cm. (12") W.
Scarce; in open water at the Kosi Barrage. Drake has upperparts and breast band black; head, neck and underparts white; cheek patch brown. Long, pointed tail important field mark. Female is brown and white with brown cheek patch. Swims and dives in large, open bodies of water. Long tail held erect only when excited. First discovered in Nepal in March 1981 by T. and C. Inskipp. Second record on 6 Feb. 1982 by A. and C. Cassels, N. Hopkins and G. Tuma. ♠ Kashmir, Nepal; breeds on arctic coasts of Europe, Asia and America, winters south 117

Black-necked Crane, *Grus nigricollis.*
915 m. (3,000') 152 cm. (5' tall) Vagrant.
Scarce; in rice fields near Begnas Tal, Pokhara Valley. Resembles Common Crane, *Grus grus* (see p. 32) but entire neck and throat black (black not restricted to throat only). Gray on face reduced to tuft behind eye. A single bird seen on two successive days and photographed on the second occasion by John Rossetti in July 1978. A most unusual record; when disturbed on the second day, the bird rose and circled up through a group of vultures and was lost to sight heading west. Call is loud and trumpet-like (AR). ♠ Nepal; Central Asia 321

Sanderling, *Calidris alba.*
76-120 m. (250-400') 19 cm. (7½") W, M.
Scarce; on sand banks of major rivers. A small, almost white wader with blackish shoulder patch and black legs. A distinct, white wingbar in flight. Very active, constantly running about at water's edge. Call: in flight a *twick twick* (Heinzel et al.). First discovered in Nepal on the banks of the Kosi on 11 Feb. 1979 and subsequently several seen along the Rapti River, Chitwan on 30 Nov. 1979 (K. Curry-Lindahl). ♠ Nepal; nearly world-wide
414

Curlew Sandpiper, *Calidris testacea.*
76-1372 m. (250-4,500') 20 cm. (8") W, M.
Scarce; on sand bars of streams and rivers. Downcurved black bill good field mark; can be separated from similar Dunlin, *C. alpina*, by all white rump (not partly dark). Often with other stints and smaller waders. First discovered in Nepal in late April 1981 at the Kosi Barrage by N. Krabbe, O. Lou, M. Henriksen. Subsequently collected by H.S. Nepali on 5 and 8 Sept. 1981 on the Vishnumati River, Kathmandu. ♠ Nepal; breeds in N. Asia, winters Europe, Asia, Africa, Australia 422

Turnstone, *Arenaria interpres.*
2562 m. (8,400') 22 cm. (8½") M.
Scarce; on gravel flats of Kali Gandaki River near Tukche. A short-legged, chunky shore bird Winter plumage (seen in Nepal) shows brown above, white below except for extensive but irregular brown pectoral band. In breeding plumage, back turns bright rufous and band black. In flight, look for white lower back, rump and tail with black V-shaped mark on upper tail coverts and black subterminal bar on tail. A single bird excellently photographed by Mark Beaman at Tukche on 14 Sept. 1973. Usually coastal. Within the past 100 years, apparently only five inland records on the subcontinent (see Ali and Ripley, 1969: 274). ♠ Nepal; North America, Africa, Asia, wintering in temperate and tropical latitudes 402

Red-necked Phalarope, *Phalaropus lobatus.*
3050 m. (10,000') 19 cm. (7½") M.
Scarce; noted from Rara Lake, Mugu District, apparently on migration. A small, gray bird with thin black bill. Very similar to Gray Phalarope, *P. fulicarius*, but latter has shorter bill, slightly yellowish at base (seen at close range). Feeds by actively swimming, often in circles, picking at insect prey. Discovered in Nepal in 1982 by D. Pritchard and D. Brearey. ♠ Nepal; breeds N. Asia and Alaska, winters along coastlines nearly world-wide 428

White-winged Black Tern, *Chlidonias leucopterus.*
915 m. (3,000') 23 cm. (9") W? M.
Scarce; a small, short-tailed tern very similar in winter plumage to Whiskered, *C. hybrida*, but slightly paler above, especially on rump. Unmistakable in black-and-white breeding plumage. Active both over shallow-water inland lakes and rivers and along coastal shorelines. First reported in Nepal (2 birds in breeding plumage) in early May 1981 at Phewa Tal Lake, Pokhara, by N. Krabbe, O. Lou and M. Henriksen. May well occur in small numbers during winter but overlooked among Whiskered Terns. ♠ Nepal; Europe, Asia, Africa, Australia 459

White-vented Needletail, *Chaetura cochinchinensis*.
152 m. (500') 20 cm. (8") R?
Occasional; in the Chitwan dun valley, often flying over water. Should also occur elsewhere in lowland Nepal. Previously synonymized with the White-throated Needletail, *C. caudacuta*, and resembles the latter but has throat dark gray-brown (not white) and vent white (not dark). In Nepal, first collected near Hetaura, Chitwan by W. Koelz in 1947 and seen repeatedly since then, mostly in Chitwan. ♠ Nepal; Nepal to S.E. Asia 689

Collared Sand Martin, *Riparia riparia*.
91-3965 m. (300-13,000') 13 cm. (5") R? M?
Scarce; noted in desert country of Mustang Dist. Slightly larger than Plain Sand Martin, *Riparia plaudicola* (see p. 157) and with *distinct* dark band across pale breast. Plain Sand Martins often have indistinct bands, so caution in identification advisable. Usually gregarious. Apparently first collected in Nepal on 15 Feb. 1938 in Morang Dist. by F. M. Bailey (T.& C.Inskipp). First recent record by Mark Beaman on 10 Oct. 1973 at Jomosom. Subsequently several reports from Jomosom area and 30-40 seen flying low over barley fields south of Lho Mantang in mid-June 1977 (Hari S. Nepali). ♠ Kashmir, Nepal; Europe, North Africa to China 910

Chestnut-backed Sibia, *Heterophasia annectens*.
2135 m. (7,000') 18 cm. (7") S.S, R(?)
Scarce; in cloud forests of far eastern Nepal. At first glance, resembles male Nepal Cutia (see p. 202) but lacks bars on flanks and tail longer. Head all black. Behavior similar to Nepal Cutia's; hunts for insects amid moss-lined tree branches. Usually in small flocks. Two birds observed in the Mai Pokhari area (Ilam Dist.) on 17, 18 Sept. 1978 by Steve LeClerq, Ridge DeWitt and RLF. Song, a four-note whistle (AR). ♠ Nepal, Sikkim; Nepal to Vietnam 1395

Black-browed Reed Warbler, *Acrocephalus bistrigiceps*.
76 m. (250') 13 cm. (5") W.
Scarce; in grass at the Kosi Barrage. A distinctive reed warbler with a conspicuous buff eyebrow under a blackish line and above a dark pre- and post-ocular stripe. Shy and skulking. First discovered in Nepal on 19 Jan. 1981 by J. Hall. Call note a *tac* (Hall). ♠ Nepal; breeding in N.E. Asia, wintering in eastern India and S.E. Asia 1555

Pied Wheatear, *Oenanthe picata*.
762 m. (2,500') 18 cm. (7") W.
Scarce; in open country of the Surkhet dun valley. A conspicuous black-and-white bird with black-tipped white tail. Variety seen in Nepal has white extending over head from forehead to lower nape. Perches upright on posts and fences, dropping to ground in search of insect prey. Discovered in Nepal at Birendranagar, Surkhet Valley on 3 Dec. 1979 by P. Hagen. Noted into Feb. and also seen in subsequent winters. ♠ Kashmir, Nepal; breeds from Turkmen S.S.R. to Ladakh, winters south in W. and C. India 1712

Dusky Thrush, *Turdus naumanni*.
1372-2745 m. (4,500-9,000') 23 cm. (9") W.
Scarce; single birds noted at forest edge or in scrub forest. A dark thrush with conspicuous buff eyebrow and pale buff throat (male). Thick black scalloping forms breast band and scaly appearance extends down sides. Also look for rufous wing. Female brownish above, with rufous wings and brown crescents on whitish breast and flanks. Possible confusion with some plumages of Black-throated Thrush, *T. ruficollis*, so identification should be made carefully. Reported in "large flocks, winter and spring" by D. Proud for the mid-1940s but not seen again in Nepal for over 30 years. An adult reported from near Lete, Mustang District on 22-23 Jan. 1979 by F. Lambert and R. Filby. Subsequent records are known. ♠ Nepal; breeds N.E. Asia, winters E. and S.E. Asia and E. India 1765

White-cheeked Tit, *Aegithalos leucogenys.*
3050-3660 m. (10,000-12,000') 10 cm. (4") R.
Scarce; in forest and scrub forest of the Chankeli Lekh, Mugu District, northwestern Nepal. Similar to Red-headed Tit, *A. concinnus*, but top of head dull rusty (not bright rusty), cheeks white (not black) and lacks pale eyebrow behind eye. Easily distinguished from Rufous-fronted Tit, *A. iouschistos*, by black (not white) bib and different head color. Usually in groups moving actively from one bush or tree to the next. Discovered in Nepal in 1982 by D.E. Pritchard and D.M. Brearey. (Kashmir, Nepal; Afghanistan to Nepal 1821

Forest Wagtail, *Motacilla indica.*
120 m. (400') 18 cm. (7") M.
Scarce; a bird of forest clearings or forest understory. A distinctive wagtail with black double breastband and peculiar lateral wagging of tail and hindparts. Usually solitary. Somewhat shy and flies up to low branches of trees when disturbed while feeding on the ground. Nepal slightly west of normal migration route but discovered in this country on 30 Nov. 1979 in Chitwan by K. Curry-Lindahl. (Nepal, Sikkim; breeds in E. and N.E. Asia, winters south to Borneo, Java and Sri Lanka 1874

Spanish Sparrow, *Passer hispaniolensis.*
76 m. (250') 15 m. (6") W.
Scarce; noted at the Kosi Barrage. Male superficially like House Sparrow, *P. domesticus*, but forehead and crown reddish-brown (not gray) and black on throat and breast more extensive, often extending down flanks. Female very similar to female House Sparrow but almost always shows some faint streaking on breast or upper flanks. Gregarious, often perching in mass on low bushes after feeding. Prefers open country dotted with bushes and fields. Discovered in Nepal in late Feb.-early Mar. 1981 by D. Mills, T. Baker and N. Preston. The winter of 1980-81 saw a severe drought in far western India and this may have driven the sparrows east. (Nepal; Europe and W. Asia south to N. Africa and India 1940

Yellowhammer, *Emberiza citrinella.*
2135-3050 m. (7,000-10,000') 16 cm. (6½") W.
Scarce; noted in scrub and fields of Jumla, west Nepal and around Kagbeni, Mustang Dist. Male has distinctive lemon-yellow head and underparts with a rufous rump. Female exhibits a variable amount of pale, greenish-yellow on head and underparts; also has rufous rump. Feeds on ground and flushes into bushes; virtually always with Pine Buntings, *E. leucocephalas*. First discovered in Nepal at Kagbeni on 25 Feb. 1981 by T. Baker. Reports now surface each winter and recently D. McCauley counted 5 birds mixed with several hundred Pine Buntings in the Jumla area (first week of Jan. 1983). (Nepal; Europe, Asia

Rustic Bunting, *Emberiza rustica.*
120-3050 m. (400-10,000') 14 cm. (5½") W.
Scarce; in old fields with other buntings. Male in breeding plumage has black head with white eyebrow starting behind eye and extending to nape. Throat white. Upperparts rusty-brown, streaked darker; underparts with rusty streaks on breast and flanks. In winter the black is replaced by brownish. Winter females hard to distinguish from other buntings in the field. Two sightings for Nepal during early 1981: P. Ewins from Rapti area, Chitwan, and T. Baker from Kagbeni, Mustang on 25 Feb. A first sighting from India also reported during this same period; no subsequent records. (Nepal; N.W. Europe east to Korea

Reed Bunting, *Emberiza schoniclus.*
915 m. (3,000') 14 cm. (5½") W.
Scarce; in reeds edging Begnas Tal in Pokhara Valley, C. Nepal. Male has distinctive head and face pattern: top of head and throat black, cheek brown, eye line and mustachial streak buff. Female very similar to female Gray-headed Bunting. *Emberiza fucata* (see p. 318) but cheeks brown (not rufous). An immature male and a female sighted on 21 Dec. 1970 by Tim Inskipp. No further records. (Kashmir, Nepal; England to Manchuria
2058 (?), 2059 (?)

Possible New Records

The following species have been reported from Nepal, but confirmatory evidence needed before they are fully admitted to the Nepal list. Details are given here in the hope of eliciting additional information.

The Siberian Crane, *Grus leucogeranus* has been reported at over 6100 m. (20,000') in the Manaslu region of C. Nepal during the second week of Oct. by Japanese mountain climbers. Their black-and-white photographs certainly show what appear to be Siberian Cranes. But as gray birds (i.e. Common Crane, *Grus grus*) flying over snow may look white, caution seems advised. A puzzle exists. If Siberian Cranes do cross over Nepal in early Oct., then where do they reside for up to six weeks before their arrival in Bharatpur, Rajasthan, India around the last week of Nov.? Their spring migration route through Afghanistan was recently confirmed by Sauie and Elliot. Clearly more data on Siberian Cranes in Nepal are desirable.

Spring sightings of the Tawny Pipit, *Anthus campestris* have been reported from Chitwan (Gunter Groh) and Shuklaphanta, W. *tarai* (RLF). This pipit is lightly streaked above and with underparts *unstreaked* (in most individuals). The possibility of confusing the Tawny Pipit with other pipits is so great, however, that we suggest confirmation in Nepal requires a specimen.

A large, pale falcon regularly seen in the Jomosom-Muktinath region of Mustang District during the past ten years may be either the Shanghar Falcon, *Falco* (*biarmicus*) *milvipes* or the Saker (Cherrug) Falcon, *Falco* (*biarmicus*) *cherrug*. Both forms often considered conspecific with Lanner Falcon, *Falco biarmicus*. To determine exact identification, good photographs or specimens desirable. Hodgson's specimens (without locality data) now in British Museum.

The Barbary Falcon, *Falco* (*peregrinus*) *pelegrinoides* noted in Manang-Mustang Districts (Thiollay). Two Hodgson's specimens probably of this race (species) collected in the Kathmandu Valley and now in British Museum (T. & C. Inskipp).

The Red-backed Shrike, *Lanius collurio*, reported from the Kosi Barrage on 20 Nov. 1975 by D. Byrne. He noted subspecies *phoenicuroides* but confirmation needed. Scully specimen of subspecies *isabellinus* in British Museum (Ripley, 1982:264). More information on this species needed.

The Eurasian Skylark, *Alauda arvensis*, previously reported from Nepal was based on a misidentification of *A. gulgula lhamarum*. However, F.R. Lambert now reports sighting one *A. arvensis* with a flock of six *A. gulgula* in the Helambu area on 4 Feb. 1979.

Radde's Leaf Warbler, *Phylloscopus schwarzi*, noted at Charali, Manang Valley on 25 Dec. 1979 (Fairbank). May occur as a rare straggler along the northern rim of Nepal.

Additional Sightings, Extensions and Corrections

As noted in the introduction (p. 16), Nepal's minimum elevation stands at only 76 meters or 250 feet above sea level. In the main text we show 122 meters or 400 feet as the minimum. Thus any bird listed for 122 m. (400') should be lowered to 76 m. (250').

Several people have suggested that some birds listed in the main text as "occasional" might best be regarded as "locally fairly common" or "locally common". Examples include the Himalayan Griffon along the Kali Gandaki Gorge, the Blue-tailed Bee-eater along streams in the western *tarai* and the Three-toed Golden-backed Woodpecker in some *sal* forests. Indeed, if one strikes ecological and habitat conditions ideal for a particular species, the frequency of that species may far exceed that of the general average. As our information increases, we expect to improve status designations.

GREBES Four Great Crested Grebes, *Podiceps cristatus* (p. 24) at the Kosi Barrage, 76 m. (250') on 2 Mar. (R. C. Gregory-Smith, 1976 : 3).
Black-necked Grebe, *Podiceps caspicus*, on Rara Lake, 3050 m. (10,000') in summer (Pritchard, Brearey).

CORMORANTS The Little Cormorant, *Phalacrocorax niger* (p. 24) appears to be "occasional" to "fairly common" in the S. E. *tarai* (R. C. Gregory-Smith, 1976 : 3) ; otherwise scarce.
A Large Cormorant, *Phalacrocorax carbo*, on Rara Lake, 3050 m. (10,000') on 23-25 Oct. 1982 (D. McCauley) and three flying over Phortse village, Everest National Park at 3962 m. (13,000') (RLF).

HERONS and BITTERNS The Eurasian Bittern, *Botaurus stellaris* (P. 28) noted in the S. E. *tarai* at 76 m. (250') (R. C. Gregory-Smith, 1976 : 4). Also recorded at Rara Lake, 3050 m. (10,000') (Pritchard, Breary), and one near Bhairhawa, C. *tarai* (K. Munthe).
Three adult Yellow Bitterns, *Ixobrychus sinensis*, seen in swampy grass, Elephant Camp, Chitwan (B. Finch).

STORKS Range of the Painted Stork, *Ibis leucocephalus* (p. 30) extended east to the S. E. *tarai* where listed as "occasional" in summer (R. C. Gregory-Smith, 1976 : 4).
A single White Stork, *Ciconia ciconia* (p. 30) seen at Jagdishpur Reservoir, 10 km. N. Taulihawa, C. *tarai*, 183 m. (600') on 05 Mar. (Jack Cox).
Adjutant Storks, *Leptoptilos dubius* (p. 32) reported as "occasional" in S. E. Nepal during the monsoons (R. C. Gregory-Smith).

CRANES Thirty-seven Common Cranes, *Grus grus* (p. 32) noted flying S. near Jomosom, Kali Gandaki Valley on 8 Oct. ; 3 more on 12 Oct. 1975 (Mark Beaman). Also, small flocks seen most winters in Chitwan Dun (RLF).

IBIS Black Ibis, *Pseudibis papillosa*, up to 792 m. (2,600') in the Surkhet Valley (P. Hagan).

DUCKS Up to 600 Lesser Whistling Teal, *Dendrocygna javanica* (p. 36) seen at the Kosi Barrage from Feb. to Apr. (R. C. Gregory-Smith).
A female Pintail, *Anas acuta* (p. 36) on lower Gokyu Lake, Everest area, 4575 m. (15,000'), May (RLF).
Up to 80 Falcated Teal, *Anas falcata* (p. 38) noted on the Kosi on 7, 8 Feb. 1974 (Madge, Dukes, Robinson and Westwood). A male seen in the Pokhara Valley in early Mar. 1977 (James Roberts) and a male on the Narayani River (C. *dun*) on 26 Feb. 1978 (John Gooders). Another 60+ at the Kosi Barrage on 12 Feb. 1979 (Lambert, Grimmett, Filby, Norton, Redman, Murphy).
Mallard, *Anas platyrhynchos* (p. 38) definitely nest on Lake Titi (S. W. flank of Nilgiri) On 11 to 13 June 1977, James Roberts counted 11 females, 7 males and 25 ducklings on the lake.
Two Common Pochards, *Aythya ferina* (p. 40) on Pangboche Lake, Everest area, 3965 m. (13,000'), May (RLF).

Three White-eyed Pochards *Aythya nyroca* (p. 40) on lower Gokyu Lake, 4575 m. (15,000'), May (RLF).

At least 6 (possibly 10-12) Goldeneyes, *Bucephala clangula* (p. 42) spent at least two winter months in the Pokhara area in 1977 (James Roberts). A single male noted on the Narayani River (C. *dun*) on 26 Feb. 1978 (John Gooders). Also noted at the Kosi Barrage, Feb. (C. Murphy, R. Grimmett).

Eurasian Shelduck, *Tadorna tadorna*, in Chitwan, Nov. 1983 (J. Halliday).

Cotton Teal, *Nettapus coromandelianus* (p. 42) apparently wander considerably as 1 male and 4 females seen on Taudha Lake, Kathmandu Valley, 28 Aug. 1976 (R. C. Gregory-Smith); a female near Dunai (Dolpo Dist.) at about 2135 m. (7,000') in Nov. 1977 (Phil Hall); a female at 3050 m. (10,000') near Pisang, Manang Valley in May (Phil Hall).

HAWKS, EAGLES and ALLIES A party of four Black-crested Bazas, *Aviceda leuphotes* (p. 44) noted on 8 May and one on 7 June 1976 in lightly forested foothills near Dharan, S. E. Nepal (R. C. Gregory-Smith). A pair noted on 22 July 1978 at edge of forest near Butwal, C. *bhabar* (Jack Cox).

A Sparrow Hawk, *Accipiter nisus* (p. 46) attacked and caught a Brandt's Mountain Finch at 4880 m. (16,000') near Gokyu, Everest area, May 1977 (RLF).

The Booted Eagle, *Hieraaetus pennatus* (p. 50) noted nesting near Braga, Manang Valley at 3850 m. (12,622'), 15 July 1977 (J. M. Thiollay).

Two Imperial Eagles, *Aquila heliaca* (p. 52) seen in migration along the Kali Gandaki Valley near Tukche on 30 Sept. 1973 (Mark Beaman). Several in migration over Pokhara Valley, early Nov. 1976 (RLF).

Numbers of Greater Spotted Eagles, *Aquila clanga* (p. 52) in migration over Pokhara Valley, early Nov. 1976, 1977 (RLF). One near Tukche, Kali Gandaki Valley on 17 Sept. 1973, (Mark Beaman).

The White-tailed Sea Eagle, *Haliaeetus albicilla* (p. 54) apparently wanders sporadically into Nepal; several additional sightings from the Pokhara area. Also one bird over Hotel Elephant Camp, Chitwan in May 1977 (C. D. Cremeans) and one (imm.) over Mohan Khola, Chitwan on 28 Feb. 1978 (John Gooders). Large eagles resting on sand of Kosi river probably this species but not positively identified (Madge, Robinson, Dukes, Westwood; RLF). Now also recorded from Kathmandu Valley (W. Sutter).

Crested Serpent Eagle, *Spilornis cheela*, up to 3352 m. (11,000') on Machapuchare (T. Lelliott).

Lammergeier (Bearded Vulture), *Gypaetus barbatus* (p. 56) noted down to 610 m. (2,000') in the Marsyandi Valley (Phil Hall). Several new records below 610 m. (2,000'), the lowest at 305 m. (1,000') at Mugling (Kathmandu-Pokhara road).

FALCONS Red-thighed Falconet, *Microhierax caerulescens* (p. 62) noted up to 1050 m. (3,442') near Pokhara (J. M. Thiollay). Several additional sightings from Pokhara Valley.

Laggar Falcon, *Falco jugger* (p. 62) noted up to 1677 m. (5,500') Kathmandu Valley (Jack Cox and Lewis Underwood). The wing linings of the bird should be quite dark as compared to the flight feathers and the bird should be described as slendered (not chunkier) than the Peregrine (Ben King).

About 150 Eurasian Hobbys, *Falco subbuteo*, collecting on telephone wires near Pokhara (about 300 m. from the steps of the Power Station) on 29-31 Oct. 1982 (J. Halliday).

Four Red-legged Falcons, *Falco vespertinus* (p. 64) seen in the Kali Gandaki Valley (Tukche) on 1 Oct. (Mark Beaman). Also, numbers seen with many Lesser Kestrels on 30 Nov. at Tumlingtar, E. Nepal (RLF). The underwing lining of male should be white (not gray) to correspond with the eastern race found in Nepal (Mark Beaman).

Nearly 100 Lesser Kestrels, *Falco naumanni* (p. 64) noted in the Pokhara Valley in late Oct. (Navin Arjal). Other records from Pokhara in Nov. and Tumlingtar, E. Nepal in Nov. (RLF). Apparently considerable numbers move through Nepal in autumn migration; fewer seen in spring. A maximum count of 340 birds at evening roost near Phewa Tal, Pokhara, on 31 Oct. 1982 (B. Finch).

The range of Hodgson's Redstart, *Phoenicurus hodgsoni* (p. 254) raised to 5032 m. (16,500') above Muktinath and lowered to 152 m. (500') in S. E. Nepal (Phil Hall).

The Blue-fronted Redstart, *Phoenicurus frontalis* (p. 254) lowered to 457 m. (1,500') in S. E. Nepal (Phil Hall).

Collared Bush Chat, *Saxicola torquata* (p. 260) lowered to 152 m. (500') in E. Nepal (Phil Hall).

Indian Robin, *Saxicoloides fulicata* (p. 260) raised to 457 m. (1,500'), E. foothills. In the male of the eastern race (found in E. Nepal), the glossy black upper parts are replaced by dark brown (Phil Hall). Noted up to 762 m. (2,500') in Surkhet Valley (P. Hagan).

Another record of Isabelline Wheatear, *Oenanthe isabellina*, from Kathmandu: on Ring Road fence on 13 Mar. 1981 (J. Wolstencroft).

An "invasion" of Eurasian Blackbirds, *Turdus merula* (p. 268) occurred across a broad range of highland Nepal during the spring of 1978 (? winter of 1977-1978). Flocks of up to 28 birds seen in the Everest National Park where they were "fairly common" in late April (RLF); additional birds in the Langtang National Park (RLF) and two birds near Jumla (Carl Friedericks and Larry Asher). All sightings in April and May.

At least 5, possibly more, Mistle Thrushes, *Turdus viscivorus* (p. 270) around Mark Beaman's camp south of Tukche and 2440 m. (8,000'), Sept. extends range east into the Kali Gandaki Valley. Range now extended east to Machapuchare (T. Lelliott).

The Dark Thrush, *Turdus obscurus*, at Gokarna, Kathmandu Valley on 20 Dec. 1978 (R. Grimmett N. Redman) and also one near Marpha (Mustang Dist.) on 27 April 1981 (J. Wolstencroft).

ACCENTORS Altai Accentor, *Prunella himalayana*, down to 1341 m. (4,400') in Rukum, 25 March 1982 (P. Hagan).

TITMICE One Fire-capped Tit, *Cephalopyrus flammiceps* (p. 280) noted near the Pelma Khola (Dhaulagiri area) on 9 April (G. B. Corbet). Two females in alders at Pakhribas, E. Nepal at 1372 m. (4,500') on 16 Jan. 1978 (R. J. Isherwood, 1978: 15). We now consider this species as occasional in the western half of the country and appearing irregularly in the eastern half.

PIPITS Eurasian Tree Pipit, *Anthus trivailis*, noted at Kosi Barrage on 10, 12 Feb. 1979 (R. Grimmett).

WAGTAILS Yellow-headed Wagtail, *Motacilla citreola* (p. 290) raised to 4697 m. (15,400') at Gokyu Lake, Everest area, May (C. Mackensie, RLF).

SUNBIRDS Range of Rubycheek, *Anthreptes singalensis* (p. 296) extended west to Tiger Tops, Chitwan National Park, Dec. (RLF). Also five in group in lower Mai Valley, E. Nepal, Mar. (RLF).

WEAVERS Streaked Weaver, *Ploceus manyar* (p. 300) reported "common" in the S. E. *tarai*; nesting from June to Aug. (R. C. Gregory-Smith).

Red Munias, *Estrilda amandava*, up to 670 m. (2,200') at Bulbuli, Surkhet in Aug. 1979 (P. Hagan).

FINCHES Range of the Brambling, *Fringilla montifringilla* (p. 300) extended east to the Kathmandu Valley. Two birds seen on top of Shivpuri, 18 Jan. 1978 (R. Jasper) and one noted near Godavari at 1525 m. (5,000') on 27 Jan. 1978 (A. D. Sudbury) during a very cold winter with much snow at high elevations in Nepal.

A male Great Rose Finch, *Carpodacus rubicilla*, down to 2622 m. (8,600') at Marpha (Mustang Dist.) on 08 Feb. 1982 (P. Pyle, C. Robson, M. Parr).

BUNTINGS Three Black-headed Buntings, *Emberiza melanocephala* (p. 316) noted on the S. E. *tarai* plain at 76 m. (250') Dec. (R. C. Gregory-Smith).

Adult and young Gray-headed Buntings, *Emberiza fucata*, common around Jumla airport; possibly nesting here (D. McCauley).

The following have supported this book project in honor of Robert L. Fleming, Sr. in recognition of his enthusiasm and love for the people and the country of Nepal.

SPONSORS

Mr. Julius Rosenwald II
Mrs. James S. Weaver
Mrs. Louis Olson
Mrs. Jane B. Dunaway
Miss Helen Fleming

CONTRIBUTORS

The Lyle Clovers
The Robert Ramsdells
The R. F. Brownie Cotes
Miss Dorothy Buckley
Mrs. Bernedene McIsaac
The Don Tarr family
The Lee Blums and Relatives
The R. Laird Harrises
Rev. Glen Ogden, Sr.
Miss Iva Fleming
Miss Alta Wade
The Ray Garlands
Miss Jenny Lind
Dr. Thelma Varian
Mrs. Thelma Fiorini
Dr. Harry Rees
The Harold Dusenberrys

The Marvin Keislars
The James Hunts, Sr.
The Rex Bells
Dr. W. G. Cooper
The Allerton Eddys
The Eric Sturleys
The W. C. Knoops
Miss Kathy O'Hare
The Wayne Doanes
The Don Milligans
The Roy Coats, Jr.
Dr. Russell Steere
The Lester C. Andersons
The Don Gebraads
Nat Hughes Bible Class, Memphis
Kalamazoo Nature Center
The T. W. deBernardis

PREFACE TO THE SECOND EDITION

NEPAL continues to be an exciting country for bird study. More exciting than we knew when BIRDS OF NEPAL first appeared. Since 1976 considerable new information has been collected by a growing number of enthusiasts and consequently the Nepal bird list has now jumped to 801 species. Similarly, range and altitude extensions have occurred. These additional data have been condensed and appear as a supplement beginning on page 321.

We would like to thank the following people for their contributions to our understanding of birds in Nepal: Navin Arjal (Kathmandu; Pokhara; Kosi Barrage), Larry Asher (Jumla), Francis Batson (S. E. Nepal), Mark Beaman (Kali Gandaki Valley), G. B. Corbet (Dhaulagiri), Jack Cox, Jr. (C. *tarai;* Kathmandu; Muktinath), C. D. Cremeans (C. *dun*), Ridge Dewitt (Kali Gandaki Valley), Carl Friedericks (Jumla), John Gooders (C. *dun*), Richard Gregory-Smith (S. E. Nepal), Phil Hall (S. E. *tarai;* Kathmandu; Muktinath), Tim Inskipp (Kali Gandaki Valley), R. J. Isherwood (Dhankuta, E. Nepal), R. Jasper (Kathmandu), Stan Justice (Jumla; Nepalganj), Julie and Penny Leslie (Annapurna area; C. *dun;* S. E. Nepal), Chris Mackensie (S. E. Nepal; Everest area; Annapurna area), Delos McCauley (C. *tarai,* C. foothills), C. McDougal (C. *dun*), Nicholas Moll (Kathmandu), H. S. Nepali (Mustang), Nigel Pedfield (Muktinath), Cliff Rice (Shuklaphanta, W. *tarai;* Annapurna area), James Roberts (Pokhara Valley), Deva Nur Singh (Jomsom), A. Dan Sudbury (Kathmandu), Amuliya Tuladhar (Kathmandu) and Lewis Underwood (Kathmandu).

We would also like to express our deep gratitude to Sally Beieler, Elizabeth Forster and Jolly Miller who assisted with distributions of the first edition.

We have been pleased with the response accorded BIRDS OF NEPAL and hope that an increased understanding and appreciation of the birds of Nepal will continue to lead to wise conservation of this valuable—and beautiful—natural resource.

BIBLIOGRAPHY

ALI, SALIM
1941. The book of Indian birds. xlvi + 162 pp. Bombay Nat. Hist. Soc., Bombay.

1949. Indian hill birds. lii + 188 pp. Oxford University Press, London.

1962. The birds of Sikkim. xxx + 414 pp. Oxford University Press, Madras.

ALI, SALIM and S. DILLON RIPLEY
1968-1974. Handbook of the birds of India and Pakistan. 10 Vols. Oxford University Press, Bombay.

BAKER, E. C. STUART
1922-1930. Fauna of British India: Birds. 8 Vols. Taylor and Francis, London.

BATES, R.S.P. and E. H. N. LOWTHER
1952. Breeding birds of Kashmir. xxiii + 367 pp. Oxford University Press, London.

BISWAS, B.
1955. Zoological results of the 'Daily Mail' Himalayan Expedition 1954: two new birds from Khumbu, Eastern Nepal. Bull. Brit. Orn. Club, **75**: 87-88.

1960-1963. The birds of Nepal. J. Bombay Nat. Hist. Soc., **57**(2) through **60**(3).

DIESSELHORST, GERD
1968. Beitrage zur okologie der Vogel Zentral-und Ost-Nepals, in Khumbu Himal, Band 2. 420 pp. Universitatsverlag Wagner Ges. M.B.H., Munchen.

DIESSELHORST, GERD and JOCHEN MARTENS
1972. Hybriden von Parus melanolophus and Parus ater im Nepal-Himalaya. J. Ornith., **113**(4): 374-390.

FLEMING, R. L. and M. A. TRAYLOR
1961. Notes on Nepal birds. Fieldiana: Zoology, **35**(8): 443-487.
1964. Further notes on Nepal birds. Fieldiana: Zoology, **35**(9): 491-558.

1968. Distributional notes on Nepal birds. Fieldiana: Zoology, **53**(3): 147-203.

FLEMING, R. L., SR. and R. L. FLEMING, JR.
1970a. Birds of Kathmandu Valley and surrounding hills: a check list. Jore Ganesh Press, Kathmandu.

1970b. Avian sap-drinkers of the Himalayas. J. Bengal Nat. Hist. Soc., **36**(1): 54-57.

1979. A checklist of the Birds of Kathmandu Valley. Avalok, Kathmandu.

FLEMING, R. L., JR.
1967. The birds of Mussoorie, U.P., India—a distributional and ecological study. Ph.D. Thesis, Michigan State University, East Lansing, Michigan.

1969. Birds of Thakkhola, north Nepal. J. Bombay Nat. Hist. Soc., **66**(1): 132-139.

1971. Avian zoogeography of Nepal. The Himalayan Review, **4**:28-33.

1973. Notes on the nest and behavior of the Yellow-browed Titmouse, Parus modestus (Burton). J. Bombay Nat. Hist. Soc., **70**(2):326-329.

1979. Birds of the Sagarmatha (Everest) National Park, Nepal. Avalok, Kathmandu.

FLEMING, R. L., JR. and HARI S. NEPALI
1972. Some birds from Nepal. J. Bombay Nat. Hist. Soc., **68**(3): 833-835.

GREGORY-SMITH, R. C. and FRANCIS BATSON
1976. Birds of South East Nepal. Mimeographed.

HODGSON, B. H.
1846. Catalogue of the specimens and drawings of Mammalia and birds of Nepal and Tibet. British Museum, London.

HOOKER, J. D.
1854. Himalayan Journals; or notes of a naturalist in Bengal, the Sikkim and Nepal Himalayas, the Khasia Mountains, etc. 2 Vols. London.

ISHERWOOD, R. J.
1978. Birds of the Pakhribas Area. Mimeographed.

LAMPREY, H. F.
1954. Birds seen above the tree-line in Tehri-Garhwal, in

the central Himalayas. J. Bombay Nat. Hist. Soc., **52**(2+3): 610-615.

LAVKUMAR, K. S.
1956. A contribution to the ornithology of Garhwal. J. Bombay Nat. Hist. Soc., **53**(3) :315-329.

LISTER, M. D.
1954. A contribution to the ornithology of the Darjeeling area. J. Bombay Nat. Hist. Soc., **52**(1) :20-68.

MacDONALD, MALCOLM
1961. Birds in my Indian garden. 192 pp. Alfred Knopf, New York.

MACKINTOSH, L. J.
1915. Birds of Darjeeling and India. 233 pp.+lxviii. Banerjee Press, Calcutta.

MARTENS, JOCHEN
1971a. Zur Kenntnis des Vogelzuges im nepalischen Himalaya. Vogelwarte, **26** :113-128.
1971b. Arstatus von Parus rufonuchalis Blyth. J. Orn., **112**:451-458.
1972. Brutverbreitung palaarktischer Vogel im Nepal-Himalaya. Bonner Zool. Beitr., **23**:95-121.
1975a. Verbreitung, Biotop and Gesang des Bambusseidensangers (Cettia acanthizoides) im Nepal. Bonner Zool. Beitr., **26**:164-174.
1975b. Akustische Differenzierung verwandtschaftlicher Beziehungen in der Parus-Gruppe nach Untersuchungen im Nepal-Himalaya J. Orn., **116**(4) :369-433.

OSMASTON, B.
1935. Birds of Dehra Dun and adjacent hills. J. Indian Military Acad., Dehra Dun.

PAYNTER, RAYMOND A., JR.
1961. Notes on some Corvidae from Nepal, Pakistan and India. J. Bombay Nat. Hist. Soc., **58**(2) :379-386.
1962. Taxonomic notes on some Himalayan Paridae. J. Bombay Nat. Hist. Soc., **59**(3) :951-956.

PETERSON, ROGER, GUY MOUNTFORT and P. A. D. HOLLOM
1954. A field guide to the birds of Britain and Europe. xxxiv+318 pp. Collins, London.

POLUNIN, O.
1955. Some birds collected in Langtang Khola, Rasua Garhi

District, Central Nepal. J. Bombay Nat. Hist. Soc., **52**(4) :886-896.

PROUD, DESIREE
1949. Some notes on the birds of the Nepal Valley. J. Bombay Nat. Hist. Soc., **48**(4) :695-719.

1951. Some birds seen on the Gandak-Kosi Watershed in March, 1951. J. Bombay Nat. Hist. Soc., **50**(2) :355-366.

1952. Further notes on the birds of the Nepal Valley. J. Bombay Nat. Hist. Soc., **50**(4) : 667-670.

1953. More notes on birds of the Gandak-Kosi Watershed, Nepal. J. Bombay Nat. Hist. Soc., **51**(3) : 653-670.

1955. More notes on the birds of the Nepal Valley. J. Bombay Nat. Hist. Soc., **53**(1) : 57-78.

1958. Bird notes from Nepal. J. Bombay Nat. Hist. Soc., **55**(2) : 345-350.

1961a. Notes on some Nepalese birds. J. Bombay Nat. Hist. Soc., **58**(1) : 277-279.

1961b. Notes on birds of Nepal. J. Bombay Nat. Hist. Soc., **58**(3) : 798-805.

RAND, A. L. and R. L. FLEMING
1957. Birds from Nepal. Fieldiana: Zoology, **41**(1) : 1-218.

RIPLEY, S. D., II.
1950. Birds from Nepal. J. Bombay Nat. Hist. Soc., **49**(3) : 355-417.

1961. A synopsis of the birds of India and Pakistan. xxxvi+702 pp. Bombay Nat. Hist. Soc., Bombay.

SCULLY, J.
1879. A contribution to the ornithology of Nepal. Stray Feathers, **8** : 204-368.

SINGH, GYAN
1961. The Eastern Steppe Eagle [Aquila nipalensis (Hodgson)] on the South Col of Everest. J. Bombay Nat. Hist. Soc., **58**(1) : 270.

SMYTHIES, BERTRAM E.
1948. Some birds of the Gandak-Kosi Watershed. J. Bombay Nat. Hist. Soc., **47**(3) : 432-443.

1950. More notes on the birds of the Nepal Valley. J. Bombay Nat. Hist. Soc., **49**(3) : 513-518.

1953. The birds of Burma. xliii+668 pp. Oliver and Boyd, London.

STEVENS, H.
1923-1925. Notes on the birds of the Sikkim Himalayas. J. Bombay Nat. Hist. Soc., **29**(3) and **30**(4-7).

APPENDIX 1: KASHMIR BIRDS

The following birds are not known from Nepal but have been recorded in the Vale of Kashmir:

Little Bittern, *Ixobrychus minutus*. Up to 1830 m. (6,000') 35 cm. (14") R. Occasional; like a small Pond Heron but black above, ochre and maroon below; a white patch on dark wings seen in flight. Young heavily streaked brown above and below. Look for it in reed beds and among aquatic vegetation at dawn and dusk near Srinagar. 55

Lesser White-fronted Goose, *Anser erythropus*. 53 cm. (21") W. Scarce; dark brown; black bars on lower breast and belly; pink bill and yellow skin around the eye. A few expected in skeins of Graylags. 80

White-headed Stiff-tailed Duck, *Oxyura leucocephala*. 46 cm. (18") W. Occasional; brown and white with white face, black on nape and base of neck. The stubby, blue bill and wire-like tail distinctive. Found on large lakes. 123

Western Tragopan, *Tragopan melanocephalus*. 1525-3660 m. (5,000-12,000') 70 cm. (28") R. Occasional; in ringal bamboo towards western edge of Vale. Like Crimson Horned Pheasant but male is darker with red confined to face, neck and middle of breast. Female gray (not rufous-brown). 285

Little Bustard, *Otis tetrax*. 46 cm. (18") W. Uncommon; partial to coarse grass areas. Buffy above, *white* below. Note spots on female and male in winter. 353

Eurasian Nightjar (Hume's European Nightjar), *Caprimulgus europaeus*. To 3050 m. (10,000') 25 cm. (10") S. Fairly common; in desert as well as forest and scrub vegetation. Winters in E. Africa. Differs from Long-tailed Nightjar in being grayer. Three white spots on primaries (not four). Call a faint *chuck-chuck-chuck*, also a sharp *choo---ee* (AR). 673

Eurasian Bee-eater (European Bee-eater), *Merops apiaster*. 1525-2135 m. (5,000-7,000') 27 cm. (10½") S. Fairly common; in open country and low foothills in the vicinity of water. Shape similar to Blue-tailed Bee-eater but distinguished from latter by its rufous-orangy nape, back and scapulars and yellow throat. 746

Eurasian Roller, *Coracias garrulus*. 1525-3202 m. (5,000-10,500') 30 cm. (12") S. Occasional; in trees and on telephone wires around fields. Differs from Indian Roller by its light brown back (not greenish), a pale blue breast (not fulvous) and blue and *black* wings. 754

Eastern Calandra Lark, *Melanocorypha bimaculata*. Up to 2745 m. (9,000') 16 cm. (6¼") W, M. Fairly common; a large plump lark with thick bill; black lines on face and throat. Flocks in fields in stony areas. 892

Pied Magpie, *Pica pica*. 1525-4117 m. (5,000-13,500') 53 cm. (21") W. Occasional to scarce; in the vicinity of upland villages (AR). Black and white with long, black tail. Also recorded from Sikkim. 1029

Rook, *Corvus frugilegus*. 1525 m. (5,000') 48 cm. (19") W. Occasional; in open cultivated areas. Resembles the Jungle Crow but face and chin unfeathered in adult birds. In groups. 1052

Jackdaw, *Corvus monedula*. 1525-3660 m. (5,000-12,000') 33 cm. (13") R. Common; around Srinagar city all year; visits upland *margs* in autumn. Resembles a small House Crow with a proportionately short bill and tail. Pale cream iris distinctive at close range. Usually in flocks. 1053

Carrion Crow, *Corvus corone*. 1525-3660 m. (5,000-12,000') 47 cm. (18¼") R. (a few), W. Occasional; in open country. Slightly less glossy and bill slightly smaller than Jungle Crow's but very hard to distinguish in field. Voice higher-pitched than Jungle Crow's and possibly the best field character. Often in pairs. 1058

Spotted Flycatcher, *Muscicapa striata*. 1525-3355 m. (5,000-11,000') 13 cm. (5") S. Occasional; in pine forest. Similar to Brown Flycatcher but has fairly distinct streaks on throat and breast; crown also dark streaked. Single or in pairs. 1403

Long-billed Bush Warbler, *Bradypterus major*. 1525-3599 m. (5,000-11,800') 13 cm. (5") R. Fairly common in Sind Valley; scuttles on ground through low vegetation like a mouse; flicks wings and tail. Similar to Chinese Bush Warbler but breast fulvous (not buffy-brown) and flanks olive-brown (not pale brown). 1491

Brook's Leaf Warbler, *Phylloscopus subviridis*. Up to 3660 m. (12,000') 10 cm. (4") S. Occasional; haunts conifer forests in summer and acacias in winter. Similar to Large Crowned Leaf Warbler but median coronal stripe indistinct and yellow (not broad and pale, bordered with olive bands). Grayish-white below (not gray) and yellowish rump. 1593

Pied Wheatear (Pied Chat), *Oenanthe picata*. 1525-3355 m. (5,000-11,000') 16 cm. ($6\frac{1}{2}$") R., W. Fairly common; in fallow fields, around cattle sheds and on rocky, barren slopes. Male black and white. Female grayish-brown or grayish-black, darker than Desert Wheatear female. 1712

Pleschanka's Wheatear (Pleschanka's Chat), *Oenanthe pleschanka*. 1525-3050 m. (5,000-10,000') 15 cm. (6") April. Straggler; in stony wasteland. Similar to Pied Wheatear but smaller and black of throat and back fringed with pale brown. Female brown and buff (not gray-brown). 1715

Eurasian Rock Thrush (Rock Thrush), *Monticola saxatilis*. Mostly above 2135 m. (7,000') 19 cm. ($7\frac{1}{2}$") M. Scarce; on rocky hillsides of Liddar Valley. Similar to Blue Rock Thrush but has a white rump and pale blue throat. Throat of female brown; buffy and brown below. 1722

White-cheeked Tit, *Aegithalos leucogenys*. 1525-3660 m. (5,000-12,000') 10 cm. (4") R. Occasional; from floor of Vale to juniper forests. Much like a White-throated Tit but has white forehead (not pale rufous). 1821

Meadow Pipit, *Anthus pratensis*. 15 cm. (6") Only one record, in grassy farming area of the Vale. Slightly more buff than Eurasian Tree Pipit; adults usually lack any streaking on breast. 1856

Forest Wagtail, *Motacilla indica*. Up to 2135 m. (7,000') 16 cm. ($6\frac{1}{2}$") M. Vagrant; on forest roads. The only dark wagtail with dark and light stripes on breast and wings. 1874

Black-and-Yellow Grosbeak, *Mycerobas icterioides*. 1525-3050 m. (5,000-10,000') 23 cm. (9") R. Fairly common; a bird of oak, deodar and pine forests. Male similar to Allied Grosbeak but has bright yellow on back (not burnt-yellow) and black thighs (not yellow). Female has abdomen and flanks buff (not olive-yellow). 1982

Red-mantled Rose Finch, *Carpodacus rhodochlamys*. 1525-4880 m. (5,000-16,000') 16 cm. ($6\frac{1}{2}$") R., W. Occasional; in bushy areas. Male resembles a large Pink-browed Rose Finch male but back rosy-brown (not brown). Female resembles female Pink-browed Rose Finch but underparts very pale, almost white (not light brown) and eyebrow much less distinct. 2018

Orange Bullfinch, *Pyrrhula aurantiaca*. Up to 3660 m. (12,000') 14 cm. ($5\frac{1}{2}$") R. Scarce; frequents juniper forests. Male orange; black wings and wing coverts; underparts pinkish-orange (not dull red and white of Red-headed Bullfinch). Female ashy-brown, fulvous below washed yellow. 2040

Ortolan Bunting, *Emberiza hortulana*. 15 cm. (6") M. Scarce; once in Vale on spring migration. Gray head, breast; yellow face, russet below. 2049

APPENDIX 2: SIKKIM BIRDS

The following birds have been recorded in Sikkim but are not yet known from Nepal:

Indian Shag, *Phalacrocorax fuscicollis*. 91-213 m. (300-700') 64 cm. (25") R. Occasional; along large rivers flowing out of the hills. Bronze and black with white neck patch and white-speckled throat. Intermediate in size between Large and Small Cormorants which it closely resembles. 27

Giant Heron, *Ardea goliath*. On seacoasts and inland lakes. 142-152 cm. (56-60") Straggler; possibly along the Teesta River. Huge gray, white and chestnut bird whose movements are not well known. 34

Blyth's Baza, *Aviceda jerdoni*. 305-1830 m. (1,000-6,000') 48 cm. (19") R. Scarce; in evergreen foothills. Larger than Black-crested Baza, brown above (not black) and breast rufous-brown (no white breast bar). Paler female has breast tan-white (not streaked). 125

Red-breasted Hill Partridge, *Arborophila mandellii*. 305-2440 m. (1,000-8,000') 28 cm. (11") R. Fairly scarce; a distinctive large chestnut bib. Found in dense evergreen forests. Call an ascending series of *quoiks* (Ali). 273

Tibetan Sandgrouse, *Syrrhaptes tibetanus*. 3660-4880 m. (12,000-16,000') 48 cm. (19") R. Occasional; a plump, pale bird with long pointed tail and much dark barring on forehead, crown and breast. Back of female barred. In small flocks in very stony country. Not very shy (Baker). 485

Tibet Owlet, *Athene noctua*. 3660-4880 m. (12,000-16,000') 22 cm. (8¼") R. Scarce; in Tibetan biotope of N. Sikkim. Whitish spots on head and back; streaked brown below. Call a plaintive *piu* (AR). 649

Hodgson's Frogmouth, *Batrachostomus hodgsoni*. 305-1830 m. (1,000-6,000') 27 cm. (10½") R. Scarce; in subtropical evergreen forests. Resembles a large, pale nightjar with indistinct white "V" on back; tail with a series of brown and gray bars. Call a long, repeated *ahwooooo* (Ali). 667

Great Blue Kingfisher, *Alcedo hercules*. 213-1220 m. (700-4,000') 20 cm. (8") R. Scarce; on shady forest streams. A large "Blue-eared Kingfisher" found in similar habitats. 721

Long-billed Calandra Lark, *Melanocorypha maxima*. Above 3660 m. (12,000') 20 cm. (8") R. Fairly common; in high marshlands and on rocky plateaus. A plump bird streaked above, pale below with a black spot on side of breast and white in tail. 893

Long-billed Wren Babbler, *Rimator malacoptilus*. 915-2745 m. (3,000-9,000') 13 cm. (5") R. Scarce; in undergrowth in rugged, forested areas. Brown, prominently streaked above and below with pale feather shafts. Long bill slightly decurved. 1193

Spotted Wren Babbler, *Spelaeornis formosus*. 2287 m. (7,500') 10 cm. (4") R. Scarce; in wet rhododendron forests among ferns and moss. Like Long-billed Wren Babbler but spotted (not streaked). 1206

Wedge-billed Tree Babbler, *Sphenocichla humei*. About 915-2440 m. (3,000-8,000') 18 cm. (7") R. Scarce; nesting in upper limit of range. A very brown head with distinctive white eyebrow. 1207

Red-fronted Babbler, *Stachyris rufifrons*. 91-915 m. (300-3,000') 11 cm. (4¼") R. Fairly common; in bamboos and dense undergrowth. Similar to *S. ruficeps* but whitish below (not pale yellow). 1209

Black-browed Parrotbill (Lesser Red-headed), *Paradoxornis atrosuperciliaris*. About 610-1525 m. (2,000-5,000') 15 cm. (6") R. Scarce; in bamboo and tall grass often with other parrotbills. Similar to Red-headed Parrotbill but smaller and with black eyebrow (not ferruginous). 1246

Red-headed Parrotbill, *Paradoxornis ruficeps*. 91-1525 m. (300-5,000') 18 cm. (7") R. Fairly common; in bamboo, cutover scrub, reeds and grass near water. Very similar to Black-browed bird but head all deep ferruginous; flanks buffy (not whitish). 1247

Gray-headed Parrotbill, *Paradoxornis gularis.* 915-1525 m. (3,000-5,000') 15 cm. (6") R. Scarce; among bamboos, bushes and low trees. Like the Black-browed Parrotbill but larger with gray head (not fulvous) and a large, black eyebrow; white below with black bib. 1249

White-browed Yuhina, *Yuhina castaniceps.* 610-1525 m. (2,000-5,000') 13 cm. (5") R. Fairly common; in scrub jungle and thin forests. White underparts like the White-bellied Yuhina but brown above (not green) with a *spotted* gray head. In restless parties up to 30 birds. Call a *chit-chit* (AR). 1363

Olive Ground Warbler, *Tesia olivea.* 120-1220 m. (400-4,000') 9 cm. ($3\frac{1}{2}$") R. Occasional; in wet, overgrown tangles in dense forest. Very similar to the Slaty-bellied Ground Warbler but has a golden-green crown contrasting with an olive-green back (Slaty-bellied has crown and back same shade). Solitary. 1472

Golden-headed Tailor Bird, *Orthotomus cucullatus.* Up to 1830 m. (6,000') 11 cm. ($4\frac{1}{2}$") R. Occasional; found in forest areas, grass and bamboo. Differs from drab Indian Tailor Bird by its rufous head; yellow rump and bright yellow abdomen. A forest rather than garden bird. 1541

Grasshopper Warbler, *Locustella naevia.* 91-3050 m. (300-10,000') 13 cm. (5") W. Scarce; in swampy ground; among reeds and tamarisk. Resembles Streaked Grasshopper Warbler but has no streaking below. 1545

Rusty-bellied Shortwing, *Brachypteryx hyperythra.* 915-2897 m. (3,000-9,500') 13 cm. (5") R. Scarce; in forest undergrowth, reeds and bamboo. Male dark blue above, *rusty* underparts and a white spot in front of eye. Female olive-brown above, pale rust below. Quite fearless. 1636

Daurian Redstart, *Phoenicurus auroreus.* 915-4270 m. (3,000-14,000') 15 cm. (6") W. Occasional; open forests, fields, around upland villages. Similar to Hodgson's Redstart but wing dark (not gray-blue) and central tail feathers black (not brown). Female has white wing patch lacking in female Hodgson's Redstart. 1677

Black-breasted Forktail (Leschenault's), *Enicurus leschenaulti.* 91-610 m. (300-2,000') 28 cm. (11") R. Occasional; along rushing rivers in forests and streams in dense jungle. Solid black back (not spotted white as Spotted Forktail). Also larger than that bird. 1687

Kessler's Thrush, *Turdus kessleri.* 2745 m. (9,000') 28 cm. (11") W. Only one record. A large black and tan thrush. Female brown below (not pale). In juniper forests. 1760

Dusky Thrush, *Turdus naumanni.* 915-3050 m. (3,000-10,000') 24 cm. ($9\frac{1}{2}$") W. Scarce; in open fields and thin forest. Resembles the Dark Thrush but is darker and has rufous wings (not brown). Often feeds on ground. Alarm note a *kvevy; spirrrr* (AR). 1765

Beautiful Nuthatch, *Sitta formosa.* 305-2440 m. (1,000-8,000') 15 cm. (6") R. Scarce; in deep forest. The only nuthatch which is blue, black and white above. 1837

Mongolian Snow Finch, *Montifringilla davidiana.* One straggler at 2745 m. (9,000') 16 cm. ($6\frac{1}{2}$") W. The only snow finch with *forehead all black* (Blanford's has black restricted to center parting). Tail brown with white subterminal band and black tip. 1956

Gray-headed Bullfinch, *Pyrrhula erythaca.* 1525-4117 m. (5,000-13,500') 15 cm. (6") R. Occasional; in forests of conifers, rhododendrons and willows. Differs from other bullfinches with its black and white lines on face and ashy-gray head, nape and back. 2038

INDEX OF SCIENTIFIC NAMES

abbotti, Trichastoma 212
Abroscopus 246
Acanthis 306
acanthizoides, Cettia 226
Accipiter 46
Accipitridae 44
Aceros 134
Acridotheres 168
Acrocephalus 236
Actinodura 206
acuta, Anas 36
acuticauda, Sterna 98
acuticaudus, Apus 152
acutirostris, Calandrella 150
adamsi, Montifringilla 298
adsimilis, Dicrurus 164
aedon, Phragamaticola 236
Aegithalos 280, 344
Aegithina 180
Aegypius 56
aemodium, Conostoma 192
aeneus, Dicrurus 164
aeruginosus, Circus 60
Aethopyga 294
affinis, Apus 152
affinis, Caprimulgus 126
affinis, Garrulax 200
affinis, Mycerobas 304
affinis, Phylloscopus 238
affinis, Seicercus 244
agile, Dicaeum 292
agricola, Acrocephalus 236
akool, Amaurornis 78
Alauda 150
Alaudidae 148
alba, Calidris 325
alba, Egretta 28
alba, Motacilla 290
alba, Tyto 118
albellus, Mergus 42
albicilla, Haliaeetus 54
albicollis, Rhipidura 224
albicollis, Rynchops 98
albifrons, Sterna 98
albiventer, Pnoepyga 188
albocinctus, Turdus 268
albogularis, Abroscopus 246
albogularis, Garrulax 196
Alcedinidae 130

Alcedo 130, 345
Alcippe 210, 212
Alectoris 66
alexandri, Psittacula 108
alexandrinus, Charadrius 84
alpestris, Eremophila 150
alpinus, Calidris 88
aluco, Strix 124
amandava, Estrilda 302
Amaurornis 76, 78
Anas 36, 38, 40
Anastomus 30
Anatidae 36
Anhinga 24
annectans, Dicrurus 164
annectens, Heterophasia 326
Anser 36, 343
anser, Anser 36
Anthracoceros 134
Anthreptes 296
Anthropoides 32
Anthus 286, 288, 344
antigone, Grus 32
apiaster, Merops 343
apicauda, Treron 100
Apodidae 152
Apus 152, 154
apus, Apus 152
aquaticus, Rallus 76
Aquila 52
Arachnothera 296
Arborophila 68, 345
Ardea 26, 345
Ardeidae 26
Ardeola 26
Arenaria 321
argentatus, Larus 96
argentauris, Leiothrix 202
arquata, Numenius 86
Artamidae 166
Artamus 166
asiatica, Megalaima 136
asiatica, Nectarinia 296
asiatica, Perdicula 70
asiaticus, Caprimulgus 126
asiaticus, Xenorhynchus 30
Asio 124
assamica, Mirafra 148
ater, Parus 278

Athene 122, 345
athertoni, Nyctyornis 132
atra, Fulica 78
atrogularis, Prinia 232
atrogularis, Prunella 274
atrosuperciliaris, Paradoxornis 345
atthis, Alcedo 130
aurantia, Sterna 98
aurantiaca, Pyrrhula 344
aureola, Emberiza 316
aureola, Rhipidura 224
auriceps, Dendrocopos 144
aurifrons, Chloropsis 180
auroreus, Phoenicurus, 346
australis, Megalaima 136
Aviceda 44, 345
avosetta, Recurvirostra 92
Aythya 40
azurea, Monarcha 222

badia, Ducula 102
badius, Accipiter 46
badius, Phodilus 118
baeri, Aythya 324
bakeri, Yuhina 208
bakkamoena, Otus 118
banyumas, Muscicapa 218
barbatus, Gypaetus 56
Batrachostomus 345
bengalensis, Eupodotis 80
bengalensis, Graminicola 234
bengalensis, Gyps 58
benghalense, Dinopium 142
benghalensis, Coracias 128
benghalensis, Ploceus 300
benghalensis, Rostratula 92
bicincta, Treron 100
bicolor, Amaurornis 78
bicolor, Dendrocygna 324
bicornis, Buceros 134
*bimaculata,
   Melanocorypha* 343
birostris, Tockus 134
bistrigiceps, Acrocephalus 326
blanfordi, Montifringilla 320
Blythipicus 146
Bombycilla 180
Bombycillidae 180
Botaurus 28

boulboul, Turdus 268
Brachypteryx 248, 346
brachyura, Pitta 148
brachyurus, Micropternus 146
Bradypterus 228, 344
brama, Athene 122
brandti, Leucosticte 308
brevirostris, Collocalia 154
brevirostris, Pericrocotus 178
brodiei, Glaucidium 122
bruniceps, Emberiza 316
brunneus, Erithacus 250
brunnicephalus, Larus 96
brunnifrons, Cettia 228
Bubo 120
bubo, Bubo 120
Bubulcus 28
Bucephala 42
Buceros 134
Bucerotidae 134
Burhinidae 94
Burhinus 94
burkii, Seicercus 244
burtoni, Callacanthis 306
Butastur 48
Buteo 48
buteo, Buteo 48
Butorides 26

Cacomantis 114
caerulatus, Garrulax 198
*caeruleocephalus,
    Phoenicurus* 254
caerulescens, Dicrurus 162
caerulescens, Microhierax 62
caeruleus, Elanus 44
caeruleus, Myiophoneus 268
cafer, Pycnonotus 182
Calandrella 150
Calidris 88
caligata, Hippolais 236
Callacanthis 306
calliope, Erithacus 248
calvus, Torgos 58
Campephagidae 176
*canicapillus,
    Dendrocopos* 138
cannabina, Acanthis 306
canorus, Cuculus 112
cantator, Phylloscopus 242
canus, Picus 140
Capella 90
capensis, Pelargopsis 130
capensis, Tyto 118
capistrata, Heterophasia 212
Capitonidae 136
caprata, Saxicola 260
Caprimulgidae 126

Caprimulgus 126, 343
carbo, Phalacrocorax 24
Carduelis 304, 306
carduelis, Carduelis 304
carnipes, Mycerobas 304
Carpodacus 308, 310,
    312, 344
caryocatactes, Nucifraga 172
*caryophyllacea,
    Rhodonessa* 40
caspia, Hydroprogne 96
caspica, Motacilla 290
caspicus, Podiceps 24
castanea, Sitta 282
castaneceps, Alcippe 210
castaneo-coronata, Tesia 226
castaniceps, Seicercus 244
castaniceps, Yuhina 346
cathpharius, Dendrocopos 144
Catreus 74
caudacuta, Chaetura 154
caudatus, Spelaeornis 188
caudatus, Turdoides 194
Centropus 116
Cephalopyrus 280
Cercomela 322
Certhia 284
Certhiidae 284
certhiola, Locustella 234
cervinus, Anthus 288
Ceryle 130
Cettia 226, 228
ceylonensis, Culicicapa 224
Ceyx 130
Chaetura 152, 154
Chaimarrornis 256
Chalcites 114
Chalcophaps 106
Charadriidae 82
Charadrius 84
cheela, Spilornis 48
chicquera, Falco 64
chinensis, Cissa 170
chinensis, Coturnix 70
chinensis, Oriolus 160
chinensis, Streptopelia 106
chirurgus, Hydrophasianus 80
Chlidonias 98
chlorolophus, Picus 140
Chloropsis 180
chloropus, Gallinula 78
Choriotis 80
chrysaea, Stachyris 188
chrysaetos, Aquila 52
chrysaeus, Erithacus 250
Chrysocolaptes 142
Chrysomma 190
chrysorrheum, Dicaeum 292

chrysotis, Alcippe 210
cia, Emberiza 318
Ciconia 30
ciconia, Ciconia 30
Ciconiidae 30
Cinclidae 272
Cinclidium 252
*cinclorhynchus,
    Monticola* 262
Cinclus 272
cinclus, Cinclus 272
cinerea, Alcippe 210
cinerea, Ardea 26
cinerea, Calandrella 150
cinerea, Gallicrex 78
cinereocapilla, Prinia 230
cinereus, Vanellus 82
cinnamomeus, Ixobrychus 28
*cinnamomeus,
    Pericrocotus* 178
Circaetus 50
Circus 60
Cissa 170
Cisticola 228
citreola, Motacilla 290
citrina, Zoothera 264
citrinella, Emberiza 327
Clamator 110
clanga, Aquila 52
Clangula 324
clangula, Bucephala 42
clypeata, Anas 40
cochinchinensis, Chaetura 326
Cochoa 262
coelebs, Fringilla 300
coelicolor, Grandala 252
collaris, Prunella 272
Collocalia 154
collybita, Phylloscopus 238
Columba 102, 104
columbarius, Falco 64
columbianus, Cygnus 324
Columbidae 100
concinens, Acrocephalus 236
concinnus, Aegithalos 280
concolor, Dicaeum 292
Conostoma 192
contra, Sturnus 168
Copsychus 252
Coracias 128, 343
Coraciidae 128
Coracina 176
corax, Corvus 174
coromanda, Halcyon 130
coromandelianus, Nettapus 42
coromandelica, Coturnix 70
coromandelicus, Cursorius 94

348

coromandus, Bubo 120
coromandus, Clamator 110
corone, Corvus 343
Corvidae 170
Corvus 174, 343
Coturnix 70
coturnix, Coturnix 70
crecca, Anas 38
Criniger 184
criniger, Prinia 232
cristata, Galerida 150
cristatus, Lanius 158
cristatus, Pavo 74
cristatus, Podiceps 24
cruentatum, Dicaeum 292
cruentus, Ithaginis 72
Cuculidae 110
cucullatus, Orthotomus 346
cuculoides, Glaucidium 122
Cuculus 110, 112
Culicicapa 224
curruca, Sylvia 236
Cursorius 94
curvirostra, Loxia 314
curvirostra, Treron 100
Cutia 202
cyaneus, Circus 60
cyaniventer, Tesia 226
cyanocephala, Psittacula 108
cyanouroptera, Minla 206
cyanurus, Erithacus 250
Cygnus 36
cygnus, Cygnus 36
Cypsiurus 154

dalhousiae, Psarisomus 148
darjellensis, Dendrocopos 144
dauma, Zoothera 266
daurica, Hirundo 156
davidiana, Montifringilla 346
decaocto, Streptopelia 106
Delichon 156
Dendrocitta 172
Dendrocopos 138, 144
Dendrocygna 36
deserti, Oenanthe 264
Dicaeidae 292
Dicaeum 292
dichrous, Perus 278
Dicruridae 162
Dicrurus 162, 164
Dinopium 142
discolor, Certhia 284
dixoni, Zoothera 266
domesticus, Passer 298
dominica, Pluvialis 84

dubius, Charadrius 84
dubius, Leptoptilos 32
Ducula 102
Dumetia 190
*dumetorum,
  Acrocephalus* 236
Dupetor 28

earlei, Turdoides 194
edwardsii, Carpodacus 310
egertoni, Actinodura 206
Egretta 28
Elanus 44
Emberiza 316, 318, 344
Emberizidae 316
Enicurus 258, 346
epauletta, Pyrrhoplectes 314
episcopus, Ciconia 30
epops, Upupa 128
Eremophila 150
Eremopterix 148
Erithacus 248, 250
erithacus, Ceyx 130
erythaca, Pyrrhula 346
erythrinus, Carpodacus 308
erythrocephala, Pyrrhula 314
erythrocephala, Garrulax 200
*erythrocephalus,
  Harpactes* 128
*erythrogaster,
  Phoenicurus* 256
*erythrogenys,
  Pomatorhinus* 186
*erythronotus,
  Phoenicurus* 254
erythropus, Anser 343
erythropus, Tringa 86
erythrorhyncha, Cissa 170
*erythrorhynchos,
  Dicaeum* 292
Esacus 94
Estrilda 302
ethologus, Pericrocotus 178
Eudynamys 110
eupatria, Psittacula 108
Eupodotis 80
eurizonoides, Rallina 76
europaea, Sitta 282
europaeus, Caprimulgus 343
Eurylaimidae 148
Eurystomus 128
excubitor, Lanius 158
exilis, Cisticola 228
exustus, Pterocles 100

falcata, Anas 38

falcinellus, Plegadis 34
Falco 62, 64
Falconidae 62
familiaris, Certhia 284
fasciatus, Hieraaetus 50
ferina, Aythya 40
ferrea, Saxicola 260
ferruginea, Muscicapa 214
ferruginea, Tadorna 36
*ferruginosus,
  Pomatorhinus* 186
festivus, Chrysocolaptes 142
flammeus, Asio 124
flammeus, Pericrocotus 178
*flammiceps,
  Cephalopyrus* 280
flava, Motacilla 290
flavalus, Hypsipetes 184
flaveolus, Criniger 184
flavicollis, Dupetor 28
flavicollis, Yuhina 208
flavinucha, Picus 140
flavipes, Bubo 120
flavirostris, Acanthis 306
flavirostris, Cissa 170
flavirostris, Paradoxornis 192
flaviscapis, Pteruthius 204
flaviventris, Prinia 232
flavolivaceus, Cettia 226
fluvicola, Hirundo 156
formosa, Sitta 346
formosae, Dendrocitta 172
formosus, Spelaeornis 345
fortipes, Cettia 226
Francolinus 68
francolinus, Francolinus 68
franklinii, Megalaima 136
Fringilla 300
Fringillidae 300, 304
frontale, Cinclidium 252
frontale, Dendrocitta 172
frontalis, Phoenicurus 254
frontalis, Sitta 282
frugilegus, Corvus 343
fucata, Emberiza 318
fugax, Cuculus 110
Fulica 78
fulicata, Saxicoloides 260
fuliginosus, Rhyacornis 256
*fuligiventer,
  Phylloscopus* 238
fuligula, Aythya 40
fulvescens, Prunella 274
fulvifrons, Paradoxornis 192
fulvus, Gyps 56
fusca, Ceromela 322
fuscicollis, Phalacrocorax 345

349

fuscus, Acridotheres 168
fuscus, Amaurornis 76
fuscus, Artamus 166

Galerida 150
Gallicrex 78
gallicus, Circaetus 50
gallinago, Capella 90
Gallinula 78
Gallus 74
gallus, Gallus 74
Gampsorhynchus 204
Garrulax 194-200
Garrulus 170
garrulus, Bombycilla 180
garrulus, Coracias 343
garzetta, Egretta 28
Gecinulus 146
Gelochelidon 98
genei, Larus 96
gentilis, Accipiter 46
ginginianus, Acridotheres 168
glandarius, Garrulus 170
Glareola 94
glareola, Tringa 88
Glareolidae 94
Glaucidium 122
godlewskii, Anthus 286
goliath, Ardea 345
Gorsachius 321
gouldiae, Aethopyga 294
gracilis, Prinia 232
Gracula 168
graculus, Pyrrhocorax 174
graeca, Alectoris 66
Graminicola 234
Grandala 252
grandis, Muscicapa 220
grantia, Gecinulus 146
grayii, Ardeola 26
grisea, Eremopterix 148
griseolus, Phylloscopus 238
Gruidae 32
Grus 32
grus, Grus 32
gularis, Francolinus 68
gularis, Macronous 188
gularis, Paradoxornis 346
gularis, Tephrodornis 176
gularis, Yuhina 208
gulgula, Alauda 150
Gypaetus 56
Gyps 56, 58

*haemacephala,
   Megalaima* 136
Haematopodidae 80

Haematopus 80
Haematospiza 314
Halcyon 130
Haliaeetus 54
haliaetus, Pandion 54
Haliastur 44
hardwickii, Chloropsis 180
Harpactes 128
heliaca, Aquila 52
hemilasius, Buteo 48
Hemiprocne 152
Hemipus 176
hercules, Alcedo 345
Heterophasia 212, 326
Hieraaetus 50
himalayana, Certhia 284
himalayana, Prunella 272
himalayana, Psittacula 108
*himalayensis,
   Dendrocopos* 144
himalayensis, Gyps 56
himalayensis, Sitta 282
himalayensis, Tetraogallus 66
Himantopus 92
himantopus, Himantopus 92
Hippolais 236
Hirundinidae 156
Hirundo 156
hirundo, Sterna 98
hispaniolensis, Passer 327
hodgsoni, Abroscopus 246
hodgsoni, Anthus 286
*hodgsoni,
   Batrachostomus* 345
hodgsoni, Muscicapella 218
hodgsoni, Phoenicurus 254
hodgsoniae, Perdix 68
hodgsonii, Columba 104
hodgsonii, Muscicapa 218
hodgsonii, Prinia 230
Hodgsonius 256
hortensis, Sylvia 232
hortulana, Emberiza 344
hottentottus, Dicrurus 162
humei, Sphenocichla 345
humilis, Podoces 172
hybrida, Chlidonias 98
Hydrophasianus 80
Hydroprogne 96
hyemalis, Clangula 324
hyperytha, Brachypteryx 346
hyperythra, Dumetia 190
hyperythra, Muscicapa 218
hyperythrus, Erithacus 250
hyperythrus, Hypopicus 146
hypoleucos, Tringa 88
Hypopicus 146
hypoxantha, Rhipidura 224
Hypsipetes 184

Ibidorhyncha 92
Ibis 30
ibis, Bubulcus 28
ichthyaetus, Ichthyophaga 54
ichthyaetus, Larus 96
icterioides, Mycerobas 344
Icthyophaga 54
Ictinaetus 54
ignicauda, Aethopyga 294
ignipectus, Dicaeum 292
ignotincta, Minla 206
immaculata, Prunella 274
immaculatus, Enicurus 258
impejanus, Lophophorus 72
imperialis, Ardea 26
indica, Chalcophaps 106
indica, Motacilla 327
indica, Sypheotides 80
Indicator 138
Indicatoridae 138
indicus, Anser 36
indicus, Caprimulgus 126
indicus, Erithacus 250
indicus, Gyps 58
indicus, Metopidius 80
indicus, Pterocles 100
indicus, Vanellus 82
indus, Haliastur 44
innominatus, Picumnus 138
inornatus, Phylloscopus 240
insignis, Saxicola 322
intermedia, Egretta 28
interpres, Arenaria 325
iouschistos, Aegithalos 280
Irena 180
Irenidae 180
isabellina, Oenanthe 264
Ithaginis 72
Ixobrychus 28, 343

Jacanidae 80
jacobinus, Clamator 110
javanica, Dendrocygna 36
javanicus, Leptoptilos 32
jerdoni, Aviceda 345
jerdoni, Saxicola 322
jocosus, Pycnonotus 182
jugger, Falco 62
juncidis, Cisticola 228
Jynx 138

kessleri, Turdus 346
kienerii, Lophotriorchis 50
Kitta (see *Cissa*)
krameri, Psittacula 108

lactea, Glareola 94
lanceolata, Locustella 234

lanceolatus, Garrulus 170
Laniidae 158
Lanius 158
Laridae 96
Larus 96
lathami, Melophus 318
latirostris, Muscicapa 214
Leiothrix 202
leptogrammica, Strix 124
Leptopoecile 246
Leptoptilos 32
Lerwa 66
lerwa, Lerwa 66
leschenaulti, Enicurus 346
leschenaulti, Merops 132
leschenaultii, Charadrius 84
leschenaultii, Taccocua 116
leucocephala, Oxyura 343
leucocephalos, Emberiza 316
leucocephalus,
 Chaimarrornis 256
leucocephalus, Ibis 30
leucogenys, Aegithalos 327
leucogenys, Pycnonotus 182
leucolophus, Garrulax 198
leucomelana, Lophura 72
leucomelanura,
 Muscicapa 216
leuconota, Columba 102
leucophaeus, Dicrurus 164
leucophrys, Brachypteryx 248
leucopsis, Sitta 282
leucopterus, Childonias 325
leucorodia, Platalea 34
leucoryphus, Haliaeetus 54
Leucosticte 308
leucura, Saxicola 260
leucurum, Cinclidium 252
leucurus, Vanellus 82
leuphotes, Aviceda 44
limnaeetus, Spizaetus 50
Limosa 86
limosa, Limosa 86
lineata, Megalaima 136
lineatus, Garrulax 194
livia, Columba 102
lobatus, Phalaropus 325
Locustella 234, 346
Lonchura 302
longipennis, Hemiprocne 152
longirostris, Arachnothera 296
longirostris, Turdoides 194
Lophophorus 72
Lophotriorchis 50
Lophura 72
Loriculus 108
Loxia 314
lucidus, Chrysocolaptes 142

lugubris, Ceryle 130
lugubris, Surniculus 114
lunatus, Serilophus 148
lutea, Leiothrix 202
luteoventris, Bradypterus 228

macei, Dendrocopos 144
macgrigoriae, Muscicapa 220
macrolopha, Pucrasia 74
Macronous 188
Macropygia 104
macrorhynchos, Corvus 174
macrourus, Circus 60
macrurus, Caprimulgus 126
maculatus, Chalcites 114
maculatus, Enicurus 258
maculipennis,
 Phylloscopus 240
madagascariensis,
 Hypsipetes 184
maderaspatensis,
 Motacilla 290
magna, Arachnothera 296
magnirostris, Esacus 94
magnirostris,
 Phylloscopus 240
mahrattensis,
 Dendrocopos 144
major, Bradypterus 344
major, Cettia 228
major, Parus 276
malabarica, Lonchura 302
malabaricus,
 Anthracoceros 134
malabaricus, Copsychus 25
malabaricus, Sturnus 166
malabaricus, Vanellus 82
malacca, Lonchura 302
malacoptilus, Rimator 345
malayensis, Ictinaetus 54
malcomi, Turdoides 322
mandellii, Arborophila 345
manyar, Ploceus 320
marginata, Zoothera 266
marila, Aythya 40
maxima, Melanocorypha 345
Megalaima 136
Megalurus 234
melanicterus, Pycnonotus 182
melanocephala, Emberiza 316
melanocephala,
 Threskiornis 34
melanocephalus,
 Tragopan 343
Melanochlora 276
Melanocorypha 343, 345
melanoleucos, Circus 60

melanolophus, Gorsachius 324
melanolophus, Parus 278
melanoptera, Coracina 176
melanotis, Pteruthius 204
melanotos, Sarkidiornis 42
melanozanthos,
 Mycerobas 304
melanozanthum,
 Dicaeum 292
melaschistos, Coracina 176
melba, Apus 154
Melophus 318
meninting, Alcedo 130
merganser, Mergus 42
Mergus 42
Meropidae 132
Merops 132
merula, Turdus 268
merulinus, Cacomantis 114
Metopidia 80
Microhierax 62
Micropternus 146
micropterus, Cuculus 112
migrans, Milvus 44
Milvus 44
minima, Capella 90
Minla 206
minutus, Calidris 88
minutus, Ixobrychus 343
Mirafra 148
modestus, Parus 280
mollissima, Zoothera 266
monachus, Aegypius 56
Monarcha 252
monedula, Corvus 343
mongolica, Rhodopechys 320
mongolus, Charadrius 84
monileger, Muscicapa 216
moniligerus, Garrulax 196
montana, Brachypteryx 248
montanus, Passer 298
Monticola 262, 344
monticola, Zoothera 266
monticolus, Parus 276
Montifringilla 298, 320, 346
montifringilla, Fringilla 300
Motacilla 290, 344
Motacillidae 286
Mulleripicus 146
muraria, Tichodroma 284
Muscicapa 214-222, 344
Muscicapella 218
Muscicapidae 214
Mycerobas 304, 344
Myiophoneus 268
Myzornis 202

naevia, Locustella 346

351

nana, Icthyophaga 54
nanus, Dendrocopos 138
naumanni, Falco 64
naumanni, Turdus 326
nebularia, Tringa 86
Nectarinia 296
Nectariniidae 294
nemoricola, Capella 90
nemoricola, Leucosticte 308
Neophron 58
Netta 40
Nettapus 42
niger, Phalacrocorax 24
nigra, Ciconia 30
nigriceps, Choriotis 80
nigriceps, Stachyris 190
nigricollis, Grus 325
nigrimenta, Yuhina 208
nilotica, Gelochelidon 98
Ninox 124
nipalensis, Aceros 134
nipalensis, Actinodura 206
nipalensis, Aethopyga 294
nipalensis, Alcippe 212
nipalensis, Aquila 52
nipalensis, Bubo 120
nipalensis, Carpodacus 308
nipalensis, Certhia 284
nipalensis, Cutia 202
nipalensis, Delichon 156
nipalensis, Paradoxornis 192
nipalensis, Pitta 148
nipalensis, Pyrrhula 314
nipalensis, Spizaetus 50
nipalensis, Turdoides 194
nisus, Accipiter 46
nitidus, Phylloscopus t. 240
niveogularis, Aegithalos 280
noctua, Athene 322
novaehollandiae,
 Coracina 176
novaeseelandiae, Anthus 286
Nucifraga 172
Numenius 86
Nycticorax 26
Nyctyornis 132
nyroca, Aythya 40

obscurus, Turdus 270
occipitalis, Phylloscopus 242
occipitalis, Yuhina 208
ocellatus, Garrulax 198
ochracea, Sasia 138
ochropus, Tringa 88
ochruros, Phoenicurus 254
oedicnemus, Burhinus 94
Oenanthe 264, 344

352

olivea, Tesia 346
onocrotalus, Pelecanus 24
orientalis, Acrocephalus 236
orientalis, Eurystomus 128
orientalis, Merops 132
orientalis, Pterocles 100
orientalis, Streptopelia 104
Oriolidae 160
Oriolus 160
oriolus, Oriolus 160
Orthotomus 234, 346
oscitans, Anastomus 30
ostralegus, Haematopus 80
Otididae 80
Otis 343
Otus 118
otus, Asio 124
Oxyura 343

pacificus, Apus 152
pagodarum, Sturnus 166
pallasii, Cinclus 272
pallidipes, Cettia 226
palpebrosa, Zosterops 296
paludicola, Riparia 156
palumbus, Columba 104
palustris, Megalurus 234
Pandion 54
papillosa, Pseudibis 34
paradiseus, Dicrurus 162
paradisi, Terpsiphone 224
Paradoxornis 192, 345, 346
Paridae 276
Parus 276, 278, 280
parva, Muscicapa 214
parvus, Cypsiurus 154
Passer 298
Pavo 74
pectoralis, Erithacus 248
pectoralis, Garrulax 196
Pelargopsis 130
Pelecanidae 24
Pelecanus 24
Pellorneum 186
penelope, Anas 40
pennatus, Hieraaetus 50
percnopterus, Neophron 58
Perdicula 70
Perdix 68
peregrinus, Falco 62
Pericrocotus 178
Pernis 44
Petronia 298
phaeopus, Numenius 86
Phalacrocoracidae 24
Phalacrocorax 24, 345
Phalaropus 325
Phasianidae 66

philippensis, Pelecanus 24
philippinus, Merops 132
philippinus, Ploceus 300
Philomachus 86
Phodilus 118
phoeniceus, Garrulax 200
phoenicoptera, Treron 102
Phoenicopteridae 34
Phoenicopterus 34
phoenicuroides,
 Hodgsonius 256
Phoenicurus 254, 256, 346
phoenicurus, Amaurornis 78
Phragamaticola 236
Phylloscopus 238-242, 344
Pica 343
pica, Pica 343
picaoides, Heterophasia 212
picata, Oenanthe 326
picatus, Hemipus 176
Picidae 138
Picumnus 138
Picus 140
pileata, Halcyon 130
pileata, Timalia 190
Pitta 148
Pittidae 148
placidus, Charadrius 84
Platalea 34
platyrhynchos, Anas 38
Plegadis 34
pleschanka, Oenanthe 344
Ploceidae 298
Ploceus 300
Pluvialis 84
Pnoepyga 188
Podargidae 126
Podiceps 24
Podicipedidae 24
Podoces 172
poecilorhyncha, Anas 38
poliocephalus, Cuculus 112
poliogenys, Muscicapa 222
poliogenys, Seicercus 244
pomarina, Aquila 52
Pomatorhinus 186
pompadora, Treron 100
pondicerianus,
 Francolinus 68
pondicerianus,
 Tephrodornis 176
Porphyrio 78
porphyrio, Porphyrio 78
Porzana 76
pratensis, Anthus 344
pratincola, Glareola 94

Prinia 230, 232
Propyrrhula 312
proregulus, Phylloscopus 242
Prunella 272, 274
Prunellidae 272
Psarisomus 148
Pseudibis 34
Psittacidae 108
Psittacula 108
Pterocles 100
Pteroclidae 100
Pteruthius 204
ptilorhyncus, Pernis 44
Pucrasia 74
puella, Irena 180
pugnax, Philomachus 86
pulcher, Phylloscopus 242
pulcherrimus,
  Carpodacus 310
pulchricollis, Columba 104
pulverulentus, Mulleripicus 146
punctulata, Lonchura 302
puniceus, Carpodacus 312
purpurea, Ardea 26
purpurea, Cochoa 262
pusilla, Emberiza 318
pusilla, Pnoepyga 188
pusilla, Porzana 76
pusillus, Serinus 306
Pycnonotidae 182
Pycnonotus 182
pygargus, Circus 60
Pyrrhocorax 174
pyrrhocorax, Pyrrhocorax 174
Pyrrhoplectes 314
pyrrhops, Stachyris 190
pyrrhotis, Blythipicus 146
pyrrhoura, Myzornis 202
Pyrrhula 314, 344, 346

querquedula, Anas 38

radiatum, Glaucidium 122
Rallidae 76
Rallina 76
Rallus 76
rapax, Aquila 52
raytal, Calandrella 150
Recurvirostra 92
Recurvirostridae 92
reguloides, Phylloscopus 242
Regulus 246
regulus, Regulus 246
religiosa, Gracula 168
remifer, Dicrurus 162
Rhipidura 224

rhodochlamys,
  Carpodacus 344
rhodochrous, Carpodacus 310
Rhodonessa 40
Rhodopechys, 320
rhodopeplus, Carpodacus 310
Rhopodytes 116
Rhyacornis 256
Rhynchops 98
richardi, Anthus n. 286
ridibundus, Larus 96
Rimator 345
Riparia 156, 326
riparia, Riparia 326
roseatus, Anthus 288
roseus, Pericrocotus 178
roseus, Phoenicopterus 34
roseus, Sturnus 166
Rostratula 92
Rostratulidae 92
rubeculoides, Muscicapa 218
rubeculoides, Prunella 274
rubescens, Carpodacus 308
rubicilla, Carpodacus 312
rubicilloides, Carpodacus 312
rubidiventris, Parus 278
rubrocanus, Turdus 270
rudis, Ceryle 130
rufa, Anhinga 24
rufescens, Prinia 230
ruficauda, Muscicapa 214
ruficeps, Paradoxornis 345
ruficeps, Pellorneum 186
ruficeps, Stachyris 188
ruficollis, Garrulax 200
ruficollis, Montifringilla 320
ruficollis, Podiceps 24
ruficollis, Pomatorhinus 186
ruficollis, Turdus 270
rufifrons, Stachyris 345
rufina, Netta 40
rufinus, Buteo 48
rufiventer, Pteruthius 204
rufiventris, Monticola 262
rufogularis, Arborophila 68
rufogularis, Garrulax 198
rufonuchalis, Parus 278
rufulus, Gampsorhynchus 204
rupestris, Columba 102
rupestris, Hirundo 156
rustica, Emberiza 327
rustica, Hirundo 156
rusticola, Scolopax 90
rutila, Emberiza 316
rutilans, Passer 298
Rynchops 98

sapphira, Muscicapa 220
Sarkidiornis 42
Saroglossa 166
Sasia 138
saturata, Aethopyga 294
saturatus, Cuculus 112
satyra, Tragopan 72
saularis, Copsychus 252
saxatilis, Monticola 344
Saxicola 260
Saxicoloides 260
schach, Lanius 158
schisticeps, Abroscopus 246
schisticeps, Phoenicurus 256
schisticeps, Pomatorhinus 186
schoeniclus, Emberiza 327
scolopacea, Eudynamys 116
Scolopax 90
scops, Otus 118
scouleri, Enicurus 258
scutulata, Ninox 124
Seicercus 244
senegalensis, Streptopelia 106
Serilophus 148
Serinus 306
severus, Falco 62
shorii, Dinopium 142
sibirica, Muscicapa 214
similis, Anthus 288
sinensis, Centropus 116
sinensis, Chrysomma 190
sinensis, Ixobrychus 28
singalensis, Anthreptes 296
sipahi, Haematospiza 314
siparaia, Aethopyga 294
Sitta 282, 346
Sittidae 282
smithii, Hirundo 156
smyrnensis, Halcyon 130
socialis, Prinia 230
solaris, Pericrocotus 178
solitaria, Capella 90
solitarius, Monticola 262
sonneratii, Cacomantis 114
sophiae, Leptopoecile 246
sordida, Pitta 148
sparverioides, Cuculus 110
Spelaeornis 188, 345
Sphenocichla 336
sphenura, Treron 100
spilocephalus, Otus 118
spilonotus, Parus 276
spiloptera, Saroglossa 166
Spilornis 48
spinoides, Carduelis 304
spinoletta, Anthus 288

spinosus, Vanellus 82
Spizaetus 50
splendens, Corvus 174
spodocephala, Emberiza 316
squamatus, Garrulax 200
squamatus, Picus 140
squatarola, Pluvialis 84
Stachyris 188, 190, 345
stagnatilis, Tringa 88
stellaris, Botaurus 28
stellata, Brachypteryx 248
stentoreus, Acrocephalus 236
stenura, Capella 90
Sterna 98
stewarti, Emberiza 318
strepera, Anas 38
Streptopelia 104, 106
striata, Lonchura 302
striata, Muscicapa 344
striatus, Butorides 26
striatus, Garrulax 196
striatus, Pycnonotus 182
striatus, Rallus 76
striatus, Turdoides 194
Strigidae 118
strigula, Minla 206
Strix 124
strophiata, Muscicapa 216
strophiata, Prunella 274
struthersii, Ibidorhyncha 92
Sturridae 166
Sturnus 166, 168
subbuteo, Falco 62
subflava, Prinia 230
subhimachala, Propyrrhula 312
subminutus, Calidris 88
subrubra, Muscicapa 214
subunicolor, Garrulax 200
subviridis, Phylloscopus 344
sultanea, Melanochlora 276
sundara, Muscicapa 220
superciliaris, Abroscopus 246
superciliaris, Muscicapa 216
superciliaris,
   Xiphirhynchus 186
Surniculus 114
suscitator, Turnix 70
sutorius, Orthotomus 234
svecicus, Erithacus 248
sylvanus, Anthus 286
sylvatica, Chaetura 152
sylvatica, Prinia 230
sylvatica, Turnix 70
Sylvia 236
Sylviidae 226
Sypheotides 80

Syrrhaptes 327

Taccocua 116
tacsanowskius,
   Bradypterus 322
taczanowskii,
   Montifringilla 320
Tadorna 36
tadorna, Tadorna 36
tanki, Turnix 70
teesa, Butastur 48
temminckii, Calidris 88
Tephrodornis 176
tephronotus, Lanius 158
Terpsiphone 224
Tesia 226, 337
testacea, Calidris 325
Tetraogallus 66
tetrax, Otis 343
thalassina, Muscicapa 222
thibetana, Carduelis 306
thoracicus, Bradypterus 228
Threskiornis 34
Threskiornithidae 34
thura, Carpodacus 312
tibetanus, Syrrhaptes 345
tibetanus, Tetraogallus 66
Tichodroma 284
tickelliae, Muscicapa 218
Timalia 190
Timaliidae 186
tinnunculus, Falco 64
tiphia, Aegithina 180
Tockus 134
Torgos 58
torquata, Saxicola 260
torqueola, Arborophila 68
torquilla, Jynx 138
totanus, Tringa 86
toulou, Centropus 116
Tragopan 72, 343
traillii, Oriolus 160
tranquebarica,
   Streptopelia 106
Treron 100, 102
Trichastoma 212
Tringa 86, 88
tristis, Acridotheres 168
tristis, Rhopodytes 116
trivialis, Anthus 288
trivirgatus, Accipiter 46
trochiloides, Phylloscopus 240
Troglodytes 272
troglodytes, Troglodytes 272
Troglodytidae 272
Trogonidae 128
Turdidae 248

Turdoides 194
Turdus 268, 270, 346
Turnicidae 70
Turnix 70
tytleri, Phylloscopus 238
Tyto 118
Tytonidae 118

unchall, Macropygia 104
unicolor, Muscicapa 222
unicolor, Paradoxornis 192
unicolor, Turdus 270
Upupa 128
Upupidae 128
urbica, Delichon 156

vagabunda, Dendrocitta 172
Vanellus 82
vanellus, Vanellus 82
variegatum, Garrulax 198
varius, Cuculus 110
vernalis, Loriculus 108
vespertinus, Falco 64
vinaceus, Carpodacus 310
vinipectus, Alcippe 210
virens, Megalaima 136
virescens, Hypsipetes 184
virgatus, Accipiter 46
virgo, Anthropoides 32
viridis, Cochoa 262
viscivorus, Turdus 270
vittatus, Lanius 158
vulgaris, Sturnus 166

wallichii, Catreus 74
wardii, Zoothera 264
westermanni, Muscicapa 216

xanthochloris, Pteruthius 204
xanthocollis, Petronia 298
xanthogenys, Parus 276
xanthonotus, Indicator 138
xanthopygaeus, Picus 140
xanthornus, Oriolus 160
xanthoschistos, Seicercus 244
Xenorhynchus 30
Xiphirhynchus 186

Yuhina 208, 346

zantholeuca, Yuhina 208
zeylanica, Megalaima 136
zeylonensis, Bubo 120
Zoothera 264, 266
Zosteropidae 296
Zosterops 296

INDEX AND CHECK LIST OF ENGLISH NAMES

ACCENTORS

- [ ] Alpine 272
- [ ] Altai 272
- [ ] Black-throated 274
- [ ] Brown 274
- [ ] Maroon-backed 274
- [ ] Robin 274
- [ ] Rufous-breasted 274

- [ ] **AVOCET** 92

BABBLERS

- [ ] Abbott's 212
- [ ] Black-chinned 190
- [ ] Black-throated 190
- [ ] Chestnut-headed Tit 210
- [ ] Chestnut-throated Shrike 204
- [ ] Common 194
- [ ] Coral-billed Scimitar 186
- [ ] Dusky-green Tit 210
- [ ] Golden-headed 188
- [ ] Golden-breasted Tit 210
- [ ] Green Shrike 204
- [ ] Jungle 194
- [ ] Large Gray 194
- [ ] Lesser Scaly-breasted Wren 188
- [ ] Long-billed Wren 345
- [ ] Nepal 212
- [ ] Red-capped 190
- [ ] Red-fronted 345
- [ ] Red-headed 188
- [ ] Red-winged Shrike 204
- [ ] Rufous-bellied 190
- [ ] Rufous-bellied Shrike 204
- [ ] Rufous-necked Scimitar 186
- [ ] Rusty-cheeked Scimitar 186
- [ ] Scaly-breasted Wren 188
- [ ] Slaty-headed Scimitar 186
- [ ] Slender-billed 194
- [ ] Slender-billed Scimitar 186
- [ ] Spiny 194
- [ ] Spotted 186
- [ ] Spotted Wren 336
- [ ] Striated 194
- [ ] Tailed Wren 188
- [ ] Wedge-billed Tree 336
- [ ] White-browed Tit 210
- [ ] White-headed Shrike 204
- [ ] Yellow-breasted 188
- [ ] Yellow-eyed 190

BARBETS

- [ ] Blue-eared 136
- [ ] Blue-throated 136
- [ ] Crimson-breasted 136
- [ ] Golden-throated 136
- [ ] Great Himalayan 136
- [ ] Green 136
- [ ] Lineated 136

BARWINGS

- [ ] Hoary 206
- [ ] Spectacled 206

BAZAS

- [ ] Black-crested 44
- [ ] Blyth's 345

BEE-EATERS

- [ ] Blue-bearded 132
- [ ] Blue-tailed 132
- [ ] Chestnut-headed 132
- [ ] Eurasian 343
- [ ] Green 132

BITTERNS

- [ ] Black 28
- [ ] Chestnut 28
- [ ] Eurasian 28
- [ ] Little 343
- [ ] Tiger 324
- [ ] Yellow 28

BLACKBIRDS

- [ ] Eurasian 268
- [ ] Gray-winged 268
- [ ] White-collared 268

BLUEBIRD

- [ ] Fairy 180

- [ ] **BLUETHROAT** 248

- [ ] **BRAMBLING** 300

BROADBILLS

- [ ] Hodgson's 148
- [ ] Long-tailed 148

BULBULS

- [ ] Black-headed Yellow 182
- [ ] Brown-eared 184
- [ ] Gray (Black) 184
- [ ] Red-vented 182
- [ ] Red-whiskered 182
- [ ] Rufous-bellied 184
- [ ] Striated 182
- [ ] White-cheeked 182
- [ ] White-throated 184

BULLFINCHES
(See Finches)

BUNTINGS

- [ ] Black-faced 316
- [ ] Black-headed 316
- [ ] Chestnut 316
- [ ] Crested 318
- [ ] Gray-headed 318
- [ ] Little 318
- [ ] Ortolan 335
- [ ] Pine 316
- [ ] Red-headed 316
- [ ] Reed 327
- [ ] Rock 318
- [ ] Rustic 327
- [ ] White-capped 318
- [ ] Yellow-breasted 316
- [ ] Yellowhammer 327

BUSH CHATS
(See Chats)

BUSH ROBINS
(See Robins)

BUSTARDS

- [ ] Bengal Florican 80
- [ ] Great Indian 80
- [ ] Lesser Florican 80
- [ ] Little 343

BUTEOS (BUZZARDS or HAWKS)

- [ ] Eurasian 48
- [ ] Long-legged 48
- [ ] Upland 48

CHAFFINCH
(See Finches)

CHATS

- [ ] Blue 250
- [ ] Brown Rock 322
- [ ] Collared Bush (Stone Chat) 260
- [ ] Dark-gray Bush 260
- [ ] Hodgson's Bush 322
- [ ] Jerdon's Bush 322
- [ ] Pied Bush 260
- [ ] White-tailed Bush 260
- [ ] White-capped River 256

CHOUGHS

- [ ] Hume's Ground 172
- [ ] Red-billed 174
- [ ] Yellow-billed 174

COCHOAS

- [ ] Green 262
- [ ] Purple 262

- [ ] **COOT** 78

CORMORANTS

- [ ] Indian Shag 345
- [ ] Large 24
- [ ] Little 24

COUCALS

- [ ] Large 116
- [ ] Small 116

COURSER

- [ ] Indian 94

CRAKES

- [ ] Baillon's 76
- [ ] Banded 76
- [ ] Brown 78
- [ ] Elwes's 78
- [ ] Ruddy 76

CRANES

- [ ] Black-necked 325
- [ ] Common 32
- [ ] Demoiselle 32
- [ ] Sarus 32

- [ ] **CROSSBILL** 314

CROWS

- [ ] Carrion 343
- [ ] House 174
- [ ] Jackdaw 343
- [ ] Jungle 174
- [ ] Rook 343

CUCKOOS

- [ ] Banded Bay 114
- [ ] Common Hawk 110
- [ ] Drongo 114
- [ ] Emerald 114
- [ ] Eurasian 112
- [ ] Himalayan 112
- [ ] Hodgson's Hawk 110
- [ ] Indian 112
- [ ] Large Green-billed Malkoha 116
- [ ] Large Hawk 110
- [ ] Koel 116
- [ ] Pied Crested 110
- [ ] Plaintive 114
- [ ] Red-winged Crested 110
- [ ] Sirkeer 116
- [ ] Small 112

CUCKOO-SHRIKES

- [ ] Black-headed 176
- [ ] Dark 176
- [ ] Large 176

- [ ] **CURLEW** 86

CUTIA

- [ ] Nepal 202

- [ ] **DARTER** 24

DIPPERS

- [ ] Brown 272
- [ ] White-breasted 272

DOVES

- [ ] Emerald 106
- [ ] Indian Ring 106
- [ ] Little Brown 106
- [ ] Long-tailed Cuckoo 104
- [ ] Red Turtle 106
- [ ] Rufous Turtle 104
- [ ] Spotted 106

DRONGOS

- [ ] Ashy 164
- [ ] Black 164
- [ ] Crow-billed 164
- [ ] Hair-crested 162
- [ ] Large Racquet-tailed 162
- [ ] Little Bronzed 164
- [ ] Small Racquet-tailed 162
- [ ] White-bellied 162

DUCKS

- [ ] Baer's Pochard 324
- [ ] Comb (Nukhta) 42
- [ ] Common Pochard 40
- [ ] Common Teal 38
- [ ] Cotton Teal (Pigmy Goose) 42
- [ ] Eurasian Shelduck 36
- [ ] Eurasian Wigeon 40
- [ ] Falcated Teal 38
- [ ] Gadwall 38
- [ ] Garganey 38
- [ ] Goldeneye 42
- [ ] Large Whistling Teal 324
- [ ] Lesser Whistling Teal 36
- [ ] Longtail Duck 324
- [ ] Mallard 38
- [ ] Merganser 42
- [ ] Pink-headed 40
- [ ] Pintail 36
- [ ] Red-crested Pochard 40
- [ ] Ruddy Shelduck (Brahminy) 36
- [ ] Scaup 40

- [ ] Shoveler 40
- [ ] Smew 42
- [ ] Spotbill 38
- [ ] Tufted Pochard 40
- [ ] White-eyed Pochard 40
- [ ] White-headed Stiff-tailed 343

- [ ] **DUNLIN** 88

EAGLES

- [ ] Black 54
- [ ] Bonelli's 50
- [ ] Booted 50
- [ ] Changeable Hawk 50
- [ ] Crested Serpent 48
- [ ] Golden 52
- [ ] Gray-headed Fishing 54
- [ ] Greater Spotted 52
- [ ] Himalayan Gray-headed Fishing 54
- [ ] Imperial 52
- [ ] Lesser Spotted 52
- [ ] Mountain Hawk (Hodgson's) 50
- [ ] Pallas's Fishing 54
- [ ] Rufous-bellied Hawk 50
- [ ] Short-toed 50
- [ ] Steppe 52
- [ ] Tawny 52
- [ ] White-tailed Sea 54

EGRETS

- [ ] Cattle 28
- [ ] Intermediate 28
- [ ] Large 28
- [ ] Little 28

FALCONET

- [ ] Red-thighed 62

FALCONS

- [ ] Eurasian Hobby 62
- [ ] Eurasian Kestrel 64
- [ ] Laggar 62
- [ ] Lesser Kestrel 64
- [ ] Merlin 64
- [ ] Oriental Hobby 62
- [ ] Peregrine 62
- [ ] Red-headed Merlin 64
- [ ] Red-legged 64

FINCHES

- [ ] Beautiful Rose 310
- [ ] Blanford's Rose 308
- [ ] Blanford's Snow 320
- [ ] Brandt's Mountain 308
- [ ] Brown Bullfinch 314
- [ ] Chaffinch 300
- [ ] Common Rose 308
- [ ] Eastern Great Rose 312
- [ ] Edward's Rose (Large Rose) 310
- [ ] Eurasian Goldfinch 304
- [ ] Gold-crowned Black 314
- [ ] Gold-fronted 306
- [ ] Gray-headed Bullfinch 346
- [ ] Great Rose 312
- [ ] Himalayan Goldfinch (Green Finch) 304
- [ ] Hodgson's Mountain 308
- [ ] Juniper (Red-fronted Rose) 312
- [ ] Mandelli's Snow 320
- [ ] Mongolian Desert 320
- [ ] Mongolian Snow 346
- [ ] Nepal Rose 308
- [ ] Orange Bullfinch 344
- [ ] Pink-browed Rose 310
- [ ] Red-breasted Rose 312
- [ ] Red-browed 306
- [ ] Red-headed Bullfinch 314
- [ ] Red-mantled Rose 344
- [ ] Red-necked Snow 320
- [ ] Scarlet 314
- [ ] Spot-winged Rose 310
- [ ] Tibetan Snow 298
- [ ] Vinaceous Rose 310
- [ ] White-browed Rose 312

FLAMINGO

- [ ] Greater 34

FLORICANS
(See Bustards)

FLOWERPECKERS

- [ ] Fire-breasted 292
- [ ] Plain-colored 292
- [ ] Scarlet-backed 292
- [ ] Thick-billed 292
- [ ] Tickell's 292

- [ ] Yellow-bellied 292
- [ ] Yellow-vented 292

FLYCATCHERS

- [ ] Beautiful Niltava 220
- [ ] Black-naped 222
- [ ] Blue-throated 218
- [ ] Brook's 222
- [ ] Brown 214
- [ ] Ferruginous 214
- [ ] Gray-headed 224
- [ ] Large-billed Blue 218
- [ ] Large Niltava 220
- [ ] Little Pied 216
- [ ] Kashmir Red-breasted 214
- [ ] Orange-gorgetted 216
- [ ] Pale Blue 222
- [ ] Paradise 224
- [ ] Pigmy Blue 218
- [ ] Red-breasted 214
- [ ] Rufous-breasted Blue 218
- [ ] Rufous-tailed 214
- [ ] Rusty-breasted Blue 218
- [ ] Sapphire-headed 220
- [ ] Slaty Blue 216
- [ ] Small Niltava 220
- [ ] Sooty 214
- [ ] Spotted 345
- [ ] Tickell's Blue 218
- [ ] Verditer 222
- [ ] White-breasted Fantail 224
- [ ] White-browed Blue 216
- [ ] White-gorgetted 216
- [ ] White-throated Fantail 224
- [ ] Yellow-bellied Fantail 224

FORKTAILS

- [ ] Black-backed 258
- [ ] Black-breasted 346
- [ ] Little 258
- [ ] Slaty-backed 258
- [ ] Spotted 258

FROGMOUTH

- [ ] Hodgson's 345

GALLINULES

- [ ] Indian 78
- [ ] Purple 78

GEESE

- [ ] Bar-headed 36
- [ ] Graylag 36
- [ ] Lesser White-fronted 343

GODWIT

- [ ] Black-tailed 86

- [ ] **GOLDCREST** 246

GOLDFINCHES

- [ ] Eurasian 304
- [ ] Himalayan (Green Finch) 304

GOSHAWKS

- [ ] Crested 46
- [ ] Goshawk 46

- [ ] **GRANDALA** 252

GREBES

- [ ] Black-necked 24
- [ ] Great Crested 24
- [ ] Little 24

GREEN PIGEONS
(See Pigeons)

GREENSHANK
(See Sandpipers)

GRIFFONS (See Vultures)

GROSBEAKS

- [ ] Allied 304
- [ ] Black-and-Yellow 344
- [ ] Spot-winged 304
- [ ] White-winged 304

GROUND PECKER

- [ ] Hume's 172

GULLS

- [ ] Black-headed 96
- [ ] Brown-headed 96
- [ ] Great Black-headed 96
- [ ] Herring 96
- [ ] Slender-billed 96

HARRIERS

- [ ] Hen 60

- ☐ Marsh 60
- ☐ Montagu's 60
- ☐ Pale 60
- ☐ Pied 60

HAWKS (also see Buteos, Goshawks)

- ☐ Besra Sparrow 46
- ☐ Shikra 46
- ☐ Sparrow 46
- ☐ White-eyed 48

HAWK EAGLES
(See Eagles)

HERONS

- ☐ Giant 345
- ☐ Gray 26
- ☐ Great White-bellied 26
- ☐ Little Green 26
- ☐ Night 26
- ☐ Pond 26
- ☐ Purple 26

HOBBYS (See Falcons)

HONEYGUIDE

- ☐ Himalayan 138

- ☐ **HOOPOE** 128

HORNBILLS

- ☐ Giant 134
- ☐ Gray 134
- ☐ Pied 134
- ☐ Rufous-necked 134

- ☐ **IBISBILL** 92

- ☐ **IBISES**

- ☐ Black 34
- ☐ Glossy 34
- ☐ White 34

- ☐ **IORA** 180

JACANAS

- ☐ Bronze-winged 80
- ☐ Pheasant-tailed 80

JACKDAW (See Crows)

JAYS

- ☐ Black-throated 170
- ☐ Eurasian (Himalayan) 170

JUNGLE FOWL

- ☐ Red 74

KESTRELS (See Falcons)

KINGFISHERS

- ☐ Black-capped 130
- ☐ Blue-eared 130
- ☐ Eurasian 130
- ☐ Great Blue 345
- ☐ Large Pied 130
- ☐ Ruddy 130
- ☐ Small Pied 130
- ☐ Stork-billed 130
- ☐ Three-toed 130
- ☐ White-breasted 130

KITES

- ☐ Black-shouldered 44
- ☐ Brahminy 44
- ☐ Dark (Pariah or Black) 44
- ☐ Honey (Buzzard) 44

LAPWINGS

- ☐ Eurasian 82
- ☐ Gray-headed 82
- ☐ Red-wattled 82
- ☐ Spur-winged 82
- ☐ White-tailed 82
- ☐ Yellow-wattled 82

LARKS

- ☐ Ashy-crowned Finch 148
- ☐ Bush 148
- ☐ Crested 150
- ☐ Eastern Calandra 343
- ☐ Horned 150
- ☐ Hume's Short-toed 150
- ☐ Little Skylark 150
- ☐ **Long-billed Calandra 345**
- ☐ Sand 150
- ☐ Short-toed 150

LAUGHING-THRUSHES

- [ ] Black-faced 200
- [ ] Blue-winged 200
- [ ] Crimson-winged 200
- [ ] Gray-sided 198
- [ ] Large Necklaced 196
- [ ] Lesser Necklaced 196
- [ ] Plain-colored 200
- [ ] Red-headed 200
- [ ] Rufous-chinned 198
- [ ] Rufous-necked 200
- [ ] Streaked 194
- [ ] Striated 196
- [ ] Variegated 198
- [ ] White-crested 198
- [ ] White-spotted 198
- [ ] White-throated 196

LEAF BIRDS

- [ ] Golden-fronted 180
- [ ] Orange-bellied 180

LEIOTHRIX

- [ ] Red-billed 202

LINNET 306

LORIKEET

- [ ] Indian 108

MAGPIES

- [ ] Green 170
- [ ] Pied 344
- [ ] Red-billed Blue 170
- [ ] Yellow-billed Blue 170

MALKOHA (See Cuckoos)

MARTINS

- [ ] Collared Sand 326
- [ ] Crag 156
- [ ] Eurasian House 156
- [ ] Nepal House 156
- [ ] Sand 156

MERLINS (See Falcons)

MESIA

- [ ] Silver-eared 202

MINIVETS

- [ ] Long-tailed 178
- [ ] Rosy 178
- [ ] Scarlet 178
- [ ] Short-billed 178
- [ ] Small 178
- [ ] Yellow-throated 178

MINLAS

- [ ] Bar-throated 206
- [ ] Blue-winged 206
- [ ] Red-tailed 206

MUNIAS

- [ ] Black-headed 302
- [ ] Red 302
- [ ] Sharp-tailed 302
- [ ] Spotted 302
- [ ] White-throated 302

MYNAS

- [ ] Bank 168
- [ ] Brahminy 166
- [ ] Common 168
- [ ] Gray-headed 166
- [ ] Jungle 168
- [ ] Pied 168
- [ ] Rosy Pastor 166
- [ ] Talking (Hill Grackle) 168

MYZORNIS

- [ ] Fire-tailed 202

NEEDLETAILS

- [ ] White-rumped 152
- [ ] White-throated 154
- [ ] White-vented 326

NIGHTJARS

- [ ] Eurasian (European) 343
- [ ] Franklin's 126
- [ ] Jungle 126
- [ ] Little (Indian) 126
- [ ] Long-tailed 126

- [ ] **NUTCRACKER** 172

NUTHATCHES

- [ ] Beautiful 346

- ☐ Chestnut-bellied 282
- ☐ Eurasian (European) 282
- ☐ Velvet-fronted 282
- ☐ White-cheeked 282
- ☐ White-tailed 282

ORIOLES

- ☐ Black-headed 160
- ☐ Black-naped 160
- ☐ Golden 160
- ☐ Maroon 160

- ☐ **OSPREY** 54

OWLS OWLETS

- ☐ Barn 118
- ☐ Barred Owlet 122
- ☐ Bay 118
- ☐ Brown Fish 120
- ☐ Brown Hawk 124
- ☐ Brown Wood 124
- ☐ Collared Pigmy Owlet 122
- ☐ Collared Scops 118
- ☐ Dusky Horned 120
- ☐ Forest Eagle 120
- ☐ Grass 118
- ☐ Great Horned 120
- ☐ Jungle Owlet 122
- ☐ Little Owlet 322
- ☐ Long-eared 124
- ☐ Scops 118
- ☐ Short-eared 124
- ☐ Spotted Owlet 122
- ☐ Spotted Scops 118
- ☐ Tawny Fish 120
- ☐ Tawny Wood 124

- ☐ **OYSTERCATCHER** 80

PARAKEETS

- ☐ Blossom-headed 108
- ☐ Large 108
- ☐ Rose-breasted 108
- ☐ Rose-ringed 108
- ☐ Slaty-headed 108

PARROTBILLS

- ☐ Black-browed 345
- ☐ Brown 192
- ☐ Fulvous-fronted 192
- ☐ Gould's 192
- ☐ Gray-headed 346
- ☐ Great 192
- ☐ Nepal 192
- ☐ Red-headed 345

PARTRIDGES

- ☐ Black 68
- ☐ Chukor 66
- ☐ Common Hill 68
- ☐ Gray 68
- ☐ Red-breasted Hill 345
- ☐ Rufous-throated Hill 68
- ☐ Snow 66
- ☐ Swamp 68
- ☐ Tibetan 68

PASTOR
(See Mynas)

PEAFOWL

- ☐ Common 74

PELICANS

- ☐ Spot-billed 24
- ☐ White 24

PEREGRINE (See Falcons)

PHALAROPE

- ☐ Red-necked 325

PHEASANTS

- ☐ Blood 72
- ☐ Cheer 74
- ☐ Crimson Horned 72
- ☐ Impeyan 72
- ☐ Kalij 72
- ☐ Koklas 74
- ☐ Western Tragopan 343

PICULETS

- ☐ Rufous 138
- ☐ Spotted 138

PIGEONS

- ☐ Ashy Wood 104
- ☐ Bengal Green 102
- ☐ Blue Rock 102
- ☐ Gray-fronted Green 100

- ☐ Hill 102
- ☐ Imperial 102
- ☐ Orange-breasted Green 100
- ☐ Pintail Green 100
- ☐ Snow 102
- ☐ Speckled Wood 104
- ☐ Thick-billed Green 100
- ☐ Wedge-tailed Green 100
- ☐ Wood 104

PIPITS

- ☐ Blyth's 286
- ☐ Brown Rock 288
- ☐ Eurasian Tree (The Tree) 288
- ☐ Hodgson's Tree 286
- ☐ Meadow 344
- ☐ Paddyfield 286
- ☐ Red-throated 288
- ☐ Richard's 286
- ☐ Rose-breasted (Hodgson's) 288
- ☐ Upland 286
- ☐ Water 288

PITTAS

- ☐ Blue-naped 148
- ☐ Green-breasted 148
- ☐ Indian 148

PLOVERS

- ☐ Black-bellied (Gray) 84
- ☐ Eastern Golden 84
- ☐ Greater Sand 84
- ☐ Kentish (Snowy) 84
- ☐ Lesser Sand 84
- ☐ Little Ring 84
- ☐ Long-billed Ring 84

PRATINCOLES

- ☐ Collared 94
- ☐ Small 94

PRINIAS (See Warblers)

QUAILS

- ☐ Black-breasted (Rain) 70
- ☐ Blue-breasted 70
- ☐ Button 70
- ☐ Common (Gray) 70
- ☐ Common Bustard 70
- ☐ Jungle Bush 70
- ☐ Little Bustard 70

RAILS

- ☐ Blue-breasted Banded 76
- ☐ Water 76

☐ **RAVEN** 174

REDSHANKS

(See Sandpipers)

REDSTARTS

- ☐ Black 254
- ☐ Blue-fronted 254
- ☐ Blue-headed 254
- ☐ Daurian 346
- ☐ Eversmann's 254
- ☐ Guldenstadt's 256
- ☐ Hodgson's 254
- ☐ Plumbeous 256
- ☐ White-bellied (Hodgson's Shortwing) 256
- ☐ White-throated 256

RIVER CHAT

(See Chats)

ROBINS

- ☐ Blue-fronted Long-tailed 252
- ☐ Dayal 252
- ☐ Golden Bush 250
- ☐ Indian 260
- ☐ Orange-flanked Bush 250
- ☐ Rufous-bellied Bush 250
- ☐ White-browed Bush 250
- ☐ White-tailed Blue 252

ROLLERS

- ☐ Dark (Broad-billed) 128
- ☐ Eurasian 344
- ☐ Indian 128

ROOK (See Crows)

RUBYCHEEK

(See Sunbirds)

RUBYTHROATS

- ☐ Eurasian 248
- ☐ Himalayan 248

- [ ] **RUFF AND REEVE** 86

SANDGROUSE

- [ ] Close-barred 100
- [ ] Imperial 100
- [ ] Indian 100
- [ ] Tibetan 345

SANDPIPERS

- [ ] Common 88
- [ ] Common Redshank 86
- [ ] Curlew Sandpiper 325
- [ ] Green 88
- [ ] Greenshank 86
- [ ] Marsh 88
- [ ] Sanderling 325
- [ ] Spotted Redshank 86
- [ ] Wood 88

SHAG
(See Cormorants)

- [ ] **SHAMA** 252

SHIKRA (See Hawks)

SHORTWINGS

- [ ] Gould's 248
- [ ] Lesser 248
- [ ] Rusty-bellied 346
- [ ] White-browed 248

SHRIKES

- [ ] Bay-backed 158
- [ ] Black-headed 158
- [ ] Brown 158
- [ ] Gray 158
- [ ] Gray-backed 158
- [ ] Rufous-backed 158

SIBIAS

- [ ] Black-capped 212
- [ ] Chestnut-backed 326
- [ ] Long-tailed 212

SISKIN

- [ ] Tibetan 306

SKIMMER

- [ ] Indian 98

SNIPE

- [ ] Fantail 90
- [ ] Jack 90
- [ ] Painted 92
- [ ] Pintail 90
- [ ] Solitary 90
- [ ] Wood 90

SNOW COCKS

- [ ] Himalayan 66
- [ ] Tibetan 66

SPARROW HAWKS
(See Hawks)

SPARROWS

- [ ] Cinnamon 298
- [ ] House 298
- [ ] Spanish 327
- [ ] Tree 298
- [ ] Yellow-throated 298

SPIDERHUNTERS

- [ ] Little 296
- [ ] Streaked 296

SPINETAILS
(See Needletails)

SPOONBILL

- [ ] Eurasian 34

STARE

- [ ] Spot-winged 166

STARLING

- [ ] Eurasian 166

STILT

- [ ] Black-winged 92

STINTS

- [ ] Little 88
- [ ] Long-toed 88
- [ ] Temminck's 88

STONE PLOVERS
(See Thick Knees)

STORKS

- [ ] Adjutant 32

- [ ] Black 30
- [ ] Black-necked 30
- [ ] Lesser Adjutant 32
- [ ] Open-billed 30
- [ ] Painted 30
- [ ] White 30
- [ ] White-necked 30

SUNBIRDS

- [ ] Black-breasted 294
- [ ] Fire-tailed 294
- [ ] Mrs. Gould's 294
- [ ] Nepal 294
- [ ] Purple 296
- [ ] Rubycheek 296
- [ ] Scarlet-breasted 294

SWALLOWS

- [ ] Barn 156
- [ ] Indian Cliff 156
- [ ] Striated 156
- [ ] Wire-tailed 156

SWALLOW-SHRIKE

(See Wood-Swallow)

SWANS

- [ ] Bewick's 324
- [ ] Whooper 36

SWIFTLET

- [ ] Edible Nest 154

SWIFTS

- [ ] Alpine 154
- [ ] Black 152
- [ ] Crested 152
- [ ] House 152
- [ ] Khasi Hills 152
- [ ] Large White-rumped 152
- [ ] Palm 154

TAILOR BIRDS

- [ ] Golden-headed 346
- [ ] Tailor Bird 234

TERNS

- [ ] Black-bellied 98
- [ ] Caspian 96
- [ ] Common 98
- [ ] Gull-billed 98
- [ ] Indian River 98
- [ ] Little 98
- [ ] Whiskered 98
- [ ] White-winged Black 325

THICK KNEES

- [ ] Eurasian (Stone Plover) 94
- [ ] Great (Great Stone Plover) 94

THRUSHES

- [ ] Black-throated 270
- [ ] Blue-headed Rock 262
- [ ] Blue Rock 262
- [ ] Chestnut-bellied Rock 262
- [ ] Dark 270
- [ ] Dusky 326
- [ ] Eurasian Rock (Rock) 344
- [ ] Gray-headed 270
- [ ] Kessler's 346
- [ ] Large Long-billed 266
- [ ] Lesser Long-billed 266
- [ ] Long-tailed Mountain 266
- [ ] Mistle 270
- [ ] Orange-headed Ground 264
- [ ] Pied Ground 264
- [ ] Plain-backed Mountain 266
- [ ] Red-throated 270
- [ ] Speckled Mountain (Small-billed Mountain) 266
- [ ] Tickell's 270
- [ ] Whistling 268

TITMICE

- [ ] Black-spotted Yellow 276
- [ ] Coal 278
- [ ] Crested Brown 278
- [ ] Fire-capped 280
- [ ] Gray 276
- [ ] Green-backed 276
- [ ] Red-headed 280
- [ ] Rufous-breasted Black 278
- [ ] Rufous-fronted 280
- [ ] Simla Black 278
- [ ] Spot-winged Black (Crested Black) 278
- [ ] Sultan 276
- [ ] White-cheeked 327
- [ ] White-throated 280

- [ ] Yellow-browed 280
- [ ] Yellow-cheeked 276

TREE CREEPERS

- [ ] Himalayan 284
- [ ] Nepal 284
- [ ] Northern (Brown) 284
- [ ] Sikkim 284

TREE PIES

- [ ] Black-browed 172
- [ ] Himalayan 172
- [ ] Indian 172

TROGON

- [ ] Red-headed 128

- [ ] **TURNSTONE** 325

TWITE

- [ ] Tibetan 306

VULTURES

- [ ] Bearded 56
- [ ] Black (King) 58
- [ ] Cinereous (European Black) 56
- [ ] Egyptian (Scavenger) 58
- [ ] Eurasian Griffon 56
- [ ] Himalayan Griffon 56
- [ ] Indian Griffon (Long-billed) 58
- [ ] White-backed 58

WAGTAILS

- [ ] Forest 344
- [ ] Gray 290
- [ ] Large Pied 290
- [ ] Pied (White) 290
- [ ] Yellow 290
- [ ] Yellow-headed 290

- [ ] **WALL CREEPER** 284

WARBLERS

- [ ] Aberrant Bush 226
- [ ] Allied 244
- [ ] Ashy Prinia 230
- [ ] Black-browed Reed 326
- [ ] Black-faced 246
- [ ] Black-throated Hill Prinia 232
- [ ] Blanford's Bush 226
- [ ] Blunt-winged Paddyfield 236
- [ ] Blyth's Reed 236
- [ ] Booted Tree 236
- [ ] Broad-billed 246
- [ ] Brook's Leaf 344
- [ ] Brown Bush 228
- [ ] Brown Hill Prinia 232
- [ ] Brown Leaf 238
- [ ] Chestnut-crowned 244
- [ ] Chestnut-headed Ground 226
- [ ] Chinese Bush 228
- [ ] Clamorous Reed 236
- [ ] Crowned Leaf 242
- [ ] Dull Green Leaf 240
- [ ] Dusky Leaf 238
- [ ] Fulvous-streaked Prinia 232
- [ ] Golden-headed Cisticola 228
- [ ] Grasshopper 346
- [ ] Gray-capped Prinia (Hodgson's Wren) 230
- [ ] Gray-cheeked 244
- [ ] Gray-faced Leaf 240
- [ ] Gray-headed 244
- [ ] Hodgson's Prinia (Franklin's Wren) 230
- [ ] Hume's Bush 226
- [ ] Jungle Prinia 230
- [ ] Large-billed Leaf 240
- [ ] Large Bush 228
- [ ] Large Crowned Leaf 242
- [ ] Large Grass 234
- [ ] Lesser Whitethroat 236
- [ ] Long-billed Bush 344
- [ ] Olivaceous Leaf 238
- [ ] Olive Ground 346
- [ ] Orange-barred Leaf 242
- [ ] Oriental Reed 236
- [ ] Orphean 232
- [ ] Paddyfield 236
- [ ] Pallas's Grasshopper 234
- [ ] Plain Leaf 240
- [ ] Plain Prinia 230
- [ ] Rufescent Prinia 230
- [ ] Rufous-capped Bush 228
- [ ] Slaty-bellied Ground 226
- [ ] Smoky Leaf 238
- [ ] Spotted Bush 228
- [ ] Stoliczka's Tit 246
- [ ] Streaked Grasshopper 234

- [ ] Striated Marsh 234
- [ ] Strong-footed Bush 226
- [ ] Thick-billed 236
- [ ] Tickell's Leaf 238
- [ ] Tytler's Leaf 238
- [ ] White-throated 246
- [ ] Yellow-bellied 246
- [ ] Yellow-bellied Prinia 232
- [ ] Yellow-eyed (Black-browed) 244
- [ ] Yellow-rumped Leaf 242
- [ ] Yellow-throated Leaf (Small Crowned) 242
- [ ] Zitting Cisticola (Streaked Fantail) 228

- [ ] **WATERCOCK** 78

WATERHEN

- [ ] White-breasted 78

WAXWING

- [ ] Bohemian 180

WEAVERS

- [ ] Baya 300
- [ ] Black-throated 300
- [ ] Streaked 320

WHEATEARS

- [ ] Desert 264
- [ ] Isabelline 264
- [ ] Pied 326
- [ ] Pleschanka's 344

- [ ] **WHIMBREL** 86

- [ ] **WHITE-EYE** 296

- [ ] **WOODCOCK** 90

WOODPECKERS

- [ ] Black-backed 142
- [ ] Black-naped 140
- [ ] Brown (Rufous) 146
- [ ] Brown-crowned Pigmy 138
- [ ] Brown-fronted Pied 144
- [ ] Darjeeling Pied 144
- [ ] Fulvous-breasted Pied 144
- [ ] Gray-crowned Pigmy 138
- [ ] Great Slaty 146
- [ ] Himalayan Pied 144
- [ ] Large Golden-backed 142
- [ ] Large Scaly-bellied 140
- [ ] Large Yellow-naped 140
- [ ] Lesser Golden-backed 142
- [ ] Pale-headed 146
- [ ] Red-eared Rufous 146
- [ ] Rufous-bellied Sapsucker 146
- [ ] Small Crimson-breasted Pied 144
- [ ] Small Scaly-bellied 140
- [ ] Small Yellow-naped 140
- [ ] Three-toed Golden-backed 142
- [ ] Yellow-fronted Pied 144

WOOD-SHRIKES

- [ ] Large (Nepal) 176
- [ ] Lesser (Indian) 176
- [ ] Pied (Flycatcher-Shrike) 176

WOOD-SWALLOW

- [ ] Ashy 166

WREN

- [ ] Wren (Winter) 272

- [ ] **WRYNECK** 138

YUHINAS

- [ ] Black-chinned 208
- [ ] Chestnut-headed 208
- [ ] Rufous-vented 208
- [ ] Stripe-throated 208
- [ ] White-bellied 208
- [ ] White-browed 346
- [ ] Yellow-naped 208

NOTES

Ficus Benghalensis   Banyan   Epiphytes
F. Religiosa   BODHI (Bodh) Buddh. at Bodh
F Elastica   Assam (WTA) RUBBER   SAYA
   Superseded by Hevea Brasilensis
Specific insect for each fig
Jack tree   Artocarpus heterophyllus fruit 70k
chaquash A. chaplaska   Jakfruit/Breadfruit
   (Moraceae)
Podocarpus Wallichianus   Large leaved
   podocarp   only natly occurring in S Indies
Bishop wood Toge Tree   Bischofia Javanica
   soft juicy cortex   rail sleepers Assam
Coral tree   Erythrina variegata Red flowers
   pepper & betel vines   origins
Tamarind   Tamarindus indica
Acac Lacc of India pour E Africa lacca Senegal
   good timber o/seed pulp c/foods

Eurasian Kestrel, *Falco tinnunculus* (p. 64) raised to 4727 m. (15,500') in the Gokyu Valley, Everest area, May (Chris Mackensie).

PARTRIDGES Common Hill Partridge, *Arborophila torqueola*, up to 3352 m. (11,000') on Machapuchare (T. Lelliott).

PHEASANTS Two males and four female Blood Pheasants, *Ithaginis cruentus*, seen in bamboo on N. side of Gurchi Lagna, north of Jumla, at 2840 m. (9317') on 22 Oct. 1982 and represents a significant westward extension of range (D. McCauley).
Impeyan Pheasant, *Lophophorus impejanus*, down to 2438 m. (8,000') in deep Feb. snow in Barun Valley (RLF).
Crimson Horned Pheasant, *Tragopan satyra*, up to 3660 m. (12,000') in much of Nepal (RLF, Lelliott).
Koklas Pheasant, *Pucrasia macrolopha*, up to 3352 (11,000') on Machapuchare (T. Lelliott).

JACANAS The Pheasant-tailed Jacana, *Hydrophasianus chirurgus* (p. 80) appears to be fairly common in the S. E. *tarai* where up to 28 birds seen in one day (Kosi Barrage area); noted between Dec. and Aug. (R. C. Gregory-Smith). Straggler noted at Rara Lake, 3050 m. (10,000') (Pritchard, Brearey).
Several records of Bronze-winged Jacana, *Metopidius indicus*, on Begnas Tal, Pokhara 915 m. (3,000').

PLOVERS Range of the White-tailed Lapwing, *Vanellus leucurus* (p. 82) extended east to Nepalganj on 01 Jan. 1977 (Stan Justice).
A single Eurasian Lapwing, *Vanellus vanellus* (p. 82) noted at Jomosom 2684 m. (8,800'), 25 Nov. 1977 (RLF).

SANDPIPERS Three Common Redshanks, *Tringa erythropus* (p. 86) at Gokyu Lake Everest area, 4697 m. (15,400'), May (C. Mackensie, RLF).
Several records of Marsh Sandpipers, *Tringa stagnatilis*, from the Kosi area and continuing reports from Chitwan.
Several reports of Dunlins, *Calidris alpinus* from Chitwan and Kosi Barrage.
Ca six Whimbrels, *Numenius phaeopus*, on 17 April 1981 on Phewa Tal, Pokhara (J. Wolstencroft).

SNIPE A single Fantail Snipe, *Capella gallinago* (p. 90) near edge of Gokyu Lake, Everest area at 4697 m. (15,400'), May (C. Mackensie, RLF).
Three to four Solitary Snipe, *Capella solitaria*, at Muktinath 3798 m. (12,460') on 16, 17 Jan. 1979 (C. Murphy) and again reported from stream near Muktinath on 01, 02 April 1981 where observed rocking on wobbly legs while feeding (J. Wolstencroft).

PAINTED SNIPE A flock of about 40 Painted Snipe, *Rostratula benghalensis* (p. 92) noted near Hotel Elephant Camp, Chitwan (A. D. Sudbury).

STILTS and ALLIES Black-winged Stilt, *Himantopus himantopus* (p. 92) seen at 3355 m. (11,000') near Muktinath on 22 Aug. 1977 (Nigel Pedfield). Illustration shows young male. Adult male loses black on head and neck. Female often has gray on head and neck (Phil Hall).
Several Avocets, *Recurvirostra avosetta*, at Saurha, Chitwan on 09 Nov. 1983 (J. Halliday).
Nine Ibisbill, *Ibidorhyncha struthersii*, together on Trisuli River on 13 March 1981 (on migration?) (R. De la Moussaye).

PRATINCOLES The Collared Pratincole, *Glareola pratincola* (p. 94) listed as "common" in S. E. Nepal (R. C. Gregory-Smith, 1976:10). Confirmation of this status designation desirable. Single adult noted from Tumlingtar, Arun Valley in May 1981 (M. Henriksen, O. Lou, N. Krabbe) and recently additional specimens (3) from Kathmandu Valley; collected on 09 Oct. 1983 by Hari S. Nepali.

GULLS and TERNS One Black-headed Gull, *Larus ridibundus* (p. 96) with 19 Brown-headed Gulls noted at over 5490 m. (18,000'), upper Dudh Kosi Valley, Everest area, May (RLF).
Nineteen Brown-headed Gulls, *Larus brunnicephalus* (p. 96) noted flying at over 5490 m. (18,000'), upper Dudh Kosi Valley, Everest area, May (RLF). Five seen on Rara Lake, 23-25 October 1982 (D. McCauley).
Great Black-headed Gull, *Larus ichthyaetus*, at Rara Lake, 3050 m. (10,000') (Pritchard, Brearey).
First specimen of Gull-billed Tern, *Gelochelidon nilotica*, from Nepal collected near Manang airport at 3352 m. (11,000') on 03 Aug. 1978 by Hari S. Nepali. Second specimen on 08 Sept. 1981 from Chobar, Kathmandu Valley, again by H. S. Nepali. Also single bird seen on 13,17 May 1981 at Phewa Tal, Pokhara (J. Wolstencroft).
Indian Skimmer, *Rynchops albicollis* (p. 98) noted from Feb. to July at the Kosi Barrage; up to 17 birds seen on one day in Mar. (R. C. Gregory-Smith).

PIGEONS About 200 Wood Pigeons, *Columba palumbus*, in Jumla area in late Dec. 1982 (D. McCauley, M. Ridley), and also *ca* 200 on Naudanda (N. W. Pokhara) last week of Dec. 1982 (T. Stowe).

PARAKEETS Slaty-headed Parakeet, *Psittacula himalayana*, up to 3261 m. (10,700') on Machapuchare (T. Lelliott).

CUCKOOS Eurasian Cuckoo, *Cuculus canorus* (p. 112) noted down to 152 m. (500'), E. Nepal (Phil Hall).
Plaintive Cuckoo, *Cacomantis merulinus* (p. 114) noted down to 152 m. (500'), E. Nepal (Phil Hall).
Drongo Cuckoo, *Surniculus lugubris* (p. 114). Young birds show thin white banding on undertail coverts and rectices; bands tend to disappear with age. Illustration shows no bands (Phil Hall).
Emerald Cuckoo, *Chalcites maculatus* (p. 114) noted at 1830 m. (6,000') near Pokhara in April (E. Forster).

OWLS A vagrant Scops Owl, *Otus scops* (p. 118) collected by Deva Nur Singh at Jomosom, Kali Gandaki Valley, 2745 m. (9,000'), Dec. Also heard up to 3292 m. (10,800') on Machapuchare (T. Lelliott).
Great Horned Owl, *Bubo bubo*, up to 3414 m. (11,200') on Machapuchare (T. Lelliott).
A Short-eared Owl, *Asio flammeus*, on 10 April 1979 at 3322 m. (10,900') and on 01 Oct. 1979 at 3261 m. (10,700') on Machapuchare (T. Lelliott).

ROLLERS A vagrant Dark Roller, *Eurystomus orientalis* (p. 128) noted at Godaveri, Kathmandu Valley, 1525 m. (5,000'), Aug. 1978 (RLF). Noted in *winter* (straggler?) at 915 m. (3,000') in Surkhet Valley (P. Hagan).

HORNBILLS The Gray Hornbill, *Tockus birostris*, up to 762 m. (2,500') in Surkhet Valley (P. Hagan).

WOODPECKERS A Wryneck, *Jynx torquilla*, at 3444 m. (11,300') on 01 May 1980 on Machapuchare (T. Lelliott).
Altitude range of Yellow-fronted Pied Woodpecker, *Dendrocopos mahrattensis* (p.144) elevated to 1525 m. (5,000') in the Kali Gandaki Valley and lowered to 152 m. (500') in E. Nepal. Female should show yellow crown with a whitish nape; the latter divided by a dark line down center (Phil Hall).

LARKS The Ashy-crowned Finch Lark, *Eremopterix grisea*, regularly seen in the Surkhet Valley up to 731 m. (2,400') (P. Hagan).

SWIFTS Black Swifts, *Apus apus* (p. 152) noted "fairly common" to "common" north of Dhaulagiri and Annapurna (G. B. Corbett: J. M. Thiollay; RLF).
White-rumped Needletail, *Chaetura sylvatica*, noted along western border at Mahendranagar on 05 Mar. 1981 with nest hole some 30 feet from ground (J. Wolstencroft).
Crested Swifts, *Hemiprocne longipennis*, up to 762 m. (2,500') in winter in Surkhet Valley (P. Hagan).

SWALLOWS and MARTINS Nearly 500 Barn Swallows, *Hirundo rustica*, at about 3660 m. (12,000') on Machapuchare and apparently on migration (T. Lelliott).
Range of Wire-tailed Swallow, *Hirundo smithii*, extended to the western border at Mahendranagar (J. Wolstencroft).
A vagrant Sand Martin, *Riparia paludicola* (p. 156) at 2989 m. (9,800') near Kagbeni Kali Gandaki Valley (Ridge Dewitt).

SHRIKES A vagrant Bay-backed Shrike, *Lanius vittatus* (p. 158) at 2684 m. (8,800') near Marpha, Kali Gandaki Valley, 28 Sept. (Mark Beaman). Regular sightings, summer and winter in the Surkkhet Valley, 731 m. (2,400') (P. Hagan).
Gray Shrike, *Lanius excubitor* (p. 158) appears to be fairly common in. C. *tarai* (Jack Cox, Delos McCauley) and occurs sporadically into the E. *tarai* (Phil Hall). Numerous records, now, from the Kosi Barrage area.

ORIOLES Additional sightings of the Black-naped Oriole, *Oriolus chinensis* (p. 160) include one in the foothills near Dharan, E. Nepal in Mar. (R. C. Gregory-Smith) and one in Kathmandu Valley, Thimi Forest. Dec. 1977 (RLF).

MYNAS The Brahminy Myna, *Sturnus pagodarum* (p. 166) now recorded sporadically from E. *tarai* and nesting near Dharan, E. Nepal in June (R. C. Gregory-Smith).

CROWS and ALLIES Plumage of the Green Magpie, *Cissa chinensis* (p. 170) reported turquoise (not green) from birds in the Birethanti area W. of Pokhara (Julie and Penny Leslie). Dietary factors may be responsible for color shift.
Himalayan Tree Pie, *Dendrocitta formosae*, down to 305 m. (1,000') in Kailali (P. Hagan).

MINIVETS and ALLIES A male Black-headed Cuckoo-Shrike, *Coracina melanoptera* (p.176) with (?) nesting material seen on 15 Apr. 1977 at Birtamore. E.*tarai* (C. Mackensie). A male noted in Feb. 1978 at Chapagaon Forest, Kathmandu Valley (Phil Hall). Several new records from Chitwan and eastern *tarai*.

LEAF BIRDS Juveniles of both Orange-bellied Leaf Bird, *Chloropsis hardwickii* (p. 180) and the Gold-fronted Leaf Bird. *C. aurifrons* (p. 180) are almost completely green.

LAUGHING-THRUSHES The Rufous-necked Laughing-Thrush, *Garrulax ruficollis*, now also known from Tamaspur, Nawalparasi Dist. where six seen on 09-10 Jan. 1979 (N. Redman and C. Murphy).

BABBLERS Several additional sightings of the Golden-breasted Tit Babblers, *Alcippe chrysotis* (p. 210) from the Annapurna region where species may be considered "occasional" (Cliff Rice; Sudbury; RLF). Also noted along the Nepal-Darjeeling border on 17 Feb. 1979 (R. Grimmett, F. Lambert).
Rufous-bellied Shrike Babbler, *Pteruithius rufiventer*, up to 3230 m. (10,600') on 23 April 1979 on Machapuchare (T. Lelliott).

FLYCATCHERS Brown Flycatcher, *Muscicapa latirostris* (p. 214) noted down to 152 m. (500') (Phil Hall).
Ferruginous Flycatcher, *Muscicapa ferruginea* (p. 214) seen between Landrung and Dhampus (Annapurna area) on 18 April 1978 (Cliff Rice). A western extension of range. And a "settled" pair in Ghasa Forest (south Mustang Dist.), spring 1981 (J. Wolstencroft). Two sightings of Large-billed Blue Flycatcher, *Muscicapa banyumas*, on the Makalu Base Camp trek at about 3352 m. (11,000') on 06, 11 May 1982 (R. Isherwood).
Red-breasted Flycatcher, *Muscicapa parva* (p. 214) noted down to 152 m. (500') (Phil Hall).
A vagrant Orange-gorgetted Flycatcher, *Muscicapa strophiata* (p. 216) noted by R. C. Gregory-Smith at 350 m. (1,150') in E. Nepal.
A pair of Sapphire-headed Flycatchers, *Muscicapa sapphira* (p. 220) noted near Ghandrung, Annapurna area, 2135 m. (7,000') on 1 April 1977 (Chris Mackensie). As this is a considerable westward extension of the range (but not out of ecological position), Mackensie reports that his sighting needs confirmation.

WARBLERS A single spotted Bush Warbler, *Bradypterus thoracicus* (p. 228) seen near Tatopani, Kali Gandaki Valley at 1220 m. (4,000') on 15 April 1977 (Cliff Rice). Also a nest found by J. M. Thiollay at 3850 m. (12,622') on 22 June 1977 on Lamjung Himal, C. Nepal. T. Lelliott reports them common on ridge west of Mardi Valley (Machapuchare area) up to 3352 m. (11,000') in June. Song is quite distinctive.
Several breeding pairs of Large Bush Warblers, *Cettia major* (p. 228) noted by J. M. Thiollay between 16 and 18 June on Lamjung Himal from 3550 to 3680 m. (11,638' to 12,067'). Also noted on Machapuchare at 3414 m. (11,200') on 13 Oct. 1979; the call is a *tip*, quite different from *C. brunnifrons* (T. Lelliott).
A Lesser Whitethroat, *Sylvia curruca* (p. 236) seen in foothills near Dharan, E. Nepal at about 701 m. (2,300') by R. C. Gregory-Smith. Also 3 noted near Tukche, Kali Gandaki Valley on 24 Sept. and one on 26 Sept. (Mark Beaman). Now several records in the hills from Kathmandu west and in the *tarai* from the Kosi Barrage west to Mahendranagar
The Smoky Leaf Warbler, *Phylloscopus fulgiventer* (p. 238) appears to breed commonly above the tree line on Lamjung Himal from 3900 to 4200 m. (12,786' to 13,770') in June (J. M. Thiollay).
Gray-faced Leaf Warbler, *Phylloscopus maculipennis*, down to 915 m. (3,000') in the Tamba Kosi Valley (RLF).
The range of the Gray-cheeked Warbler, *Seicercus poliogenys*, extended west to Nayathati (Ulleri area of Annapurna), 2438 m. (8000'); in mixed flock on 05 Feb. 1982 (P. Pyle).

THRUSHES and ALLIES A single Gould's Shortwing, *Brachypteryx stellata* (p. 248) noted in Gauchar Forest, Kathmandu Valley at 1281 m. (4,200') in July (Lewis Underwood, Phil Hall).
The discovery of pairs of Rufous-bellied Bush Robins, *Erithacus hyperythrus* (p. 250) on Lamjung Himal between 3350 and 4100 m. (10,983' and 13,443') on 20, 21 and 27 June by J. M. Thiollay extends the range westward and upward.
Numerous Grandalas, *Grandala coelicolor* (p. 252) down to Lukla airstrip, 2806 m. (9,200'), Everest area, in May after heavy snow (C. Mackensie, RLF). Others down to 2135 m. (7,000') in Feb. snow storm in Barun Valley (RLF).
The altitude range of the Black Redstart, *Phoenicurus ochruros* (p. 254) extended up to 5337 m. (17,500') on the Thorongla above Muktinath and down to 76 m. (250') in the E. *tarai* (Phil Hall).